MISCARRIAGES OF JUSTICE

Many innocent people are imprisoned in British jails, some for exceptionally long terms, because the police handling the investigation misconstrued the actions of suspects, or because faulty and misleading evidence was presented at the trial, or because the defence case was inadequately argued. The adversarial system of justice in the UK puts innocent people at an inbuilt disadvantage. They may be less concerned with putting forward a good case because they put their trust in the legendary infallibility of British justice.

Bob Woffinden demonstrates that this infallibility is merely a myth. Another assumption is that mistakes made at the original trial will be put right at appeal. In fact mistakes are often perpetuated. No branch of government is responsible for miscarriages of justice.

The result, as Bob Woffinden demonstrates in this survey of post-war injustices, is that even where wrongful verdicts are conceded by the administration – such as in the Timothy Evans case – it is often as a result of intensive campaigning: thirteen, in that case. The overwhelming majority of miscarriages of justice are never put right.

About the author

Bob Woffinden was born in 1948. He took a politics degree at Sheffield University and from 1973 to 1978 was Associate Editor of *New Musical Express*. *The Illustrated Encyclopaedia of Rock*, which he co-authored with Nick Logan, won the Libraries' Association of America Award for the best non-fiction book of 1976 in the arts field. Since 1978 he has worked as a freelance journalist, contributing to newspapers and magazines including the *New Statesman*, for which he wrote a series on 'Innocent Women in Prison' in 1985. He also writes regularly for *The Listener*. Bob Woffinden lives in London with his wife and two children.

Miscarriages of Justice

Bob Woffinden

CORONET BOOKS
Hodder and Stoughton

For Anne

First published in Great Britain in 1987 by Hodder and Stoughton Limited

Coronet edition 1989

Printed and bound in Great Britain for Hodder and Stoughton Paperbacks, a division of Hodder and Stoughton Limited, Mill Road, Dunton Green, Sevenoaks, Kent TN13 2YA (Editorial Office: 47 Bedford Square, London WC1B 3DP) by Cox and Wyman Limited, Reading, Berks. Photoset by Rowland Phototypesetting Limited, Bury St Edmunds, Suffolk.

British Library C.I.P.
Woffinden, Bob, *1948–*
    Miscarriages of justice.
    1. England. Criminal law. Justice.
    Miscarriages, 1945–1985
    I. Title
    344.205

ISBN 0-340-42406-0

'I regard injustice, or even the risk of injustice, perpetrated in the august precincts of a court of law, with calm consideration and time for reflection, as utterly repellent.'
— Peter Ustinov, *Dear Me*

'The test of a country's justice is not the blunders which are sometimes made but the zeal with which they are put right.'
— Cyril Connolly, *Sunday Times*,
15 January 1961

Contents

Introduction

THROUGHOUT MY lifetime there always seems to have been at least one rumoured miscarriage of justice nagging away at the public conscience. It was the Timothy Evans case in the fifties and the A6 murder throughout the sixties. Innumerable cases gave rise to concern in the seventies: Luvaglio–Stafford, the Luton post-office murder, the Maxwell Confait murder, and others highlighting mistakes in identification evidence. In more recent times, there has been the Carl Bridgewater murder, and those particularly disturbing examples of judicial waywardness collectively termed the Irish cases.

Many of these injustices have been individually examined in books, of which Ludovic Kennedy's *Ten Rillington Place* is the most renowned. The Timothy Evans case which it analysed did result in an executive pardon. That was the end result not just of Kennedy's impressive work, but of painstaking and dedicated campaigning by a large number of people over *thirteen years*. From 1953 there had been a general public suspicion, shared by a great many MPs, that something had gone dreadfully wrong: so why had it taken until 1966 to rectify a palpable injustice?

Further, that was one of the few *causes célèbres* of this kind which did win an acknowledgment that justice had miscarried. The capacity of the UK judicial system for finding fault with itself is remarkably limited. Even in Britain, few institutions can match its sublime complacency. An elaborate constitutional machinery, specifically designed to detect and rectify errors in the criminal justice system, does exist. Yet a particular case of injustice would not normally come to public attention until *after* it had exhausted the appeal process. So why did the Court of Appeal, the theoretical safeguard built into the judicial system, malfunction so regularly?

This was the crux of the problem. Why, after I and perhaps millions of others had become genuinely convinced of the innocence of a convicted person, and after public and parliamentary pressure had been exerted, were the authorities hardly ever able to do anything about it?

It seemed to me invidious to tackle miscarriages of justice individually; to all appearances, they were accumulating faster than ever. Why was there the yawning gap between what the higher courts of appeal were supposed to be doing and what they in fact were doing? Had the process of judicial review of criminal cases seized up?

I started work on this book frenetically, trying to examine every major post-war case in which a miscarriage of justice had been widely suspected. I wanted to satisfy myself that there had been something genuinely awry with the verdict, and also to be able to provide sufficient information to convince readers. More importantly, I wanted to show which avenues had been explored in each case in an attempt to right the wrong.

Two conclusions soon became clear. Firstly, that just about every case which had been cited as a putative miscarriage of justice was an actual one; and, secondly, that the notion of covering all the post-war cases in one book was absurd. There were far too many.

At least, though, the initial burst of research had given me a valuable perspective. The scale of the problem has been consistently underestimated, both by the general public and by every political party.

My aim, therefore, was two-fold: to provide a cross-section of post-war miscarriages of justice – to explain how they occurred, and to convince the reader (as I was convinced) that they were genuinely errors of justice; and then to show what happened afterwards – to demonstrate how the avenues of redress theoretically available to wrongly convicted prisoners have failed, and how those specifically charged with administering the post-trial tier of the judicial process have discharged their primary duty inadequately.

Some readers may consider this criticism trenchant; I do not believe that it is misplaced. One problem in the past has been that journalists have worked on one specific case. Naturally, they have striven not to jeopardise its chances of ultimate success by directly criticising the legal and political authorities who, after all, are the arbiters of a prisoner's petition. It is an open secret that nothing is guaranteed to alienate them more than media scrutiny of (they would dub it interference in) their affairs. Consequently, journalists and politicians, who may have strong reasons for attacking the judiciary, have generally refrained from doing so. Due deference has been rigorously observed.

This approach, it seems to me, has been misguided. First of all, it has not actually proved efficacious in the majority of cases. More importantly, the fact that journalists and authors have so readily agreed to temper their criticism may be, as Geoffrey Robertson and Andrew Nicol have written, "one reason why the British media has so signally failed to make much contribution to improving the standards of justice". (*Media Law*, Sage Publications, 1985)

In fact, the process of judicial review of criminal cases is hopelessly inadequate, and that may as well be said. Appeals at first instance are invariably a waste of everybody's time, as I intend to explain. If a media campaign subsequently develops around a particular case, the Home Office will usually spend months and months deciding to set up a secret police inquiry which will then spend months and months determining that there was nothing wrong with the convictions in the first place.

This is not justice, it is administrative casuistry. The longer the Home Office, the police and the judges expect to get away with it, the more complete will be the ultimate evaporation of public faith in the system.

In a *New Statesman* article, "A System of Injustice" (29 June 1984), I gave notice of my intention to write this book. As a result, a number of people contacted me, most of them with haunting, heartbreaking tales. I would like to thank them all. Many apologies to those whose cases I have not been able to pursue.

The following people have all rendered assistance of some sort to my cause: Leah Levin and Peter Ashman of Justice; Duncan Campbell, of the *London Daily News*; Jonathan Caplan; Tim Caulfield; Sister Sarah Clarke of La Sainte Union Des Sacres Coeurs; Lord Devlin PC; John Disher; Harry Disley; Frank Dowling; Harold Evans; Lord Fitt; Paul Foot; Lord Gardiner; Ivan Geffen; Lord Gifford QC; E. D. Gilbert; Peter Hill; Rt Hon Roy Jenkins PC; Rita Lillington; Robert Lizar; Alastair Logan; Bryan Magee; Annie and Paddy Maguire; Wendy Mantle; Michael McMahon; Chris Mullin; Sir David Napley; Paddy O'Connor; Tim Owen; Lord Paget QC; Ian Peddie; Gareth Peirce; John Platts-Mills QC; Tom Sargant; Pyare Shivpuri; Paul Sieghart QC; Richard Spence; Elizabeth Thompson; Keith Verrinder; Ann Whelan; and Martin Young. I'm indebted to them all. None, of course, bears any responsibility for my conclusions, let alone my mistakes. I must add that as the book contains strong criticism of the operation of the Court of Appeal, I naturally applied for permission to interview the registrar of the Court. The request was, however, refused.

I'd like to thank Colin Honnor for taking up the idea, and Ion Trewin and Carola Edmond for seeing it through. I have used the British Library in Great Russell Street and the Newspaper Library in Colindale, the Court of Appeal library, Marylebone public library, and the internal BBC library: my thanks to all the staff concerned.

LONDON
JANUARY 1987

Part One

Selected Cases 1946–86

One

Timothy Evans

People in the case

Timothy Evans — hanged for murder of his daughter
Beryl Evans — wife of Timothy
Geraldine Evans — baby daughter of Timothy and Beryl
Mr Justice Lewis — judge at Evans trial
Christmas Humphreys KC — prosecuting counsel
Malcolm Morris — defence counsel
John Christie ⎫
Ethel Christie ⎭ — ground-floor residents at 10 Rillington Place
Mr Kitchener — first-floor resident at 10 Rillington Place
Mrs Probert — Evans' mother
Mr and Mrs Lynch — Evans' uncle and aunt
Mr Willis ⎫
Mr Jones ⎬ — building workers employed at 10 Rilling-
Mr Anderson ⎭ ton Place
Joan Vincent — friend of Beryl Evans
Muriel Eady — murder victim of John Christie
Mr Justice Finnemore — judge at Christie trial
Sir Lionel Heald — Attorney-General; prosecuting counsel
at Christie trial
Chief Inspector Griffin — police officer in charge of Christie
inquiry
James Chuter Ede — Home Secretary 1945–51
Sir David Maxwell-Fyfe
(later Lord Kilmuir) — Home Secretary 1951–4
Sir Hugh Lucas-Tooth — under-secretary of state at Home
Office 1952–5
John Scott Henderson — appointed to undertake first inquiry
Dr Odess — GP for Christie
Dr Jack Hobson — consultant psychiatrist
Dr Teare — Home Office pathologist
Sydney Silverman — MP; co-author of *Hanged – and
Innocent?*

Reginald Paget QC — MP; co-author of *Hanged – and Innocent?*

George Rogers — MP for North Kensington

Michael Eddowes — solicitor; author of *The Man on Your Conscience*

Ian Gilmour — MP; editor of the *Spectator*

John Grigg — editor of *National & English Review*

Ludovic Kennedy — author of *Ten Rillington Place*

Sir Frank Soskice — Home Secretary 1964–5

Herbert Wolfe — industrialist; campaigner

Harold Evans — journalist; editor of the *Northern Echo* and the *Sunday Times*

Eric Lubbock — MP for Orpington

Mr Justice Brabin — appointed to undertake second inquiry

THE FILE on the Timothy Evans case was opened on 30 November 1949 when he walked into the police station at Merthyr Vale, South Wales, and told the duty constable that he had put his wife's body down a drain. He was taken to Merthyr Tydfil, where he made a statement to Detective Constable Evans and Detective Sergeant Gough. They alerted the police at Notting Hill in London and a number of men were sent round to 10 Rillington Place, where Evans lived. It took three of them to lift the manhole cover outside the house. There was no sign of a body.

When this news was relayed to Evans, he made a second statement. He reiterated that his wife was dead and declared that she had died when Mr Christie, the downstairs tenant, had unsuccessfully tried to cause her to abort.

The local police returned to Rillington Place and searched Evans' flat. They also interviewed Christie at length in the police station, and simultaneously a statement was taken from Mrs Christie at home. The police were still in the dark. They didn't even know whether or not a crime had been committed.

Physically, Evans was small and slight; mentally, he was retarded. He was illiterate, immature and irresponsible. Lying came more naturally to him than telling the truth. However, he was not without some savvy. He was employed as a driver by Lancaster Food Products, and knew his way round London. He patronised a couple of local pubs and was generally regarded as innocuous. The priest who saw him in prison noted that "He has always seemed to me a meek and mild person whom I cannot imagine doing anything violent."

Evans was born in Merthyr Vale on 20 November 1924. His father walked out on the family before his birth and was never heard of again. In 1929 his mother, Thomasina, married Penry Probert, and in 1935 the family – Evans had two sisters – moved to West London.

On 20 September 1947 Evans married eighteen-year-old Beryl Thorley. The following year they moved into their top-floor flat at Rillington Place. Already resident there were a middle-aged couple, the Christies, who occupied the ground floor and had use of the patch of dirt that could barely be described as a garden; and Mr Kitchener, an elderly tenant in poor health, who was on the first floor. The Evanses' daughter, Geraldine, was born in Queen Charlotte's Maternity Hospital in October 1948.

On 2 December 1949 the police, still without knowing quite what they were looking for, searched Rillington Place thoroughly. This time, the bodies of Beryl Evans and her baby daughter were discovered in the wash-house at the back. Evans was escorted back to London, and was photographed being led from Paddington Station.

At Notting Hill police station, he was shown the two piles of clothing taken from the bodies. He was charged with the murders of his wife and daughter, and during the night made two statements admitting to the crimes. These sealed his fate.

At his trial, which opened at the Old Bailey on 11 January 1950 before Mr Justice Lewis, he was indicted on the sole charge of the murder of his baby daughter Geraldine (*see* page 13). Christmas Humphreys was the prosecuting counsel. Malcolm Morris defended Evans, who now reverted to his second Merthyr Tydfil statement in which he blamed everything on Christie. The latter, however, installed as chief prosecution witness, was winning the court's sympathy with suitably embellished biographical snippets about how he had been badly injured in the First World War, and how he had served during the Second as a special constable. Such details had the happy effect of diverting attention from his own criminal record, which included one conviction for assault on a woman.

Evans was found guilty and sentenced to death. His appeal was heard on 20 February before the Lord Chief

Justice (Lord Goddard), Mr Justice Sellers and Mr Justice Humphreys, the father of the prosecuting counsel. The family was in accord: Evans was guilty. His appeal was rejected, and he was hanged at Pentonville on 9 March 1950.

The public gave the matter little further thought until 24 March 1953 when a new tenant moved into Christie's Rillington Place flat. He opened up an alcove in the back of the kitchen and found the bodies of three women. A nationwide search ensued for John Reginald Halliday Christie. He was found a week later, not far away, on the Embankment near Putney Bridge.

By this time, the police had discovered more bodies. Mrs Christie was under the floorboards of the front room; the remains of two women were buried in the garden. In custody, Christie confessed to the murders of seven women in all: the six whose bodies had just been found, and Beryl Evans.

In September 1949 Beryl Evans had discovered that she was pregnant again. This alarmed her. She and Timothy were already living beyond their means. Now she would have to give up her part-time job in Ladbroke Grove. Their flat was tiny, and in any case, one child probably seemed enough of a headache. Evans, who loved Geraldine dearly (as, of course, did Beryl), was less concerned about the turn of events, and would not countenance Beryl's suggested remedy of an abortion. (Evans was a Catholic, though not a practising one.) In increasing desperation, she turned for assistance to several people, among them Mr Christie.

Christie indicated that he had some medical knowledge, and would be prepared to perform an abortion. He tried to persuade Evans that he had the credentials to do the job. He had had medical training, he said, and showed Evans one of his books. This was an ordinary St John's Ambulance first-aid manual, but one book was much the

same as another to Evans. He remained sceptical, however, and told Christie he didn't want anything to do with
it. Since Evans remembered Christie as saying that "with
the stuff he used, one out of every ten would die of it",
his coolness was perfectly understandable.

Nevertheless, Beryl arranged the abortion with Christie.
On the morning of Tuesday 8 November she insisted that
Evans, on his way out to work, should call in to Christie
in the downstairs room that everything was all right; and
that if he didn't, then she would. Poor, feckless Evans told
Christie, as he had been instructed, and went to work.

When he came home that evening, Christie followed
him up to his flat. "It's bad news; it didn't work," he said.
Beryl had, he explained, died while the abortion was
in progress. Christie showed him the body on the bed.
Absolving himself not just of murder but even of surgical
incompetence, he further told Evans that "her stomach
was septic-poisoned" and "another day, and she'd have
gone to hospital".

No doubt he impressed upon Evans, who was infinitely
suggestible, several not necessarily compatible considerations: that he, Christie, would be suspected and face grave
punishment – merely because of his infinite kindness in
helping out the young couple upstairs; that Evans, who
had been having rows with Beryl, would be suspected; that
he would 'expose' Evans if he did not agree to what he,
Christie, advocated.

Christie said he would deal with the body, and "dispose
of it down one of the drains". He would also try to think
of what to do about Geraldine. In the meantime, he started
trying to carry Beryl's body downstairs to Kitchener's flat
– which was empty, Kitchener being in hospital throughout
this period.

The effort was beyond him. Evans heard him "puffing
and blowing" on the stairs. He came out and helped his
wife's murderer to move her body down to the first floor.

That night Christie and Ethel, his wife, heard noises in
the flat above; or so they said. If this was true, it must

have been Evans stumbling about, saying goodbye to his wife. They had had their arguments – which married couple hasn't? – but had been fond of each other nevertheless.

In the morning, Evans fed Geraldine and set off for work. On his way out Christie told him that he thought he knew of a couple in East Acton who would be prepared to look after the baby. When Evans returned home in the evening, Christie said he had arranged everything with this couple, who were unable to have children themselves. Christie said they were to knock three times, and he would let them in.

On Thursday 10 November, therefore, Evans again fed the baby and left out her clothes. He never saw her again. That evening, Christie said that the couple had collected her.

Christie had decided to persuade Evans to sell his effects and move out of London. Throughout this period, Christie was abetted in his wickedness by several strokes of remarkable good fortune. Having committed one of the most foul crimes imaginable, and murdered a baby in her cot, he was delighted to learn that Evans had just lost his job. The latter was accordingly quite amenable to suggestions that he should leave London for a while.

After the traumatic events of the week, it must have been a blessed relief for Evans simply to be able to run away. He disposed of his furniture for £40 and left London in the early morning of Tuesday 15 November, on the 12.55 a.m. from Paddington. He changed at Cardiff and, in those pre-Beeching days, arrived at the home of his uncle and aunt, Mr and Mrs Lynch, in Merthyr Vale at 7 o'clock in the morning.

Evans told a garbled story to explain his sudden appearance, and took refuge there. On 23 November, anxious about Geraldine's welfare, he returned to London. Christie stalled, told Evans he couldn't see her until she had settled in, and sent him back to Wales.

By this time his aunt and uncle were becoming apprehensive. Mrs Lynch wrote to her sister-in-law, Mrs Probert.

When the reply reached Merthyr Vale on 30 November, the Lynches realised that Evans had been telling them a string of lies. The game was up for him.

Had the circumstances surrounding the deaths of Beryl and Geraldine Evans been properly investigated at the time, Evans would never have hanged. The problem was that the police regarded him from the outset as the villain. That is the significance of the photographers at Paddington Station. At that point, the police had Evans on a holding-charge of stealing a briefcase. The press did not happen to be in the right place at the right time, however, just to snap a petty thief. They were there because the police had tipped them off that the man was guilty of sensational crimes.

Nor was it only the police who jumped to conclusions. Evans' solicitors clearly didn't imagine that their client had a case. His barrister was probably equally pessimistic, although he did put up a spirited defence based on Evans' second Merthyr Tydfil statement in which he referred to Christie's failed attempt at an abortion. It is, nevertheless, exceptionally difficult for a defendant to accuse the major prosecution witness of the crime. (Elizabeth Thompson faced a similar hurdle; *see* Chapter 8.)

Critical pieces of evidence were ignored, the most important being provided by workmen from a building company, Larter's, who were carrying out repairs on the premises throughout the week in which Beryl and Geraldine were murdered. Most significantly, they had been using the wash-house all the time, storing their tools there.

The three men and the office manager all made what the police presumed were going to be routine statements about their movements there that week. Once they had finished, however, it was clear that these statements, far from being throwaway cards in the prosecution's hand, were actually aces for the defence.

On 11 November all but one of the men left the premises.

At that time, to quote Mr Jones, the plasterer's mate, "there was definitely nothing whatsoever in the wash-house". This would seem the kind of positive and unambiguous statement for which the police would be grateful. It is, moreover, inconceivable that Jones could have been mistaken. Like good workmen, the Larter's team had thoroughly tidied up after completing the job. The wash-house had been properly swept out.

This evidence, however, flatly contradicted Evans' Notting Hill 'confessions'. According to these he had put Beryl's body there on the 8th, and Geraldine's on the 10th.

It was, perhaps, possible to argue that Evans had committed the murders, but had been wrong in the details of his 'confession'. The account of the carpenter, Mr Anderson, removed that possibility. He had stayed after the others to finish work in the hallway. He had taken up some floorboards on the 11th, and given them to Christie on the 14th. He identified these floorboards as the wood which had been used to conceal the bodies. Since Evans had left Rillington Place on the afternoon of the 14th, this evidence virtually exculpated him.

The most indulgent interpretation of the actions subsequently taken by the police is that nobody on the case was alert or intelligent enough to realise the full implications of these statements. Two of the workmen were taken back to the police station to make second statements. They were kept waiting about three hours before they said more or less what the police wanted them to. They did so partly out of sheer frustration, and partly because they couldn't believe it made any possible difference anyway.

These fresh statements may have served the purpose of the police, but they were palpably nonsense. Mr Jones now said that he had collected his tools on the 11th, "not taking any particular notice of the wash-house at the time". The wash-house was such a small, confined area that the bodies, had they been there, must have been noticed.

A second piece of police deviousness was far more serious. They asked Larter's for the men's work-sheets.

All except one were duly returned. The missing one detailed the work undertaken by Mr Willis, the plasterer, and showed that he had inspected the wash-house *after* the time when Evans said he had left the bodies there. It was evidence of exceptional importance, but it was never seen again.

A third reprehensible matter was the way the police handled the carpenter's evidence. No statement was ever taken from Mr Anderson.

Other pieces of evidence should have been adduced in Evans' defence. Joan Vincent, one of Beryl's close friends, went up to the Evanses' flat at lunchtime on 8 November. She found she couldn't open the door, apparently because someone was holding it on the other side. She assumed that Beryl did not wish to see her, and went away again. A feasible assumption is that she arrived when Christie had just committed the murder.

This provided another illustration of how the police tried to dispose of 'inconvenient' evidence. They attempted to persuade Mrs Vincent that this had occurred the day before. However, the fact that the front door to the house was wide open argues against this. It suggests that the builders were on site, and they did not arrive until Tuesday, the day of Beryl's death.

Later in the week, Vincent paid a second visit. On this occasion, Christie told her that Beryl and the baby had gone to Bristol. Had this evidence been assimilated, it should have saved Evans, since what Christie said contradicted what he later told the police.

Maureen, Evans' younger sister, also joined the search for the family. When she went round to Rillington Place the following week, Christie and his wife each gave differing accounts to her of the 'departure' of Beryl and Geraldine. "Well, one of you is lying," she said as she walked away.

Other salient points were neglected. When police originally searched Evans' flat they found a newspaper cutting about the notorious Stanley Setty torso case. This seemed to suggest that Evans was a man with murder on his mind.

It should have provided quite contrary indications: Evans couldn't read and would have had no use for or understanding of it. Presumably it had been planted there by Christie.

There was also a small but significant contradiction in the statements Christie and his wife made when they were interviewed separately at the very beginning of the investigation – if 'investigation' is not too generous a description of the superficial review of events undertaken by the police.

Clearly, Evans' two Notting Hill confessions told most heavily against him. There are, however, abundant reasons for questioning their accuracy. For a start, the phraseology seems unlikely to have been Evans'. He is recorded as saying not that he had rows with his wife about their debts, but that he "accused her of squandering the money". The statements are sprinkled with such relatively articulate comments, and suggest that someone was putting words into his mouth.

Taken line by line, the statements give details that are frequently incorrect; taken as a whole, they don't make sense.

Point 1: it would have been impossible for Evans to have placed his wife's body in the wash-house without Christie or his wife being aware of it. (If they had heard the noise in the flat upstairs, as they said, why hadn't they heard anything when the frail Evans was supposed to have lugged his wife's body downstairs and right past their bedroom door?)

Point 2: neglected babies can make an unbelievable amount of noise – yet during two whole days, when she was left on her own, this baby apparently disturbed neither Christie nor his wife.

Point 3: during three weeks in November, Christie did not discover the bodies himself (nor, for that matter, did his dog).

Evans' Notting Hill statements were made when he was in extreme shock and distress, emotionally vulnerable and even more suggestible than usual. Until he was taken into

Notting Hill police station, he had no idea that his beloved daughter was dead. As he later explained, "The police caught me for a statement when I was upset."

In contravention of the judge's rules, no time was logged at the end of Evans' second Notting Hill statement, made on 2 December. Three years later, the police insisted that it had been taken down between 10.00 and 11.15 p.m. This also fuels suspicion about its reliability. The statement seems too lengthy to have been made, and laboriously taken down, and then read back to Evans, all in seventy-five minutes. It took more than twice that time to take down the second Merthyr Tydfil statement, which was of equivalent length. To judge from newspaper reports of the time, Evans was still being questioned long past midnight.

There is no good reason to doubt his second Merthyr Tydfil statement. On being informed that his wife's body was not, after all, down a drain, he must have been very puzzled. His earlier statement had been made solely with a view to protecting Christie. Once he knew that Christie had deceived him, he had no inhibitions about telling the truth. That is what he did. He was probably feeling no overwhelming anxiety. The local police were not hostile and seemingly behaved with the utmost probity. The statement has an inherent plausibility. For example, Evans said that Christie had told him that his wife's body was "septic-poisoned". It is difficult to understand how such a term could have appeared in Evans' vocabulary, if not in just the manner he said.

It should also be remembered that Evans made that statement on 30 November 1949, and did not see it again. In his evidence in court, on 12 January, he deviated from it not one whit. Had he been lying in Merthyr, would he have been able to recall his lies so accurately?

Twice during the trial Christie came perilously close to exposure. For example, he said in evidence that Evans had told him on Wednesday of the departure of his wife and child. In his original statement to the police, he said Evans had told him this on the Tuesday. More significantly,

Malcolm Morris cross-examined Christie about Evans'
testimony, during which the latter had said that Christie,
in trying to persuade him to permit his wife's abortion,
had shown him the "medical textbook". Christie denied
all this. In that case, Morris asked Christie, how could he
possibly have known that you possessed such a book? It
was a pertinent question, one to which Christie was unable
to supply an answer.

Those investigating the case might also have noticed that
in Mrs Christie's original statement she said that she and
her husband had been using the wash-house daily to obtain
water, which seems logical enough. From the committal
hearing on, she changed tack, saying "the wash-house was
never used".

With the fates apparently so collectively deployed
against him, poor Evans was entitled to all the disinterested
assistance which it is in the power of the English judiciary
to provide. He received none. The judge undermined
Evans' slender chances of an acquittal still further by
deepening confusion over what he had said with regard to
each of his four statements. He "grossly distorted the
truth", as the author Ludovic Kennedy recorded in *Ten
Rillington Place*.

One other matter didn't figure at all in Evans' trial, but
was certainly relevant. This was the curious affair of the
skull of Muriel Eady, one of the two women whom Christie
murdered in 1943, and whose bodies he buried in his
garden. At the time that Evans was being questioned in
Merthyr Tydfil, and Notting Hill police were searching
Rillington Place, Christie's dog unearthed the Eady skull,
hardly a timely discovery. He waited until it was dark, and
then took the skull and threw it into the shell of a bombed
house in St Mark's Road, a few minutes' walk away. It
was discovered by children some days later and reported
to police. A pathologist examined it, and a local coroner
determined that it was the skull of a bomb victim.

This was police work that mocked the description 'detection'. Had no forensic scientist anything to say about the

condition of the skull – about whether it had been buried in earth rather than rubble, for example? If it had lain there since the house was bombed – in the 1940 blitz – how was it that in *nine years* it hadn't previously been discovered? Murder investigations were then proceeding at a nearby house – did nobody at all consider that an interesting coincidence?

Christie's assertion in 1953 that it was he who had killed Beryl Evans discomfited, but was not an immediate disaster for, the legal and political authorities. As frequently happened in capital murder cases, Evans was charged with only one offence. (This manoeuvre was partly to husband resources, and save court time and public money; partly to allow the Crown, in the event of an acquittal, to bring alternative charges against the defendant.) Because the charge ensured that he could neither expect jury sympathy nor plead mitigating circumstances, he was accused, and duly convicted, of the murder of his daughter, not of his wife.

Even so, Evans had originally been committed at the magistrates court on both charges. At the outset of his trial, Mr Justice Lewis ruled that evidence regarding his wife's murder was admissible. Since the prosecution was able to supply a motive for Beryl's murder – domestic stress brought on by her propensity to accumulate debts – but not one for the infanticide, the evidence was obviously telling. Furthermore, the appeal court rejected Evans' appeal on the grounds that the evidence provided in the 'confessions' was "highly relevant . . . with regard to the whole matter relating both to the wife and the child". The fact that he had not been executed for Beryl's murder was therefore merely a technicality. His presumed responsibility for her death had been writ large throughout the judicial process from start to finish.

There was a certain level of official embarrassment – Evans' conviction had been secured through his own 'confessions'; three years later, someone else was confessing to Beryl's murder – so the police simply issued a press statement saying there was no connection between the two cases.

Like Evans, Christie was charged with just one murder; unlike Evans, he was charged with killing his own wife, whose body had been found under the floorboards of the front room. The trial opened at the Old Bailey on 22 June 1953 before Mr Justice Finnemore. It was not the first major news story of that eventful month – the coronation and the conquest of Everest had preceded it – but while it lasted, the trial overshadowed everything else. Public interest was intense.

The prosecution was led, significantly, by the Attorney-General, Sir Lionel Heald, who did his utmost to quell the gathering speculation. "Have you any ground from your inquiries," he asked Chief Inspector Griffin of the Hammersmith police force, "for believing that the wrong man was hanged in the Evans case?" "None at all," was the confident reply.

Suspicions were not allayed that easily. The Christie trial abounded with references to Evans, whatever Inspector Griffin might have said. In his final speech, Heald allowed the political sensitivity of the business to surface briefly. "I think you [members of the jury] will understand how, especially in my position . . . in a governmental position – it is most important that nothing avoidable should be said in Court which might cast an unjustified reflection on the administration of justice . . . it is most important that one should scrutinise most carefully what is and what is not proved with regard to a case of that kind."[1]

As a rule, the authorities in Britain go to quite extraordinary lengths to preserve the fiction that legal and political issues are wholly separate. This was a rare acknowledgment that they intersect. With this gentle warning to the jurors, Heald was vouchsafing an all-too-rare elucidation of the first principle of British justice: there must be no political embarrassment.

Almost all the subsequent failures to rectify wrongs inflicted by the judicial process may be attributed to the meticulous application of this principle.

Christie's defence of insanity was unsuccessful. Found guilty, he was sentenced to death.[2]

By now, three things were abundantly clear. First: it seemed an incredible coincidence that two stranglers, who were killing people in exactly the same way, should, unknown to each other, have been living in the same house at the same time, disposing of the bodies of their victims in precisely the same way. Second: if Evans was guilty, then it was uncanny that he should have chosen to accuse of his crimes perhaps the one man in the country who was strangling people in exactly that fashion. Third: if Evans was guilty, then Christie would have had no reason to lie at his trial – but in the light of his own trial, it was now obvious that he had lied throughout.

Within twenty-four hours of the Christie trial, MPs – all of whom, at this stage, came from the opposition (Labour) benches – were demanding an inquiry into the circumstances of Evans' conviction. Sir Hugh Lucas-Tooth, under-secretary of state at the Home Office, told Sydney Silverman, untiring opponent of capital punishment, and George Rogers, the MP in whose North Kensington constituency Rillington Place was located, that the Home Secretary, Sir David Maxwell-Fyfe, was "giving urgent consideration to the matter".

Urgency is a relative concept, and nowhere is it more relative than in the Home Office. On 25 June Christie was sentenced to death. On 30 June his execution was fixed for 15 July. On 6 July, with time fast running out, Maxwell-Fyfe told the Commons that he had appointed John Scott Henderson QC, the Recorder of Portsmouth, to head an inquiry into the Evans and Christie trials and "to report whether there is any ground for thinking there may have been a miscarriage of justice".

Because Maxwell-Fyfe was adamant that it could not be a public inquiry, MPs were immediately apprehensive. He did, however, reassure them that the conduct of the inquiry would be "according to the rules of natural justice".

Scott Henderson was to be assisted by George Blackburn, the assistant chief constable of the West Riding of Yorkshire, and G. A. Peacock, a Treasury solicitor. Anthony Wedgwood Benn, MP for Bristol South-East, wondered whether there should be any lay assessors, as the Home Office, the legal profession and the police were all interested parties. Maxwell-Fyfe responded that he had done all he could to ensure that the inquiry was "of the most impartial and thorough nature", and generally pooh-poohed the anxieties that were being expressed on the opposition benches. "It will be a poor day for Great Britain," he said, "when we cannot find men in this country who are prepared to undertake an inquiry and come fearlessly to the conclusion to which the facts point without any regard for the consequences of opinion."

The Scott Henderson report was published on 14 July 1953, a poor day for Great Britain. Its conclusions were that the case against Evans was "an overwhelming one"; that Christie's statements that he was responsible for the murder of Beryl Evans were "not only unreliable but untrue"; and that "there is no ground for thinking that there may have been any miscarriage of justice in the conviction of Evans."

To reach these categorical conclusions, against which not only a mass of evidence but also plain common sense militated, Scott Henderson can only have sifted the available information in the most selective manner. He disregarded evidence which might have benefited Evans, such as that of the workmen and Joan Vincent, and gave added weight to that which seemed to incriminate him (for example, the spur-of-the-moment reactions of his family, when they were as much in the dark as everybody else; Scott Henderson even published a private letter written by Evans' mother without having received permission to do so). On the other hand, he submitted Christie to the gentlest of interrogations, and that only after the police had already visited Christie in prison and told him there was no evidence that he had murdered the baby Geraldine.

Scott Henderson was able to 'confirm' Evans' guilt by perpetuating, or even inventing, misconceptions – most notably the 'irresistible inference' that Evans could not have known the details of the murders and disposal of the bodies revealed in his 'confessions' unless "he had first-hand knowledge of the crime".

In fact, evidence given at Evans' trial had indicated that he might well have been told these details by the police before embarking on his 'confession'; and, in any case, because the times of his statements were not correctly logged, it is impossible to know to what extent words might have been put into Evans' mouth. The most important point, surely, is that the Evans 'confessions' contained not a single detail about the crimes that was not already known to the police. Evans could have inferred virtually everything from the pitiful piles of clothing at the police station. The 'confession' of George Beattie, made a quarter of a century later, seems to have been obtained in very similar circumstances.[3]

Scott Henderson also referred to the newspaper cutting about the Setty murder discovered in Evans' flat to suggest that he, Evans, was copying the crime – in other words, drawing precisely the wrong inference from the evidence, just as the police had done. There was less reason for Scott Henderson to overlook the obvious, especially since by then it was known that Christie did collect newspaper cuttings.

During Christie's Old Bailey trial, two mistakes in evidence had perpetuated the myth of Evans' guilt. Dr Odess, the GP whom the hypochondriac Christie regularly visited, said that Christie had complained of fibrositis throughout November 1949. (Christie always pretended that he was in too much pain to be able to lift a body.) This was an error. Dr Odess apologised to Scott Henderson, explaining that Christie only complained of fibrositis on Saturday 12 November; and that this could have been caused by lifting a heavy weight. Odess, however, agreed that he was no specialist, and Henderson ignored the point.

The second mistake occurred when Heald said that Evans had lied about the abortion, and that this was accordingly indicative of his guilt. This point was crassly reiterated in the Scott Henderson report: "the most material fact is that no interference with Mrs Evans' pregnancy was attempted". No one had ever actually supposed that Christie *was* an abortionist; only that he had pretended to be one to gain access to Beryl Evans. In an unavailing attempt to lend credibility to his conclusions, Scott Henderson advanced the theory that Christie would have wanted to confess to as many murders as possible in order to strengthen his insanity plea. (In which case, might not he have confessed to the murder of the baby Geraldine, since nothing could have been more insane than that? But there were many, many questions which did not apparently occur to the Recorder of Portsmouth.)

Even apart from all this, Scott Henderson had conducted the inquiry in a manner which could legitimately be described as bullying. Counsel for the Evans family were not permitted to cross-examine, they were excluded from hearing the evidence of witnesses they themselves had suggested calling, and Scott Henderson refused to put to Christie and other witnesses questions which they had proposed.

Dr Jack Hobson, consultant psychiatrist at the Middlesex Hospital, saw Christie in prison and probably got closer to him than anyone else. In the last interview he had with him, Christie said, "I seem to remember something about the baby . . ." Hobson is convinced that he would have learned the circumstances of the baby's death – "something that now we shall never know, for I was prevented from interviewing Christie again".

When the Scott Henderson team talked to Christie, Hobson's presence at the interview was expressly forbidden. He was seen twice by the inquiry team, but "on neither occasion was I allowed to volunteer information nor to be asked questions other than those chosen by Scott Henderson himself".[4]

This was the inquiry which, the Home Secretary had reassured MPs, would be conducted "according to the rules of natural justice".

Leaving aside both the way in which the inquiry was conducted, and the report itself, it is sufficiently scandalous that its publication was timed to thwart the attempts of MPs and others who did want to get at the truth. MPs received copies less than twenty-four hours before Christie was due to be executed, and the Speaker refused to accede to frantic requests for it to be debated immediately.

During those dramatic days in June and July, the Home Secretary displayed what in different circumstances might have seemed a wholly proper humanitarian concern for a man under sentence of death. He refused to offer him unjustified hope, or to prolong the agony, by postponing the execution. It might equally have been argued, however, that in these circumstances, in which Christie had knowingly played such a central role in sending an innocent man, an unwitting Sydney Carton, to the gallows in his place – in such exceptional circumstances, the postponement of his execution would be one extra cross he would just have to bear.[5]

In the end, then, the debate took place on 29 July, a fortnight after the one man who knew exactly what had happened had been eliminated from further inquiries.

Geoffrey Bing QC, MP for Hornchurch, led the onslaught on the Scott Henderson report, delivering a lengthy speech which Michael Foot described as "one of the most formidable which had been delivered in this House for many years". Bing considered the report unsatisfactory in every respect. "It was unfortunate," he commented, "that the Home Secretary presented it to parliament without either explanation or opportunity for debate. The whole of the report was shot through with prejudice and evidence of all sorts of irregularities"; the manner in which it had been written was "most deceptive and improper".

Reginald Paget said it deliberately concealed the truth and was dishonest. Michael Foot, at his most abrasive in those days, argued bluntly that "it was not worth the paper it was printed on", and Aneurin Bevan pledged that MPs would persist in the matter until justice was done.

Maxwell-Fyfe, himself a barrister, rose to the defence both of the report ("what we all want is the truth. I believe that on this occasion we have got it"), and of the integrity of Scott Henderson("there is not a scintilla to support the attack on his motives and methods").

The House was not at all convinced. "We are not attacking this report because it does not disclose the truth," countered Paget; "we are attacking it because it deliberately conceals the truth. We are attacking it not because it is mistaken, but because, we say, it is dishonest." Sydney Silverman pointed out that the administration would be understandably reluctant to admit to such a fatal failing in the judicial process; but that the administration of justice could survive such an admission. What it could not survive was the possibility that people might begin to doubt "not its infallibility, but its integrity. If we allow people to believe that, having made the error, all the resources of the community are being employed to hush it up, then indeed confidence in the administration of justice will be undermined."[6]

Altogether, the debate showed the Commons at its most purposeful and impassioned in its defence of the concept of justice; and at its most penetratingly critical of executive shortcomings. The authorities were clearly so rattled that the story took another extraordinary turn on 14 September when Scott Henderson attempted to answer his many critics with a supplementary report.

Now, referring to the original statements of the workmen, Scott Henderson blithely wrote, "there was no reason why [they] should have been made available to the defence"; referring to the disappearance of the crucial time-sheet, he submitted, "I did investigate that, and satisfied myself that the police had no responsibility for [its] disappearance".

Scott Henderson also claimed not to have seen a statement, apparently in Christie's own handwriting, in which he described how he had murdered Beryl Evans. (It had been published in the *Sunday Pictorial*.) "Why not?" Paget wanted to know. "If Scott Henderson did not know it, his ignorance can hardly have been shared by anyone else in England." Overall, he concluded, "this even more unsatisfactory addendum to an unsatisfactory report makes a proper public inquiry all the more essential."[7]

One bizarre development succeeded another. The Home Secretary attended a reconstruction of the taking of Evans' statements at Notting Hill, which purported to demonstrate that the police had timed them accurately. Despite this – or, perhaps, because of it (the affair was surely more indicative that the cover-up was proceeding apace than that the police had behaved punctiliously) – the storm refused to abate. A further eighteen questions awaited the attention of Maxwell-Fyfe when parliament reassembled after the summer recess, and on 5 November the supplementary Scott Henderson report was debated.

MPs who were demanding an inquiry into the inquiry won no concessions from the government, but did have the satisfaction of making their case in an extra-parliamentary context. During the course of the decade a gap formed between the bureaucratic line on Timothy Evans (he was guilty), and what a growing section of the public perceived the truth to be (he was innocent). Ewan MacColl, one of Britain's leading folk-singers, composed an angry song about the case:

> They sent Tim Evans to the drop
> For a crime he didn't do;
> 'Twas Christie was the murderer
> The judge and jury too.[8]*

This was rather hard on the jury, who could hardly have been expected to weigh evidence that had been concealed from them; and somewhat lax on the officials involved. Among these, though, one man of honour was found: Chuter Ede, the Home Secretary who had sanctioned the execution in 1950. He conceded that a dreadful mistake had been made, and joined with those campaigning for posthumous justice for Evans.

In 1955 Michael Eddowes' *The Man on Your Conscience*, the first of the genuinely influential books on the case, was published.

This generated renewed interest in the affair. Ian Gilmour (of the *Spectator*), John Grigg (*National & English Review*) and Linton Andrews (*Yorkshire Post*) jointly wrote to *The Times*, arguing that the reputation of the police force was now at stake.[9] Its efficiency was in doubt because Christie, who had a bad criminal record, had been taken on as a special constable during the war; and its fairness was in question because the police knew at the time of Evans' trial that Muriel Eady's skull had been dug up in Christie's garden. This had been gleaned from *Scotland Yard*, a book published the previous year, 1954, by Sir Harold Scott, former chief commissioner of the metropolitan police.

The assistant commissioner of the London CID immediately responded that this was not true; Sir Harold had been mistaken.[10] Gilmour and co. retorted that this threw further doubt on the competence of the metropolitan police, since Scott's book had ostensibly been written from police records.[11] If those at the top made such errors at leisure, what debacles were those below likely to perpetrate in moments of stress?

Gilmour and Grigg developed their arguments in a pamphlet, "The Case of Timothy Evans: An Appeal to Reason", published by the *Spectator* in 1956.

Ludovic Kennedy's *Ten Rillington Place* was published at the beginning of 1961. The book provided a comprehensive analysis of the case. Its main virtue was simply that it assembled all the known facts, and did so in such an illuminating and compelling manner.

Nevertheless, Kennedy did have some cards of his own to play. In particular, he demonstrated that the onset of Christie's fibrositis coincided with the time when he must have moved the body of Beryl Evans from Mr Kitchener's flat to the wash-house. This point had previously been discussed by Dr Odess and Scott Henderson. When, however, Odess agreed that he was not a specialist, Scott Henderson, determined to leave no stone turned in his pursuit of the truth, abandoned the matter. Kennedy did what was logical and took the available information to five leading specialists, each of whom independently asserted that the condition was most likely to have been caused by the lifting of a heavy weight.

Kennedy also adduced evidence buried in Evans' solicitors' brief to counsel. This was a reference to the fact that at the committal hearing, Dr Teare, the Home Office pathologist, appeared to suggest that there had been posthumous penetration of Mrs Evans. At the time, the *defence* was concerned that this evidence should not be placed before the crown court on the grounds that it made a sickening case even more repellent. However, Kennedy asserted that it was evidence which removed all trace of suspicion from Evans who could, after all, have had sex with his wife while she was alive; only the necrophiliac Christie needed to wait for the opportunity until she was dead. (Had a swab been taken of Beryl's vagina, the whole issue would have been put beyond doubt from the start.)

In a letter to the *Sunday Times*, Dr Teare fiercely disputed all this. "These interpretations are quite contrary to my belief," he wrote, "and have resulted in a complete distortion of my evidence."[12] Kennedy riposted that the brief to counsel had definitely stated that at the magistrates court Dr Teare had "purported to suggest" that there might have been an attempt at sexual penetration after death.[13] Evans' solicitors could not have invented this. (Suppose they had; it was extraordinary that it should have coincided

so precisely with what was subsequently learned of
Christie's gruesome behaviour.) Kennedy also made the
point that the explanation which Dr Teare now advanced
for a bruise on Beryl's vagina differed from that given in
his deposition eleven years earlier.

By this stage, Maxwell-Fyfe had become Lord Kilmuir,
and was Lord Chancellor. The Home Secretary was R. A.
Butler. Two stalwarts of the Evans campaign, George
Rogers and Sydney Silverman, asked if he would now
order a fresh inquiry into the case. Butler stalled, saying
on 26 January 1961 that, although he was not convinced
of the value of a fresh inquiry, he was "examining carefully
the recently-published book".

Butler's final reply on 16 March ruled out a further
inquiry – partly on the grounds of the inconclusiveness of
the exchange of letters in the *Sunday Times* between
Kennedy and Teare. "It seems clear," he said, "that no
definite deduction about the circumstances in which Mrs
Evans met her death can now be drawn from the medical
evidence."

"I have given careful consideration," Butler continued,
"to the suggestion that Evans should be granted a free
pardon. There is no precedent for recommending a
posthumous free pardon and the legal powers to do so are
doubtful. In any event a free pardon cannot be granted
without a certainty which is not possible in this case."[14]

Throughout the long history of the struggle to clear
Evans' name, the bureaucratic stratagems to evade logical
inferences and muzzle rational argument were shameless.
Even in such a context, however, Butler's statement was
the most disgraceful of all. Confronted with the pellucid
argument which Kennedy had advanced, the Home Office
simply abandoned its position and fell back to a new line
of defence. As a military manoeuvre, it might well have
been admirable; as a device for keeping at bay the uphol-
ders of those values which the Home Office was supposed
to have been protecting, it was scandalous. It is appalling
that we allow ourselves to be governed in such a manner.

There were now, it seemed, three wholly new reasons why nothing could be done about Evans' case: (i) there was no precedent; (ii) the legal powers to do so were "doubtful"; and (iii) there could be no "certainty".

Each of these could easily have been countered: was there any precedent for hanging an innocent man? If the legal powers to remedy, as far as decently possible, such a monstrous injustice were "doubtful", then should not fresh ones be taken? "Certainty"? This is something not given to man. It is in humble recognition of this that the law has never pretended to have anything to do with "certainty".

The Home Office, though, does have the knack of making common-sense arguments seem ridiculously inappropriate.

The anger on the opposition benches grew. "This case will not lie down," declared Patrick Gordon Walker, MP for Smethwick, on 15 June. "It will not be stifled by authority. The weight of opinion that Evans was wrongly convicted is increasing and will increase. Sooner or later justice will be done." Sir Hugh Lucas-Tooth, still stonewalling on behalf of officialdom, dismissed Kennedy's *tour de force* as "tendentious", a book which "has misled a great many people". For good measure, he added that "it was an extraordinary coincidence that two stranglers should be living in the one house at the same time, but there was no reason why it should not have occurred."

The 15 June debate was lengthy and absorbing. Chuter Ede's contribution was especially moving, for he, more than anyone, had cause to wish that there was no need for the debate at all. Prior to becoming the first post-war Home Secretary, though, he had been Butler's parliamentary private secretary during the passage of the 1944 Education Act, and a close relationship existed between them. Ede revealed that on an earlier occasion Butler had approached him privately about the matter, but more recently Butler had said to him, "I am advised that I cannot say that this man Evans was innocent."

Ede then took up this newly introduced notion that there was no precedent. "We are concerned here today not so much with the law as with justice. One of the difficulties for all of us, whether we be lawyers, magistrates or ministers of the Crown, is to reconcile law and justice. If one has to go, let us be quite certain that, for the safety of the State, it must not be justice."

Another member to speak in the debate was Sir Frank Soskice. "I desire to make a most earnest appeal to the Home Secretary," he said, "to accept the suggestion that there should be a further investigation into the circumstances of this case . . . If ever there was a debt due to justice, and to the reputation both of our own judicial system and to the public conscience of many millions of people in this country, that debt is one that the Home Secretary should now pay."[15]

By the time the case was next raised in parliament, in 1965, a Labour government had taken office. Soskice was himself Home Secretary. Now, surely, was the moment for the hypocrisy and procrastination to be swept away.

Not a bit of it. The script was the same as before; only the roles had been reversed. *Conservative* MPs in opposition now tried valiantly to extract common sense from a stubborn *Labour* administration.

On 4 February 1965 Ian Gilmour, by now MP for Norfolk Central, asked the Home Secretary if he would make an official declaration of Evans' innocence. Soskice replied that, even if the innocence of Evans were to be established, he had no power to do any such thing. Gilmour pressed him. "Would the Home Secretary not agree that virtually nobody outside the Home Office has serious doubts about the innocence of Evans? Will he not accept that until the Home Office is prepared to make this declaration and stop taking refuge in technicalities, its word on similar matters will inevitably lack weight?"

"I pressed for an inquiry when this was previously debated," admitted Soskice. "That was three or four years ago. I do not think that an inquiry would serve any useful purpose at this stage. I think it would be kinder not to express views one way or the other."[16]

At least no one could ever claim that the Home Office lacked effrontery: it was now issuing guidelines on the matter of *kindness*. The debate was concluded but the matter was not closed.

"Why has there been this change of attitude?" inquired the Liberal peer Lord Byers in the Lords on 18 May. "The Home Secretary has reached the conclusion that it would be impossible to reach any definite conclusion," replied government spokesman Lord Stonham, clearly not a man to shun contradictions.

Lord Brockway pointed out that both Soskice and the Foreign Secretary – Patrick Gordon Walker – had, as opposition MPs, firmly committed themselves to the Evans campaign. He urged the government to reconsider: it was a matter of justice.

"Justice," responded Stonham, "that is precisely our difficulty in this case. The Home Secretary does not believe that a further inquiry could make anyone certain of the guilt or innocence of Evans."

"This is a very weak answer," Byers retorted. "Is he satisfied with the Scott Henderson report? They [Labour MPs and peers] were not, up to the time they came into office."[17]

Why, indeed, was Soskice so ready to step straight into the shoes of his Conservative predecessor?

Meanwhile, we shall encounter Lord Stonham again. He had further weak answers to deliver.

For some, Soskice's hypocrisy was the last straw. In Darlington, an industrialist, Herbert Wolfe, had been convinced by Kennedy's book. He had arrived in this country in 1933, a refugee from German state injustice. Unlike many of the natives of his adopted country, he found the concept of British justice infinitely precious. He did not take it for granted.

He wrote an article on the Evans case and sent it to the editor of his local paper, the *Northern Echo*. Local newspaper editors are rarely in a position to exert a critical influence on political events. But this editor was Harold Evans, quickly to become the outstanding journalist of his day (as editor of the *Sunday Times*).

"After receiving Wolfe's article," he said, "I got hold of Kennedy's book. I read it on the train to London, and became so angry I wanted to pull the communication cord. I thought, this is an outrage; something must be done about it."

Something was done about it. Even though Darlington had no conceivable connection with the tragic story of his namesake, Evans took up the "Man on Our Conscience" theme. "I published something every day for months," he wrote.[18] "Members of my staff were furious about the campaign. When I went on holiday, they tried to drop it. I came back and reinstated it."

The campaign was conducted with vigour, skill and remarkable pertinacity. Wolfe telephoned people incessantly; Evans produced pamphlets; MPs were lobbied. Eric Lubbock (then Liberal MP for Orpington, now Lord Avebury) and Lord Chuter Ede, as he by then was, were especially valuable allies. On 28 July 1965 a campaign committee was formed in London, with Ludovic Kennedy as its chairman.

To announce the launch of this committee, a press conference was called. Journalists were asked to assemble in a Notting Hill pub, and from there were taken to the house where the murders had been committed: 10 Rillington Place. By that stage, the property was owned by Michael Eddowes, who had been campaigning with devoted zeal for over a decade. His purpose in purchasing the house was to maintain it as it was, and thus to demonstrate that its mere physical properties (even apart from other considerations) were sufficient to discredit the prosecution case presented at Evans' trial: because the house was so small, Evans would not have been able to carry the body of his wife past Christie's room without disturbing him; the bodies could not have remained undetected in the wash-house; and so on.

However, with about twenty pressmen tramping round the house and the back yard, the West Indian tenants suddenly took umbrage at this unexpected invasion of their privacy. They locked in the journalists and refused to return the key. Evans vividly remembers shouting to a passing policeman through the letter-box, explaining that Eddowes was the legal owner of the house, and that they all wanted to be let out of it.

Because of this bizarre and, perhaps, eerie experience the press conference undoubtedly received greater coverage than otherwise. Shortly afterwards, Evans wrote to the Prime Minister, Harold Wilson, who promised that the government would intervene. Lubbock headed an all-party delegation of MPs to the Home Office. Finally, on 19 August, Soskice agreed to set up another inquiry, chaired by Mr Justice Brabin.

If the Scott Henderson inquiry had been conducted *prestissimo*, Brabin's was, by contrast, *adagio* in the extreme. Brabin himself was away on holiday at the announcement of the inquiry. Admittedly, there was by now no special need for urgency; but equally, it was hard to understand why fourteen months were needed to produce this second report.

The inquiry lasted thirty-two days, took over a million words in evidence, was completed on 21 January 1966, and the report finally published on 12 October 1966.

In a last bizarre twist to this astonishing saga, it reached a conclusion which no one could have anticipated. Christie had indeed killed the baby Geraldine, the crime for which Evans was hanged; but Evans himself had killed Beryl, his wife. A technical miscarriage, therefore, but a perfect example of rough justice.

"Whereas all those who had previously studied the case," wrote Ludovic Kennedy, "were agreed that whoever had done one murder had done both, Brabin produced the novel idea that while Evans had probably not murdered the baby, he probably had murdered his wife. This certainly was an arresting theory, especially as there was virtually no evidence to support it."[19]

On closer examination, it could be seen that Brabin had made some startling assumptions *en route* to this innovatory conclusion. Take, for example, Brabin's comments about Mrs Christie's evidence regarding the wash-house. In her statement to the police on 5 December, she had said, "We have been using this place daily for the purpose of getting water for rinsing the slop pail"; in her deposition, barely a fortnight later, she said, "I didn't use the wash-house at the back. The boiler was out of order and hadn't been used for years." These, surely, would appear to be incompatible statements. Brabin, though, set to work to reconcile them. "I would have *thought it obvious*," he wrote, "that she was saying no more than that she did not use the wash-house as a wash-house but with the other tenants used it as a water-point." (Author's italics.)

I can hardly believe that anyone would have agreed with Brabin that *it was obvious* this is the correct interpretation of what Mrs Christie had been saying. There is, moreover, a corollary. If those wash-house statements are reconciled, then it becomes necessary to explain how Mrs Christie failed to notice the bodies there. "I see no reason why it [Beryl's body] should not have gone undetected by Mrs Christie," Brabin blithely reported. "I say that the probability is that both these men [Christie and Evans] killed and that both killed by strangulation using a ligature."

For some, that was the end of the matter. "There seems little more that the Home Secretary can do," said *The Times*.

It should be recorded that there were two positive aspects to Brabin's report. It concluded that no jury could possibly have convicted Evans of either murder had all the evidence been available; and, in its entirety, it was so palpably absurd that no one believed a word of it. The

British public could distinguish three new levels of deceit: lies, damned lies, and official inquiries into the Evans case.

It was against this background that the next, and closing, development took place: on 18 October it was announced from Buckingham Palace that the Queen had granted Evans a posthumous free pardon.

That was it. Simple, really. Roy Jenkins, who had replaced Soskice as Home Secretary in December 1965, had shown that, *pace The Times*, there was something he could do. He could discharge the functions of his office honourably; quite a revolutionary notion for a Home Secretary. At a stroke he restored to the English judicial system a little of the decency, dignity and common sense of which innumerable legal and political mandarins had, during 13 years of officially prescribed fecklessness, managed to deprive it. The Royal Courts of Justice were not reduced to rubble; public confidence in the administration of justice did not evaporate overnight. But post-war Britain had hanged its first innocent man. Or so everyone was persuaded to think.

Two

Walter Rowland

People in the case

Olive Balchin — murder victim
Walter Rowland — charged with her murder
David Ware — confessed to murder of Balchin
Mr Justice Sellers — trial judge
Kenneth Burke — defence counsel
Basil Nield KC — prosecution counsel
Edward MacDonald — licensed broker; prosecution witness
Elizabeth Copley — waitress; prosecution witness
Norman Mercer — licensee; prosecution witness
Rita Leach — prosecution witness
Dr Jenkins — pathologist
Dr Firth — forensic scientist
Norman Jones — police sergeant in Stockport
Frank Beaumont — landlord at Rowland's lodgings
Henry Somerville — defence witness at appeal
Mrs Coppock — pub landlady; defence witness at appeal
J. C. Jolly KC — head of inquiry
Superintendent Barratt   ⎫
Detective Inspector Hannam ⎭ — assistants to Jolly
Wilfred Gosling — pub landlord; witness at inquiry

EVANS, THOUGH, was not the first. That distinction belongs to Walter Rowland, who was hanged at Manchester's Strangeways prison on 27 February 1947.

The body of Olive Balchin was discovered at 11.00 on a Sunday morning, 20 October 1946. A prostitute who had apparently left Birmingham three months earlier, she had been murdered the previous evening on a bombed site in Deansgate, in the heart of Manchester.

Her death had been especially violent. She had been savagely beaten about the head with a hammer. There could be no doubt about the murder weapon: it was lying, covered in blood, close by the body; or that it was newly purchased: the brown paper in which it had been wrapped was also conveniently discarded, in a corner of the site.

A week later Rowland was charged with the murder. His trial opened before Mr Justice Sellers at Manchester assizes on 12 December 1946.

According to the prosecution, Rowland was identified by three separate witnesses in circumstances which had a direct bearing on the case; he knew Olive Balchin, had admitted to being with her on the Friday, and furthermore to making a reference to seeing her again the day she died; and he not only had a strong motive for killing her, but agreed that he was in the frame of mind in which he easily could have murdered her.

Perhaps the most crucial evidence against Rowland – apart from that which he obligingly offered himself – was provided by Edward MacDonald, who owned what was then termed a licensed broker's business (a second-hand shop) at 3 Downing Street, in the Ardwick district. After photographs of the murder weapon appeared in local newspapers, he came forward to identify it. He explained that it was immediately recognisable because it was a special type, a leather-dresser's hammer. He had purchased it on the morning of Saturday 19 October and displayed it for sale in his shop window at 3.30 p.m.

At 5.40 a man came in and asked to buy it, saying that he needed it for "general purposes". MacDonald hastened to explain that it was not a general-purpose hammer. The customer remarked that it would nevertheless suit his purpose. He handed over 3s 6d and left with the hammer wrapped in a length of what MacDonald described as brown crêpe paper, torn from a roll in the shop. He was also able to identify the paper.

On 27 October Rowland was placed in an identity parade at Bootle Street police station. MacDonald picked him out without difficulty.

The prosecution averred that Olive Balchin was seen three times that Saturday evening. About 9.15 she stopped a woman named Rita Leach in the street and asked to be directed to Deansgate. Mrs Leach walked with her part of the way. She subsequently identified Balchin from the hat and coat she had been wearing.

Elizabeth Copley gave evidence that at 10.30 p.m. three people – a young woman, an elderly woman, and a man carrying a brown-paper parcel – came into the Queen's Café in Deansgate, where she was a waitress. She described the man as having black hair, and said he was wearing a dark suit, but had neither mackintosh nor hat. She said that he seemed surly and taciturn. He just had a cup of tea. The two women had something to eat. At 11.00 they all left. She could be reasonably certain of these times; a clock was prominently placed in the café, which was doing only light business at that hour.

Mrs Copley, too, attended an identity parade on 27 October. She walked down the line three times, before picking out Rowland, saying, "That looks like the man, but I'm not sure."

Around midnight on the Saturday, Norman Mercer, the licensee of the local pub, said, he was out walking his dog. At the corner of Deansgate and Cumberland Street, adjacent to where the body was discovered the next morning, he noticed a couple apparently arguing.

He was taken to the mortuary on the Sunday – 20 October – and identified Olive Balchin as the woman. It was difficult to recognise her at all, she was so battered, but Mercer also identified her coat, which had distinctively large buttons. He later picked out Rowland as the man at an identity parade in Strangeways prison, on 4 November.

Rowland was sleeping at the Services Transit Dormitory when the police arrived late at night on 26 October to take him in for questioning. He made a statement agreeing that on the Friday night he had seen Olive Balchin, whom he knew as 'Lil'. Moreover, he had mentioned that he might see her on the Saturday. He maintained, though, that this was not a firm arrangement, just a way of saying ("a figure of speech") that he would probably bump into her again.

Earlier that day Rowland had begun having treatment for venereal disease. He suspected Balchin, with whom he had twice had intercourse, of having infected him, and admitted great animosity towards her. "If I had been sure it was her, I would have strangled her," and "If she gave it to me, she deserved all she got," were remarks attributed to him. He denied neither. (As it transpired, poor Olive Balchin was clean; Rowland had picked up his syphilis in Italy.)

This, broadly, was the case on which the prosecution relied. It must be added that Rowland was a man with a criminal record. He had been convicted of murder in 1934, when he was found guilty of strangling his baby daughter. The jury recommended mercy. Rowland received a life sentence, but was released in 1942 so that he could enlist. He was demobbed in 1946. Thus he had at the time of his arrest in October 1946 enjoyed only three months of civilian liberty since 1934. Even in that brief period, he had already been involved in a couple of skirmishes with the law.

As the identification evidence mounted, the police must have assumed they had the whole case sewn up. Rowland even created further difficulties for himself, giving an incorrect address for, and time of arrival at, the lodgings where he had spent that Saturday/Sunday night; then refusing to disclose exactly where he had been.

He explained that he had given the first address, 36 Hyde Park, in error. He had stayed there on the Sunday, so this mistake seems plausible enough. When he did remember, he decided to keep the information to himself until he had seen his solicitor; he could tell the police were building a case against him, and wanted to retain some cards in his hand.

When Rowland did say his piece, this was how he accounted for his movements on that Saturday. Around lunchtime, he said, he had been with "the boys in Liston's bar". He had then "knocked about town" until going to a post office to collect washing which his mother had done for him. It had not arrived, so he decided to go home to collect it. 'Home' was New Mills in Derbyshire, about ten miles away. He went by bus and arrived there about 7.45 p.m. He had a meal, changed his brown-striped shirt for a blue one, picked up his washing – two shirts and a pair of overalls – and caught the bus back to Manchester. (He explained he had not wished to stay the night at his parents' house because of his venereal condition, though doubtless he also relished the prospect of Saturday night on the town.)

Unfortunately, the bus he caught wasn't going into Manchester city centre, but terminated at Stockport, where he decided to go into the bottom Wellington for a drink. (The pub, in Mersey Square, Stockport, was built on two levels with separate entrances; hence the top and bottom Wellington.) He then caught a bus into Manchester, got some fish and chips, found somewhere to stay, popped out for a few minutes to slake his thirst after the greasy supper, returned, and went to bed.

In the gulf between the prosecution and defence cases, doubts about whether Rowland could have committed the murder rest on four points: (i) uncertainties surrounding the identification evidence; (ii) unexplained gaps in the prosecution scenario; (iii) the complete absence of forensic evidence in circumstances where the chances of detection by such means could have been considered very high; and (iv) the corroboration of his alibi which Rowland was able to provide.

As in the Hanratty case (*see* Chapters 3 and 4), and all too many others besides, identification evidence is rarely clear-cut. In this trial, oddities were apparent from the outset.

When Edward MacDonald originally came forward, he gave police this description of the man: aged 28–32, 5'7"/ 8", medium build, very pale face, thin features, clean shaven, quietly spoken, no hat, wearing a white shirt with a white collar, a dark tie, dark suit, and a dark fawn cotton raincoat. He was of clean and respectable appearance.

Norman Mercer likewise provided an immediate description. The man was, he said, 30–35, 5'7", with a full round face, clean shaven, dark hair, dressed in a blue suit, of clean and tidy appearance.

Elements in these are, of course, incompatible. Did the man have a thin or round face? Was his complexion fresh or pale? It is the shade of hair, though, that is most interesting. MacDonald, apparently, did not mention this at all, though he subsequently added that the man was "on the dark side". That's two votes for dark hair, and one, Elizabeth Copley's, for black. Rowland was fair haired. He was also sallow, and looked old for his age, which was 38.

How Rowland's hair could have been described as "dark" or "black" became one of the crucial arguments of the trial. Each of the three witnesses explained the discrepancy in court by saying that Rowland's hair had been greased, and thus appeared darker than it was.

Rowland was adamant: he never used hair grease. The prosecution countered with two witnesses who said that Rowland did grease his hair. It was apparent, however, that neither knew him well. The landlords of the lodgings where Rowland had stayed that weekend were not even asked whether he greased his hair.

The hair-grease theory was clearly intended to divert attention from what was, from the prosecution's point of view, a crack in the witnesses' evidence. The crux of the matter is that three people, two of whom had the opportunity of observing the man relatively closely, independently mentioned dark hair; and Rowland had light hair. Even if, moreover, it had been well-greased at the time, why had none of the three thought to mention this in their original statements?

Elizabeth Copley had the best opportunity of identifying the man. She was working in the well-lit café where he was sitting for half an hour. There are, however, several striking features about her testimony, not the least being that she did give a description of the man to the police, but the prosecution refused to produce it.

Significantly, 19 October was her first day back at work after a three-month break. The police, making routine inquiries, visited the café to ask whether any strangers had been there. Yes, she said: this party of three.

Point 1: one would have thought that most of the customers would have been strangers to her, anyway.

Point 2: two of this group were not, it transpired, strangers to her at all. After picking out Rowland at the identity parade, she remembered, she said, that she had seen him in the café twice before. Rowland readily agreed that he had been there previously (though not on the night of the murder). In her testimony in court, Copley further said that she had seen the old lady before. So it is odd that she did not recognise either of them during the half-hour they spent in the café.

In another striking aspect of her testimony she referred no fewer than six times to the woman she identified as Balchin as "a young girl" and once as a "young woman". She did add that she was about her own age (38), but looked young, and had tinted her hair auburn. When Dr

Jenkins, the pathologist, examined the body, he described Olive Balchin as follows: "a woman of 40–50, yellow hair turning grey, a few septic teeth in the lower jaw, none on the upper".

Can this be the same woman? (Copley identified her from a retouched photograph of the body. Unlike Rita Leach, she was not asked to identify the dead woman's hat and coat.) As before, there were those who tried to reconcile this serious discrepancy. The fact, though, should not be obscured by ingenious theories. The murdered woman, whose youth seemed a long way behind her, was repeatedly described in evidence as "a young girl"; or so we are asked to believe. It was not unusual for a trial to contain a solitary unexplained piece of evidence; it was extraordinary for one to contain such an accumulation of irreconcilable features.

It seems almost unnecessary to add that the defence produced a witness who also claimed to have seen the party of three in the café; and who asserted positively that Rowland was not the man.

Mercer's identification of the couple presents a different problem. In the mortuary, he identified Olive Balchin as the woman he had seen the previous evening on the street corner. He did say, however, that the woman was not wearing a hat.

Rita Leach had given explicit evidence that the woman she met was wearing a hat; at the trial, Elizabeth Copley said that the woman had placed her hat on the chair beside her (although she had not mentioned this at the magistrates court); and Olive Balchin's hat had been discovered with her body. Yet Mercer had not noticed a hat. He ventured in court that perhaps the hat could have been worn well back on the head. Photographs of the hat, however, reveal this to be improbable.

MacDonald identified Rowland immediately. His evidence seemed the most straightforward of all. In this trial, though, nothing was straightforward. In the witness-box, he described the conversation that had taken place with the man who bought the hammer, about the fact that it was required for "general purposes". This was news to all those in court. MacDonald had not previously mentioned it either in his deposition or in the magistrates court. When asked why, he replied, "Because I was told that this must not be spoken until later." It is a great pity that Rowland's counsel, who ignored the point, did not attempt to establish exactly what this meant.

Moreover, MacDonald's identification of Rowland was not as consistent as it seems. In the magistrates court, he was at first unable to see the man to whom he had sold the hammer. Rowland was sitting with his solicitor, not standing in the dock. There are conflicting versions of what happened next, but it seems that MacDonald was only able to identify Rowland once the prosecuting counsel had asked him, Rowland, to stand. At his trial, Rowland said, "He did not pick me out until I was pointed out to him."

While it is logical to assume that the man to whom MacDonald sold the hammer was the man who committed the murder, it is not logical to assume that this man was Rowland. Two further matters beg to be raised. Mac-Donald referred to the mac – "a dark fawn cotton raincoat" – of the man in his shop: a very precise description. No other evidence was offered to show that Rowland had a mac. Neither Copley nor Mercer saw their man wearing a mac; and the landlord where Rowland stayed the night said he did not have one with him. Secondly, Rowland brought back with him from his mother's a parcel of washing. The landlord said he remembered it that evening, and that it was the sort of parcel which could have contained two shirts and a pair of overalls. So Rowland, if he had the hammer wrapped in brown paper, and his washing wrapped in brown paper, must have had two parcels. Copley mentioned only one parcel. Mercer had not seen a parcel at all.

The scenario which the prosecution wove around the testimony of its three witnesses is also oddly incomplete. The murdered woman had been sighted at 9.15; then, in the company of the man presumed to have been Rowland, between 10.30 and 11.00; and again with him at midnight. What happened in the intervals between these sightings? How was it that no one else saw the couple?

We now arrive at the most extraordinary, the most glaringly suspect part of the prosecution case. Elizabeth Copley referred to a group of three in the café: the man who may have been Rowland; the "young girl" who may have been Balchin; and an older woman – "well over 60, she might have been going on 70" – who spoke with an Irish accent and whom Copley had seen before. During Copley's evidence, the judge, Mr Justice Sellers, inquired about this lady, "Is she in court?" Prosecuting counsel replied, "No, my Lord". That was the sum total of the attention the court paid to the matter.

Who was this woman? What was her relationship with the others? If she had been with the killer and his victim within an hour or so of the murder, as the jury was asked to believe, her evidence must have been highly material, to say the least. But she was never produced nor her absence explained. Nothing more about her was ever learned.

There was practically no forensic evidence to link Rowland with the crime. The Home Office scientists could only muster: a solitary blood stain on one of his shoes, and spots of blood on his handkerchief; particles of dust and rubble in his trouser turn-ups; and a few grey hairs on Rowland's coat which could have been Balchin's.

In truth, this added up to no evidence at all. The blood on the handkerchief should not have been mentioned; under cross-examination police confirmed that it was Rowland's own, the result of a cut while being shaved in prison. The blood spot on the shoe was too small to be grouped; that could be attributed to the same cause.

Analysis showed that the dust and rubble was consistent with its having come from a local bombed site, but there were limitless innocent explanations of this, especially in the case of a man like Rowland who "knocked about town".

The mention of the grey hairs illustrated just how low an uneasy prosecution will occasionally stoop. The forensic scientist said in court that the hairs were "consistent with hair having come from the deceased, but I cannot put it any higher than that – no definite identity". So this is pretty shaky from the outset. Let us assume, nevertheless, that the hairs actually were Balchin's: Elizabeth Copley's testimony becomes even more unlikely. These were all, we have it on good authority, grey hairs. Since grey hairs have traditionally been regarded as a sign of ageing, it is even more improbable that a grey-haired woman would be so consistently and deliberately referred to as "a young girl".

As frequently happens, though, the forensic evidence was more interesting for what it didn't reveal. Like hundreds of thousands of others, Rowland had only one suit at the time: his demob suit. It was subjected to meticulous analysis, but not a single spot of blood was ever found on it. Yet when the police inaugurated the murder inquiry, the pathologist told them that the murderer, and his clothing, would probably have been drenched in blood spurting from the woman's head.

Nor was any evidence offered about fingerprints. (Rowland had no gloves, and his prints were on file.) This, too, is extraordinary. Police knew that because the brown-paper wrapping had borne the impression of the hammer, but was free of blood stains, the hammer was unwrapped when it had been so savagely wielded. The force of the blows indicated that it must have been grasped very tightly. It was discarded immediately after the attack, and there must have been fingerprints on it. Obviously, they weren't Rowland's. If his prints had been there, they would, in the circumstances, have been conclusive proof of his guilt.

Rowland's alibi was that during the period in question

he had gone for a drink in the bottom Wellington in Stockport, had travelled into Manchester, and got a room for the night. One of the details he could remember from his Wellington visit, he said, was that as he came out of the toilet he noticed two police officers pass through the pub from the top to the bottom Wellington. It was then closing time: 10.30.

It is a lucky man – or so one would imagine – who can rely on the police to corroborate his alibi. At the trial, Sergeant Norman Jones of the local force gave evidence that on that Saturday evening, in company with a colleague, he had entered the top Wellington, passed through into the bottom Wellington, and then out into the street.

This evidence availed Rowland little – primarily because the judge seemed determined to misconstrue it. At the outset, he invited the prosecution to object to its admissibility. Then, while Jones was describing the interior lay-out of the Wellington, the judge grumbled, "I cannot see any relevance at all in how a house in Stockport is constructed." But it was highly relevant: the pub was unusual in that it contained what seems almost to have been a thoroughfare. If the police had passed through at that time, but in a different direction, Rowland would have been undone. If he was deliberately faking an alibi, it must have taken supreme nerve for him to have expected the police to do it for him. Yet in every detail, Sergeant Jones precisely substantiated Rowland's story.

Rowland was hardly better assisted by his own counsel, who forgot to ask Sergeant Jones the actual time of his inspection of the Wellington, hardly an immaterial point. To establish it, he had to ask the judge's permission for leave to recall the witness. "If I had thought it was relevant," remarked the judge, "I would have assisted him; since I did not, I did not. You can ask him." Permission was grudgingly granted. According to Jones' note-book, he made his visit at 10.32. This gave Rowland's alibi the precise corroboration it desperately needed; but how could the members of the jury have been expected to recognise that, when the judge was virtually inviting them to disregard this extremely important evidence?

It was true that Rowland could have been drinking in Stockport at closing time and still, if Mercer's midnight identification was reliable, have committed the crime. However, it was agreed that Rowland had not arrived in Stockport from Derbyshire until after 10 o'clock, and the police had gone to some lengths to demonstrate that, if the first bus had arrived early, and the 10.04 for Manchester left a little late, then Rowland would have been able to make the connection and be in the Queen's Café by 10.30. (It is frequently a feature of miscarriage-of-justice cases that police will demonstrate how inherently unlikely journeys might actually have been made; the Luvaglio/ Stafford case (*see* Chapter 5) and the Guildford pub-bombings (*see* Chapter 13) provide further examples.)

If Rowland had stayed drinking in Stockport, this would have created great difficulties for the prosecution, because Elizabeth Copley's entire testimony would have to be discarded. And if someone who had the best opportunity of seeing Rowland had wrongly identified him, might not others, seeing him in less favourable circumstances, also have done so?

Having at first given inaccurate information about where he stayed on the Saturday night, Rowland subsequently provided the address: 81 Brunswick Street, Chorlton-on-Medlock, Manchester. The landlord, Frank Beaumont, gave evidence in court. He recalled Rowland arriving there that evening and asking for a room; and that at the time he remembered Rowland had stayed there on a previous occasion (which Rowland himself had forgotten until reminded of it).

He corroborated Rowland's story: that the latter turned up at 11.15, went out for a few minutes to get a drink, returned, and went to bed. Rowland was in the house when he, Beaumont, locked up at 11.40.

At the trial he was questioned about whether it would have been possible for Rowland to have left the house in the night and return unnoticed. Beaumont replied that it would have been possible, although no one unfamiliar with the house would necessarily have been aware of this. (This theory, too, would have begged a fresh series of questions about the prosecution scenario. In any case, if Rowland had taken the room to give himself an alibi, why was he unable to remember it when police questioned him?)

The landlord also produced his register to show that Rowland had signed in, in his own name, on 19 October. Unhappily, the register also showed Rowland as having *left* on the 19th. Although Basil Nield KC, prosecution counsel, spent much time and effort suggesting that this was of great significance, Beaumont said simply, "Yes, that's an error – I didn't know it was disputed."

The landlord was adamant that the events he described had occurred on a Saturday. Upset by the tenacity of prosecuting counsel in cross-examining him, he felt the need to say it loud and clear, "Walter Graham Rowland definitely did arrive on the Saturday."

Two points must be made here. The first is that the landlord was not believed; Rowland, after all, was found guilty. No one, however, has been able to explain why Rowland should have sought – and been able to obtain – an alibi from someone he hardly knew and who could have had no conceivable reason for helping out a murderer. (Certainly not money; Rowland was impoverished.) Secondly, the prosecution was able to offer no theory, let alone a verifiable account, of where else Rowland might have spent the night.

Rowland's movements throughout the rest of the week, until his arrest, were precisely catalogued; there was no dispute about them. He signed registers correctly, in his own name, and on one occasion asked to leave a parcel with the manager at the hostel where he was staying. Had he committed the murder, he must have known that, with his record, and as someone who had associated with Balchin, he would be a prime suspect; but he behaved as though nothing untoward had occurred.

The final point is that Rowland vigorously contested the
police version of the self-incriminating interview he had
with them. He argued that although he had actually said
some (though not all) of the things attributed to him, the
police had set them in a different and, for him, far more
damaging context.

Despite all this evidence which the defence tendered,
and despite the holes in the prosecution case, Rowland
was found guilty on 16 December. After that, his previous
record was disclosed, and must have been sufficient to
quell any lingering courtroom doubts about the rightness
of the conviction.

Rowland, who had strenuously maintained his innocence throughout, continued to do so. Asked if he had
anything to say before sentence of death was passed, he
delivered a moving, off-the-cuff speech which ought to be
famous in the annals of British justice:

> I have never been a religious man, but as I have sat
> in this Court during these last few hours the teachings
> of my boyhood have come back to me, and I say in
> all sincerity and before you and this Court that when
> I stand in the Court of Courts before the Judge of
> Judges I shall be acquitted of this crime. Somewhere
> there is a person who knows that I stand here today
> an innocent man. The killing of this woman was a
> terrible crime, but there is a worse crime been (sic)
> committed now, my Lord, because someone with the
> knowledge of this crime is seeing me sentenced today
> for a crime which I did not commit. I have a firm
> belief that one day it will be proved in God's own time
> that I am totally innocent of this charge, and the day
> will come when this case will be quoted in the courts
> of this country to show what can happen to a man in
> a case of mistaken identity. I am going to face what
> lies before me with the fortitude and calm that only a
> clear conscience can give. That is all I have got to say,
> my Lord.

Rowland's legal advisers announced immediately that they would appeal, and that they would bring forward additional evidence to support their client's contention that he was in the bottom Wellington in Stockport at 10.30 that Saturday evening.

Even while frantic efforts were being made in this direction, however, a fresh development apparently greatly strengthened Rowland's chance of a successful appeal. Someone made a detailed confession to the murder.

David John Ware was the same age and height as Rowland, though his hair was a different colour: his was dark. He was serving a sentence in Walton prison, Liverpool, when he made a statement on 22 January 1947, admitting that he had carried out the crime for which Rowland was then under sentence of death. Two days later he made a further statement to Inspector Stainton and Detective Constable Douglas Nimmo of Manchester police who had conducted the murder investigation. Later, he made a third statement, in which he elaborated on particular points, to Rowland's legal advisers. At these times, he indicated that he felt in need of psychiatric help. Indeed, he had been in Buckinghamshire mental hospital, and had also been discharged from the army on the grounds of mental ill-health. He was described then as suffering from manic depressive psychosis.

Ware's story opened in Stoke-on-Trent on the morning of Friday 18 October when he had stolen some money from the Salvation Army hostel where he was casually employed. He said that he walked to Longton, got a bus to Uttoxeter and then went by train to Manchester, arriving about 7.30 p.m. He picked up a girl and spent the night with her. He explained that on the Saturday he purchased the hammer, for the purpose of robbery, at a shop on the main road from the railway station to the Hippodrome theatre. He then met the woman he referred to as Olive

Balshaw and took her to a small picture-house near Belle Vue.

About nine o'clock they left, had a cup of coffee in the café opposite the cinema, and caught a bus to Piccadilly. According to Ware's second statement, this is what happened next:

> I decided to spend a while with her. The spot where we stopped was a place or building that I took to be bombed in this war. We went inside the ruins and stood for a short while near the entrance. We were quite close to each other & being so near she took the opportunity of going through my pockets. I was aware of this but did not show her. I was ate up with hatred & felt immediately that I'd like to kill her. I realised I had the hammer so suggested that I'd like to make water & went further in the building. In there I took the brown paper off the hammer & threw it in the corner.

Ware then went on to describe how he murdered her.

> . . . I repeated the blows. Blood shot up in a thin spray. I felt it in my face and then I panicked. I threw down the hammer and left everything as it was. I made no attempt to get my money. I ran & ran zigzag up & down streets I didn't know eventually getting to a railway station which I was told was Salford. I was frightened of going on the station so I decided to go to Stockport. I got into a tram but was told I would have to go by bus. I slept at a lodging-house there.
>
> On Sunday I tramped to Buxton & on to Chapel-en-le-Frith where I stayed the night at the Institution. On the Monday I hitch-hiked to Sheffield. I took the belt off my mac and threw it away together with my cap. I did this to alter my appearance. I later read in the newspapers that the wanted man had not been

wearing a hat and I realised I had made a mistake in
throwing my cap away.

I surrendered myself to the police for the offence I
had committed in Stoke as a cover-up. I thought I
would be safer from possible detection in the hands
of the police or in prison than I would be if I were
wandering about.

In the statement which Ware made to Rowland's legal
advisers, he provided a greater depth of background information. In his description of where he purchased the
hammer, for example:

The shop was on the left-hand side of the road some
little distance after passing under the bridge which
passes over the road below the railway station. The
road declines from the railway station and a little
further down from the shop it inclines to the Manchester Hippodrome.

About going with Balchin to the cinema:

We got on a tram-car, the indicator of which said
Belle Vue. We left the tram at the stadium and then
walked up the road for quite a long way until we came
to a third-rate picture house on the right-hand side of
the road.

Ware was unfamiliar with Manchester, having previously
visited the city on only two occasions, each time for a
couple of hours. As it finally stood, the statement went
into considerable graphic and geographic detail about the
crime itself, and the events either side of it. In all this
detail, Ware in no respect departed from the facts of the
crime as they were known to the authorities.

He explained his delay in coming forward by saying that
while on remand he read that the body had been found
and that the police anticipated making an arrest. "I then

purposely avoided reading the newspapers, as I did not want to read anything more about the murder." He said that he had heard about Rowland's conviction from a fellow prisoner on 18 January. As a result he made his short statement to the governor on 22 January and, two days later, elaborated on it to police and Rowland's legal advisers.

This created a fascinating situation for the appeal, which was listed for 27 January, immediately after the weekend. It was, though, adjourned, while further inquiries were made.

In any criminal case, the defence is handicapped by having to rely on whatever scraps of information the police and prosecution may choose to feed it. It does not usually have any resources, either in finance or manpower, to pursue its own investigations. In the Rowland case, the police simply supplied the defence with a list of people from whom statements had been taken. Some of these statements were highly favourable to Rowland, but the defence had no means of discovering this. In the context of English law, this is a manoeuvre which has been frequently employed.

As it happened, the defence made encouraging progress anyway. Rowland's mother had earlier put out an appeal for the man to whom her son had sold cigarettes in the Wellington to come forward. (The pub itself did not sell cigarettes.) The man, Henry Somerville, did so. On that Saturday, he had just been to the local cinema to see a Dick Powell film. He identified Rowland as the man who had sold him ten Woodbines for 10½d. The landlady, Mrs Coppock, recalled the incident. The manager of the Plaza cinema, Walter Ellwood, was also recruited to the defence cause, so that he could confirm part of Somerville's evidence.

All this, and Ware's confession too.

The Lord Chief Justice, Lord Goddard, Mr Justice Humphreys and Mr Justice Lewis heard the appeal on 10 February. They refused to hear Ware's evidence; declined to hear Mrs Coppock's evidence; and dismissed the appeal.

Rowland was understandably stunned. "I am an innocent man," he declared. "This is the grossest injustice which has ever occurred in an English court. Why did you not have in court the man who confessed to the crime? I am not having justice because of my past. I am innocent before God."

The winter of 1946/7 was particularly severe. The coal industry was unable to meet the increased demand for power. As a consequence, the Ministry of Fuel was forced to impose energy cuts, and the first was made on 10 February. Most of Rowland's appeal was accordingly heard by candlelight. The occasion could have been furnished with no more apt metaphor: the judges seemed hopelessly in the dark, both about the particular circumstances of this case and about the duties and responsibilities of their high office.

Mr Justice Humphreys, in delivering judgment, argued that the alibi evidence merely confirmed evidence already offered at the trial and, in the opinion of the court, would not have affected the jury. Permission to call Mrs Coppock had been denied on the grounds that she was available for the original trial, but Rowland's counsel had neglected to call her.

As regards Ware's evidence, Humphreys continued, the court had determined that it was not the proper tribunal to hear this.

"If the Court had allowed Ware to give evidence and he had persisted in the expression of guilt, the Court would have been compelled to form some conclusion as to his guilt or innocence and to express that opinion in open court. In effect therefore the Court would have been engaged in trying not only Rowland but also Ware, thereby usurping the functions of a jury . . . As a result of their judgment Ware might have had to stand trial on a charge of murder. In that event, the finding of the Court could not fail to be prejudicial to his chance of an impartial trial."

This may seem deluded reasoning today; it was widely perceived to be deluded at the time. After all, the matter to hand was whether circumstances had been prejudicial to Rowland's actual trial, not Ware's hypothetical one.

"The judgment was questioned," wrote Sydney Silverman, "on the grounds that the Court had misdirected itself as to what was the issue before it."[1] The judges seemed to believe that Rowland could not be acquitted on Ware's evidence unless Ware was, in effect, convicted. But they were not being asked to reach any conclusion about the guilt or innocence of Ware and would, of course, have been quite wrong to do so. If Rowland was acquitted, then there would be some discomfiture at the heart of any future trial of Ware. That would be the unfortunate but inescapable by-product of the review process; but it would not be the process itself which discomfited Ware – it would be his confession, made entirely voluntarily.

Would a jury have convicted Rowland had it been aware of Ware's evidence? That was the issue to which the judges should have addressed themselves. If Ware gave evidence and the judges believed it, or if they found it *capable of belief*, then they must acquit Rowland. A sufficient measure of doubt would have been introduced into the case. That was the law then; it remains the law today.

The legal establishment is notoriously keen to cite legal precedent. The appeal judges here could have referred back to an analogous case from 1932 (though on a much less serious charge), which Sydney Silverman uncovered. Then, a conviction had been quashed on appeal as a result of the confession of someone not previously implicated in the crime.

The Rowland case had provided the Court of Appeal with the perfect opportunity to demonstrate the efficacy of the constitutional process of judicial review. The opportunity was spurned; instead, the judges abdicated their responsibilities. Humphreys concluded the judgment by saying that the three of them "are not unmindful of the fact that there exists an authority in the person of the

Home Secretary who has far wider powers than those possessed by this Court; who is not bound, as we are, by rules of evidence; and who has all the necessary machinery for conducting such an inquiry as is here asked for."

In the week-long interval between the abrupt dismissal of the appeal and the explanation of the reasons for it, enlightened legal opinion seemed in favour of the Attorney-General passing the appeal to the House of Lords on a point of law, which would perhaps have been the most satisfactory course of action. Once he had been so publicly invited to set up an inquiry, however, the Home Secretary immediately responded. On 21 February he asked the experienced barrister J. C. Jolly to investigate Ware's confession and any other material which had become available since Rowland's conviction. There was, though, little time left; the execution was fixed for 27 February.

Ware was taken to Strangeways prison, where Rowland was imprisoned and where Jolly held his inquiry throughout the weekend of 22/23 February. Rowland, who played no part in it, had to sweat the whole thing out. With the publication of the Jolly report on 26 February, his worst fears were realised.

Jolly put forward three reasons for rejecting the possibility that Ware could have murdered Olive Balchin: (i) Ware's disavowal of his confession; (ii) identification; and (iii) additional circumstances. The rationale behind each is tortuous to the point of perversity.

With regard to the first point, Jolly reported, "After persisting at first in maintaining that his former statements as to the murder were correct, Ware admitted that they were false, saying, 'I'd better turn it in'."

Reading between the lines, this suggests that Ware was virtually talked out of his confession. Presumably he was asked if it was true, and he indicated that it was. The question must have been repeated, and the reply reiterated; how long this continued for is not known. No independent witnesses were present at the interview.

In a fresh statement from Ware, appended to the report, he gave an alternative version of events over that weekend and explained what induced him to make his 'false' confession.

This substitute statement is a glorious muddle. It is dated incorrectly. It begins, "On the 19th of October I was in Manchester, arriving by train from Uttoxeter at 7.30 p.m. or thereabouts . . ." Ware refers to his movements that evening and throughout the following day. Now, the 19th was the Saturday. It therefore becomes clear that the date mentioned initially should have been the 18th. Otherwise Ware would have been doing a host of things, like going into Woolworth's for his lunch, which he could not possibly have done on a Sunday.

So, an honest mistake had been made. It would hardly be worth mentioning, were it not for two weighty considerations that flow inevitably from it. A man's life hinged on the outcome of this inquiry. Jolly referred to the "heavy and responsible duty" of undertaking it. Surely such an enterprise, if properly carried out, should have been immune from such slipshod errors. Secondly, one of the points on which Rowland's trial had turned was whether or not he had spent the night, as he said, at 81 Brunswick Street. Because of the accident of the wrong date appearing in the register, the prosecution was able to undermine the credibility of the alibi. The very same factor now turns up here. When it is put in the scales against Rowland, it is as heavy as lead; when it is put in for him, it is of no account at all.

In his substitute statement, Ware gave a rambling account of what he was supposed to have done on the Saturday. He went to the cinema in the afternoon: "I paid 2/9d for my seat which was well down on the ground floor. I cannot recall the title of the picture but to the best of my memory it was a war-time picture with aeroplanes and parachutists; there was nothing outstanding in the programme which I can remember." It was the last cinema visit Ware would have made – he had been in prison since

– but he seemed unable to come up with a single hard fact about the film. Anyone passing the cinema could presumably have gleaned as much, if not more, from the stills displayed outside the theatre as Ware apparently did from sitting through the programme.

Yet Jolly is convinced. This is the truth.

In the evening, Ware now said, he went to the Oxford pub in Oxford Street and stayed there "until the house closed". He gave sketchy descriptions of some other customers. Rowland said he was in the Wellington in Stockport and was able to produce witnesses who corroborated his story. Ware's pub story, by contrast, was less detailed to begin with, and was corroborated by no one.

Yet Jolly is convinced. This is the truth.

Later, Ware had to look for somewhere to stay. "I knew I should not get a bed in Manchester, but knew I should get one at Stockport, so decided to go there while someone was up." Ware did not explain how he, a stranger in town, had arrived at this conclusion, especially since he had actually stayed in Manchester the previous evening.

Yet Jolly is convinced. This is the truth.

Ware concluded his revised statement: "On the Monday, I bought a *Daily Herald*. I read about the Manchester murder and this was the first I knew about it. Having read of the murder and noticed the description of the suspect it struck me how much I was like him." He said he then decided to concoct his confession story, and apologised because, "I didn't realise the serious consequences it might entail."

It is true that the mentally unstable might confess to crimes in which they were not concerned; in the Appeal Court the Lord Chief Justice had said, "It is not unusual for all sorts of confessions to be made by people who had nothing to do with a crime." Here, what was unusual, unprecedented even, was the overall plausibility of the confession statements. That, indeed, was the basis on which the business was taken so far. It is inconceivable that any stray lunatic who wanted to confess for the hell of it would have been able to provide such persuasive and compelling details of the crime.

Jolly did not consider it at all inconceivable.

"I am satisfied that these details are such as could have been derived from newspaper reports, statements inserted at the instance of the police, discussions with prisoners who were received in prison after the murder, and from his own imagination.

"It is noteworthy that Ware described the woman as Olive Balshaw, a name by which she was described in the press."

It is indeed noteworthy, but hardly in the way in which Jolly maintained. The press did, indeed, take about forty-eight hours to name the victim correctly. (For example, *The Times* initially referred to her as "Balshaw' and "Balshin".) After that, there was no further confusion. If Ware had been assiduously following the story in the press for the purpose of fabricating a confession, as Jolly averred, it is absurd to imagine that he would have been able to display such an impressive knowledge of the crime, and yet get the victim's name wrong.

The original statements have the ring of authenticity. Ware had said that after he hit Balchin, "I felt the blood shoot up in my face." Now, that seems a particularly vivid detail. It was certainly not taken second-hand from press reports. All right, he could have obtained it, as Jolly insisted, "from his own imagination". But it did dovetail *exactly* with what the pathologist said. Most people would have considered it accurate, persuasive, and conceivably derived from first-hand experience. Most people, but not Jolly.

Ware, having retracted his original confessions, was placed in an identity parade before the three witnesses who had given evidence at Rowland's trial. Jolly spoke to the second-hand dealer first: "Mr MacDonald, you have already stated during the course of these proceedings that a man bought a hammer in your shop on 19 October at about 5.40. You have stated that man is the man Rowland.

Now, I want you to walk along the line where those men are standing, and tell me whether you see anyone there who in any way resembles the man Rowland whom you have already identified. You understand?"

MacDonald, Copley and Mercer had all given their evidence in good faith, and each had identified Rowland. They may have been – surely were – mistaken, but they were not dishonest. They would naturally be reluctant to rescind or amend their testimony and lay themselves open to, at best, public humiliation and, at worst, charges of perjury. In this difficult situation, Jolly could have put them at their ease. Instead, he spread the psychological intimidation as thickly as possible.

They all said there was no one who looked like Rowland.

Ware had been put on parade, and had not been picked out; the witnesses had not been asked to do so. It was a subtle manoeuvre, which would have reinforced their natural resistance to changing their evidence. Only then were they individually confronted with Ware and asked the salient question: whether they recognised him. All said not. For good measure, MacDonald added, "He is not the man – nothing like him, sir."

Poor Jolly: he had arrived at a logical contradiction. He accepted that Ware had been encouraged to make his confession "because I was so well-fitted with the description of the man wanted for the murder". There are three separate references to this in the substitute statement, which Jolly found to be truthful. Now, witnesses were saying, "He is nothing like the man."

Jolly moved on to consider the additional circumstances. Clearly, there was a disparity about the timing. In his first short statement Ware said he murdered Balchin at about 10 o'clock. No time is subsequently mentioned, but about 10.30 seems to be indicated. Jolly adduced fresh evidence from another pub landlord, Wilfred Gosling, who reported that he took his dog for a walk over the bombed site at 10.30 that evening – and there definitely wasn't a body there then.

The first point that struck me about this evidence was the remarkably strange time for a publican to be out walking his dog: closing time on a Saturday night. Even if the evidence is taken at face value, however, it hardly has the weight which Jolly attaches to it. It doesn't invalidate anything in Ware's original confessions, since he was never specific about a time.

Jolly's report also included a statement from Dr J. B. Firth, director of the forensic laboratory at Preston. He examined Ware's clothes at the end of January, and made the scarcely dramatic discovery that the trouser turn-ups contained "the usual type of fibre stuff commonly found in trouser turn-ups". Note the time-gap in the forensic tests – Rowland's clothing was examined within a week, Ware's three and a half months later. Yet spots of blood would still be detectable three months later, so what did Dr Firth have to report?

"There is no evidence of bloodstains on Ware's trousers."

Perhaps the Preston forensic team was under the impression that Ware was wearing nothing but trousers at the time; somehow I doubt it.

The man who bought MacDonald's hammer was wearing a "dark fawn cotton raincoat". This, as it transpired, was an accurate description of Ware's mac; no one saw Rowland wearing a mac. Why, then, was Ware's mac not forensically examined? Because analysis might have yielded results the authorities were determined not to discover? (Nor do Ware's jacket and shoes appear to have been examined.)

This is especially interesting because we know – it is in the Jolly report – that Ware's mac did have blood stains on the sleeve. Needing to explain these, the substitute Ware statement offered:

I used to wear my raincoat whilst doing the mailbags and I accidentally got some spots of blood on the front of it. [He explained that he had pricked his finger.]

When I was preparing my mind to confess to this murder I deliberately put spots of blood on the lower forearm of the two raincoat sleeves. I later washed these spots off with a piece of wet rag and burnt some of them off with the tip of a cigarette.

Unpicking such testimony should have been meat and drink to an experienced barrister. If Ware was actively concocting a false confession, as he said, thinking it "worthwhile being hung to be a hero", why did he attempt to eradicate the blood spots? Wasn't this rather the action of a guilty man attempting to destroy genuinely incriminating evidence? How was it that Ware was wearing his mac in the prison workshops?

In connection with the Jolly report, two concluding points must be made. The first is that Ware explained originally that he surrendered to the Sheffield police "as a cover-up".

This is perfectly plausible.

According to the substitute statement, "I thought of the idea of confessing to this murder and I decided to surrender . . . for stealing the money at Stoke. I hoped the police would also suspect me of the Manchester murder . . . "

This is simply implausible.

If he was not guilty of the Balchin murder, why did he need to give himself up at all? A spell in prison would hardly have facilitated his plans for making a bogus confession. And if he was surrendering in the hope of being suspected, why did he not confess then, or at least drop a few hints?

The second point is the matter of where Ware lodged on the Saturday night. He originally said he stayed at 7 Great Egerton Street, Stockport. Two police officers checked up on the house, confirmed that Ware had arrived there between 11.15 and 11.30 (which tallied with his statements), that he had stayed the night and had signed the register.

In connection with investigations for the Jolly inquiry,

Detective Inspector Herbert Hannam of the metropolitan police returned to the lodging-house but was unable to verify Ware's story, because, as he later reported, "Following the inspection of the lodging-house register by the police subsequent to Ware's confession, the book was destroyed." Jolly adds parenthetically: by the proprietor.

The register signed by Rowland was, amongst other things, taken to Preston for forensic analysis and produced as an exhibit in court. The one signed by Ware was, Jolly would have us believe, casually destroyed. But guest-house registers are not usually discarded within two months of their expiry. They are retained for a period as a record of guests and, perhaps, for the very reason that pertained here – namely, that they might prove of assistance in some criminal investigation. Presumably the police who originally visited Ware's lodgings would have made it clear that the register could be needed in further inquiries. The fact that Jolly records that it has been destroyed, without further comment or reproach, suggests that the destruction of a vital piece of documentary evidence suited him very well.

Jolly was assisted by two officers from the Metropolitan Police, Superintendent Barratt and Detective Inspector Hannam. Hannam's subsequent career was a chequered one. He proved an adept manipulator of the press, "apparently for his own glorification rather than for any assistance which it could give to the investigation", according to Lord Devlin.[2] In *Two Men Were Acquitted*, the *Daily Express* chief crime reporter Percy Hoskins recalled that Hannam's method of conducting the police investigation into the 1953 Teddington towpath murder case was "at best, unsavoury"; and that Hannam was held in such low esteem on the *Express* that the paper was prepared to back Hoskins in 1957 in his unpopular defence of Bodkin Adams, the doctor hounded to the Old Bailey (and almost to the scaffold) by Hannam.[3]

The Jolly report illustrates that British justice is sometimes blind. When Jolly reported to the Home Secretary that "there are no grounds for thinking that there has been any miscarriage of justice in the conviction of Rowland", he was misinforming him; and the misinformation led inexorably to the death of an innocent man.

Kenneth Burke, Rowland's counsel, made last, despairing efforts, sending telegrams to Arthur Greenwood, the Lord Privy Seal, and a number of MPs; but to no avail. Rowland was hanged on 27 February 1947. "I know I die for another's crime," he wrote in his last letter to his mother. The crimes, in fact, of a number of people, prominent among whom was John Catterall Jolly.

Ware said several times, both when confessing to the crime and when denying it, that he thought he needed psychiatric treatment. After his involvement in the Rowland case, he did have a further three spells in mental hospitals. On 2 August 1951 he walked into a Bristol police station and said, "I have killed a woman. I don't know what is the matter with me. I keep having an urge to hit women on the head."

He hadn't killed anyone, not quite. At Bristol assizes on 16 November 1951 he was found guilty but insane of the attempted murder of Adelaine Fuidge. He was sent to Broadmoor, where he hanged himself in 1954.

After Ware's conviction, there were questions in parliament. By then, though, Sir David Maxwell-Fyfe had been appointed Home Secretary. He assured MPs that "there is nothing in the recent charge brought against Ware to require any further action", since his confession to a remarkably similar crime in 1947 had already been the subject of "an exhaustive inquiry' by Mr Jolly.

"The late Jolly was known to me for nearly 30 years," continued Maxwell-Fyfe, "as one of the most careful and conscientious men at the Bar. The results of his inquiry showed he had taken immense pains on the subject, and there was no reason to throw doubt on his conclusion."[4]

Hardly surprisingly, MPs were not satisfied with this

reply. Sir Hartley Shawcross, Attorney-General at the time of the Rowland case, asked, "Does the Home Secretary accept that the police had evidence favourable to Rowland that they failed to disclose to the defence, and does he agree that it is the paramount duty of the prosecution and the police in all criminal cases to disclose all information, whether favourable or unfavourable, to the defence?"[5] Maxwell-Fyfe responded that he was certainly in agreement with the last part of the question and, with regard to the rest, muttered vaguely about having inquiries made. In fact, the matter was never raised again – largely, one suspects, because soon the Evans and Derek Bentley cases merited greater attention.[6]

One last point on this particular case. Walter Rowland was undoubtedly a tough customer who could, and had, put himself about. There is something fundamentally incongruous about his purchasing a hammer for 3s 6d. He was penniless; no one ever suggested otherwise. The day before the murder he had sold a pair of black shoes for "the price of a packet of fags"; one of the reasons he went to meet "the boys in Liston's bar" was to borrow money off them.

Even if he had determined to kill Olive Balchin, why on earth would he have bought an expensive hammer for the purpose when he could have murdered her, as it were, for free? On the other hand, David Ware did have money burning a hole in his pocket: the 'hot' money stolen from the hostel in Stoke.

Three

The A6 Murder (i)

People in the case

Michael Gregsten — murder victim
Valerie Storie — Gregsten's companion
James Hanratty — charged with murder of Gregsten
Mr Justice Gorman — trial judge
Michael Sherrard — defence counsel
Graham Swanwick QC — prosecution counsel
Sidney Burton — farm labourer, first scene-of-crime arrival at Deadman's Hill
John Kerr — undergraduate, scene-of-crime arrival
Harry Hirons — garage attendant where murder car stopped for petrol
James Trower ⎱
John Skillett ⎬ — witnesses to arrival of murder car in east London
Edward Blackhall ⎰
Peter Alphon — original murder suspect
Janet Gregsten — widow of Michael Gregsten
William Ewer — brother-in-law of Janet Gregsten
Audrey Willis — resident of Old Knebworth, Herts., possibly confronted by A6 killer
Meika Dalal — victim of assault by man claiming to be A6 killer
Mrs Lanz — proprietress of Old Station Inn, Taplow
Michael Fogarty-Waul — local resident in Dorney area
Detective Superintendent Acott — policeman in charge of murder inquiry
Detective Sergeant Oxford — assistant to Acott
Edward Milborrow — senior police officer at Deadman's Hill
James Hanratty ⎱
Mary Hanratty ⎰ — parents of James Hanratty
Charles France — friend of Hanratty; prosecution witness
Carol France — daughter of Charles France
William Nudds — police informer; prosecution witness

Louise Anderson — antique dealer in Soho, friend of
                          Hanratty; prosecution witness

Roy Langdale — prisoner; prosecution witness

Jean Justice — amateur criminologist; author of *Murder
                    versus Murder*

Jeremy Fox — barrister; friend of Monsieur Justice

Olive Dinwoodie — sweetshop assistant; alibi witness

Grace Jones — Rhyl landlady; alibi witness

Margaret Walker ⎫
Ivy Vincent   ⎪
Christopher Larman ⎬ — alibi witnesses in Rhyl
Trevor Dutton   ⎭

Robert Fish ⎫
Henry Parry ⎭ — residents of Rhyl

Joe Gillbanks ⎫
Frank Evans ⎭ — private detectives hired by defence

R. A. Butler — Home Secretary at the time of the crime

Niall MacDermot QC — MP; prosecution counsel at commit-
                              tal hearing

Fenner [Lord] Brockway — MP for Slough; subsequently
                                  member of the House of
                                  Lords

Louis Blom-Cooper — author of *The A6 Murder*

Tony Mason — freelance journalist in Slough

Lord Russell of Liverpool — author of *Deadman's Hill*

Paul Foot — author of *Who Killed Hanratty?*

Lord Stonham — under-secretary of state at the Home Office
                      1964–7

Detective Chief Superintendent Nimmo — head of two in-
                quiries into Rhyl alibi

Chief Inspector Mooney — Scotland Yard policeman, in-
                volved in Alphon telephone case

Lewis Hawser QC — appointed to undertake solo inquiry

THE A6 MURDER – the crime itself, the search for the killer, the trial and the protracted aftermath – developed into the most extraordinary saga. A generation later, it continues to exert a strong fascination. The whole story is so bizarre and complex that virtually the only absolutely safe conclusion is that the man convicted of the crime, James Hanratty, had nothing whatever to do with it.

Shortly after 9.00 on the evening of 22 August 1961, Michael Gregsten and Valerie Storie, colleagues at the Road Research Laboratory at Langley, near Slough, went for a drink together at the Old Station Inn, Taplow. Gregsten was living apart from his wife and two children; Storie was the girl with whom he was having an affair. They were using a car which belonged, jointly, to Gregsten's mother and aunt. It was a grey Morris 1000 (Morris Minor), one of the most popular cars of its day.

From the pub they drove to Dorney. Just outside the village a cornfield stretched to the banks of the Thames and was, especially on summer evenings, a favourite spot for courting couples. Gregsten and Valerie Storie had previously been there together several times.

Just after darkness fell, there was an alarming tap at the driver's window. A man pointed a gun at them, said, "This is a hold-up", took charge of the ignition keys and slipped into the back seat of the car. He ordered Gregsten to drive further into the field, where they remained for about two hours. At roughly 11.30 p.m. they began a circuitous journey, skirting the north-west fringes of London: from Slough to near London Airport (as Heathrow was then still known), Harrow, Stanmore, to St Albans and thence on to the A6 to Luton and Bedford.

The gunman did not allow the couple to turn round and look at him. He did offer a few scraps of information about himself, suggesting that he had spent a considerable time in custody and had recently "done the lot" (criminal slang for serving a complete sentence – i.e. receiving no remission), and inviting Valerie Storie to call him "Jim". The car stopped at least twice: once at a garage, and once at a milk machine.

After passing through the village of Clophill, the gunman ordered Gregsten to pull into a lay-by on the brow of Deadman's Hill and to turn the car round so that it faced back in the direction of Luton and London. The gunman then decided it was time to tie up his hostages. Gregsten at this point attempted a sudden manoeuvre with a duffle-bag, to try to disarm him. It failed. Instead, the precipitate move served only to alarm the gunman, who reacted by firing instantly. He killed Gregsten with two shots into his head. Then, after a furious argument with Valerie Storie, he forced her into the back seat and raped her. He subsequently compelled her to help him drag Gregsten's body from the car. Storie, sitting beside her dead companion, implored the killer to leave and, at his request, twice showed him how to work the gears of the car. After a few moments of apparent indecision, he suddenly fired several shots at her, left her for dead, and drove off.

It was, of course, a shockingly brutal crime.

On the morning of Wednesday 23 August, James Trower, on his way to work in an engineering factory in Redbridge, stopped to pick up a friend and noticed a grey car being driven incompetently. There was an awful grinding noise whenever the driver tried to change gear. Edward Blackhall and John Skillett, also on their way to work, similarly noticed the grey Morris 1000 which nearly collided with both their own and another car, and changed traffic lanes indiscriminately. Skillett became so annoyed that he drew his own car level at the Gant's Hill roundabout, and asked Blackhall to wind down his passenger window so that he could shout a few choice words across to the driver. The latter just laughed, and continued driving erratically. Skillett and Blackhall last saw the car when it cut across oncoming traffic and, without signalling, turned right off the dual carriageway.

Meanwhile, Valerie Storie, crippled but still alive, had been found by a farm labourer called Sidney Burton. John Kerr, an Oxford undergraduate doing a traffic survey as a summer vacation job, arrived shortly afterwards. He flagged down passing cars, and asked their drivers to telephone for the police and an ambulance. He himself remained in the lay-by to comfort Storie. On the back of one of his enumerator forms he wrote down the first, embryonic description of the killer: "staring eyes, light, fairish hair". He also made a note of Valerie Storie's name, address and height, and the number of the missing car.

The crime received saturation publicity. Thursday morning's newspapers reported that the couple had picked up a hitch-hiker, and the RAC issued a public warning, advising motorists not to offer lifts to strangers. This initial elementary error presaged an accumulation of misinformation that dogged the inquiry throughout.

The hitch-hiker theory automatically eliminated two considerations: that the couple had been anything other than arbitrary victims; and that the liaison between them was at all significant. Although the mistake was admitted within a few days, it remained in the public consciousness, and the police never seemed to deviate from the assumption that they were searching for some kind of wild, sex-crazed killer.[1]

The first suspect, Peter Louis Alphon, was taken for interview at Blackstock Road police station, Highbury, north London, on Sunday 27 August. One of his fellow guests at the Alexandra National Hotel in Seven Sisters Road, Finsbury Park, reported that he had been behaving very strangely since the murder. He had hardly left his room, and had been pacing up and down in an agitated fashion, muttering to himself.

Alphon was able to provide an alibi; on the Tuesday evening he had seen his mother, and spent the night at the

Vienna Hotel in Sutherland Avenue, Maida Vale. He
was not, apparently, asked to explain either his strange
behaviour or why he had registered under the name of
Frederick Durrant. But at this stage there was nothing to
connect him with the crime.

Alphon left the station, but returned the following day
to ask if anything further was required of him. It wasn't.

At this point Miss Perkins, the schoolmistress with a
well-developed sense of civic responsibility who had
brought Alphon to the attention of the authorities, passes
from the story, unrecognised and unrewarded.

James Hanratty entered the picture in circumstances
which the least realistic thriller-fiction writer would be
ashamed to invent. Janet Gregsten, the murdered man's
widow, saw him walking in the arcade in Swiss Cottage,
north London, where her brother-in-law, William Ewer,
owned an antique shop. She had an immediate intuition
that Hanratty was the A6 killer. "That's the man. He
fits the description. But it's more than that. I have an
overpowering feeling that it is him."[2]

The strange thing about Janet Gregsten's intuition, even
apart from its fantastic implausibility, is that Hanratty did
not fit the description of the murderer. She claimed that
her attention had first been drawn by Hanratty's "blue,
staring eyes"; yet all the descriptions which had been
circulated referred to "deep-set brown eyes".[3]

Hanratty walked into a dry-cleaner's opposite, and Ewer
later went in himself to ask questions. On the basis of
his sister-in-law's assertions, he decided to keep a sharp
look-out for Hanratty. The following day he came across
him in a Finchley Road café. Ewer contacted Scotland
Yard. A squad car was despatched, and the police made
some inquiries of their own. Then, still tracking Hanratty,
Ewer went into the shop of a business associate, Mrs
Louise Anderson, in Greek Street, Soho. Curiouser and
curiouser: Mrs Anderson knew Hanratty well and had
frequently given him shelter.

There were two other puzzling developments. On 24

August, the day after the murder, an unknown man held up a lady, Audrey Willis, living in Old Knebworth, Hertfordshire. He produced a gun and demanded money and food, which she handed over.

On 7 September, a Richmond housewife, Mrs Meika Dalal, let into her house a man answering an advertisement for a room to let. She showed him the upstairs room, where he attempted to assault her, shouting, "I am the A6 killer." She struggled free, and screamed, and he raced out of the house.

The details of both incidents were filed with the A6 murder documents.

The murder weapon had been found almost straight-away, in the early evening of 24 August, under the upstairs back seat of a number 36A London Transport bus. It was lying underneath a handkerchief, together with some loose bullets and boxes of ammunition. On 11 September, two cartridge cases from bullets that, police forensic experts were able to determine, had been fired from the same gun, turned up in the Vienna Hotel, Maida Vale. Just another of the many incredible features of the case is that while Alphon was registered at that hotel on the night of the murder, Hanratty had stayed there the previous evening. It was in Hanratty's former room that the cartridge cases were discovered.

The police nevertheless fixed on Alphon as their prime suspect. William Nudds, a regular police informer who changed aliases as frequently as most men change underwear, happened to be then working at the Vienna. He made a statement, which incriminated neither Alphon nor Hanratty. This was hardly of much use to the police. He then obligingly withdrew it in favour of another, which made it clear that Alphon had not spent the murder night in his room. The police also learned that Alphon, whose father, though retired by then, had worked as a records clerk in Scotland Yard, had not met his mother on the murder evening after all; she admitted that she hadn't seen him for some time. Alphon's alibi was comprehensively smashed. Furthermore, he had been behaving strangely, and he did fit the original description of the killer tendered by Valerie Storie at Bedford General Hospital. The identi-kit picture which she had sanctioned resembled Alphon remarkably closely.

Probably the police had some further information which they have never disclosed – an underworld tip-off, perhaps. Certainly, just a month after the murder, the police officer in charge of the inquiry – Detective Superintendent Basil Acott – thought he knew his man. He was so positive that he launched a public appeal through television and the newspapers to find him. It did not prove difficult. Alphon phoned two national dailies from outside Scotland Yard, and then surrendered himself.

The following afternoon, Saturday 23 September, Alphon was put in an identity parade at Cannon Row police station. Mrs Dalal named him as the man who had attempted to molest her. Mr Blackhall, whom police regarded as the most observant of the early-morning witnesses, picked out someone else, and was quickly ushered out. He later said that parade procedure had not been properly explained to him beforehand; that he was unsure whether he was expected to indicate one man or more than one; and that had he reached the end of the line, where Alphon had positioned himself, he might well have picked him out. Nudds, the police informer, picked out two men, one of whom was Alphon.

That afternoon's edition of the *Evening News* announced dramatically that Alphon "is expected to travel to Ampthill this evening" – i.e. to be charged with murder. This was premature. There was first a crucially important identity parade before Valerie Storie at Guy's Hospital on Sunday morning.

She identified a Spanish sailor as the A6 murderer, and the case against Alphon collapsed.

The next day, 25 September, discussions took place between police and officials from the Director of Public Prosecutions (DPP). The results of this meeting were never made public, but it can safely be assumed that a decision was taken not to proceed with a case against Alphon. In the absence of an identification from Valerie Storie, the chances of a successful prosecution were slender.

The police therefore went back to the accommodating William Nudds, who withdrew his second statement and made a third, resurrecting the essential elements of the first. On the same day, it is thought that Charles 'Dixie' France went to Scotland Yard with a postcard he had received from Hanratty, who was then in Ireland.

Scotland Yard would have had a relatively detailed file on James Hanratty, who had spent most of his adult life in prison. He first came before the courts in September 1954, when he was eighteen, on a charge of taking and driving away a motor car. On that occasion he was placed on probation, but he subsequently served two prison sentences – for, respectively, house-breaking and car-stealing – before, in March 1958, he received a severe sentence: three years' corrective training, again for car-theft. He earned no remission, was released on 24 March 1961, and returned to London.

In July he met Charles France, who became a business associate, or at least its underworld equivalent. He helped Hanratty to value his takings from the burglaries which he had resumed as soon as he was freed, and introduced him to middle-men. Hanratty regarded him and his family as close friends, occasionally took out Charles's daughter, Carol, and frequently lodged with them during the summer of 1961. The Frances lived in the same Swiss Cottage area of north London in which William Ewer had his shop, and Hanratty was staying with them when Janet Gregsten first proclaimed him the killer.

If France did go to Scotland Yard about Hanratty on his own initiative, then it is extraordinary, because at that time nothing had been announced publicly to connect Hanratty with either the Vienna Hotel or the crime itself.

It would, however, explain why the police visited his parents, James and Mary Hanratty, the following day,

26 September. The police told them that their son was suspected of running cars over to Ireland, but within a few days they learned the real reasons for the visit: that he was wanted for questioning about the infinitely more serious matter of the A6 murder. Naturally, they believed him innocent, and on 3 October James Hanratty snr went to Scotland Yard with a birthday card he had received from his son. It was postmarked London. Acott, at that time scouring Ireland for his suspect, returned to base.

Hanratty, learning on the grapevine that he was very much a wanted man, telephoned Acott, stressing his innocence. He refused to give himself up, however, because he knew he would be charged with house-breaking, and was fearful of another long stretch inside. On 7 October he stole a Jaguar car, drove to Manchester and then caught a train to Liverpool. He contacted Acott again, explaining that he was trying to establish an alibi in Liverpool, but was having difficulty in doing so because the three men he had been with on the night of the murder would not allow their names to go forward in his defence; this was, said Hanratty, because they were 'fences' – i.e. receivers of stolen goods.

On 9 October he went to a hairdresser's, where his naturally fair hair, which had been dyed black since early in August, was now bleached. It was a visit which was to have disastrous consequences for Hanratty and which in any case did not serve its fundamental purpose of providing him with a disguise. He was apprehended by Blackpool police two days later.

Acott was telephoned at 2 a.m. He and his assistant, Detective Sergeant Oxford, drove through the night, and began interviewing Hanratty at 7.45 a.m. on the morning of 12 October. At that stage the evidence against him was only circumstantial: Hanratty had stayed in the hotel room in which incriminating cartridge cases were subsequently found; the murder weapon had been discovered underneath the back seat of a bus – which was, as Hanratty had once explained to Charles France, a convenient place to dispose of the unwanted spoils of robberies; and Hanratty to some extent fitted the description which the murderer had provided of himself.

Hanratty participated in his first identity parade on 13 October. Two witnesses – John Skillett and James Trower – picked him out; two – Edward Blackhall and Harry Hirons, an elderly garage attendant who had refuelled the murder car – did not. This was encouraging enough for the police. They must have been jubilant when Valerie Storie identified him at a parade in Stoke Mandeville Hospital on Saturday 14 October.

He was charged with murder the same day. After a preliminary hearing at Ampthill magistrates court from 22 November until 5 December, it was decided that there was a case to answer. Hanratty was sent for trial at the Old Bailey. On 2 January 1962, however, the case was recommitted to Bedford, where it opened on 22 January. After what had been the longest murder trial on record, the jury found Hanratty guilty on 17 February, and he was sentenced to death. The Court of Appeal upheld the verdict and sentence on 13 March. Hanratty's last hope came and went on 2 April, when the Home Secretary, R. A. Butler, discovered no grounds for granting a reprieve. Hanratty, who had protested his innocence throughout, was hanged at Bedford on 4 April 1962.

We can now be certain that Hanratty was innocent. In the first place, his alibi stood up to examination. He claimed that on the day of the crime he travelled to Liverpool by train, that he left his case (containing stolen jewellery) at the station, asked directions in a sweetshop along the Scotland Road, and spoke to someone on the steps of a billiard hall.

All three elements in this Liverpool alibi received corroboration. The most remarkable evidence was provided by the lady serving in the sweetshop, Mrs Olive Dinwoodie. Yes, she did remember a man who looked like Hanratty asking directions. (She identified him positively at Bedford.)

What made her evidence especially problematic for the prosecution was that she had worked in the shop as a holiday relief for only two days: on Monday 21 August and Tuesday 22 August. Since the prosecuting counsel, Graham Swanwick QC (later Mr Justice Swanwick) had already been able to account fully for Hanratty's movements on the Monday, this pinned down the date to the Tuesday, and should in itself have been sufficient to save Hanratty from the gallows, since the time of the incident was estimated at close to 5 p.m. – and even Swanwick admitted that Hanratty could not therefore have been in the vicinity of Slough a mere four or five hours later.

The effect of this, however, was vitiated by the initial absence of corroboration for Hanratty's alibi for the evening. From the outset, in his first conversations with Acott, he'd maintained that he'd stayed in Liverpool with three men. One week into the trial, he changed his story. He said he'd spent the evening in Rhyl. He told his solicitors that if he was to go into the witness-box and face a testing cross-examination from the prosecution counsel, then he must be able to tell the absolute truth. He had previously lied about his whereabouts because he thought he might easily be able to 'acquire' an alibi in Liverpool, whereas he couldn't remember precisely where he'd spent the night in Rhyl. He knew merely that he wandered round as darkness fell, searching with some difficulty for a room for the night (it was still the summer season). Eventually he'd found a bed in an attic room containing a green bath, in a boarding-house somewhere behind the railway station. (The trains could be heard, but not seen.)

Hanratty's counsel, Michael Sherrard, and the rest of the defence team were dismayed. They explained the seriousness of such a fundamental shift in his position. Hanratty was adamant; it had to be the truth, the whole truth and nothing but the truth.

The two men working on behalf of the defence in

Liverpool were instructed to switch their attentions to Rhyl. Joe Gillbanks and an assistant, Frank Evans, began knocking on the doors of boarding-houses in Rhyl. The owners were asked, simply, if they had a green bath in the attic.

Just like Hanratty's story about the sweetshop (which the police had investigated) this must have seemed a hopeless task. Just like the sweetshop, however, it came up trumps. Mrs Grace Jones, the landlady of "Ingledene", South Kinmel Street, confirmed not only that she had a green bath in the attic, but that she had let the room in just the circumstances described to someone who she thought was Hanratty.

The problem for the defence, as it turned out, was that Mrs Jones, in taking sympathy on someone looking for shelter late in the day, had probably been overfilling her guest-house; otherwise Hanratty would hardly have been allocated what seems to have been a bathroom with a bed in it. Because what she had to offer was so far from ideal, she allowed Hanratty to leave what luggage he had while he searched – unavailingly – for somewhere more suitable.

In the event, the prosecution, using the underhand trick of appropriating Mrs Jones' registers (tactics which earned a rebuke from the judge), was able to imply that Mrs Jones had been fiddling her books, and thus to inflict damage on her credibility as a witness. (Mrs Jones subsequently suffered a nervous breakdown as a result of her experiences at the trial.) Other guests staying in "Ingledene" at the time were brought forward; none could remember having seen Hanratty there.

It was unlikely that they would have done so. Hanratty, who stayed there for two nights, was a sort of supplementary visitor and, the house already being officially full, he breakfasted at the back in the family's own rooms.

Nor was Mrs Jones the only landlady who was able to substantiate Hanratty's alibi. Others could recall his making inquiries about a room for the night. Margaret Walker made a statement saying she had been approached by

Hanratty. In her case, she could pinpoint the date because of a family tragedy that was expected to take place, and did take place, on the following Friday. When Hanratty came up to her she had just been discussing this with her son, who always visited her on Tuesdays. Ivy Vincent corroborated this, saying that Hanratty had asked her about bed-and-breakfast, but that she had been unable to put him up.

Christopher Larman also encountered a man he thought was Hanratty. He, too, could remember the precise date of the chance meeting because he was embarking on a valedictory tour of Rhyl pubs before leaving the town the next morning. He made a statement at Staines police station, but it probably arrived too late to assist the defence at the trial.

Trevor Dutton, a poulterer from Kinmel Bay, had been approached by someone trying to sell him a gold watch. He thought the person was Hanratty, and he was able to check the date by his bank deposit book. He volunteered a statement to the police in Abergele.

Because of Hanratty's late switch of alibi, much of this information was not properly assimilated in time to be presented at the trial. Even at the appeal, though, Hanratty's legal advisers decided not to press forward with it, almost certainly because of the way in which Mrs Jones' credibility had been demolished at Bedford. The defence instead used as the main plank of its appeal the argument that the judge had misdirected the jury. It was a much more hazardous line of attack: Mr Justice Gorman had been a model of impartiality.

It should nevertheless be stressed that Hanratty's Rhyl alibi depends not on statements made several years after his execution (as sometimes seemed to be the case, since it was during the years 1966–8 that newspapers were most active in pursuing the Rhyl connection); but on statements made at the time, either in response to defence inquiries or from a sense of civic responsibility. Once Hanratty revealed where he really was on the evening of the murder his story was readily corroborated by a number of independent witnesses.

Prosecution counsel will generally try to undermine alibi evidence by alleging that it was bought; indeed, Hanratty had originally tried to do that very thing. In the event, his alibi was substantiated by a number of people who would have no possible motive for assisting a particularly vicious killer. Quite the reverse. They were – with due respect – just the sort of people who would have no natural sympathy with a common criminal like Hanratty: the last people from whom he would have sought a fraudulent alibi.

Everything Hanratty said stood up in court. He never stumbled in cross-examination, although he was pitting unschooled wits against an experienced barrister. (Incidentally, Swanwick's junior at the trial was Geoffrey Lane, who took silk two months later and is today the Lord Chief Justice.) Nothing was shown to be in any way false or contradictory. Even when explaining his criminal undertakings, Hanratty was wholly truthful. He maintained, for example, that he had stolen a black jacket because he had ripped his own. (At this stage the prosecution was trying to establish that he had swopped clothes because his own were blood-stained.) The police could find no evidence of a jacket having been stolen. By investigating Hanratty's story more carefully, however, the defence was able to show that it was entirely true.

Why should he even have tried to concoct an alibi initially? Niall MacDermot QC explained in the House of Commons: "The answer to that is simple. He could not count on alibi evidence in the sense of having someone to call to testify where he was at the time of the murder. A person of low intelligence finding himself in that situation, knowing himself unlikely to be believed, particularly when he has a criminal record, would tend to construct a false alibi."[4]

In the final analysis it is tragically ironic that Hanratty's behaviour over his alibi should have proved so damaging for him, since, however apparently perverse, it was the action of an innocent man. A guilty man would presumably have tried far more strenuously than Hanratty apparently did to establish a fake alibi. (At the time, Hanratty had sufficient funds available – the proceeds of his house-breaking – to offer reasonably attractive inducements.) At one stage, the prosecution vaguely mooted the idea that Hanratty might somehow have traced a lookalike in the north-west and was merely relating the movements of this second person. The suggestion was ridiculous.

Let us suppose, though, that Hanratty actually was guilty of the A6 murder. He invents a vague story about going into a sweetshop to ask directions, knowing that if its vagueness makes it well-nigh impossible to prove, it is equally impossible to disprove. But – a miracle happens! A middle-aged lady corroborates his story exactly. A solitary miracle, however, is insufficient. He accordingly formulates a new cock-and-bull story about having been in Rhyl. What then happens? A shower of miracles! Honest citizens step forward eagerly to confirm exactly the story of this sadistic killer.

The notion is ludicrous. There is only one explanation: on 22 August 1961 Hanratty caught a train to Liverpool, and from there went on to Rhyl where he spent the evening and the following day. Just as he said he did. His alibi was watertight.

The second compelling reason for believing in Hanratty's innocence concerns the car.

The murderer asked Valerie Storie to show him how to work the gears. This she did. It then stalled, and he had to ask her again. Finally, after shooting her, he drove off.

Three hours later the car was still being driven so ineptly that the murderer was endangering his chances of making good his escape. Witnesses who saw the car in the early-morning traffic noticed it particularly because of the dangerous manner in which it was being driven. John

Skillett, for example, was so annoyed that he pulled alongside to remonstrate with the driver. The murderer would have wanted at all costs to avoid drawing attention to himself; yet that is precisely what he was doing. Furthermore, when the car was discovered later in the day it was found to have dents in the back and the bumper that had not been there at the time of the murder. Clearly, it had suffered some damage *en route* from Deadman's Hill, even while the roads must have been almost empty. The only explanation is that the murderer had no motoring skills. This, indeed, was the first genuine clue to his identity which the police possessed.

Hanratty was a semi-professional car thief who had been found guilty of stealing cars on three occasions. Early in September he had realised a personal dream by buying a car of his own, a Sunbeam Talbot. The police had initially told his parents that he was wanted for running cars over to Ireland. While evading arrest by Acott, he had stolen a Jaguar in London and driven to Manchester.

Though he might not bother with matters like driving licences and car insurance, Hanratty undoubtedly knew how to handle cars. It is implausible that someone so experienced would have needed to seek advice about how to put a humble Morris Minor through its paces; it is inconceivable that three hours after setting out in it he would be driving so badly that he risked immediate discovery. Not only was the car being driven badly; John Skillett and Edward Blackhall testified that the driver was also displaying an acute lack of road sense, yet Hanratty had driven all over the country in stolen cars.

There is a final, admittedly less persuasive, point. The murderer/driver had not made good time in escaping the scene of the crime. Hanratty would surely have reached east London more quickly, and thus have safely abandoned the vehicle before potential witnesses were up and about.

* * *

The prosecution case against Hanratty rested almost entirely on identification evidence, which provides notoriously fallible grounds for conviction.

In this case, the identifications should have been regarded with particular caution since no one, not even Valerie Storie, got a good look at the man. She admitted as much. (It should be remembered that although she had spent several hours in close proximity to him, they were entirely hours of pitch darkness. During the time the three of them had been together in the car, the gunman had not allowed Gregsten or Storie to turn round.)

Valerie Storie's positive identification of Hanratty should have been weighed against not just this consideration, but also the facts that he did not match her original description of her attacker, and that she had picked out someone else at a previous identity parade.

It has been suggested that she could hardly have failed to identify Hanratty at Stoke Mandeville. She would have been aware from the newspapers – which, as a hospital patient, she would have had plenty of time to read – that the new police suspect had dyed hair; and, unhappily for him, Hanratty's hair colouring looked most unnatural under the harsh hospital lighting. Secondly, Storie's identification was made only after she had asked everyone in the parade to say, "Be quiet, will you, I am thinking". The murderer had used this phrase several times and his Cockney accent – noticeable in his pronunciation of 'thinking' as 'finking' – had made it especially memorable.

Aural identification is even more risky than visual identification, since it is highly probable that a guilty person will make some effort to disguise the natural timbre of his voice; also, what had actually distinguished the murderer's voice had been his Cockney accent – and there is no evidence that the identity parade (held in Buckinghamshire) contained a single Londoner other than Hanratty.

For all this, however, Valerie Storie was clearly a forceful and impressive witness, and Hanratty's case ultimately foundered on the rock of her unwavering evidence.

The other identification evidence came from witnesses who had seen the car being driven so awkwardly the morning after the crime.

Hanratty had first been placed in an identity parade on 13 October at Bedford. Two witnesses failed to pick him out. Harry Hirons, the elderly garage attendant, had never been confident of his ability to recognise the man whom he had only glimpsed through the back window of the car. However, Edward Blackhall, the passenger in Skillett's car, had been regarded by police as a vital witness. This was because of his acute observation of the car itself; because he was the one who reported the matter; because Skillett had been furious with the driver of the murder car, whereas Blackhall had stayed calm; and, because Skillett had been driving, giving Blackhall the better opportunity of studying the car and its occupant.

The two who did pick out Hanratty were Skillett and James Trower. The police had not previously thought them key witnesses; neither had attended the Alphon parade.

Trower would not have been able to see the driver properly at all, and his evidence was contradicted by the friend whom he drove to work. (Also, Trower had previously picked out three suspects from police files. Two were discovered and eliminated, and the third, being in prison at the time, had the perfect alibi.) Skillett could not possibly have got as good a view of the driver as Blackhall, who has always maintained that it was not Hanratty.

Blackhall also told Paul Foot, author of *Who Killed Hanratty?*, that Skillett said to him, as the two walked away from the Bedford court, "Well, it must have been Hanratty because otherwise the police would never have arrested him."[5]

The remainder of the prosecution case presented equally grave doubts. The evidence of the cartridge cases in the hotel room and of the gun underneath the back seat of a bus seems damning. On examination, however, it is rather less so. The discovery of the cartridge cases was particularly curious. There was no suggestion that a gun had been fired in the room. Hanratty, therefore, must have fired the gun somewhere else and retained the cartridge cases. Why? For what purpose had the gun previously been fired? And if the murderer initially took such care to retain the cartridge cases, why should he then have so carelessly left them in so prominent a position in the room? Moreover, how had they managed to remain undisturbed for so long – from 22 August to 11 September – at a time when hotels are supposed to be doing good business?

Similarly, why should a ruthless murderer, knowing himself to be the most wanted man in Britain, have carefully disposed of the murder weapon in such a way that it was almost bound to be discovered within a few hours? Wouldn't he rather, say, have thrown it into the Thames?

There is one logical explanation. The cartridge cases and the gun were planted to incriminate Hanratty. He was, after all, an ideal person to frame; just the sort of small-time crook who might have difficulty explaining to the police exactly what he was doing on a particular evening.

The person who planted the evidence could well have been Charles France. Hanratty had confided to him that a convenient place to dispose of unwanted baubles from jewellery robberies was underneath the upstairs back seat of a bus. France was therefore able to dispose of the murder weapon in such a way, and at a later date pass on Hanratty's comments, suitably embroidered, to the police.

Planting the cartridge cases must have been relatively easy. The hotel was hardly the Dorchester; rooms were frequently left unlocked, staff were not always about. Planting the murder weapon must have been more difficult; it could hardly have been done during the rush hour, only when the bus was carrying few, if any, other passengers. It therefore follows that the conductor might have been able to give helpful descriptions of passengers during quiet periods.

The point seems especially germane in view of an incident on 13 March 1962, when Hanratty's case went to appeal. Once the appeal had been dismissed, a lady sitting in the public benches stood up and shouted, "It's not true, he didn't do it. Ask the conductor on the 36 bus."

This is perhaps the single most fascinating feature of the entire case. No one who has subsequently researched the A6 murder has been able to identify this lady, or to suggest how she could have acquired her information. Neither has the bus conductor – conductress, actually – been traced since all that is known about her is that she was called Pat.

The police interviewed 'Pat' and took a statement from her, but they neither identified her nor produced the statement. She was never brought to court, presumably because her knowledge would not have buttressed the prosecution case. The defence did not attempt to trace her because it was not appreciated that her evidence might be significant. The lady in the Appeal Court, therefore, knew something which even those closely involved with the case did not suspect. Who she was, and why she was so certain that what the conductress knew established Hanratty's innocence, remain impenetrable mysteries.

Leaving aside the identifications, the majority of the evidence given against Hanratty in court was offered by people who, like France and William Nudds, made their living in that twilight zone between the legal and the illegal. In this context it is hardly surprising that a figure almost mandatory in miscarriage cases briefly threw his sinister shadow across the courtroom: the prison grass.

Roy Langdale had been convicted of various offences twelve times in the previous eight years. One of his crimes had been maliciously assaulting a fellow prisoner in Wormwood Scrubs in 1958. In November 1961 he was being held on remand in Brixton prison at the same time as Hanratty, and subsequently claimed that Hanratty had openly confessed to him of having committed the A6 murder.

Unfortunately, his evidence was full of holes which the defence was able to expose, and was even contradicted by two other prisoners. Langdale had described walking alongside Hanratty in the exercise yard; the others insisted this had never happened. Hanratty himself told his defence that he couldn't remember anybody of that name. Nobody at all could be found to support Langdale's story.

In the end the judge, and even the prosecution, made it clear to the jury that Langdale's evidence must be treated with the utmost caution. Nevertheless it must have been damaging, if only because Hanratty's protestations of innocence had hitherto seemed credible precisely because they had been so consistently voiced. Langdale's statement opened a chink, however small, in Hanratty's strongest line of defence.

The British legal system is full of mechanisms which apparently protect the innocent and ensure that the course of justice is rigorously and transparently pursued. The rule against hearsay evidence is one such. It is hard to understand why such safeguards are not extended to prevent the admissibility of prison evidence, which can hardly ever be above all suspicion. Hanratty's case illustrates this perfectly. The two prisoners who spoke up on his behalf had no possible ulterior motive for doing so; Langdale had. At the time of his remand in Brixton, he had been charged with forgery and, in view of his record, seemed likely to be sent down for some time. He got three years' probation.

There was one further instance of the prosecution resorting to disreputable tactics. The first people to find Valerie Storie after the murder were Sidney Burton and John Kerr. On the back of one of his traffic enumerator forms, Kerr had written down the features of the killer which came most readily to Storie's mind. The form thus represented the first sheet of what was presumably destined to become a mountain of paperwork. Kerr handed it to a senior police officer at 8.00 a.m. that same morning.

When Kerr was giving his evidence at the committal proceedings, the magistrates asked to see this exhibit. Naturally, the prosecuting counsel assented. However, following a conversation with police officers, there was some hesitation before counsel admitted that the important document was "not available". He could not account for its absence.

At the trial proper, the prosecution, still unable to produce the missing evidence, reacted by trying to discredit Kerr. Swanwick submitted him to some uncomfortable questioning, and inferred that the shocking nature of the events must temporarily have unhinged him. Perhaps he had merely imagined passing on this form to the police?

Swanwick then questioned Police Inspector Edward Milborrow, the senior police officer at Deadman's Hill, and asked if he had been able to trace the form. Milborrow replied that no policeman there had received anything from Kerr. However, he had discovered a form which fitted Kerr's description at the county surveyor's office. This document was produced, and identified as one of Kerr's enumerator forms. On the back, the registration number of a car had been written, and there were also some scribbled figures; but no prototype description of the murderer.

However, Kerr adamantly rebutted Swanwick's suggestions that this must be the form to which he had referred in his evidence. He explained that he did not write his figures or letters as they appeared on the newly produced sheet, and that in any case the registration of the murder car was incorrect (the numbers and letters had been reversed).

To begin with, it may have been thought merely unfortunate that the police should have mislaid the very first piece of paperwork they received. The crude substitution, however, exposed the attempt to doctor the evidence. It was highly convenient that Kerr's document should have gone AWOL, because it would have significantly weakened the prosecution case. Within hours of the murder, at a time when she was, according to the consultant orthopaedic surgeon at Bedford Hospital, *compos mentis*, Storie had described the murderer as having "light, fairish hair". Hanratty's hair, at that time, was dyed black.

This apparently irrelevant exchange about a traffic enumerator form should itself have been sufficient to alert the jury that there was something distinctly devious about the prosecution case.

Altogether, then, Swanwick's version of events raised more questions than it answered; but it seems even more comprehensively flawed when one considers the evidence he didn't provide. He could offer no clue as to when Hanratty might have planted the gun; how he might have acquired it; what he did on the day the crime commenced, and for three days afterwards; how he might have made his way to the cornfield, and for what reason; why a sex-crazed murderer should have procrastinated for over five hours – on all these points, he could only conjecture.

This leads to the final reason why Hanratty did not commit the A6 murder, which is simply the inherent implausibility of it. The prosecution could never provide a rational motive, other than that it was some kind of irrational sex attack. Hanratty had a history of crime, and so the police knew quite a lot about him. His record showed that he had no convictions for violence, and he was not the sort to have possessed a gun. Still less was he a likely sex-attacker. There was no evidence of emotional or psychological instability to suggest that he might ever have behaved in that fashion. Far from being sex-starved, he seemed at ease with the opposite sex, had occasional girlfriends and was also a regular client of one of Soho's call-girls.

In fact, one of the awful Catch 22s of the A6 murder saga is that psychiatrists who examined Hanratty after his conviction declared him perfectly sane, and therefore fit to hang. But of course he was sane. He was innocent. Many had thought the terrible crime the work of a madman. If the psychiatrists had therefore been examining the actual killer it is conceivable that their medical verdict would have been one of insanity, which would have saved him from the gallows.

Four

The A6 Murder (ii)

SPECULATION SURROUNDING the A6 murder did not die with Hanratty. For the next fourteen years it positively raged. Even apart from the baffling absence of motive to account for the crime which Hanratty was supposed to have committed, there were too many loose ends. Two factors in particular, though, ensured continuing interest in the case.

In the first place, there was the understandable determination of James Hanratty snr to clear his son's name. When they had been alone together in prison his son had given him his word that he was totally innocent. From that point, Mr Hanratty's faith in James never wavered, and he did all he could to obtain posthumous justice for him. The A6 murder committee was formed, and remained in existence until the mid-seventies.

Secondly, there was the not insignificant consideration that someone else kept confessing to the crime.

The committal proceedings at Ampthill and the trial at Bedford were both avidly followed by M. Justice. The son of a Belgian diplomat, Jean Justice was a kind of prosperous drop-out who was in the happy position of having both the time and the money to be able to indulge his whims. He had a passionate interest in the law. The A6 murder fascinated him and in company with his friend Jeremy Fox, a barrister, he travelled north from London in those winter weeks of 1961–2 to attend the court hearings.

From quite early on, Justice had been persuaded of Hanratty's innocence. The original police suspect, Peter Alphon, was now installed in a comfortable hotel near London Airport – a change from the unprepossessing establishments he had been frequenting in August – and Justice began to make regular contact with him.

Though distant initially, Alphon quickly proved companionable. He was a former public-schoolboy who received a small allowance from his family and had never been in regular employment. He was deeply lonely, and it was perhaps not surprising that a close relationship with Justice developed.

Justice guessed that he probably knew something about the crime: the police had at one point been positive enough that Alphon was the culprit to embark on a full-scale nationwide search for him; and yet the reasons Acott gave in court for eliminating him from police inquiries seemed oddly insubstantial.

On 20 February 1962 Alphon playfully handed Justice a drawing. Within a tangle of lines, Justice could discern the name PETER MCDOUGAL. (Alphon, by then at the Regent Palace Hotel in the centre of London, had registered in his solicitor's name of McDougal.) On the reverse, a word could be picked out from a background confusion, perhaps as a particular shape is distinguished in a colour-blindness test. The word was MURDERER. At the bottom of the page was written BEDFORD.

Justice was naturally taken aback. He had not previously suspected Alphon of having committed the murder. Alphon would not let him retain the drawing, but five days later Justice succeeded in dispossessing him of it. He then used it to try to prevent the forthcoming execution of Hanratty.

The police were not interested. Mr Justice Christmas Humphreys, however, did agree that in some circumstances it could be regarded as a confession. Jean Justice also contacted Fenner Brockway, the MP for Slough, in which constituency the crime had originated. Henceforward Brockway followed the case closely. He indicated to the Home Office that Alphon might be prepared to confess to prevent Hanratty's execution. Such earnest endeavours, however, came to naught.

This is not to suggest that Alphon viewed Hanratty's approaching demise with unconcern. On the contrary, he wrote to the *Daily Express* arguing in favour of a reprieve; and in two other respects he seems to have tried, albeit obliquely, to persuade the authorities to think again about condemning Hanratty.

His harassing phone calls seem to have been instrumental in the suicide of Charles France, who gassed himself in Acton, west London, on 16 March. Surely somebody in the corridors of power must have thought it strange that one of the main prosecution witnesses should take his own life within three days of the dismissal of Hanratty's appeal? It was also strange that just two days before the execution, someone again threatened the resident of Old Knebworth, Audrey Willis, with a gun and demanded cash and food and drink. This duplicated almost exactly the incident which had occurred at the same house on 24 August the previous year, and which the police and the press had at the time linked with the A6 murder of the previous day. Mrs Willis was fairly certain that the same man was involved on each occasion. (She had attended one of the Hanratty identity parades, and confirmed that it had not been him.) Perhaps the intruder was Alphon.

For the rest of the decade Alphon maintained an erratic but unbroken dialogue with those who remained interested in the case, in the course of which his confessions became more and more explicit. His behaviour was always unpredictable, and prone to wild excesses, and he would mercilessly hound his telephone contacts, just as he had apparently hounded Charles France.

On the first anniversary of the murder, he visited Hanratty's parents at their home, took out his chequebook and offered compensation for the death of their eldest son. Naturally, he was thrown out, but the following day there was a fracas between him and them at Green Park tube station. The Hanrattys were on their way to meet Jean Justice at the Ritz Hotel in Piccadilly to discuss the case. Alphon had met Justice earlier in the morning, and had tracked him there. The scuffle made all the news-

papers, and was another of the incidents which kept the
A6 affair in the public eye.

Justice had by now satisfied himself that Alphon was the
real murderer, and had even obtained from him a set of
handwritten notes, outlining the course of the crime. One
of Alphon's comments referred to leaving Slough dog-
track for the cornfield after watching a greyhound called
Mentals Only Hope compete.

After some months, the nervous strain imposed by
Alphon's regular companionship became unbearable, and
Justice resolved to cease personal contact with him. He
did, however, remain in telephone contact, and at the
suggestion of Brockway and Martin Ennals, secretary of
the National Council for Civil Liberties, decided to start
recording the frequent and lengthy conversations.

Justice had not been the sole recipient of these. Alphon
also plagued the Hanrattys with calls that were invariably
anonymous and mostly silent. On one occasion, however,
he did speak: "I am the A6 killer, Mrs Hanratty, and I'm
coming to get you."

On the evening of 17 May 1963 he introduced himself,
and had a long conversation with James Hanratty, in
the course of which he confessed to the crime for which
Hanratty's son had hanged. He also learned, to his evident
dismay, that his conversations with Justice were being
tape-recorded, and bitterly reproached Justice for his
duplicity.

The first book about the case appeared in the spring of
1963. It was a Penguin Special, *The A6 Murder: Regina v.
James Hanratty; The Semblance of Truth*, written by the
distinguished QC and legal commentator, Louis Blom-
Cooper. He argued that, the continuing disquiet notwithstanding, Hanratty had been guilty and thus there was no
need for public hand-wringing over the business.

Nobody familiar with the case believed any longer that
it was that simple. Jean Justice, Jeremy Fox, and Tony
Mason, a freelance journalist from Slough who had
thought Hanratty innocent all along, put together a de-

tailed memorandum on the case including the drawing, the confession notes and transcripts of the telephone conversations. It was sent to Fenner Brockway at the House of Commons. He diligently set about arousing parliamentary interest in the case, and ensured that a copy of the memo was sent to every MP, over one hundred of whom signed his Commons motion calling for an inquiry.

The matter was debated in the Commons for the first time on 2 August, just before the summer recess. Brockway's speech touched on the confession notes, the inadequate reasons given for Alphon's elimination as a suspect, the factors which all along had pointed to Hanratty's innocence, and the tape-recordings. Other speakers who expressed concern were Chuter Ede; Tory MPs Peter Kirk (Gravesend) and Dr Donald Johnson (Carlisle); and Labour MPs Eric Fletcher (Islington, East) and Niall Mac-Dermot QC (Derby, North), the original prosecuting counsel in Hanratty's case at the magistrates court.

Kirk was especially interested in the evidence of Michael Fogarty-Waul, who lived in a caravan close to the Dorney cornfield. Fogarty-Waul recalled giving a lift to a man from Slough dog-track some days before the murder; and to seeing the same man some months later, just after Hanratty had been found guilty. He said the man looked like the actor Sidney Tafler (a description which could have fitted Alphon) and was adamant that it had not been Hanratty. He had reported the original incident after the murder; and the second one immediately it happened, but police had not pursued the lead.

The then Home Secretary, Henry Brooke, responded by trying to use his authority to quell the burgeoning speculation. He pointed to a discrepancy in the confession notes. The timing of the races at Slough dog-stadium on that evening showed that Alphon would not have had time to leave to commit the crime after watching the dog called Mentals Only Hope race.

The point was strictly correct, but hardly sufficient to dispose of the alternative-killer theory. It needed to be backed up by other substantial points. The rest of the speech, however, was less than persuasive. Brooke maintained that the evidence of the car-driving eliminated Alphon from consideration, since he did not hold a licence and therefore could not drive. This was patently ridiculous. The car-driving evidence was important – but it should, as we have seen, have eliminated Hanratty. It did fit Alphon who, though without a licence, proved himself on the one occasion he had got behind the wheel of Justice's car to be a driver more willing than able: just like the murderer.

Brooke also suggested that Alphon "had a complete alibi for the crime. It is beyond challenge that [he] was occupying a room at the Vienna Hotel in London at the time of the murder".[1] As Home Secretary, therefore, he declined to reopen the case.

That evening, a disappointed Brockway appeared on ITN's news programme, and said that he thought Mr X, the term which had concealed the identity of Alphon during the parliamentary debate, had committed the A6 murder. Through his solicitors, Alphon issued writs against Brockway and ITN, alleging libel on the grounds that sufficient people were aware to whom Mr X actually referred. The writs were never pursued.

The desultory telephone relationship between Alphon and Justice was maintained. On 18 March the following year, 1964, Alphon added two important glosses to his confession by providing the motive for the murder and naming the man who had commissioned the crime. The motive was to sunder Gregsten and Valerie Storie, so that Gregsten would return to his wife and children. The murder was only committed when Gregsten's resolve to remain with Storie proved unshakeable.

Alphon had at last provided the crime with a gruesome rationale. In those far-off days of 1961, when society was less inured to extra-marital relationships, the explanation had its own nefarious logic. It also dovetailed with information about earlier attempts to separate Gregsten and

Storie, of which the general public could hardly have been aware.

Justice's own book, *Murder versus Murder*, published in Paris, and *Deadman's Hill: Was Hanratty Guilty?*, written by Lord Russell of Liverpool, appeared in 1964 and 1965 respectively. They were the first full-length accounts of the whole affair which presented forceful arguments for Hanratty's innocence.

In October 1964 a Labour government had been returned. Fourteen months later, in December 1965, Roy Jenkins replaced the ineffectual Sir Frank Soskice as Home Secretary. It was an appointment which put fresh heart into those campaigning for posthumous justice for Hanratty. Jenkins had been one of the signatories of the 1963 Commons motion calling for an inquiry and during the March 1966 election campaign he still appeared sympathetic to this course of action.

A motion tabled by Lord Russell calling for a public inquiry into the A6 murder was debated in the House of Lords on 4 August 1966 (again, coincidentally, just before the summer recess). By that time the two main adversaries of the earlier Commons debate, Fenner Brockway and Henry Brooke, had both been elevated to the Lords. Each reaffirmed his previous stance.

The closing contribution of the debate came from Lord Stonham, parliamentary under-secretary at the Home Office. He told the House that "the Home Secretary would now anxiously study the debate and the arguments". While not altogether excluding the possibility of an inquiry, however, he did argue forcibly against one. Yet his speech was no more convincing than previous pleas to let the matter rest. Furthermore, he concluded in extraordinary fashion by explaining that Alphon had had an alibi for the evening of the murder, as he had seen his mother then. As Paul Foot has written, this was incredible. Alphon claimed at the time of his very first interview to have been in the hotel and to have seen his mother on that evening. The police quickly discovered that neither alibi could be substantiated, and on that basis launched their highly publicised nationwide search for him. Two years later, the then Home Secretary revived the 'hotel' alibi; now, five years later another prominent Home Office official had resurrected the 'mother' alibi. The first had occurred under a Conservative administration, and the second under a Labour one. Had a confessed murderer ever before received such generous cross-party assistance from parliament?

The media's reporting of the aftermath of the A6 murder trial had hitherto been both sporadic and sceptical. Now, the story suddenly became hot news again. The immediate cause was a court appearance by Alphon. For two years, ever since he had disclosed his intention of publishing a book about the case, Lord Russell had been tormented by phone calls that were either silent or else abusive and threatening. The caller – who else? – was Alphon. The police, however, displayed no enthusiasm for prosecuting him, despite repeated complaints, until the Lords debate enabled Russell to bring the whole business into the open. Within a month Alphon was brought to court and charged with making phone calls that contravened the Post Office Act. He was fined £5 and bound over to keep the peace.

In the ensuing months, the media provided three major contributions to the growing debate. Paul Foot wrote a lengthy article in *Queen*. He made use of the Alphon– Justice tapes and publicly named Alphon as the killer – the first time this had been done outside the protection of parliamentary privilege. The BBC's prestigious *Panorama* programme examined the case in detail, and so did the *Sunday Times* colour magazine in December.

Perhaps surprisingly, Alphon agreed to be interviewed at the BBC studios for *Panorama*. The interview must rank as one of the most bizarre in the BBC archives. When Alphon arrived, the reporter – John Morgan – surprised him by playing extracts from the telephone tapes. Alphon reacted by maintaining that he and Justice had merely been discussing a book project; Morgan retorted that he'd never known a book being planned in quite such an excitable, almost hysterical, manner.

Even in such potentially damaging circumstances, Alphon couldn't resist talking about what had happened in the murder car. His impression of those hours – based, he now claimed, entirely on supposition – seemed plausible. There was also a glaring reference to the fact that Gregsten had "come" back to the car; surely someone hypothesising about the crime would have said that Gregsten had "gone" back to the car.

Panorama, however, ultimately proved reassuring for those disposed to believe in the near-infallibility of British justice. After all, Alphon disclaimed all connection with the crime; and Valerie Storie, also interviewed by Morgan, reiterated her certainty that Hanratty was the murderer.

One substantial problem, though, had been raised by both *Panorama* and the *Sunday Times*: the Rhyl alibi. Other newspapers joined the hunt and despatched correspondents to North Wales. In the face of mounting media pressure, the Home Office made a tactical concession. On 30 January 1967 Jenkins announced that Detective Chief Superintendent Douglas Nimmo, the head of Manchester CID, would conduct an inquiry specifically into the alibi. The Home Secretary detailed Nimmo's brief in the Commons: "to investigate the claim that James Hanratty was at Rhyl on 22–23 August 1961; to take statements from all relevant witnesses; and to make a report to the Home Secretary".

Nimmo stayed in Rhyl from 9 to 15 February, and interviewed a number of people who had seen Hanratty there in August 1961. None was legally represented; nor were independent observers present. The report, 250,000 words in length according to some, was handed in to the Home Office on 23 March.

At length, a number of newspapers got hold of what

were clearly well-informed leaks, and reported that Nimmo had been unable to substantiate the alibi.

This advance publicity alarmed Hanratty's parents, who had imagined that the inquiry might simply be the mandatory bureaucratic prelude to their son's pardon. Accordingly, they visited Rhyl themselves and, while the official report remained ostensibly under wraps, took statements from witnesses to demonstrate how persuasive the alibi was. This material was published in the *Sunday Times* on 11 June 1967.

The Home Office then sent Nimmo back to Rhyl on 13 July to make another inquiry. On this occasion Lord Russell ensured that interviews took place only in the presence of an independent observer, Mr B. Berkson, a solicitor from Birkenhead. The witnesses were only too ready to comply with this. They had already felt their integrity slighted by what they had gathered of the contents of the first report. Afterwards, Berkson told the press: "There has been some clarification of the earlier statements the ladies made which in my view adds to their stature. I am satisfied that there is cause for a public inquiry and I think that a jury that had heard the ladies' evidence would have come to the conclusion that Hanratty was in Rhyl that night."[2]

The second Nimmo report was delivered on 21 July. Once again, a deafening silence emanated from the Home Office.

Infuriated by the procrastination, Lord Russell called a press conference in Rhyl on 31 July. He informed the assembled journalists that he suspected his telephone was being tapped. Clicking noises on the line had first aroused his suspicions. Then, at the time of the second Nimmo inquiry, he had two telephone conversations with Mrs Margaret Walker in which he advised her not to see Nimmo without an independent witness. Mrs Walker told Nimmo of the *first* conversation; yet he later let slip a remark which indicated that he was aware of *both*.

Nor was this the only telephone hazard for Lord and

Lady Russell. In defiance of the court injunction of August 1966, Alphon was continuing to plague them with hostile calls. He seemed almost a law unto himself – ceaselessly provoking the authorities, yet always escaping censure. This time, though, he tempted fate too far. In the spring of 1967, when he was served with a police summons, he realised he was in deeper water than he'd imagined.

Thus, he played the card he had always threatened to use. On 12 May, the very day on which he should have been at Marylebone magistrates court to answer the summons relating to a breach of his recognisance of the previous year, he gave a press conference in Paris. He publicly admitted to the A6 murder. "I killed Gregsten and half-killed Miss Storie. It's not my fault. I can't shoot a gun very well. This is my confession. I have never confessed before." He said his purpose was "to expose British justice as a sham".[3]

The proceedings were witnessed by an inspector from the Metropolitan Police, stationed in Paris on Interpol liaison duties, and a detective-sergeant sent over from London. They made notes, and reported back to the metropolitan police commissioner.

The following day, Alphon spoke on the telephone from Paris to Paul Foot, and gave a detailed account of the crime, which was published in the *Sunday Times* (14 May 1967).

Alphon explained that he and Charles France had been two members of a three-man conspiracy. The third man had previously tried to end Gregsten's affair with Valerie Storie, and had finally offered Alphon £5,000 to do the job once and for all. The contract money was to be paid into Alphon's account at Lloyd's Bank – the Law Courts branch, ironically. France had acquired the gun, and Alphon had fired two practice shots at the Cumberland Hotel, Marble Arch, subsequently handing the cartridge cases to France. Alphon agreed that all three knew Hanratty ("a stupid little crook"), and thus it was suggested that he could make some vague pretence to be him, but it was only afterwards that he realised the others intended framing Hanratty. That was why, explained Alphon, he'd pestered France with the phone calls that probably led to his suicide.

The third man had shown Alphon the cornfield that was the scene of Gregsten and Storie's trysts, and Alphon had twice reconnoitred the area, which in any case he knew well, having lived there during the war. On the evening of 22 August 1961, he had made his way to the cornfield from the dog-track at Slough. He climbed into the car, and during the next five hours allowed Gregsten two opportunities, as he saw it, to walk away; but Gregsten returned both times. The actual murder occurred, when it did, almost as self-defence, "but it wasn't accidental because I was going to kill them anyway". He drove the car to Redbridge, and made his way from Ilford to Warwick Avenue. He had a wash and breakfasted at the Vienna Hotel, and then caught the train to Southend, for a pre-arranged meeting with France. He returned the gun, he said, and then travelled back to London and booked in at the Alexandra National Hotel in Finsbury Park. He was still there when the police interviewed him about the crime four days later.

No one, of course, can say for certain that this is the truth, but it is a plausible account of the crime. Nobody had previously been able to provide that.

ITN subsequently interviewed Alphon for its magazine programme, *Dateline*. He repeated his confession, though in the course of the televised interview said that he had fired only once at Gregsten and that he had not reloaded the gun when firing at Valerie Storie. Each of these observations was at variance with the known facts of the crime.

Alphon moved from Paris to Dublin, and returned to England in the summer. He resumed his routine of annoying Lord Russell with telephone calls, all of which were meticulously logged. Finally, on 2 September, he surrendered himself to Chief Inspector Mooney at Scotland Yard, asking for the case, which on 12 May was ordered to lie on the file, to be tried.

For the offence, Alphon was fined £11, and additionally £10 of his original £50 recognisance was estreated. The Marylebone magistrate had been lenient. He had clearly been sympathetic to the arguments advanced by Mooney, who tried to show that Alphon had been persecuted by people (Russell, Jean Justice, *et al.*) who were themselves obsessed with the A6 murder. Further, Mooney told the court, Alphon himself was indubitably innocent: "I know where he was at the time of the murder".

"I hope," the magistrate told Alphon, "that what has been said in court today will finish for good all these stories that have been put about saying you had a hand in the murder. I can see no reason why anybody from now on will have cause to say you did the murder."[4]

The court case had been yet another extraordinary twist in the A6 saga. Mooney seemed to have discovered a cast-iron alibi for Alphon which had eluded all those who had investigated the case during the previous six years. It is remarkable that alibi evidence produced so belatedly should be deemed so persuasive, especially since, as Paul Foot wrote, Mooney could produce neither evidence nor witnesses to back it up.

In the event, Alphon spurned the hand that Mooney offered, and quickly reverted to the path he had trodden so consistently since the murder. On 1 October he wrote to Roy Jenkins to demand an inquiry into the whole A6 affair.

The Home Secretary now had before him both the evidence of the Rhyl alibi, presumably documented in the Nimmo reports, which should have indicated that Hanratty hadn't done the murder; and the evidence of the Alphon confessions, indicating that he had.

On 1 November Roy Jenkins provided a written answer in the Commons. He declined to hold an inquiry into the matter. "Detective Chief Superintendent Nimmo has made detailed and exhaustive investigations covering all possible lines of inquiry into the alibi. Mr Nimmo's thorough investigations have found nothing to strengthen the evidence called at the trial on Hanratty's behalf, and no further evidence which, if put before the jury, might have influenced the verdict.''

Thus did the honest and disinterested statements of a number of responsible and respectable citizens of Rhyl receive short shrift from one of the most able members of the government.

"He [Alphon] has withdrawn his earlier confession,'' Jenkins added. "Neither his confession nor other allegations about his part in the case are supported by new material of substance . . . I have accordingly decided that there are no grounds for taking any further action in this case.''[5]

In May 1968 the A6 murder committee made its own independent inquiries. It was only at that stage that the witness evidence of Trevor Dutton came to light. He, remember, had made a statement to the police in Abergele prior to Hanratty's execution, but had heard nothing at all in the intervening years. He had certainly not been interviewed in either of Nimmo's investigations.

Later in that year the committee learned of the evidence of Christopher Larman. He had made a statement to the police in Staines, but had never afterwards been contacted. In the meantime, he had emigrated to Australia.

Consequently, Nimmo had not bothered to pursue this lead either. His two reports hardly justified the absolute confidence – "detailed and exhaustive'', "thorough'', "covering all possible lines of inquiry'' – which the Home Secretary placed in them.

Who can tell how many other witnesses there might have been? Paul Foot, for example, learned only in 1970 of the testimony of Robert Fish, who had directed a man looking for lodgings in August 1961. This was the first the Hanratty supporters knew of his existence, as the Rhyl police had never passed on his statement to the defence (and yet he *had* been seen by Nimmo). Might there, perhaps, have been other witnesses who simply did not wish to get involved? Henry Parry, the landlord of the Windsor Hotel directly opposite Mrs Jones's guest-house, said merely that he made a statement to the police at the time, and wished to take the matter no further.

On 16 November 1967, just over two weeks after the disappointment of Jenkins' Commons statement, David Frost's *The Frost Programme* devoted an entire edition to the case. Alphon originally agreed to appear and to stand by his Paris confession. A fee was negotiated, but he pulled out. Frost, at that time near the height of his celebrity, had a reputation as a forceful and tenacious interviewer.

On 15 December Alphon repeated his demand for an inquiry to the new Home Secretary, James Callaghan. He denied that there had ever been any valid retraction of his Paris confession. In September 1968 he wrote again, baldly admitting the crime. Lord Brockway applied once more in parliament for an inquiry on 27 November; once more, he was rebuffed by Lord Stonham. The under-secretary revealed to the Lords that by that stage Home Office material on the case amounted to 198 files.

Every time Alphon was baulked or ignored, he was forced to push the boat out a little further. On 7 March 1969 he named the third man in a letter to Callaghan. This did not stir the authorities. Neither did the continued activities of the A6 committee, which included regular gatherings at Speakers' Corner in Hyde Park (legal) and demonstrations outside the Houses of Parliament (quite definitely illegal). No arrests, however, were made until 28 November.

At about that time the Hanrattys seemed to have been put in touch with a new and important ally – John Lennon, who with his wife Yoko Ono generated more publicity at that time than virtually anyone else in the world.

Lennon and Ono enthusiastically espoused the Hanratty cause. They talked of making a film, among other things, to publicise the injustice. When attending the première of *The Magic Christian*, a film starring Peter Sellers and his Beatle colleague Ringo Starr, Lennon unfurled a banner proclaiming "Britain Murdered Hanratty".

Unfortunately, this intervention was not as auspicious as it must originally have seemed to the Hanrattys. During this period the Lennons tended to become passionately fired – momentarily, at least – with almost any radical cause, and so the A6 murder was absorbed into a ragbag of fashionable socio-political concerns.

Nevertheless, they kept their promise to the Hanratty family by completing a 40-minute colour film about the campaign for an inquiry. This received its first public showing on 17 February 1972 in the crypt of St Martin-in-the-Fields, Trafalgar Square, London.

There had been so much publicity, but so little to show for it. Spirits, however willing, started flagging. In *Who Killed Hanratty?* Paul Foot conceded that "publicity about and public interest in the case were lower in the first nine months of 1970 than at any other time since the murder".[6]

No one, however, could doubt either the resourcefulness or the pertinacity of Mr and Mrs Hanratty. In November 1970 they took out a High Court writ against Lord Butler, the Home Secretary who had sanctioned their son's execution, alleging that he negligently failed to consider the arguments for a reprieve, and claiming damages for "grief and agony". However sincerely felt, this course of action was always likely to prove unavailing. It was inconceivable that the courts would allow a suit of this nature to proceed.

The Hanrattys' case was presented in court by Gershon Ellenbogen. "The Home Secretary had before him material not before members of the jury when they reached their guilty verdict. That material should have been the subject of an inquiry, such as that conducted in *R. v. Rowland* (1947). An inquiry would have cast such doubts on the verdict that a reprieve would have been almost inevitable."[7] This was perhaps a tenable argument, but it must have come as no surprise when Lord Denning, Lord Justice Salmon and Lord Justice Stamp effectively tore up the writ in the Appeal Court. "No action for damages for negligence can lie against the Home Secretary, nor can the courts inquire into, let alone pass an opinion on, the way the Crown prerogative is exercised."[8]

Interest in the case was rekindled in May 1971 in response to the publication of Paul Foot's cogent and compelling book, *Who Killed Hanratty?* It was favourably received, and there was a particularly generous review from Louis Blom-Cooper in the *Observer*. He conceded that the conclusions reached in his own earlier book had been "rash".

There was considerable agitation in parliament. Lord Brockway had renewed his call for an inquiry even prior to the book's appearance in the shops. Over eighty backbench MPs of all parties endorsed a proposal for a fresh initiative. Among them were Joan Lestor, who had been Brockway's successor as member for Eton and Slough, Phillip Whitehead and Patrick Gordon Walker.

The Home Secretary, Reginald Maudling, confirmed that he had been sent a copy of the book. He said that, "In the light of this, and the voluminous reports available to me, I shall consider whether there is any fresh information which would justify action on my part."[9] Former Home Secretary James Callaghan appeared to suggest that his own views on the matter had modified. "If he [Maudling] reaches the conclusion that there should be a fresh public inquiry," he said, "I should not want to dissent from that merely because a different conclusion was reached earlier."[10]

In the wake of the publication of the book, and its serialisation in the *Sun*, more evidence emerged. Mrs Lanz, the proprietress of the Old Station Inn, Taplow, made a statement. She said that Gregsten and Storie often popped in for a drink and "were well known to me and my family". On the evening of 22 August 1961 they dropped in, and left at about 9.00. The man she now knew as Peter Alphon (he was using a pseudonym at the time) was also in the pub. He left by the back exit, with a blonde lady, about half an hour after Gregsten and Storie. In the spring of 1962 Jean Justice and Alphon had visited the pub together, and she had then confirmed to the former that she remembered Alphon from the previous summer.

Her testimony was therefore based not on recollections a decade later, but on what she knew at the time of the trial. "We were the last people to see Michael Gregsten alive," she told the *Sunday Times*, "yet we never gave formal statements to the police or were called at the trial."[11]

A few days prior to Hanratty's execution, she had been so alarmed about the possibility of a miscarriage of justice that she and a member of her family had visited Staines police station to make her statement. (Nor was she the only one thus disturbed; Christopher Larman had rung the *Daily Mirror* to ask how he could use his information to prevent the execution.)

Mrs Lanz's testimony could be compared with the deposition of Michael Fogarty-Waul. The importance of those statements becomes even more pronounced when one considers that neither police nor prosecution nor the Home Office had been able to produce a single witness (Valerie Storie excepted) who had ever seen Hanratty in the vicinity of Dorney Reach.

Maudling gave uncommitted replies to further questions in parliament from Joan Lestor, Phillip Whitehead and others on 24 June and 22 July. The Home Office gave the clamour plenty of time to subside. Its decision against an inquiry was not announced until 28 October. Maudling said he did not believe that "any judicial tribunal can be expected to arrive at a convincing opinion as to the facts on the basis of the recollection of witnesses as to specific details ten years after the event". Nor did he consider the new book – in spite of "very extensive research" – to have been particularly illuminating. "Foot has not had full access to all the available material, and in some respects his arguments are based on premises that are not supported by the facts."[12]

It was over a year before this longest running of all

murder mysteries received another fascinating twist. Lewis Chester disclosed in the *Sunday Times* (16 December 1972) that he had assembled fresh information about the identikit picture of the A6 killer.

In two quite distinctive ways, Hanratty had never fitted the original description of the wanted man. In the first place, Valerie Storie had referred to "light, fairish hair" when she had spoken to John Kerr, the undergraduate whose traffic form had afterwards disappeared, whereas Hanratty had dark hair at that time. Secondly, the original reports referred to "deep-set brown eyes". It wasn't for some days (until 31 August) that Storie first alluded to "icy-blue saucer-like eyes", which Hanratty's were.

The identikit system of tracing wanted men had only been introduced to this country earlier in 1961. Chester took the original identikit which Storie had approved (and which bore a remarkable resemblance to Peter Alphon) to Hugh C. McDonald, a US law enforcement expert who had devised the identikit system and trained British police officers in its use. McDonald confirmed that the method had worked largely because of its flexibility. There were, for example, no fewer than 104 codings for types of eyes. He said that both the identikits which the police had issued in August 1961 (one composed almost entirely with Storie; the other drawn up with the aid of the witnesses who had seen the car driver in the morning) depicted dark eyes – code number E49. Had the police wanted to illustrate large, light eyes then code number E10 would have been selected instead.

Chester further discovered that the "brown eyes" aspect of this description had been radioed back to Bedfordshire police headquarters from the scene of the crime. It remained part of the official description for eight days, until detectives amended it to "blue eyes".

This research triggered a further flurry of activity. In October 1973, a report by McDonald on the identikit evidence was submitted to the Home Office. Campaigners, however, began to feel more optimistic once a new Labour

government had been installed in March 1974. One of the
new cabinet ministers, Shirley Williams, had earlier, as
shadow Home Secretary, publicly told the A6 murder
committee that the case for an inquiry "has now been
made out". Jean Justice seemed buoyant when he told *The
Times*, "We have now got the broad-based support that is
always essential in these cases. It took 15 years and an
all-party delegation before the Timothy Evans case was
rectified. The precedents in that case are encouraging for
us."[13]

In those spring months, the campaign received fresh
ammunition. Valerie Storie's first statement to the police
came to light. (It was unearthed by a diligent local journalist.) There was no mention of the colour of the eyes.
This didn't resolve the blue/brown argument one way
or the other, but it was a significant omission; at the trial,
Graham Swanwick, prosecuting counsel, affirmed that
"the blueness of the eyes left a deep imprint on her
mind".

Far more significantly, however, Storie said at that time,
with events fresh in her mind, "After he shot Mike, he
told me to call him 'Jim', *but I don't think that was his
name*." (Author's italics.) This rider was not mentioned
during any of Storie's court appearances; yet it was exceptionally important. At the trial, the prosecution emphasised the significance of the name. Equally, Acott gave it
as one of the reasons for the elimination of Alphon as a
suspect.

Finally, on 2 August 1974, there was a breakthrough, of
sorts. The Home Office announced that Lewis Hawser
QC had accepted an invitation to make an independent
assessment of what it termed "relevant material".

The hundred-page Hawser report was published on 10
April 1975. It came as a bitter, bitter blow to those who
had campaigned so assiduously for so long on Hanratty's
behalf. "The case against Hanratty remains overwhelm-

ing," concluded Hawser, "and the additional material set into the framework of the case as a whole does not cast any real doubt upon the jury's verdict."

Early the following year, Hawser was involved as defence counsel in a much publicised case: the prosecution of the then Liberal party activist Peter Hain on a trumped-up charge of attempting to rob a Putney branch of Barclays Bank. Hawser defended his client superbly. Hain's admiration for him was unbounded: "Those in court saw one of the country's top barristers in full flow as, bit by bit, he teased out the inconsistencies and downright contradictions in the prosecution case."[14]

How sad that he was unable to tease out any of the inconsistencies and downright contradictions in this prosecution case; how strange that he seemed temporarily bereft of his outstanding forensic abilities. A few examples must necessarily suffice to demonstrate the inadequacy of his report.

Most notable was the treatment of the Liverpool sweetshop incident. "I have investigated this in considerable detail," Hawser wrote, "because it is a matter of crucial importance." So, indeed, it is. The reader will recall that Olive Dinwoodie identified Hanratty as having briefly come into the shop while she was serving there. The difficulty for the prosecution was that the encounter could only have occurred on Monday 21 or Tuesday 22 August. Hawser asserts positively that it took place on the Monday. "He [Hanratty] performed the classical false-alibi trick of relating a true incident but putting it one day later than it actually occurred."

This is preposterous reasoning. The theory raised two quite fundamental problems. According to the Hawser scenario, Hanratty travelled to Liverpool to construct a false alibi; he exchanged a few fleeting words with an elderly lady in a small shop on the Scotland Road, the precise location of which Hanratty could not afterwards recall; he didn't even bother to purchase anything in the shop; he returned straightaway to London; and neither on the outward nor return journey was noticed by anyone else at all.

Nor is that all. At the trial the prosecution had produced seven witnesses to account for Hanratty's movements throughout that day – in London. So was Hawser suggesting that a number of prosecution witnesses had been either lying or mistaken; and, moreover, had all been lying or mistaken in precisely the same respect – namely, having imagined seeing Hanratty in London at a time when he was actually in Liverpool?

In any case, Hawser tried to have it both ways. One of these witnesses was Carol France. Elsewhere in the report Hawser used her testimony to buttress the prosecution case. "Evidence was called by the prosecution that he [Hanratty] was at the Frances' house on Monday 21 August . . . Miss France in particular was able to speak of the date with a special degree of certainty as she had a tooth out." There was, indeed, documented proof of this visit to the dentist's.

So, between 4.00 and 5.00 p.m. on Monday 21 August 1962, Hawser had managed to place Hanratty simultaneously in London and Liverpool. Far from teasing out contradictions in the prosecution case, Hawser was supplementing them with a few of his own invention.

Accordingly, it is not clear whether Hawser accepts or rejects Carol France's evidence. Elsewhere, certainly, he is only too ready to rely on it. In respect of Hanratty's driving ability, for example, he accepted without demur her evidence ("he drove zig-zagging from side to side up the road"), while rejecting the deposition of Hanratty's cousin, Eileen Cunningham ("he was a very good driver").

Hawser found Christopher Larman's evidence unacceptable partly because the latter was apparently strengthened in his belief that he had seen Hanratty in Rhyl after seeing his picture in the papers. When considering the identification evidence of *prosecution* witnesses, however, Hawser fully understood such reactions: "people's ability to describe a person they have seen is often a good deal less than their ability to recognise the face when they see it again."

One of the reasons advanced for dismissing Alphon's confessions was that he, Alphon, said he had a drink before waylaying Gregsten and Valerie Storie. She, though, had given no evidence to indicate that the murderer had been drinking. Hawser completely ignored the fact that Gregsten and Storie had themselves been in a pub for some time. Those who have not been in contact with alcohol can readily detect it on the breath of others; those who have are less likely to do so.

As for the experiences of Meika Dalal and Audrey Willis, Hawser commented "these incidents suggest that one or it may be two other persons were claiming to be the A6 murderer". The vision of a pack of pseudo-A6 killers wandering round the country petrifying housewives is farcical.

The saddest thing of all was the readiness with which the Hawser report was accepted by the Home Secretary, by parliament and by the press. Only *Private Eye* repudiated it as comprehensively as it deserved (under the fitting headline, "Hung, Drawn and Hawsered").[15]

From the time of the hunt for the A6 murderer in September 1961, and for the rest of the decade, Alphon expended much emotional energy in fanning the flames of the unofficial inquiries into the crime. If he wasn't guilty, then the explanations usually offered for his behaviour are that he did it for publicity and money; that, having been interviewed about it shortly afterwards, he became obsessed with the crime; or that he was a crank.

Even if he were a crank, it would not automatically exclude the possibility of his having been the murderer. But in any case, mental instability is too facile an explanation. There was clearly method in Alphon's madness. Whenever he indicated that he was the culprit, he left himself an

escape-route just in case the authorities should take him
seriously. For the drawing that first alerted Jean Justice,
he referred to himself as Peter McDougal; in the confession
notes that he compiled, he made a mistake about
the greyhound called Mentals Only Hope; in the ITN interview after his Paris confession he made two significant
errors in his description of the crime (errors which would
have been obvious to anyone who had followed the case
closely).

Evidence concerning his finances tends to refute the
obsession theory. In August 1969 he asked his bank to
send Paul Foot details of his account for 1961 and 1962.
These revealed that during the six months after the murder
his account was swollen by roughly £7,500. Approximately
£2,500 of this was known to have been the accumulated
payments made to him by several newspapers. That left
£5,000 – which coincidentally is the size of the purse he
said he'd been promised for carrying out the crime. He
didn't tell anyone he had been paid £5,000 until 1967, and
he didn't sanction the release of his bank statements until
1969 – which is significant because banks retain individual
details of all account transactions for six years, after which
they are destroyed. This, then, was a further instance of
Alphon claiming culpability for the crime, while safeguarding himself against prosecution for it.

Assuming, still, that Alphon was merely obsessed with
a crime he did not commit, that obsession can be dated
back at least to 7 September 1961, when he attempted to
assault Mrs Dalal. (She readily identified Alphon; the
incident took place in broad daylight and lasted a few
minutes.) So, those who canvass the 'obsession' theory
must explain how, in the coming months, he was suddenly
able to acquire such a large sum for the purpose of giving
credibility to his bogus confession; and why, having satisfactorily achieved this, he was so judiciously patient in
releasing the information.

The theory that he behaved as he did simply for money or
publicity is easily repudiated. Prior to his Paris confession,

Alphon ignored numerous opportunities to sue for libel; and if he was merely a ghoulish publicity-seeker, why did he back off *The Frost Programme* which, because of its fashionableness, would have provided him with more and better publicity than anything else?

Something else is strange. Why did the authorities time and again treat him with such leniency? Successive opportunities to administer condign punishment were spurned. It seems as though they were desperate to avoid committing him to prison, the one place where he would presumably have found a deeply sympathetic audience for his exposure of "British justice as a sham".

Perhaps, then, Alphon was the murderer. His confessions, whether made calmly or hysterically, sometimes contained nebulous hints either that he was concerned to right the terrible wrong done to Hanratty; or, alternatively, that, having perpetrated such infamous villainy, he felt cheated of his enduring notoriety, his place in the chamber of horrors.

The question of Alphon's guilt is debatable; the question of Hanratty's innocence is not. In August 1966 Lord Stonham told parliament that "if, on studying this again, there was solid reason for thinking that there has been a miscarriage of justice, no effort must be spared to get at the truth". What the whole episode demonstrated was the reverse: that where a miscarriage of justice has occurred, no effort must be spared by the legal and political authorities to prevent the truth from being publicly revealed. For Home Office ministers to say, as Reginald Maudling did in October 1972, that Paul Foot had not had access "to all the available material" just about takes the biscuit, bearing in mind the iron determination with which they have withheld it from him (and from anyone else eager "to get at the truth").

If the papers are released, as the Home Office magnanimously promises, in 2061, a hundred years after the event, at least posterity will have the satisfaction of knowing what actually happened. In the meantime the crime remains the most tantalising of modern real-life murder cases; a case which began when a man died violently on Deadman's Hill and which was given its unique character when the search for justice was taken up by a man called Justice.

Five

The Angus Sibbet Murder

People in the case

Angus Sibbet — murder victim

Michael Luvaglio }
Dennis Stafford } — charged with murder

Lord Justice O'Connor — trial judge

Rudolph Lyons QC — defence counsel (Stafford)

Raymond Dean QC — defence counsel (Luvaglio)

Henry Scott QC — prosecution counsel

Vince Landa — club-owner; Luvaglio's brother

Dr John Hunter — local GP

Dr Jack Ennis — police pathologist

Tom Leak — coal miner who discovered the body

Selena Jones — cabaret singer; girlfriend of Stafford

Pat Smithson — former wife of Stafford

Matthew Dean — doorman at Bird Cage Club

Dorothy Brady — visitor to Bird Cage; defence witness

Robert Anderson — near neighbour of Luvaglio; defence witness

Francis Camps — Home Office pathologist

Geoffrey Rhodes — MP for Newcastle East

Sir David Napley — solicitor for Luvaglio

Joseph Stafford — father of Dennis Stafford

David Lewis }
Peter Hughman } — authors of *Most Unnatural*

Leslie Parker — coal miner; defence witness

Alan Wood — coal miner; defence witness

James Golden — colliery blacksmith; witness

Arthur Bowman — consultant engineer

Patricia Walpole — defence witness

Nora Burnip — farmer's wife; witness

Doreen Hall }
Joyce Hall } — girlfriends of Sibbet

PC John Ainsworth — police constable; witness

AT 5.15 A.M. on a cold morning in January 1967, Durham coal miner Tom Leak was cycling home from his night's shift at the local pit. In South Hetton, just past Pesspool Bridge, he noticed a Mark X Jaguar saloon car, poorly parked, about fourteen inches from the kerb, and also damaged. Snow covered the back window, bonnet and much of the top. He cupped his hands and peered into the car through the near-side passenger window. A man was lying across the back seat.

Leak opened the door, said loudly, "Hey, mate, you can't park there," and shook his left leg. As he did so, Leak realised that the man was dead. He hailed three passing colleagues, also going home, and they called the police. A local GP, Dr John Hunter, was then summoned, though the police advised him not to touch the body. It was clear that the man, who had been shot three times, was a murder victim.

Seventeen hours later, Michael Luvaglio and Dennis Stafford were taken in for questioning.

Luvaglio, a devout Roman Catholic, was born into an Anglo–Italian family just before the outbreak of the Second World War. He was the second son; his brother, Vince, was four years older. Vince changed his surname to Landa and made a fortune in the north-east, largely through profiting on one-armed-bandit machines. Through his company, Social Club Services Ltd, he also owned a number of night clubs. He lived in some style, on an estate just outside Bishop Auckland, and had persuaded his parents and his brother to join him in the north-east. By then, in the mid-sixties, Michael had done National Service in the RAF and subsequently worked as a printer.

Dennis Stafford had a rather more chequered history. Born in 1934, the son of a well-to-do London bookmaker, he left school at 16 and started his own fruit-machine company. He quickly made his mark on the club scene, but was arrested after becoming involved in a burglary. The car he was driving at that point was found not only to be stolen but also to contain a Luger pistol, and he received a harsh seven-year sentence. He was then only 22. (He always maintained that the Luger, a relic of National Service days, which he said he kept at home, had been planted in the car.)

However, he went over the wall of Wormwood Scrubs on 8 November 1956, and escaped to Newcastle, where he passed himself off as the managing director of a buying agency. He began to prosper, and in February 1957 moved to Trinidad. After 136 days of freedom, he was arrested there. He fought the extradition order, unsuccessfully, and arrived back in England in a blaze of publicity on 10 June 1957.

He had to answer further charges in Newcastle – of conspiracy to defraud and obtaining goods by false pretences – and was jailed for an additional 18 months. He was sent to Dartmoor. After 6 months, he escaped from there also, in company with another prisoner who was later found drowned in a reservoir. There was evidence that Stafford had tried hard to resuscitate him.

Six weeks later, he was recaptured in Leicester Square, London. This time he served out his sentence, although he was allowed out in October 1962 to marry a Gateshead girl, Pat Smithson. In March 1964 he was freed, but later that year he received fresh sentences for stealing a car and possessing a pistol within five years of release from prison.

When he came out he returned to Newcastle with Selena Jones, a leading cabaret singer. Landa appointed him manager of his newly opened Piccadilly Club, which was soon gutted by arson in what was assumed to be an act of gang warfare. Landa then gave him alternative employment, booking acts into his clubs.

Another of Landa's employees was Angus Sibbet. A well known personality on the north-east club circuit, he

counted Tom Jones and Englebert Humperdinck among
his friends. He had once served in the army in Korea but,
like Stafford, had a prison record, having been sentenced
to twelve months for receiving. He was employed collect-
ing the takings from Landa's fruitmachines – a job which
seemed to support a comfortable lifestyle and which was, as
Sir David Napley has noted, "pregnant with possibilities".[1]
Just so; it was Sibbet's body which Leak discovered in the
back of the Mark X on that morning in January 1967.

On the third day of the new year Luvaglio and Stafford
returned together from Majorca, where they had spent a
holiday with their girlfriends, Luvaglio's parents, and his
brother Landa at Landa's villa. Michael Luvaglio immediately made arrangements to see Sibbet, a close colleague,
over a business matter. They talked the next afternoon,
though without finalising their plans. A further meeting
was therefore arranged for 12.30 a.m., on what would by
then be 5 January, at the Bird Cage Club.

Luvaglio's own car was undergoing repair, but he was
able to borrow his brother's E-type Jaguar, for which
Stafford fortuitously possessed a spare key. The E-type,
too, was at that time in the garage, having been serviced.
Landa wouldn't be needing it himself as he had returned
to Britain with the others only for discussions with his
accountant in London and was due to fly back straightaway
to Majorca.

At 11.30 that evening, Luvaglio and Stafford left
Stafford's home in Peterlee and drove to Luvaglio's house
in Chelsea Grove, Newcastle to collect an international
telephone call from Landa at midnight. Had Landa placed
that call, his brother would not have spent eleven unhappy
years in prison. Since he didn't, Luvaglio and Stafford
merely drove on to the club for the appointment with
Sibbet.

It wasn't their night, for Sibbet didn't show up either.
Luvaglio tried to reach him by telephone, though without
success.

At 2.00 a.m. Stafford went to get some duty-free

cigarettes from the car, and noticed that it had been
damaged by a car running into the back of it. He
mentioned this to Matthew Dean, the doorman, who
recollected hearing a noise some twenty minutes earlier.
The two discovered tyre tracks in the snow in the road,
from which it appeared that a vehicle had collided with
the Jaguar outside the club, and then reversed out into
the middle of the road. Thus: Dean had heard the noise;
he had seen the damage to the car within seconds of
Stafford; and he had noticed the tyre marks. This was
important independent evidence.

Subsequently, at about 2.15 Luvaglio and Stafford gave
up and went home – first to Luvaglio's place in Chelsea
Grove to check if Landa had called (he hadn't); and then
back to Peterlee, where Luvaglio spent the rest of the
night.

In the light of morning, Stafford thought the damage to
the car not too severe, but he knew that Landa would be
upset, so he put it back into the garage in Sunderland from
which he had collected it only the previous day. He also
took some clothes in for cleaning: suits, shirts and his
laundry from the Majorca trip.

During the day, at Landa's company offices, they
learned from newspaper reporters – trying to contact
Landa – of the murder of Sibbet. They went to the flat of
the garage proprietor to watch the early-evening news on
television. Afterwards, Luvaglio felt ill, and at 7 o'clock
he went to bed.

Meanwhile the police had received a phone call which
enabled them to focus their inquiries. The caller, who
declined to give his name, told them that they would be
well advised to inspect a damaged, red E-type in a
Sunderland garage. The police took the hint, and discovered that damage on the E-type corresponded to some
of the damage on Sibbet's car.

It is sound professional practice for the police sometimes
to rely on what is nebulously described as "information
received"; but in this instance they seem never to have

suspected that the information might not have been wholly disinterested.

Luvaglio and Stafford were taken in for questioning at 10.20 that evening, the former being roused from bed. Both wore the same suits they had worn throughout the previous day. They were subsequently charged with murder.

The case came to trial unusually speedily and opened at Newcastle assizes on 7 March 1967 before Lord Justice O'Connor. The prosecution case was thought to be weak, and Luvaglio and Stafford were assumed to have an unbreakable alibi.

The Bird Cage Club is 16½ miles from South Hetton, and a police car had covered the distance in 46½ minutes. Although it was suggested that an E-type could have done it faster, the pathologist estimated the time of death at between midnight and 4.00 a.m., and gave evidence to this effect at the committal proceedings. Since Luvaglio and Stafford had arrived at the Bird Cage within a few minutes of 12.30, this meant that they had an alibi for the period during which the murder was committed.

The only way the prosecution could make headway, therefore, was by somehow introducing even more elasticity into the already imprecise medical evidence tendered regarding time of death. This, with the assistance of the judge, it managed to do. In an extraordinary part of the trial, the police pathologist, Dr Jack Ennis, at first reiterated his original time-of-death estimate of midnight –4.00 a.m., and then went on to state, "If you wish to pin me down to a time, I would say round about twelve o'clock." During the course of his testimony, he effectively contradicted himself; if midnight was the mean time, why was his estimate not 10.00 p.m.–2.00 a.m.? In conclusion, and at the judge's suggestion, he did change his estimate to 11.00 p.m.–2.00 a.m. (The judge actually noted down 11–3, and later had to be corrected.) Dr Ennis explained to Rudolph Lyons QC, Stafford's counsel, that he had changed his estimate for two reasons: "one was the remarkable rate of cooling which had taken place in this particular body and secondly I was not aware at the time I completed my report that in fact *rigor mortis* was confirmed at 6 o'clock in the morning [i.e. by Dr Hunter]."

By the 'remarkable rate of cooling' he meant that the body had cooled less quickly than one would expect, given the weather conditions. (There were still 6 °F of frost at 8 o'clock in the morning.) This was because it was "in a car which must have been warm for the first part of the cooling period". He imagined that the interior was warm for "two to four hours" after the car stopped. How did he explain that? "The heater was still functioning . . . that is yet another of the peculiar air conditions in the car." How long had the heater been blowing hot air through the car after the engine cut out? "At least half an hour."

Even Jaguar cars are not capable of that. A company expert reckoned the period would be "a minute".[2]

So Ennis was completely wrong about the heater. In his assessment of the 'peculiar air conditions' in the car, he was also wrong about the windows. He did not realise, until it was pointed out to him in cross-examination, that both off-side windows were open to the elements (one shattered by a bullet, the other wound right down). These were two serious errors. As a pathologist, he was professionally negligent in three other respects. Although he arrived at the murder scene at 8.05 a.m., he did not take a body temperature until he began his postmortem examination at 1.15 p.m.; and he *estimated* Sibbet's weight, instead of taking it accurately (body weight being another important factor in cooling).

Basing his calculations on this series of misconceptions and inadequate information, Ennis estimated a rate of cooling of 2.6 °F per hour, which gave a time of death of about midnight. Even on a figure of 3.0 °F, death would have occurred at 2.00 a.m., and Luvaglio and Stafford would have been in the clear. At that time, the rate of cooling of bodies per hour in snow was calculated by the leading pathologist, Dr Keith Simpson, at 3.6 °F.

Ennis' fifth blunder was not to ascertain the precise nature of the tests which 'confirmed' *rigor mortis*. Had he done his homework on this point, he would have learned that, according to Dr Hunter's evidence to the magistrates court in Peterlee, no test for *rigor mortis* was made. At the trial, Hunter changed his evidence. He said that he took hold of the left leg and "raised it to ascertain the presence of *rigor mortis*". Hunter, though, was a GP, not a pathologist. He was specifically asked not to interfere with the body, so it is regrettable that he felt obliged to exaggerate the thoroughness of his inspection.

It is more than likely that *rigor mortis* had not set in when Hunter looked at the body. Tom Leak said that the left leg was stretched along the back of the seat and that he moved it. By the time the police photographer arrived on the scene, the left leg was bent. As David Lewis and Peter Hughman wrote:

> Whether Leak or somebody else bent it is beside the point. What matters is that if *rigor mortis* had been present in the leg at 5.15 and if, some time before Dr Hunter's examination, the limb was bent, *rigor mortis* would have been destroyed and could not have been felt in the left leg, *the only limb* used by Dr Hunter to test for it.[3]

Professor Francis Camps, the distinguished pathologist, later confirmed, "There must be some error here."

So this aspect of the prosecution case – the time of death – was based on wholly erroneous medical and scientific assumptions. Its other main stanchion was the apparent collision between Sibbet's Mark X and the E-type which Luvaglio and Stafford had borrowed. Six-tenths of a mile along the A182 from where the Mark X was discovered police found fragments of glass, metal and plastic in the road. The glass had come from the Mark X offside window and the plastic perspex from the E-type. At this scene there were also five spent cartridges; three of the bullets had been fired into Sibbet, and the other two, one of which had shattered a rear window, into the car. Further debris – glass and plastic – was found a little way up a small lane leading off the main road.

Subsequent forensic tests showed that specks of green paint on the red E-type had come from the green Mark X; and that particles of red paint on the Mark X had come from the E-type. Luvaglio and Stafford were able to offer no explanation of this, the piece of circumstantial evidence which ultimately damned their case.

With this ammunition, metaphorically speaking, the prosecution put forward its interpretation of events: the two cars were driven in convoy south along the A182 and collided; either Luvaglio or Stafford got out and fired five shots at Sibbet, killing him; one of them then drove Sibbet's car, with his body in it, and the E-type behind, or in front; they turned down Pesspool Lane to clean out the murder car and dispose of incriminating evidence and then returned to the main road. The Mark X, due to overheating caused by radiator damage in the collision, stalled at the bridge in South Hetton; Luvaglio or Stafford, whoever it was, then abandoned the car and got back into the E-type; they drove together to the Bird Cage Club.

Three factors, which had nothing to do with the evidence itself, handicapped the chances of the successful presentation of the defence case. The first was the fact that the trial was held in Newcastle, where feelings were running high about what many felt to be the city's rising tide of gangsterism. "There was much press comment both before and after the murder about the corruption of club officials by people hiring out fruit-machines. Social clubs had been burnt down and there was talk of gangland warfare . . . public comment before the trial showed all the traces of a typically Northern puritanical backlash," wrote Geoffrey Rhodes MP in the *New Statesman*.[4]

Then, there was Stafford's public profile as a notorious criminal, of which the jury would inevitably have been aware. His exploits had been extravagantly publicised, and in 1965 Pat Smithson had sold the story of their high-life together to *Tit-Bits* (in those days a magazine with a healthy circulation and a scandal-sheet reputation).

Thirdly, the judge, realising that his own peroration fell plumb on 15 March 1967 – the Ides of March – found gratuitous historical allusions irresistible. In a summing-up which affronted traditional concepts of British justice, he referred to the betrayal of Julius Caesar by Brutus – "*Et tu, Brute?*" – and of Christ by Judas Iscariot, mentioning these as parallels of the violently sundered friendship between Sibbet and Luvaglio.

Luvaglio and Stafford were found guilty, and sentenced to life imprisonment, the death penalty having been abolished in November 1965.

Had the jury been more accurately directed, they would surely have been acquitted straightaway. The most obvious gap in the prosecution case was the absence of motive. Why would Luvaglio have wanted to kill his friend and colleague? Henry Scott QC, prosecuting, admitted that he could offer no reason, but added that "whoever killed Sibbet had a very real and sinister motive for doing so".

Rudolph Lyons QC pointed out other omissions in the case against the defendants: there was no suggestion that either of them had a gun; or that either behaved in anything other than a normal manner in the hours after the murder; and there was no forensic evidence at all.

The clothes which Stafford took in for cleaning on the morning of 5 January were recovered by police. Among them were three suits. In one of the jacket pockets of one of these, forensic experts discovered traces of red paint and plastic. Stafford explained in court that he took his laundry to the car in the morning, put it in the boot, then inspected the previous night's damage to the car, and tried to straighten the number-plate. After that, he went through the pockets of the suits he was taking to the laundry to make sure they were empty. The forensic scientist giving evidence for the Crown agreed that this was an entirely acceptable explanation of the presence of the paint particles.

Like the dog that didn't bark in the night, this fact should have been of fundamental significance in the analysis of the crime. Had Stafford been guilty, then surely his motive in taking clothing to the cleaners immediately afterwards was to destroy forensic evidence linking him to the crime. If so, he was thwarted because police recovered the clothes in time. There was nothing, however, to link him to the crime. Altogether, police took for examination 62 items of Stafford's clothing and 11 of Luvaglio's; nothing at all was found. Further, it was unchallenged in court that, when taken in for questioning, both men were wearing the suits they had worn the previous evening.

There was simply no evidence to link Luvaglio and Stafford with either Sibbet, or the Mark X, or the scene of the crime. There was no mud or grass on them, though a great deal on Sibbet. Nor was there anything to link Sibbet with their E-type (there was not even recent grass debris on the car wheels). The conditions were ideal for the gathering of weighty forensic evidence. The absence of any at all was so telling it should not merely have acquitted Luvaglio and Stafford; it should have ensured that all charges against them were dropped at the outset.

In the circumstances, it is not surprising that the rest of the prosecution scenario was riddled with illogicalities. Robert Anderson, a company director who garaged his car near Chelsea Grove, testified that he noticed the E-type outside the house at midnight, a time of which he could be certain since it was ten minutes after television close-down. Angus Sibbet did not leave another club, La Dolce Vita, until about 11.20, so that even on the basis of the Crown evidence he could hardly have arrived in South Hetton before midnight.

Luvaglio and Stafford, according to the prosecution theory, committed the murder and then raced at breakneck speed to arrive at the Bird Cage Club in time for their prearranged 12.30 appointment, and thereby establish an alibi. A number of people were up and about on that cold January morning. No one saw an E-type being driven at 70 mph or over – a speed which, given the snow-covered roads, would have been practically suicidal.

Both cars were damaged visibly and, in the case of the saloon, audibly as well. According to the Jaguar company expert, it would have developed a knocking noise after the collision. It would also have a body in it. Why would the defendants have turned off a small dark lane on to a well-lit main road to drive through a village which, because so many of its inhabitants were employed at the local coal mine, generated an unusual level of night-time activity? Why, in any case, the desperate rush to establish an alibi when, for all they knew, the body might be discovered straightaway? Had Luvaglio and Stafford committed the murder, and accordingly realised the significance of the damage to the car, is it likely that they would have drawn the attention of the garage proprietor to the crime by watching news of it on his TV set?

Luvaglio and Stafford were never able to explain how the two cars could have tangled. One theory is that the E-type could have been taken while they were both inside the Bird Cage. Was there any evidence for this?

There was. It was provided by Mrs Dorothy Brady, who explained that she had been called because her daughter worked in a solicitor's office and had been able to inform the defence of her evidence. That night, Mrs Brady, with a friend, had visited the club at 12.35 and noticed the red E-type outside. When she left at 1.15, it was no longer there. Most people probably notice an ostentatious car like a red E-type anyway. It was especially likely that Mrs Brady would have done so, since she worked at the garage where the car was frequently cleaned. She had even re-marked as she left, "Mr Landa's car is not there now." The prosecution was unable to persuade her that she had got her dates confused; she was adamant that she could

remember the night exactly because of its proximity to the
New Year celebrations.

Taken together, the evidence of Mrs Brady and of
Matthew Dean, the club doorman, should have exonerated
Luvaglio and Stafford. It is astonishing that the judge
placed such little weight on their combined testimony.

Luvaglio and Stafford's application for leave to appeal
against conviction was dismissed on 26 July 1968. They
were also refused leave to call further evidence. Lord
Justice Edmund Davies, who heard the appeal application
together with Lord Justice Fenton Atkinson and Mr Justice
Waller, did criticise aspects of the judge's summing-up –
rebuking him, for example, for his emotive references to
Christ and Julius Caesar; and averring that overall it "could
have been expressed in more balanced terms". However,
he found the circumstantial evidence relating to the collision between the two cars adequate to sustain the prosecution case.

Prior to the appeal, Luvaglio had turned for assistance
to David Napley, plain 'Mr' in those days, yet already
established as one of the country's pre-eminent solicitors.
With characteristic assiduity, he set to work on behalf of
his client. Over months and years, a mass of fresh evidence
was brought to light, all of it extremely persuasive of the
innocence of the two convicted men.

In October 1969, Joseph Stafford delivered a petition
on behalf of his son to 10 Downing Street. *The Times*
noted the solicitous attitude of the prison authorities at
Parkhurst, where the Staffords were given the use of an
interview room to draw up the petition and a 50-page
dossier of fresh evidence.[5] However, Prime Minister
Harold Wilson was unable to be of assistance.

In 1971, the public pressure was stepped up. Napley
argued in the *Law Society Gazette* in June that he was
certain of Luvaglio's innocence and that there was a need
both for a public inquiry by the Home Office, and for a

parliamentary debate, to secure the reform of judicial
review procedures. "Michael Luvaglio, however, must not
be left behind prison bars while the slow processes of
reform fashion a means to justice," he concluded.

At the end of the month, Home Secretary Reginald
Maudling met an all-party group of peers and MPs who
were disturbed about the case. The deputation was led by
Geoffrey Rhodes who, as Labour MP for Newcastle East,
represented Luvaglio. Writing in the *New Statesman*,
Rhodes argued the need for inquiries into both the police
investigation of this case and the methods of operation of
the Court of Appeal. David Lewis and Peter Hughman
collaborated on the illuminating book, *Most Unnatural:
An Inquiry into the Stafford Case*, which was published as
a Penguin Special and serialised in the London *Evening
News*. Just prior to his death in 1970, Bertrand Russell
described the imprisonment of Luvaglio and Stafford as
"intolerable". Thirty-six criminologists, meeting in conference at York University, signed a petition to the Home
Secretary.

The case became a *cause célèbre*, especially in the north-
east. Geoffrey Rhodes disclosed that he had received
anonymous correspondence advising him to pursue his
interest in the case no further. A letter, postmarked Leeds,
said, "Do not interfere with this matter of the Luvaglio–
Stafford conviction. There are very big fish involved. It is
nothing to do with an MP."

Rhodes said he had only decided to make this public
after learning that similar threats had been made to BBC
personnel investigating the case for the late-evening programme, *24 Hours*. It was alleged that members of the
team had been tailed; that one had been told by telephone
to "lay off"; and that hotel rooms had been ransacked.[6]

On 23 August 1971 Napley sent the Home Secretary a
detailed memorandum. Maudling, who had personally
given much support to the Luvaglio and Stafford campaign

when a shadow minister, now adhered dutifully to the Home Office practice of never providing a reply the next day or week if it is possible to provide one the next year.

After he had been prodded yet again, via a letter in *The Times* signed by a number of distinguished figures (Lords Chorley, Donaldson, Foot, Norwich and Willis; Baroness Wootton and Dame Irene Ward; Tom Sargant, of Justice; the Bishop of Wakefield; Richard Crossman and C. H. Rolph, editor and deputy editor respectively of the *New Statesman*), Maudling finally acceded to the growing public clamour.[7] Not, however, by ordering a public inquiry. On 11 February 1972, the Home Office announced that it had been decided to refer the case back to the Court of Appeal.

Luvaglio and Stafford were thus obliged to resubmit their petition to the same legal process which had already failed them, but with one significant difference. Whereas the Appeal Court had previously declined to hear fresh evidence, this time it was virtually instructed to do so.

However, on 12 May 1972 Mr Justice James ruled that the new evidence should be heard, prior to the appeal itself, before an appeal judge sitting as an examiner. There was provision for this procedure in the 1968 Criminal Appeal Act, but to call it unusual fails to drive home the point: the last time it had been used was in 1924 (under a previous appeal act). Moreover, the examiner, Mr Justice Croom-Johnson, decided that it should be a closed hearing. Accordingly, even before this stage of the appeal process could begin (and by this time nine months had passed since the Home Office had referred the case back), counsel for the appellants had to go to appeal to plead that all this new evidence should be heard in open court.

This was one argument which Lewis Hawser QC for Stafford, and John Mathew QC for Luvaglio, did win. Lord Widgery, the Lord Chief Justice, sitting with Mr Justice Melford Stevenson and Mr Justice Brabin, ruled that "the principle to be applied is that the examination should take place in open court unless the examiner thinks that the ends of justice will not be served by sitting in open court". The critical test, let it be noted, was which method best served "the ends of justice".

So, Croom-Johnson was overruled. The new evidence from sixty-three witnesses was heard from 14 to 30 November 1972, and it was heard in public.

The most important body of evidence came from thirty-three witnesses, nearly all of them miners, who said they had noticed the Mark X Jaguar parked in South Hetton in the early hours of the morning. Yet, prior to Tom Leak, no one had either spotted any damage to the car, or seen a body in it.

The damage, though not extensive, was certainly apparent: the radiator grille was badly punctured, the offside head-lamp smashed, the bonnet cover pushed in and the rear offside window broken. Leslie Parker, a miner, said it was an event to see a Mark X Jaguar in the village. He noticed it parked near the railway bridge while cycling to work, but it was undamaged and unoccupied. Another miner, Alan Wood, said that he looked into the car from several positions while on his way home from work. There was no one in it. The windows were not broken or wound down, and the bonnet was warm. Similarly, a long-distance lorry driver and a colliery deputy both said there was no damage to the car when they saw it parked at 2.30 a.m.

Of these thirty-three witnesses, all of whom were available for cross-examination by Crown counsel, fourteen said there was no damage, although they might not have noticed if there had been; ten claimed they thought they would have noticed damage, but were uncertain whether there had been any; nine, however, said they were positive that they would have noticed damage, and that they did not notice any. Moreover, four of these nine said they had inspected the car with care. Some had been car enthusiasts. Alan Wood had memorised all but one figure of the vehicle's number from the registration plate which was immediately below the supposedly damaged radiator grille.

The two most individually important witnesses were James Golden, a colliery blacksmith, and Nora Burnip, a farmer's wife, both of whom appeared for the prosecution at the original trial. Golden was cycling home from work when he was passed by two Jaguar cars (one, an E-type, the other a saloon). However, he could say no more than that. He neither saw nor heard anything unusual; nor did he overtake a stationary car. The Crown attempted to explain this gap in the evidence of one of its main witnesses by alleging that Golden would not have been able to see the Jaguars turning off the main road into Pesspool Lane. Chief Superintendent Kell, in charge of the murder inquiry, gave evidence on this point. However, the defence brought forward Norman Bennett, a respected local surveyor, who confirmed that Golden would undoubtedly have been able to see the cars turn off the road.

Investigations subsequent to the trial confirmed both that police evidence on this matter was totally inaccurate; and – the central point – that the defence was able to establish, mathematically, that Golden must have been cycling past the scene at almost the instant when, according to the prosecution, Luvaglio and Stafford murdered Sibbet; yet he saw and heard nothing. (Nor did the driver and conductor of a late-night bus perceive anything strange on their journey.)

At about midnight, Nora Burnip's husband switched off the bedside light and glanced at the alarm clock. Twenty minutes later, still awake, she heard two sharp cracks outside the house. They were so startling that she got up to look out of the window. She could see nothing, but a haystack obscured her view of the main road. The next day, after hearing of the murder, she volunteered a statement to police, who accordingly conducted an inch-by-inch search of the road outside the farm. There they discovered the pieces of plastic and glass debris from which they ascertained that the two cars had collided. They determined that the accident and Sibbet's murder took place on the stretch of road hidden from Mrs Burnip's view by the haystack.

Once they leapt to that conclusion, what Nora Burnip

didn't hear became more important than what she did. The prosecution alleged that the murder was committed at 11.50. At that time, she and her husband were still awake. Neither heard anything – no shots, no car accident.

Of the additional witnesses, one man, driving past the stationary Mark X at about 12.45 a.m., said that he was waved on to overtake the car – i.e. that at that time someone was sitting in the driver's seat. Patricia Walpole corroborated the earlier testimony of Robert Anderson, saying that she and her mother saw Luvaglio's E-type parked in Chelsea Grove after midnight.

A ballistics expert affirmed that the only realistic explanation for the position of the cartridges in the road was that they were deliberately placed there. Arthur Bowman, a consultant engineer, observed that some of the damage to the E-type was malicious and not impact damage.

The pathologist, Dr Ennis, stated that he varied his original estimate of time of death after being informed that *rigor mortis* was confirmed at 6 a.m. On the other hand, Dr Hunter, the man who supposedly 'confirmed' it, was recalled, and had to agree that no question of *rigor mortis* arose when he looked at the body. Professor Francis Camps, offering retrospective pathological advice as best he could in the circumstances, concluded from the available evidence that the mean figure for time of death was 1.30 a.m.

The appellants' counsel complained that the police had been selective in passing on information. The prosecution dropped some witnesses because their evidence did not tally with its case, and their statements were never served on the defence. Prime amongst them was Tom Leak, the man who had discovered the body, though the defence had managed to find out about him in time for the original trial. More witnesses of whose statements the defence had not previously been aware were traced by Napley; others only came to light from 1972 when the Newcastle police finally did begin to surrender to the defence statements they had taken during their 1967 inquiries.

The appeal proper should have been heard on 15 January 1973. It wasn't, because two of the three judges due to hear it were ill. Lord Widgery, the Lord Chief Justice, recovered to be able to take his place alongside Lord Justice James the following day; but Mr Justice Croom-Johnson remained indisposed and Mr Justice Eveleigh was drafted in instead. The one judge who had heard all the fresh evidence did not hear the appeal. The three who did were provided with transcripts of the testimony of the sixty-three witnesses.

On 23 January Lord Widgery dismissed the appeals. The Lord Chief Justice argued that the fresh evidence had not disturbed the prosecution case. He agreed that there were "improbable features" and "unanswered questions" on both sides, but averred that "the verdicts are not held to be unsafe or unsatisfactory merely because certain elements of the prosecution case have not been fully established".

That James Golden must have been cycling past at the moment when the murder must have been committed; that the weight of medical evidence now suggested that Sibbet was killed after, not before, midnight; that a witness like Alan Wood, who was not only observant but interested in cars, should have noticed no damage to the Mark X Jaguar: all these points, Widgery conceded, did enhance the case for the defence. He reasoned, however, that it was fundamental to any consideration of the crime that there was a collision between the cars. Accordingly, he concluded, "the inference of guilt is irresistible".

The nub of the prosecution case was that Sibbet was murdered at almost precisely 11.50 p.m. His car, with his body in it, was abandoned by Pesspool Bridge, having by then been in collision with Luvaglio's E-type. That was the argument which the jury accepted. Two factors crucial to it are: the time of death; and the state of the car in those hours before Tom Leak arrived. Any evidence which cast serious doubt on the reliability of either automatically undermined the entire prosecution case.

The defence sent such prosecution props flying like skittles. They were replaced by judicial sophistry, always more than a match for logical argument in the Court of Appeal.

"Great effort has been put into challenging the pathological evidence," Widgery noted, "but the circumstances of the case were never such as to enable pathologists to give a time of death which could have a conclusive bearing on the case." If the judge at the assizes had said that, the case against the two men – depending, as it did, on a more-or-less exact time of death – must surely have collapsed.

Thirty-three witnesses had noticed no body in the car. "The Court had not been surprised," said Widgery. "The body was pushed well down, and no one was looking for a body. They were looking for a sick or perhaps drunken man sitting in the car." In the absence of testimony to support his judgment, Widgery was using his imagination to construct some.

Neither had the thirty-three noticed any damage to the car. "It is odd to say the least of it that all these men, some of whom were interested in motor cars and paying close attention to this car, should have walked past it and not seen the damage. But we do not find it an impossible proposition to put forward." At a stroke, the evidence of thirty-three witnesses was dismissed.

It is worth studying this aspect of the case from the opposite point of view. The prosecution case was predicated on the basis that a damaged Mark X Jaguar was parked by a railway bridge in South Hetton for over five hours. It was the middle of the night, but so many local people were working night shifts that there was a considerable amount of pedestrian activity. During that time, no one noticed any damage to the car. The prosecution could bring forward *not one witness* to say the car was damaged.

Patricia Walpole's recollection that the E-type had been parked outside Luvaglio's house when she returned home from work just after midnight was very persuasive because her precise movements that evening were corroborated by supplementary testimony (for example, from the manager of the bowling alley where she had been working late). Widgery observed that "such a respectable witness, speaking so directly in favour of the defence, is a matter of consequence, and we have treated it as such". Hardly; the evidence was disregarded on the basis that the jury had already disregarded parallel testimony and "you do not necessarily improve the strength of your evidence merely by multiplying the numbers", a quaint legalistic notion.

Fresh arguments were advanced regarding the entire absence of any forensic evidence, such as the transfer of fibres. The Court did not consider this "a potent factor".

There was no attempt even to deal with Arthur Bowman's evidence: "this is largely a technical matter and it is very difficult for us to take an accurate view". The ends of justice will never be served if judges refuse to consider matters because they are "technical" or "difficult". In any case, the arguments were straightforward enough, and had already been painstakingly and properly explored in the Lewis/Hughman book.[8]

The defence had not called a witness on this matter at the trial, because its importance was not then appreciated. Bowman, however, detailed nine separate aspects of the prosecution collision theory which were not explained by the evidence. The original prosecution case was that the cars had collided on two occasions. Bowman averred that there must have been three separate bumps, and that even then there was some damage for which he could not account; for example, the obliteration of the rear light and flasher lenses on each side of the sports car when the surrounding areas were unmarked. He felt this – the aspect which most directly linked the E-type with the Mark X – could only be explained by a deliberate action, like striking them with a hammer. Similarly, there was no possibility that the E-type could have caused all of the damage to the Mark X radiator.

At the trial, Nora Burnip's evidence became an embarrassment for the prosecution, which was unable to account for it and yet could hardly dismiss it. She said what she had to say clearly, consistently and unequivocally; and she had led the police to vital evidence. Yet the decision of the jury effectively relegated her evidence to the side-lines; it became maverick testimony. Highly trained legal minds, surely, would restore it to a central position, where it belonged. Widgery's verdict? "Mrs Burnip should stay where she was at the trial – she is an unanswered question."

Altogether, there was, as Hugo Young wrote in the *Sunday Times*, "no subtle forensic examination – just the blunt instrument of judicial assertion".[9]

In their prolonged efforts to demonstrate that they were wrongly convicted, Luvaglio and Stafford encountered two formidable obstacles. The first was that the police had in their possession an additional piece of evidence which pointed to their guilt. Fleet Street knew of this too, and it is inconceivable that the judiciary would have been unaware of it.

The evidence was a note left by Sibbet for one of his girlfriends, Doreen Hall, saying that he had a meeting with Luvaglio on the night in question – which was already known; but that the meeting was at 11 o'clock.

The note could not be produced in court because Sibbet could not be cross-examined about it. It might even have predisposed those undertaking the murder inquiry to consider Luvaglio and Stafford as the guilty men and to ignore other leads. Perhaps it is one of the ironies of the case that a piece of hearsay evidence which could not be admitted in fairness to the defendants played a part in securing their convictions. Had it been admitted, it could easily have been disposed of.

Although married, Sibbet had several mistresses and was in the habit of leaving misleading notes to allay the suspicions of one or another of them. (The defence did make sure that this aspect of his behaviour was revealed in open court, but the apparently incriminating note could not be referred to.) In another piece of unexplained trial testimony, to which insufficient attention was paid, Joyce Hall (sister of Doreen, and another of Sibbet's conquests) revealed that when she arrived home that morning at 2.20 a.m., the bed was disturbed. She later learned that Sibbet had arrived there from La Dolce Vita with a girl in tow. Two men who lived in the same house agreed that Sibbet arrived there after leaving the club – another indication that he could not have been murdered in a spot sixteen and a half miles away before midnight.

The other problem was that Luvaglio and Stafford were never able to offer a complete and convincing alternative version of how the E-type which they were using had collided with Sibbet's Mark X; or, indeed, of how Sibbet might have died. No theory was advanced either at the trial or on appeal before Mr Justice Edmund Davies. One was put forward at the 1973 appeal, but Widgery had little difficulty unpicking it.

On 26 February 1973, Luvaglio and Stafford went back to the Court of Appeal, seeking leave to appeal to the House of Lords against the decision of the court a few weeks earlier not to quash their convictions. Only if a case has raised some specific point of law which requires clarification by the House of Lords, the ultimate legal authority in the British constitution, may appellants be granted leave to take their suit there. The ruling of the three appeal judges – Widgery, James and Eveleigh – in this matter was as bewildering as the appeal verdict itself. They ruled that the Luvaglio and Stafford appeal *did* raise a point of law of general public importance; but they nevertheless declined to allow the men to pursue it in the Lords.

The only option now open to Luvaglio and Stafford was to petition the appeal committee of the House of Lords. The point of law which required clarification was whether or not the Appeal Court was right to attempt to fit the fresh evidence into the framework of the whole of the evidence originally called at the trial. Many lawyers argued that, if weighty new evidence emerged, either the appeal should be upheld or, at the least, the case sent for retrial before a jury. On 12 April the appeal committee did rule that it was a proper case in which to grant leave to appeal.

The appeal opened on 11 July, and ended six days later when their lordships decided to ponder their verdict over the summer holidays. Judgment was delivered on 18 October. The appeals were unanimously rejected. Furthermore, the Lords effectively broadened the powers of the Court of Appeal by arguing that appeal judges were correct in determining for themselves the evidential value of new testimony, in the context of the whole case.

"The 1968 Act gave wide powers to the Court of Appeal," emphasised Viscount Dilhorne, "and it would be wrong to place any fetter or restriction on its exercise. The Act did not require the court, in making up its mind whether or not a verdict was unsafe or unsatisfactory, to apply any particular tests.

"Parliament had in terms said that the court should only quash a conviction if, there being no error of law or material irregularity at the trial, 'they think' the verdict was unsafe or unsatisfactory." In other words, the Court of Appeal was a law unto itself, and that was right and proper.

Dilhorne then turned to the case under discussion. "The House had to consider, as had the Court of Appeal, whether there was any possible explanation of the proved facts which was consistent with the appellants' innocence." Really? The onus seemed to have changed. No longer was it a question of proving guilt, but of proving innocence. The law was being turned inside out: by the highest constitutional authority in the land.

Dilhorne said that because the jury returned a verdict of guilty, "it followed that the damage to the car and Sibbet's death must have occurred before 12.30 a.m." However, he continued, "the evidence by Mr Golden and

calculations based on it were *wholly insufficient* to raise
any doubts." (Author's italics) This was interesting, since
it contradicted the Court of Appeal. Even Lord Widgery
had admitted that Golden's evidence "did go into the
scales for the defence", which presumably meant, if it
meant anything at all, that it was of sufficient weight to
raise *some* doubts.

ilhorne concluded by saying that all extra evidence
availed the appellants nothing – his conclusion being that
"the E-type and Sibbet's car collided and Sibbet was murdered on the A182 where the debris was found shortly
before midnight".

The whole thing had been an extraordinary exercise in
judicial myopia. Dilhorne said that while he had of course
striven to reach his own opinion on the basis of the facts,
he "was fortified in his conclusion by the fact that the Lord
Chief Justice and five Lord Justices reached the same
conclusion". Lord Diplock said he had "no doubt' as to
the appellants' guilt. Lord Cross averred that "the balance
remained overwhelmingly in favour of the Crown and on
the totality of the evidence a doubt as to the appellants'
guilt would be unreasonable". Lords Pearson and
Kilbrandon gave their assent to these astonishingly sweep-
ing judgments.

It is hard to say which causes more sadness: that two
innocent people can spend twelve years in prison; or that
the English law can be reduced, *in extremis*, to such sublime
and pompous foolishness. Sir David Napley has written:
"It is legalistic dogma of this sort which has done so much
to lower the reputation of our courts among laymen, and
as a result contributed to an increasing disrespect for
the rule of law generally."[10] In the case of Luvaglio and
Stafford, the Appeal Courts entirely failed to perform their
specific function. Far from serving "the ends of justice",
the judicial system was used to frustrate them.

Any one of a number of threads of evidence should have
been sufficient to exonerate Luvaglio and Stafford. There
are abundant persuasive factors in addition to all those

already discussed. Fresh blood stains were noticed on a directory in the telephone kiosk near where the Mark X was abandoned. These were grouped as A MN; blood which matched Sibbet's. The prosecution had said nothing about his making a phone call. Also, there was fresh blood on the carpet covering the transmission tunnel of the Mark X. This was group A MM: not Sibbet's, then. Neither was it Luvaglio's (group O); or Stafford's (again, group O). This was evidence only an unusually obtuse investigative team could have disregarded. A quantity of cigarette stubs was found with the debris in the lane – though of a brand which none of those presumed to have been there smoked. Headlamp glass was discovered on the main road by the Burnips' farm with the debris from the supposed collision between the Jaguars; but this was not glass fitted to Jaguars.

Even two policemen gave testimony that refuted the prosecution theory. At 12.20 that morning, PC John Ainsworth saw a Jaguar saloon turn out of Pesspool Lane with a red Mini behind it. No one else gave evidence concerning a red Mini, but it is a model about which a policeman is unlikely to be mistaken. Another police officer reported from the scene of the crime that blood was still dripping from Sibbet's body at 5.30 a.m.; evidence which, if true, also demolished the prosecution theory about time of death.

The murder of Angus Sibbet remains one of the unsolved mysteries of English crime. At the 1967 trial, Raymond Dean QC showed great prescience in describing it as a riddle which would never be solved. "There are too many pieces of the puzzle missing," he said, "and too many that do not fit."

Such a wretched business had an unsavoury postscript. In June 1979 the two men were released, Luvaglio having obtained an Open University degree during his imprisonment. On 7 September 1980 the *News of the World* published a 'confession' by Dennis Stafford, who said he'd killed Sibbet after Luvaglio had gone to bed.

The story had a veneer of credibility. On closer examination, though, it was revealed to be spurious. Napley and
Luvaglio put out a press statement drawing attention to
some discrepancies. This assessment was confirmed three
weeks later, on 28 September, when the *Sunday People*
revealed that Stafford had invented the entire confession
because the *News of the World* had paid him handsomely
to do so; £10,000 was the figure mentioned. "I only did it
for the money," explained Stafford, "and to prove how
hypocritical the system is and how people will believe what
they want to believe. We did not commit the murder and
the evidence and facts of the case remain as they were."[11]

Six

The Luton post-office murder (i)

People in the case

Reginald Stevens — murder victim

David Cooper (John Disher)

Michael McMahon ⎱
Patrick Murphy ⎰ — jointly charged with murder of Stevens

Mr Justice Cusack — judge

Margaret Crawley ⎱
Peggy Calvert ⎰ — scene-of-crime witnesses

Kenneth Isaac — witness to the gang's arrival

John McNair ⎫
Edward Seal ⎬ — witnesses to the gang's getaway
Herbert Andrews ⎭

Alfred Mathews (Elliott) — chief prosecution witness

Michael Good — East End gangster

Terence Langston — Good's brother-in-law

Detective Chief Superintendent (later Commander) Kenneth
    Drury — policeman in charge of murder inquiry

Detective Sergeant John Hill — policeman engaged in inquiry

Albert Elliott ⎱
Reg Elliott ⎰ — brothers of Alfred Mathews

Thomas Weyers ⎱ — prisoners giving evidence for the
Derek Jackson ⎰   prosecution

Stephen Murphy — father of Patrick Murphy

Marlene Baker — girlfriend of Patrick Murphy

Morris Lerman — Hackney tailor; alibi witness for Cooper

Roderick Firmstone — assistant to Lerman

William Slade — alibi witness for Cooper

Fred Lawrence — alibi witness for Cooper

Richard Hurn — alibi witness for McMahon

Terence Edwards — alibi witness for Murphy

Mrs Brooks — witness to Mathews' departure

Donald Leek — witness to gang's M1 journey

Terence Leonard ⎱
Frederick Stephens ⎰ — witnesses against Mathews

James Wilkinson — witness against Mathews

James Humphreys — underworld associate of Drury
William Thomson — journalist who interviewed Mathews
Tom Iremonger — MP for Ilford North
Bryan Magee — MP for Leyton
Michael Spicer — MP for Worcestershire South
Dr Oonagh McDonald — MP for Thurrock
Gareth Peirce — solicitor for Cooper
Wendy Mantle — solicitor for McMahon
Bryan Anns QC — counsel for Cooper
Bryan Capstick QC — counsel for Cooper
David McNeill QC — counsel for McMahon

FROM START to finish, the Luton murder case was a complete balls-up. The criminals who planned and carried out the crime; those who investigated it; those who assessed it for the Director of Public Prosecutions; those entrusted with the responsibility of reviewing the case afterwards: all behaved with gross incompetence.

For David Cooper and Michael McMahon, who paid with their liberty for the professional inadequacies of others, it seems only to be adding insult to injury to have to report that the crime of which they duly became indirect victims was not even a particularly intriguing one.

At about 6.10 p.m. on 10 September 1969 sub-postmaster Reginald Stevens was shot dead in his car in a Luton car-park. Few crimes could have been more clumsy (the murder was apparently accidental) or more self-defeating. The four gangsters had been hoping to bully him into handing over the post-office keys. In killing him, they had automatically aborted their mission. They had not even got close to the High Town Road post-office that was their target. Moreover, their getaway plan was now in tatters. Betraying a lack of common sense more readily associated with comedy film gangsters than real ones, they'd driven to Luton in their own cars.

These – a Vauxhall and a red sports car – had been left in the station car-park. The men had driven to Barclay's Bank car-park, where Stevens habitually left his car, in a stolen green van. Thus, in between committing the murder in the second car-park, and driving back in rush-hour traffic to the first, they were observed by a number of people.

Kenneth Isaac, who was doing some paperwork in his car, noticed the little convoy of three – Vauxhall, van, sports car – arrive in the station car-park. The Vauxhall parked next to him. He observed the driver to be "in his late 40s or early 50s, with greying hair". The passenger seemed to be wearing a "darkish blue overall".

Margaret Crawley and Peggy Calvert, neighbours who were talking together, heard the noise of the shot which killed Stevens. From a distance of about sixty-five yards, they saw a man running to the van as it was pulling away. Mrs Crawley admitted, however, "I wouldn't recognise him again."

John McNair and Edward Seal both saw the van in transit between the car-parks. It could hardly have escaped McNair's attention; it was exiting the bank car-park across the pavement. He remembered something of its driver, whom he afterwards described as thin-faced with a very pale complexion, and wearing a "trilby-type hat". He also saw a man clinging to the side of the van, and was struck by his "dark blue raincoat". Subsequently, the van almost collided with a car driven by Seal, who said its driver had a thin face and was aged between forty and forty-five.

Now, as the men prepared to make a hurried exit from the station car-park, they were again noticed by Isaac. More importantly, their departure was monitored by Herbert Andrews. He saw four men get out of the van, and gave brief descriptions of three of them. The first was in his mid-twenties, and wearing a navy-blue boiler suit; another was about thirty, neatly dressed with fair hair. A third was "in his late 40s, well-built, with greying hair in a swept-back style".

This man, together with the one dressed in blue, got into a Vauxhall. The other two got into a red sports car. The men, clearly in a state of agitation, abandoned the van. Andrews became justifiably suspicious. As a responsible citizen he jotted down the number of the Vauxhall: 5075 MW. (In fact, it was 5075 MV.) He was unable to discern the number of the sports car, but ventured that it had an 'E' suffix, with digits that included '5' and '1'.

The murder aroused understandable national outrage. The Postmaster-General, John Stonehouse, put up a reward of £5,000 for information leading to the capture of those responsible. This ought not to have been an unduly difficult undertaking. The police not only had various descriptions of the men; they had the registration number from Andrews. They could hardly have dared hope for so much so soon.

The Vauxhall car was found in Stoke Newington, north-east London. It belonged to Alfred Mathews (also known as Elliott), who lived in Bow in east London. The police knew quite a lot about him. He had convictions for house-breaking, assault, theft and using explosives. He had pre-viously robbed a post-office and had an underworld reputation as a good getaway driver. The car, curiously, had been wiped clean of fingerprints. Even more curiously, its ownership had been transferred the day after the murder to a non-existent person at a non-existent address.

Mathews, however, did not seem to be available for interview. He had gone away, according to his wife; she did not know where.

The police had other leads. A pair of spectacles and a trilby hat were found in the station car-park close to the green van. Also, Herbert Andrews originally said that the sports car carried a Mercedes badge on the front. After carefully studying photographs of the various models, how-ever, he affirmed that the car was almost certainly a red MG with a hard top. Most importantly, the murder weapon was found. A sawn-off shotgun, it had been put into a brown hold-all and tossed over on to the railway embank-ment.

It was traced to Michael Good, an East End gangster. He was already facing robbery charges, but was out on bail at the time of the Luton crime. His wife told police that when her husband was in custody she had passed his gun on to her brother, Terence Langston. He was taken in for questioning, but denied knowledge of the crime.

The trail grew cold. The police had a great deal of information, but were unable to make headway with any of it. Beyond the strong inference that the operation had been mounted by an East-End gang, they had learned little.

At that time, post-office raids were in vogue among London's criminal community. There had lately been two: at Newington Green on 20 May, and at Middleton Road on 7 July (both in the same Dalston/Stoke Newington area of London). Patrick Murphy owned a red and white Triumph sports car which had been used in the second raid. It had been on loan to a friend, but Murphy was observed on the day of the raid in the company of two men subsequently convicted of the crime. Murphy initially faced charges which were later dropped. In connection with the first raid, however, he was put on an identification parade at Wood Green police station. He was picked out and as a result charged with the offence. He was given bail.

Two other young men, Michael McMahon and David Cooper (whose real name was John Disher) were soon caught up in inquiries about the London post-office robberies. Cooper drove a red Mercedes convertible (i.e. soft top), registration number DAH 996B. McMahon was put on an identification parade in connection with a whole series of post-office robberies, but not one of over twenty witnesses picked him out. He was nevertheless charged with being in possession of stolen furniture. While out on bail, he was summonsed to answer, at Thames magistrates court on 10 September, another charge of dishonestly handling stolen goods. Cooper's flat, like McMahon's, was raided by police. Nothing was discovered to incriminate him in any significant criminal activities, but he was charged with being in possession of a stolen washing-machine. His court appearance was scheduled for 11 September.

These three – Murphy, McMahon and Cooper – soon became the focus of police attention. None was a pillar of rectitude; each had a criminal record. The previous offences, though, had been relatively minor. There was nothing to indicate that they were moving up into a higher division. However, the man in charge of the murder investigation, Detective Chief Superintendent Kenneth Drury of Scotland Yard's Flying Squad, could point to a number of grounds for his suspicions: Cooper owned a red Mercedes sports car; he did know Mathews, and indeed had carried out a small jewellery robbery with him earlier in the year; he was friendly with Murphy and McMahon; Murphy had been arrested and charged with one post-office robbery; and McMahon was on the list of suspects for another.

Throughout October, Murphy, McMahon and Cooper became increasingly uncomfortably aware that the police were interested in them in connection with the Luton crime.

All this time, Mathews was in hiding. He stayed with a friend, spent some time in Eastbourne with his wife, and finally holed up in Ilford at the house of his brother, Albert Elliott. How the police failed to find him is one of the major mysteries of the case. It was, however, typical of the overall level of efficiency with which the investigation was conducted. This only took a decisive step forward on 22 October when Elliott telephoned the police to tell them where they could find his brother.

This should have been the prelude to the successful unravelling of the case. For a start, Mathews was a grey-haired, thin-faced man in his early fifties. Witness descriptions pointed to him as the driver of the van. At the outset, McNair had picked him out (from a selection of photographs) as the driver, and Mathews' record confirmed the likelihood of this. His car had been involved, and the obviously bogus transfer of ownership only increased suspicions. Forensic science tests might also have established a link between Mathews and the discarded hat and spectacles.

Mathews was taken into custody. At his interview at Luton police station, he tried to persuade Drury that he knew nothing of the crime. He said it must have been carried out by the person to whom he sold his car. Only someone of bottomless gullibility could have believed this.

In any case, statements taken simultaneously from his wife and brother gave the lie to it. Mathews was in deep trouble.

The case, however, was never resolved satisfactorily. No one who committed the brutal Luton murder ever served a day in prison because of it. Mathews, despite the accumulation of evidence against him, was never even put on an identification parade.

Drury seemed possessed of an *idée fixe* about Murphy, McMahon and Cooper. Considerations such as hard evidence were quite unable to dislodge it. So, all that was required was Mathews' cooperation. If he would identify those three not merely as his accomplices, but as the actual protagonists, he could turn Queen's Evidence (referred to as QE) and escape totally the consequences of his criminality.

Mathews drank from the poisoned chalice; with what enthusiasm, it is hard to tell. Drury later admitted in the *News of the World* that he had been "leaned on a bit".[1] Even a man like Mathews must have had misgivings about what he was doing. In the early hours of 25 October he made a lengthy statement, in which he gave himself a peripheral, unknowing role in the crime; on 3 December he elaborated on it.

As a result, Mathews, Murphy, McMahon and Cooper appeared together to face murder charges at committal proceedings in Luton on 15 December. On the strength of Drury's recommendation to the DPP, however, no evidence was offered by the Crown against Mathews, and the charge against him was dismissed.

Just before their trial commenced, the three remaining defendants were offered a deal. If they would change their pleas to guilty, the charges would be reduced to manslaughter. Being innocent, they all naturally rejected the offer out of hand. It is an incident, though, which provides a sidelight on the built-in absurdities of the judicial system. Had they committed the crime, then, knowing the strength of Mathews' evidence, the three would gratefully have accepted the deal. Because they were innocent, they were convicted of a far more serious crime than they would have been if they were guilty.

The trial opened at the Old Bailey on 26 February 1970. Mathews, the main prosecution witness, gave evidence on oath that he agreed to go to Luton merely to help pick up some parcels from the railway station, for which he would be paid £10. By the time he realised he'd been duped, he was on his way up the M1. When they reached Luton, he told the jury, the others had gone on ahead of him. He was asked to keep a look-out on a shop he belatedly realised was a post-office. As he hadn't been to the bank car-park he didn't know what had happened there, though it was clear when he was picked up again that something had gone very wrong. The three, one of whom was covered in blood, came tearing up to him in the van. He said he heard the words, "Get going, you have shot him", and that he was bewildered and terrified. He wanted to drive off on his own. However, in the station car-park the man in blue, wiping blood from himself, had forced his way into the Vauxhall. Half a mile outside Luton, though, Mathews was able to get rid of him. He said he got home about 8 p.m., and was unaware of what had actually happened until he saw *News at Ten*.

This was the statement, subsequently termed the "parcels story", on which he had been allowed to turn QE. It is amazing that anything so feeble, so transparently concocted, should have been accepted by the DPP. Two years later, Bertie Smalls, the notorious bank-robber, turned QE. His impressively detailed statement contained an abundance of information which the police would not otherwise have been able to obtain. It was demonstrably advantageous for the Crown to strike a deal. In this case, there were no such extenuating circumstances to bring Machiavellian logic to bear on an ethically dubious practice. The end result of this QE deal was the violation of the fundamentals of the English judicial system: the freedom of the guilty was bartered for the imprisonment of the innocent.

Mathews' second, embellishing, statement filled out the roles the three defendants supposedly played. Murphy was cast as the driver. Mathews ascribed to him the glasses and trilby he had himself been wearing. He alluded also both to McMahon's navy-blue boiler suit, and to the fact that John (Cooper) had been driving the red sports car. Three innocent people had been given character parts in a murder story.

Somewhat disconcertingly, this fresh 'evidence' conflicted with much of the actual evidence the police had already gathered. No problem; the latter could be, and was, doctored to suit.

For example, Mrs Crawley was prevailed upon to reconsider her original statement. Her response was extraordinary. She made thirteen additional ones. She began by professing to have noticed two men other than the running man of her original statement. By 25 October she had provided graphic descriptions of all three, an extraordinary feat for a woman who, in her immediate recollection of the incident, had noticed only one man, and him so distantly that she would be unable to recognise him again. She picked out McMahon at an identity parade on 31 October.

The police chose not to reveal that on 14 October Mrs Crawley and Mrs Calvert had been shown photographs of a number of suspects. Each had independently picked out a man who had nothing to do with the crime; neither reacted to photographs of Murphy, McMahon or Cooper.

The new Crawley evidence was tendered on the day that Mathews made his first statement. The day after he made his second, Andrews' memory, too, was coincidentally jolted. The red sports car which he had previously identified as an MG he now obligingly re-identified as a Mercedes. To his credit, though, he stuck to his story in other respects: that the car had a hard top, that its registration suffix was 'E'; and that its numerals included '5' and '1'. If he was right in just one of these three features about which he remained so unshakeable, then Cooper's car was not the one at Luton.

McMahon, Cooper and Murphy thus had pitted against them not only the dishonest, ulterior statements of Mathews; but also the disingenuous, albeit disinterested, statements of important independent witnesses. A third thread of disreputable evidence was cynically woven into this shoddy: statements of fellow prisoners.

McMahon was held on remand in Leicester prison. There, he found himself billeted next to Thomas Weyers and Derek Jackson. They candidly confessed guilt in their own cases; McMahon adamantly maintained innocence in his.

The latter was accordingly surprised to learn that Jackson had made a statement to police, saying that McMahon had readily admitted his guilt in prison. McMahon was perturbed, but asked his solicitor to contact Weyers, who was by then at liberty again. Sadly, by the time she did so, Weyers, too, had already made a statement. According to this, McMahon had not merely admitted his guilt, but had actually relayed precise details of his movements throughout that day. The Himalayan improbability of this didn't noticeably occur to anyone in court. Prisoners might well admit guilt to each other; what they would never do is discuss the commission of the crimes in the cut-and-dried fashion of a police statement: "left court at 2.30, arrived home at 2.50, had a cup of tea, left home at 3.10", etc. Moreover, Weyers mentioned that McMahon had told him that the target post-office contained £26,000. The figure was spot-on. As McMahon pointed out, how, even if he had been one of the gang, could he possibly have known that? Obviously, Weyers' information had been fed to him by police.

It was disgraceful that the prosecution should have sought to rely on the evidence of a man like Weyers. He was not a reputable witness because, sadly, he was not in full possession of his mental faculties. When his own case went to appeal, within three months of this trial, Mr Justice

Geoffrey Lane remarked, "it is *quite plain* that when he is released he will need assistance . . . There is no power in this Court to order compulsory after-care, but we hope he will take the opportunity of undertaking voluntary supervision." (Author's italics.)

Other trivial pieces of prosecution evidence were presumably put forward on the theory that many a pickle makes a mickle. For example, a pillow-case was produced. This had supposedly been found on the railway embankment next to the brown hold-all, and supposedly contained hairs which *could* have come from Cooper's Golden Labrador.

This kind of evidence should set alarm bells ringing in a perceptive jury. It proved nothing, as a diffident scientific witness admitted: Golden Labradors are hardly uncommon, and in any case, dog hairs cannot be subjected to fine analysis like human ones. (Moreover, Mathews kept a dog – though this was concealed from the jury.) The fact that it was brought forward at all merely threw into sharp relief the absence of genuine forensic evidence. There was nothing to link the defendants with the abandoned van, or the gun, or the scene of the crime, although McMahon, for example, had provided samples of his hair, blood and saliva.

The prosecution said that when Murphy was arrested on 29 October he had straightaway produced a written alibi statement for 10 September; and that when he was later taken for an identification parade, he spent some minutes beforehand combing and apparently restyling his hair. Why, the prosecution asked, would an innocent man behave like this?

Again, this was disingenuous. The police knew that Murphy had received abundant indications that he was a prime suspect for the Luton crime. Innocent or guilty, he would have been foolish not to take precautions.

One of the host of reasons why Mathews' statement was ridiculous was that both McMahon and Cooper had to make court appearances around the day the crime was committed. McMahon's case was listed for that very afternoon. He would hardly have double-booked himself by arranging a major robbery then. Likewise, Cooper was due in court the following morning. At 4.00 p.m. that afternoon he had phoned his solicitor, at her request, in connection with it. According to Mathews, they were all *en route* to Luton at the time the call was placed.

Considerations such as these pointed to the absurdity of the prosecution case. In demonstrating that court appearances seemed not to be the rarity for the defendants that they are for the average member of the public, however, they were hardly likely to benefit the defence.

Neither McNair nor Seal was called as a witness by the prosecution. Their evidence would have conflicted with the picture it was trying to paint. Their names were, however, passed to the defence. Each was contacted by solicitors; each independently contacted the police; each was told there was no need to respond as statements had already been taken from them. Thus, one of the defence's strongest cards was neutralised. Only afterwards did defence solicitors establish the immense importance of the McNair and Seal testimony. Seal was shown a picture of Murphy, and said he definitely wasn't the driver of the van; and, later, one of Mathews, and indicated that he was. McNair, of course, had already identified Mathews as the driver.

Ultimately, the defence had to fall back on the argument that none of the three could have committed the crime, as they all had perfectly good alibis. They had spent the entire day in London.

After his court appearance, McMahon, with his father and Fred Lawrence (who had acted as bail sureties) had met Cooper, who had driven them home. Lawrence left almost immediately. McMahon spent the rest of the afternoon watching horse-racing on television. (It was the day of the St Leger.) His father, a bus conductor, left home at 4.00 p.m., and his mother went out shopping. Shortly after 5.00 p.m., McMahon went to his girlfriend's flat, twenty minutes' walk away. They had a meal, and later in the evening went out for a drink.

Cooper, having dropped off McMahon, had visited a friend in Haggerston – an area of north-east inner London – and telephoned his solicitor. He then went to his tailor, Morris Lerman, in Mare Street, Hackney, to be fitted for a new suit. He arrived back home at 5.30, and at 6.30 was back in Hackney, now with his brother. He spent the evening drinking in local pubs with a friend. The following morning, he made his court appearance. (After another remand, he eventually received a twelve-month suspended sentence.)

Murphy was then living in Haggerston with his girlfriend, Marlene Baker, and her parents. He too, with Marlene, her father and a friend, spent the afternoon glued to the horse-racing. At 4.30 he drove off to see his father in Ilford. He arrived soon after 5.00, and had tea with his father, Stephen Murphy, and stepmother. Later on, he returned to Haggerston and, in the evening, went out with Marlene.

The obvious problem with these alibis, complete as they were, was that nearly all the people able to give evidence were either family or close friends: the very people of whose evidence a jury is invariably advised to be sceptical. There were two exceptions – Cooper's solicitor and, more importantly, his tailor. Here, the prosecution got in first. Drury tried his best to persuade Morris Lerman to alter his evidence. He did not really succeed, but he did manage to introduce a degree of uncertainty into what was basically straight-forward testimony. Lerman was then entered as a prosecution witness.

If defence counsel had had the opportunity of working out beforehand how Lerman's evidence could have been better employed to Cooper's advantage, it might have been a different story. Drury's prompt intervention denied them that.

At the trial, the Crown tried to make it appear that Lerman was not providing an alibi for Cooper; under cross-examination, he made it clear that he was. He said he could pinpoint Cooper's visit to his shop by reference both to Cooper's court appearance the following day, which had been a subject of conversation between them, and also to the imminence of the Jewish New Year.

Consequently, the alibi evidence came to nothing. Jury members were left with the apparent enigma of Mathews. Whatever conclusions they reached about him, it would have been extremely difficult for them to reject his evidence out of hand. In his summing-up Mr Justice Cusack explained that Mathews would have to be "wicked, beyond belief" to have invented the participation of the others, thus inviting the jury to assume that this was unthinkable.

On 19 March Cooper, McMahon and Murphy were found guilty and given mandatory sentences of life imprisonment. Cusack added, however, that he would recommend that each serve a minimum of twenty years. "I think it necessary that this matter should be dealt with in a way which will bring home to those disposed to carry firearms that they must receive such sentences as will express the strongest possible public disapproval and horror, and may serve to deter other people."

Since the greatest deterrent to crime is the certainty of capture, the outcome of the trial was to afford the greatest possible encouragement "to those disposed to carry firearms".

Ultimately, the alibi evidence was a source of strength, not weakness. Close family and friends will almost always do what they can to rally round those wrongly imprisoned. In this case, natural loyalty was buttressed by additional considerations: hurt pride, because their own testimony had plainly not been accepted; and searing outrage. They *knew* their kith and kin were innocent: hadn't they themselves been with them throughout the period of the crime? No miscarriage of justice campaign was ever launched on a surer knowledge of absolute innocence.

Seven

The Luton Post-office
Murder (ii)

THE CASE went to appeal, as cases do. Defence lawyers had by then learned the precise nature of the testimony which Seal and McNair would have given in court had defence lawyers not been forestalled in their efforts to call them. The evidence of both pointed directly to Mathews as the getaway driver.

Equally importantly, Stephen Murphy, Patrick's father, pursuing an assiduous solo investigation, had contacted Mrs Brooks, one of Mathews' next-door neighbours in Roman Road, Bow. She had witnessed the departure of the gang. According to her, Mathews left the house with three other men at 3.30 in the afternoon of 10 September 1969, carrying a brown hold-all which he put into the boot of his car. (The gun was later discovered in a brown hold-all.) Her statement was doubly intriguing because she had never been interviewed at all by police carrying out the murder inquiry.

But in February 1971 the Luton post-office murder was not yet popularly established as in any sense 'a special case'. Notwithstanding the newly adduced evidence, Lord Justice Fenton Atkinson, Mr Justice Lyell and Mr Justice Mars-Jones determined that Cooper, McMahon and Murphy "were all three rightly convicted of the crime of murder".

The court noted that it had to consider evidence from three new witnesses. "One was a lady, Mrs Brooks, from whom a statement had been taken several months afterwards which, if it was true, entirely conflicted with Mathews' account of how this expedition set off. We have considered her statement with some care, the circumstances in which it was taken, the length of time afterwards, and we feel it is not in the circumstances likely to be credible."

This was disingenuous of the judges. They ought not to have dismissed this statement because of "the length of time afterwards' without going on to ask themselves why a statement had not been taken from her within days of the crime. At the very least, it exposed the investigation as ridiculously inadequate, and should have raised grave doubts about police proficiency.

The judges rejected the testimony of Seal and McNair, not because it was untruthful, but because it was considered unavailing: ". . . once one assumes, *as we all do*, that the jury *clearly* must have reckoned that Mathews was very much more deeply in this than he said, and whether he was the actual driver of the van, or exactly what part he was playing, perhaps does not matter". (Author's italics.)

Yet if Mathews had imputed an untruthful role to Murphy, what was there to have prevented him from similarly inventing other parts of his story? More crucially, weren't their Lordships guilty of jumping to conclusions? To use their own word, they *assumed* that the jury acknowledged Mathews was more deeply implicated than he was admitting. It was the likely interpretation, of course, but it was hardly proper to say more than that. The jury might alternatively have found it hard to credit that the DPP would be so cavalier as to grant a brutal murderer immunity from prosecution.

So, the imprisoned men could expect to make headway only in an extra-judicial context.

From the moment of the convictions Stephen Murphy worked tirelessly on behalf of his son. He gave up his job to campaign (and subsequently retrained as a taxi-driver). He leafleted everyone he encountered, hoping against hope that his outline of the case would jog someone's memory and that the million-to-one chance would turn up. Unbelievably, it did.

Terence Edwards, a sewing-machine mechanic who knew the Murphy family, saw Patrick Murphy in London at 4.30 on the afternoon the murder took place. He had just bought a sewing-machine in Dalston and was about to cross the road to get a birthday card for his brother when Murphy drove past in his distinctive red-and-white sports car. (Murphy advertised the fact that he was an Arsenal supporter.) Edwards yelled out, but Murphy did not notice him.

This testimony corroborated what Murphy had said at the trial: *viz*. that at the time he was going to Ilford. Further, the accuracy of Edwards' memory was confirmed by the records of the sewing-machine shop.

As a result of continuing coverage in *Private Eye*, two London criminals, Terence Leonard and Frederick Stephens, came forward. They said that a year before the Luton murder Mathews had asked them to form a team with him to rob the sub post-office in High Town Road. Such evidence demolished the 'parcels story'.

An unexpected development then set the whole business in a fresh light. On 27 February 1972, the *Sunday People* published a front-page story about Drury, who had been promoted in April 1971. This disclosed that he and his wife had recently returned from a holiday in Cyprus with James Humphreys and his wife. Humphreys, a notorious under-world character, was a Soho strip-club proprietor and pornographic bookshop owner with a number of convictions. A judge had once described him as "a hardened and dangerous criminal". He was certainly strange company for the new Commander of the Flying Squad to be keeping.

Publicly, Drury was as bland as could be, saying he had no qualms about what had happened. His superiors responded less phlegmatically. On 6 March Drury was suspended from duty, and on 30 April he resigned from the force. In September he was named in an Old Bailey trial as one of seven senior Metropolitan Police officers in the pay of a crooked car dealer.

In the light of this, pressure for a review of the case understandably increased. It swelled still further after the transmission of *Midweek* (BBC 1) on 25 October 1972, in which reporter Tom Mangold probed the evidence that had recently emerged. Most of it benefited Murphy, whose alibi evidence was by now substantial. His father was exceptionally forceful; a plumber who had been working in the Murphy household at the time was equally adamant about Patrick's presence there; and now there was Edwards: all prepared to testify to having seen Murphy in the London area at a time when the legal process had deemed him to be committing a murder in Luton.

Mathews' elder brother, Reg, told Mangold that he strongly suspected that Mathews had told a string of lies in court. Terence Langston, who had initially been unable to assist the police in their inquiries about the gun, now agreed that he had lent it to Mathews and another man and they had collected it from his home. Even more revealingly, he said that Drury had tried unsuccessfully to persuade him to give evidence that he had lent the gun to Murphy.

On 9 November the Home Secretary, Robert Carr, was questioned in the Commons by Tom Iremonger, Conservative MP for Ilford North. Iremonger, at this point the most prominent of the fifty-plus MPs who had expressed support for the campaign to reopen the case, had first brought the existence of the Edwards alibi to the attention of Carr's predecessor, Reginald Maudling, in December 1971. Now he wanted to know why it was taking so long to reach a decision.

"A statement was obtained from the new witness," answered Carr, "and my department has undertaken a full review of other aspects of the case with a view to assessing the significance of the statement. I am studying the reports I have received, and also the transcript of a recent television programme. I hope shortly to reach a conclusion on this complex case."

Iremonger got his reply on 7 December, twelve months after he had originally raised the matter. Murphy's conviction was referred to the Court of Appeal.

A further delay followed. Lawyers considered the terms of the Home Office's reference too restrictive. These pertained solely to Edwards, the new witness. The defence

team was keen to incorporate additional post-trial evidence
also. The Home Office, though, was firm: the basis of the
appeal should be the new evidence of Edwards; nothing
more, nothing less.

As it happened, this was enough. On 13 November
1973, the appeal judges – Lord Widgery, Lord Justice
Stephenson and Mr Justice Browne – perceived Edwards
to be "a man of good character", and quashed Murphy's
conviction. "Because Edwards made a favourable impression upon us, we find it necessary to abandon our
somewhat cynical original view of this story. Because
Edwards' evidence has made us feel that the identification
of Murphy by Mathews was unsafe, we have decided that
this appeal must be allowed," explained Widgery.

"The decision was manifestly right," Lord Devlin later
wrote. "A case that is based on a single dubious witness is
too weak to sustain a fresh wound."[1]

The champagne, though, stayed on ice. For a start,
Murphy was not released from prison. After the Luton
trial, he had received a concurrent twelve-year sentence
for the Newington Green robbery. Thus, a single victory
was insufficient: he needed two. Secondly, Cooper and
McMahon were emphatically denied the opportunity of
deriving personal elation from the outcome of Murphy's
appeal. "The Court has been concentrating entirely on the
case of Murphy," stressed Widgery. "It has not had before
it the cases of Cooper and McMahon, and it expresses no
view about those cases, except to say that it should not be
assumed that the Court's views expressed today necessarily
mean that Cooper and McMahon's convictions are in any
way rendered unsafe."

This was judicial obtuseness with a vengeance. Tom
Sargant, secretary of Justice, indicated as much in a letter
he wrote to Robert Carr: "By the judgment of the Court,
Mathews was proved to have been a false witness who
committed perjury in respect of all that he said at the
trial about the involvement of Murphy. It is therefore a
justifiable inference that he also gave false evidence about

Cooper and McMahon, and without this evidence the case against them would never have got off its feet. This was plainly the opinion of the trial judge."

It was not only Mathews whose testimony was impugned by the Court's verdict. At the trial, Drury gave evidence of a discussion in which Stephen Murphy inquired if there was any possibility of his son also turning QE. Murphy emphatically denied that such a conversation had taken place. Drury was called to the witness-box "to prove the conversation" (as the first Appeal Court put it). Naturally, this sabotaged Murphy's forceful alibi evidence for his son.

Now that the alibi was judicially vindicated, the inference was inescapable: the police officer in charge of the investigation had committed gross perjury at the trial.

As a result of the general election of February 1974, the Labour party was narrowly returned to power. Roy Jenkins was reinstalled at Queen Anne's Gate, the home of the Home Office. On 29 May he referred the cases of Cooper and McMahon back to the Court of Appeal. The letter of reference to the registrar of criminal appeals made it clear that the decision had been reached in the light of the quashing of Murphy's conviction.

Cooper and McMahon were by now provided with the services of first-rate solicitors, Gareth Peirce and Wendy Mantle, respectively, and the groundwork for the defence was painstakingly prepared. At a private hearing in chambers on 16 December 1974, Lord Justice James directed that the prosecution must provide answers to three crucial questions:

(i) In what circumstances was the decision made to call Mathews for the Crown?

(ii) Which names and addresses of witnesses and/or statements were disclosed to the defence by the prosecution?

(iii) What rewards, and in what circumstances, were paid by the Post Office to witnesses in this case?

When the answers were provided in January, the defence suddenly had a volume of unanticipated evidence at its disposal. The answer to the first question was the least important, for the time being anyway: Drury himself had initiated moves to drop charges against Mathews who would have known at least a fortnight in advance that he would emerge scot-free. At the trial, Mathews had refuted suggestions that such was the case; so this, at least, nailed one of his lies.

In response to the second question the police were obliged to hand over what was euphemistically termed the 'non-material file' on the case. "It would have been dynamite at the trial," said Peirce. "We discovered that the prosecution had failed to disclose the existence of over 800 statements taken within days of the murder, many of which suggested a very different course of events and cast of characters than that portrayed at the trial."

No fewer than thirteen of these statements had been made by Mrs Crawley. The defence had not previously imagined that her testimony, like clay on a potter's wheel, had been so studiously shaped.

Witness descriptions of the sports car and its driver indicated that the car was an MG (in line with Andrews' original firm identification) and not a Mercedes (as Cooper's vehicle was). Donald Leek, who worked then at the 'K' garage on the North Circular Road, remembered the convoy of three cars – the green van, red sports car, and Vauxhall – pulling in. (Interestingly, even Mathews' statement confirmed that the cars had stopped there. He would have had no need to lie about that.) Leek stated that the sports car definitely had a hard top, and that its driver was a swarthy, Mediterranean-looking individual. Cooper was eliminated on both counts: he was pasty-faced and balding; his car, a convertible. A number of other people endorsed Leek's evidence, including many who had spotted that the sports-car driver was of foreign appearance.

When corresponding with McMahon, Wendy Mantle had asked him to brace himself for the information about the distribution of the £5,000 Post Office reward money.

This is how it was divided:

	£
Alfred Mathews	2,000
Albert Elliott	500
Michael Good	500
Thomas Weyers	500
Derek Jackson	500
Herbert Andrews	400
Kenneth Isaac	200
Margaret Crawley	200
Peggy Calvert	200

The final sums had been allocated by Post Office management, but Drury had made the recommendations.

The list revealed that the whole business was more corrupt than anyone had previously suspected. The genuine members of the public – the last four names on the list – received the smaller amounts. Of these, Calvert and Crawley were together when the crime occurred, but contradicted each other under oath. Calvert picked out members of the public at the Cooper and McMahon identity parades; and the conduct of Crawley, who had been so ductile in police hands, was naïve, to say the least.

The other five on the list shared 80 per cent of the money. Since the Crown had attempted to portray Mathews as Cooper's innocent dupe, it is difficult to understand why Elliott had been rewarded so handsomely for turning in his 'innocent' brother. Weyers and Jackson received money for perjuring themselves. That left Mathews himself and Michael Good. Mathews had been involved in the original crime; so, surely, had Good (of whom more anon).

Had public funds ever been put to more nefarious use?

The Luton murder case went to appeal, for the third time, on 10 February 1975. The barristers representing Cooper and McMahon, Bryan Anns QC and David McNeill QC, hoped that the judges would permit the cross-examination of Mathews and would also admit as evidence the testimony of William Thomson, a journalist to whom Mathews had indicated that his reward money had been split 50/50 with Drury.

They were disappointed. Lord Widgery, Lord Justice James and Mr Justice Ashworth refused permission for Mathews to be cross-examined, saying that such a course of action could be countenanced only in an 'exceptional case'. Nor would they hear Thomson's statement. The testimony of Leonard and Stephens was rejected because "we find it incredible that 21 months or so before the event Mathews could have nominated as the place at which the sub-postmaster would be held up the car-park in which he was in fact shot". Within twenty-four hours the appeals were roundly dismissed.

Lord Justice James, giving judgment, advanced two logically incompatible propositions. He said that the jury must clearly have accepted that Mathews had been more centrally involved than he was prepared to admit; and that, in identifying Murphy, Mathews was not necessarily lying, but could have been mistaken.

Now, common sense dictated that if the 'parcels story' were correct, Mathews might have been mistaken about Murphy; if, on the other hand, he was one of the confederates engaged in a planned robbery, then he would know who his accomplices were. Not even Lord Justices of Appeal can have it both ways.

Bryan Magee, then the Labour MP for Leyton, had attended the hearing at the invitation of Cooper, one of his constituents. He was baffled by the findings of the third court and shocked to discover for himself what passed for 'justice' in the higher courts of the land. The performance of the judges – Magee later wrote that "their combination of complacency, brutal indifference and lack of common sense was one I was unprepared to encounter"[2] – handed Cooper a valuable ally. From that time on, Magee worked unstintingly to right a wrong.

He was not alone. By this stage, the press (which took its fourth-estate responsibilities more conscientiously in those days) was up in arms. The case received considerable publicity from, among others, *The Times*, the *Guardian*, the *Sun* and the *News of the World*. McMahon fuelled further interest by writing to *The Times*. (When the letter was published, the prison authorities demanded to know how he had contrived to smuggle it out.)

Magee and the Conservative MP Michael Spicer (whose Worcestershire South constituency took in the Long Lartin prison, where McMahon was held) retained hopes that something more could be done. Alex Lyon, minister of state at the Home Office, who had an impressive grasp of the details of the case, nevertheless felt bound to disappoint them.

The *News of the World* then reported a matter which may have had a bearing on the case: Detective Sergeant John Hill, who had worked for Drury, had received a two-year prison sentence for corruption, and been dismissed from the force in August 1972.[3]

On 5 May *Panorama* (BBC 1) weighed in with a typically thorough investigation, with Magee, Tom Sargant and Sir David Napley as studio guests. The programme was transmitted only four days before the hearing of an application to take the case to the House of Lords. Since the judiciary is notoriously allergic to media interest in its affairs, the timing was unfortunate. Cooper and McMahon, though, were grateful for what the BBC was doing for them; so they were unlikely even to attempt to frustrate its arrangements. The *Panorama* broadcast inspired fresh Fleet Street interest. Predictably, at the end of the week, Cooper and McMahon lost their chance to go to the Lords. The application was dismissed by the same three judges who had so controversially dismissed the appeal earlier in the year. Lord Widgery noted that they were not obliged to give their reasons, and did not give any.

In November the ever-resourceful McMahon was frustrated again. The Law Society turned down an application for legal aid that would have enabled him to pursue a civil writ for damages against Mathews.

Something else happened that year: James Humphreys, Drury's underworld associate, made a statement saying that Drury told him he had "a good drink" from the Luton reward money (i.e. that he pocketed much of it himself).

No one could ever accuse the police of over-zealousness in their pursuit of wrong-doing among colleagues. Despite the revelations over four years earlier about Drury's conduct, he had not been prosecuted for any offence. After this fresh assertion by Humphreys, however, corruption charges were at last preferred against him. In June 1976 he was committed for trial.

By then, a fresh alibi witness for Cooper had come forward.

William Slade had at the time of the crime been a partner in Cooper's father's window-cleaning business. By 1976 he had retired to run a hotel in Cliftonville, Kent. His evidence was that on that particular September day, six and a half years earlier, he had just come from a bookie's when Cooper pulled up in his red Mercedes. They went into a café, and had a cup of tea together while Slade worked out his betting slips. At 5.00 p.m., Cooper left to visit his tailor's, not far from Slade's office. Later that evening, at about 6.45, after he left work, Slade again saw Cooper, and his brother Tony, outside an amusement arcade (though they did not see him).

The appearance of such significant alibi evidence so late in the day was bound to be treated with scepticism. Nevertheless, it could not be dismissed out of hand. The problem was that Slade always felt uncomfortable with Cooper's father, and accordingly deferred to him. Cooper's father knew that Slade could alibi his son, but told him not to get involved. "He was a bit strange, my old man," explained Cooper. "He simply thought the whole thing was bad for business. He wasn't worried about me; he'd never had anything to do with me."

Consequently, Slade had said nothing. As the years passed, it troubled his conscience – but, equally, he was embarrassed about admitting that he had not spoken up when he should have done. The evidence only came to light when Cooper's brothers found themselves drinking in the same pub as Slade's son.

Cooper has never been able to recall the incident. The café was one that he, and those employed in his father's business, used regularly. "I was always in there, but I can't remember being there with Slade on that particular day." Cooper had never needed to think too hard about his alibi, simply because he had one.

Roy Jenkins now referred the case once more to the Court of Appeal. To pre-empt the court's customary tactic of taking a blinkered view of the affair, Jenkins itemised three factors which he specifically requested that it should take within its purview. Firstly, the judges were asked to evaluate the evidence of Slade; secondly, that in view of the previous deposition of William Thomson, the recent statement of James Humphreys should be made available to them; thirdly, the court was told, as bluntly as was constitutionally decent, that it must cross-examine Mathews.

Even before the appeal took place, there was a further intriguing development. James Wilkinson, a fellow prisoner, told McMahon that he knew Mathews; that when he heard about the Luton crime he straightaway connected Mathews with it, because of an earlier conversation with him; and that at that time Mathews himself possessed a red MG sports car. The solicitors took a statement from Wilkinson. They also arranged to bring forward evidence from Roderick Firmstone, Morris Lerman's assistant, to confirm Cooper's original trial alibi.

On 12 July 1976 appeal no. 4 opened before Lord Justice Roskill, Lord Justice Lawton and Mr Justice Wien. The

Crown QC tried to argue once again that Mathews could not be cross-examined, on the basis of the previous 'exceptional case' ruling. Lawton responded, "This is the first time that this Court has twice had a case referred back to it, and you say this is not exceptional?"[4] At long last, Mathews was heard again.

After the week-long hearing, the judges held their fire. Roskill's judgment was finally delivered on 22 July. The judges rejected the evidence of Slade and Wilkinson, argued that Drury had not omitted to put up Mathews for identification for any discreditable reasons, and said that although Murphy's conviction had been quashed, it did not follow that he was innocent.

So far, so bad. Roskill did, however, agree that the convictions had been founded largely on Mathews' evidence. In court, Lawton described part of it as "a cock-and-bull story". Roskill seconded this in his judgment, saying "that he [Mathews] had lied in certain respects is beyond question". If the appellants thought they were home and dry, however, they could not have been more mistaken. "Each of us watched him [Mathews] closely while he was giving his evidence," declared Roskill. "The conclusion each of us independently reached on the vital part of his story was that he was clearly telling the truth . . . we see no justification for disturbing the verdicts which in our view were entirely correct."

Appeal court judges have frequently displayed an ignorance of what goes on in the real world outside and occasionally delivered judgments that defy rational analysis. Never have they made such conspicuous fools of themselves as they did on this occasion.

Objections to the findings of the fourth court are inexhaustible. It is hard to know where to begin. Perhaps the most significant point is that the judgment contradicts common sense. To say that Mathews was telling lies throughout, but that the convictions which rest on his evidence are 'entirely correct' is fatuous. The whole *raison d'être* of the jury system is that a person stands trial before a random selection of the common people who can apply their collective common sense to weigh the evidence for and against. Given the case as it now stood, no one could have believed for a moment that any jury would have brought in a guilty verdict. "To most sensible, rational people a verdict which depends on the evidence of a man like Mathews, in the circumstances in which he gave that evidence, cannot be safe," argued *The Times*.[5] This, for the judges, should have been the crux of the matter.

In assessing Mathews' credibility for themselves, the judges exceeded their constitutional powers. "The judges' job was not to ask themselves whether they believed or disbelieved a particular witness, or other proffered evidence," *The Times* again commented, "but to consider what the jury at the trial, if presented with that evidence, might have done. They effectively imposed their judgment on the value of the new evidence, instead of asking whether the jury might not have come to a different verdict. It is not a technical point. It goes to the root of the English system of criminal justice."[6]

Even if it had been right for the judges to substitute themselves for the jury, they might at least have heard the appellants' evidence also, and tested its veracity. What they had done was akin to convicting a defendant after hearing the prosecution case only: as complete a betrayal of the criminal justice system as is possible to imagine.

But suppose that all of this was somehow in order; that their Lordships had been granted dispensation to overturn centuries-old judicial practice: what on earth were they thinking of to determine that Alfred Mathews carried any credibility at all?

People forced into the position of having to tell a string of lies can, for example, deliver a kind of highly sophisticated circumlocution. This option was not available to Mathews who took refuge in the imprecision of the inarticulate. In the main, he stuck as closely as possible to the bones of his script. However, when required to elaborate on the ancillary details, those minutiae of experience that serve to verify the whole, he was left floundering. Questions were wittingly misunderstood, or responses shrouded in vagueness.

Nevertheless, counsel for Cooper and McMahon, Bryan Capstick QC and David McNeill QC, did manage to elicit a great many points of significance. Mathews' account of his first interview with Drury bore no resemblance to the police record of it. He contradicted himself about his actions following the supposed ejection of McMahon from his car in Luton. At the trial, he said that he tried to make his way back to the scene of the crime (to report what had happened to the police); at the appeal, he said that he drove away from Luton as quickly as possible. He contradicted himself, too, about when he had abandoned his Vauxhall.

The route which Mathews claimed the convoy had taken to the M1 made no sense at all. Confronted with this, he simply stonewalled, and said, "I am not too familiar with north London", a likely story.

He had, so he said, begun to have misgivings about the Luton trip when driving there. Since he was alone in his own car, why had he not simply turned off the M1?

"I am not familiar with the road, I could not say."

Would it matter, counsel pressed, whether or not you were familiar with the road?

"I think it does matter," responded Mathews, "if there are no interceptors and one is in thought. There is a tint on many incidents like that."

At this point, Mathews was really floundering.

McNeill asked him about the fake transfer of ownership of the Vauxhall: "Did your wife complete the form at your dictation?"

"In my detention?" Mathews replied.

For barristers trained to employ *le mot juste*, it was gruelling stuff.

"I have to put this to you," counsel said. "Before you

dumped your own Vauxhall you wiped it clean of finger-prints?"

"No," retorted Mathews. "I had no reason to, I did not do that."

Here, Mathews was in dangerous waters. He was contesting the evidence not of other witnesses, but of forensic science. The car had been carefully wiped clean of finger-prints. Who else but Mathews would possibly have done that? At the trial, moreover, he had referred to McMahon forcing his way into the car, and wiping blood from his hands. The examination of the car revealed this, too, must have been a fabrication.

Let us momentarily put Mathews to one side, and consider the evidence of one independent witness: Herbert Andrews. His presence of mind in taking down the number of Mathews' Vauxhall had led the police straight to the car (and should have led them straight to the gang), despite a small error in his recollection of the registration letters. He was adamant about three aspects of the sports car: that its figures included a '5' and a '1', that its suffix was the letter 'E', and that it had a hard top. None of these corresponded with Cooper's car.

The Crown had relied completely on one part of the evidence of an important, disinterested witness, while rejecting as completely another part. This illogicality was compounded by the fact that the 'hard top' evidence was borne out by other witnesses, such as Donald Leek; and contradicted only by Mathews, whose evidence on this point should have put even more severe strains on judicial credulity. Because he had referred in his original statements to Murphy "jumping into the car", he had no option but to persist with the 'soft top' line. In a faltering attempt to reconcile the disparity, he blithely told the appeal court that, "He [Cooper] must have put one on [i.e. a soft top] on the way or something. But I didn't notice him do it."

And so it went on and on. Cherer and Co. of Clifford's Inn, shorthand writers to the Court, took down reams of barefaced lies.

On one matter, Mathews was unable to give false evidence (though this did not prevent him from trying): his own criminal record. He had been convicted of explosives offences in 1954, and sentenced to eight years in prison; in 1963 he had been sentenced to two five-year, and one two-year, terms, all concurrent, on similar charges. In 1968, he had been put on probation for three years.

Boldly signposted as the issues were, Roskill, Lawton and Wien nevertheless seemed incapable of grasping them. Like Mr Justice Cusack, they seemed to find it "beyond belief" that everything could have been invented. Yet, as *The Times* pointed out, "Mathews had a strong motive to lie, by implicating innocent men, both so that the full story of his own part would not be revealed: and through fear of the consequences if he named the men who were involved."[7]

The cross-examination of Mathews regarding the reward money drew blood. It was alleged that at the same time as paying in his £2,000 reward he had withdrawn money from his account, in order to split the proceeds with Drury. Mathews emphatically denied this – only to learn that the Court was empowered to order the release of the relevant bank statements. These duly revealed that the £2,000 deposit was made at the same time as a £700 withdrawal.[8]

Moreover, Mathews insisted that there was no reward at all: he had received this money merely as compensation for loss of work and inconvenience resulting from his decision to turn QE and the consequent need for a constant police presence. (Yes, that's correct: within two months of effecting a murder which provoked national outrage, he was receiving 24-hours-a-day police protection.)

"I have classed that [the money] as the expenses I lost during the police stay at my house," explained Mathews. "I would not have received this as part of a reward." The judges attributed this attitude to 'vanity'; he could not admit that he had got the money for grassing on his colleagues.

There is an all-too-obvious alternative explanation. It

was not vanity, but self-deceit. Mathews could not bring himself to admit that he had not only incriminated innocent men, but had taken his thirty pieces of silver for doing so.

Nearly two years later, Lord Devlin, one of the most highly regarded legal authorities in the country, made a characteristically incisive intervention into the affair. In a lecture delivered at All Souls College, Oxford, on 2 May 1978 he candidly said that McMahon and Cooper had been betrayed by the legal process. "They have not been convicted by a jury which has heard substantially the whole of the relevant evidence; I also say that just as they have been tried in form only and not in substance, so their appeal has been only in form." Devlin was especially critical of the judgment of the fourth court, and distinguished four grounds on which it had been defective:

(i) in reaching its decision in the way it did, the court had usurped the function which constitutionally belonged to a jury.
(ii) the court had overlooked the requirements of natural justice.
(iii) the decision of the fourth court was inconsistent with that of the second (which had quashed Murphy's conviction).

In the judgment, Lord Roskill said that the judges' decision must depend on the view they took "of the veracity of Mathews' incrimination of the appellants and of Murphy". Here, at least, he was right about something: Mathews' evidence was clearly indivisible. The only respect in which this could have changed would have been if Mathews himself, when appearing before the fourth court, had been able to explain how he could have been mistaken in his identification of Murphy, and yet veracious beyond possibility of error in his identification of Cooper and McMahon.

Mathews, however, made no attempt to distinguish between the identifications. He positively reiterated that

Murphy had been involved, as this extract from the evidence shows:

> "Just so that I can understand what your present position is," began Bryan Capstick, "you are completely wrong, are you, about Mr Murphy?"
>
> "No, I was not wrong," replied Mathews.
>
> "You say he was with you on that day?"
>
> "I say he was with me."
>
> "You had every opportunity to see him?"
>
> "Every opportunity."
>
> "No conceivable question of mistake arises here at all?"
>
> "Regarding who?"
>
> "Murphy."
>
> "No, none whatsoever."

Nothing could have been clearer.

The fourth court was thus saying, Devlin maintained, that the second court had been wrong. He added, "It is not possible to exact public respect for a system of justice which allows life sentences to depend on accidents of this sort."

(iv)   "In pursuing their self-appointed task of assessing the truthfulness of Mathews, [the fourth court] thereby disqualified themselves from the job they should really have been doing.

"What was wanted from the Court of Appeal was not confirmation that Mathews appeared from his demeanour to be a truthful witness. What was wanted was an answer to the question whether, however convincing Mathews might sound, it was safe to act upon the evidence of a habitual liar, who even at the trial had not come clean, who was an accomplice almost uncorroborated, and who had turned Queen's Evidence in the hands of a police officer who was not above suspicion."[9]

*   *   *

The Roskill verdict attracted, as it was bound to do, an almost unanimously hostile reaction. This was of little comfort either to Cooper and McMahon, who remained in prison, or to Roy Jenkins, who had imagined that they would be freed. They petitioned him for mercy; but he felt that as he had invited the Appeal Court to consider the case, he could not now flout its authority by ignoring its verdict and releasing them.

Nor was this the only cul-de-sac. McMahon and Cooper were again refused leave to take their case to the Lords. For good measure, McMahon was also refused permission to take a lie-detector test.

Bryan Magee, still working hard for Cooper, and Dr Oonagh McDonald, Labour MP for Thurrock, who had similarly involved herself on McMahon's behalf, formed a committee in May 1977 in a concerted campaign to achieve justice. Tom Sargant was involved; as were the energetic solicitors of the men. "Even the authorities of the prison in which one of them is held," wrote Marcel Berlins in *The Times*, "have made it clear by their conduct towards him and his family that they regard him as guiltless."[10]

Meanwhile, there had already been two fresh developments, each of them significant.

The police officer "not above suspicion", as Devlin had so scrupulously put it, was, of course, Drury. On 7 July 1977 he was jailed for eight years for corruption.[11] He was thereby conscripted to the ranks of a prison population that included not only Cooper and McMahon, but also John Stonehouse, who had put up that wretched money on behalf of the Post Office. In August 1976 Stonehouse had been sentenced to seven years' imprisonment for a total of eighteen offences, including theft and false pretences.

Drury was the thirteenth senior Metropolitan Police officer to be imprisoned on charges relating to pornography activities in Soho.[12] James Humphreys, who claimed to have had dealings with forty senior Yard officers, said that at one stage he had been paying Drury £100 per week.

Humphreys, extradited from Holland in January 1974, had been sentenced to eight years' imprisonment for wounding. Publicly, he maintained that he had been framed by police in revenge for his part in Drury's downfall.

After Drury's trial and conviction, the Home Secretary, Merlyn Rees, said that Humphreys would be eligible for special remission in view of the evidence he had given against Drury and the others. (Rees had succeeded Jenkins as Home Secretary in September 1976.) On 24 August 1977, seven weeks after the Drury trial, Humphreys was released from prison by the exercise of the Royal prerogative. In a fresh statement, he referred again to Drury's practice of appropriating sums intended as reward money.

At the time of the fourth court, Drury's trial was still pending. Indeed, Roskill and his colleagues had been most solicitous in ensuring that nothing was said which might prejudice it. Now, both due process of law and executive actions had determined that Humphreys was telling the truth.

Then, another alibi witness came forward.

On 10 September 1969 two people acted as bail sureties for McMahon when he attended an afternoon hearing at Thames magistrates court: his father, and Fred Lawrence. After the hearing, they were met by Cooper, accompanied by his dog, in his red Mercedes. He drove them back to the McMahons' home. When they arrived, Lawrence left on his own.

Almost immediately, he encountered an old friend, Richard Hurn. They discussed returning to look at Cooper's car, which at that point was up for sale. Hurn, who wanted to replace his Volvo, had been impressed by it. In the event, they didn't inspect the car, and after chatting, they parted.

Lawrence subsequently served a two-year prison term. He lost touch with Hurn, who had moved out of the district by the time he was released. They did not bump into each other again until February 1977, when, inevitably, they discussed the circumstances of their last meeting. Hurn recalled that after seeing Lawrence that day he had noticed (but not been noticed by) McMahon, who was walking up Kingsland Road in Shoreditch. He remembered the incident, he said, because he had been regretting not pursuing his interest in the car. When he saw McMahon a second time – he mistakenly thought McMahon, not Cooper, owned it – he would have taken the matter up, but his bus arrived.

The story dovetailed with McMahon's trial testimony that at that time he had been walking to his girlfriend's flat. Hurn could not recall the date of the incident, which could be fixed only by cross-reference to Lawrence's testimony.

Wendy Mantle took statements from Hurn and Lawrence, and forwarded them without delay to the Home Office. On 15 December, almost nine months later, Merlyn Rees reached a decision on the matter. As Home Secretary, he could have ordered the Court of Appeal to review the case yet again; or he could have taken the matter into his own hands. He did neither. He merely asked the court *for an opinion on the new evidence*; whether it would "regard itself as required to receive it, if a further appeal was ordered". Considering the tangled history of this case, it was an absurdly abject response.

Replying to Dr McDonald in the Commons, Brynmor John, minister of state, explained that the court had already had four opportunities to study the case: "it would not be right to put it in the position of having to go into the whole matter yet again on the basis of evidence which, at the end of the day, it might feel unable to receive."[13] In this instance the Home Secretary's reference was made under section 17(1)(b) of the 1968 Criminal Appeal Act; all previous references of cases had been under section 17(1)(a).

The matter was determined on 11 April 1978 by Lord Widgery, Lord Justice Eveleigh and Mr Justice Milmo.

The Appeal Court had already made itself a laughing-stock over this case. Could it possibly find new ways of disgracing itself?

The court decided that the proposed alibi evidence "should properly be rejected as not likely to be credible". If received, said Widgery, it would afford no ground for allowing the appeal. The reasons for its verdict are worth quoting:

> The fresh evidence tendered is valueless for the purposes of section 17, unless it tends to show that McMahon was at an inhibiting distance from Luton at the time of the murder. Further, it is now revealed that Lawrence was at the Central Criminal Court during the trial as a potential (though uncalled) alibi witness for McMahon. His two statements are inconsistent with each other as to his means of transport to and from the court. The fresh evidence to which the reference relates does not justify an inference that the events referred to took place on 10 September 1969 . . . It describes in detail events which occurred some years ago. Despite intense efforts to find alibi evidence to support McMahon, the evidence was not previously forthcoming.

The reasoning behind *all* these propositions is faulty.

(i)   The notion that the 5.00 p.m. alibi in the centre of London was "valueless' because it did not show the person to be "at an inhibiting distance' from a 6.00 p.m. date in Luton caused much amused despair among members of McMahon's defence team. What did the Lord Chief Justice imagine? That McMahon could have slipped into a handy telephone kiosk and emerged as Superman, perhaps?

Assuming that the Lord Chief Justice did not entertain this possibility, how was McMahon supposed to cope with London rush-hour traffic and reach Luton in an hour? Had

Lord Widgery ever been introduced to the dubious delights of the North Circular Road?

The journey could not be done now, and it could not have been done then.

(ii)   Lawrence had not been cited as an alibi witness for McMahon at the 1970 trial, but as an alibi witness for Cooper.[14]

This may seem a distinction without a difference, but it is fundamental because, in law, each defendant is entitled to an individual defence.

Moreover, even had the judges been correct in this assumption, it would still have been irrelevant. The point is that Lawrence could not then possibly have been aware of Hurn's evidence. Between April 1977, when Hurn's statement was taken and passed to the authorities, and December, when the Home Secretary acted, this new evidence was examined on behalf of the criminal justice department at the Home Office by the police. Detective Chief Superintendent Roy Ranson of Scotland Yard interviewed Hurn and Lawrence separately. When the judges deliberated, therefore, they had in front of them the testimony of Hurn and Lawrence; and Ranson's evaluation of it as evidence. (Counsel were not on hand to tender advice; section 17(1)(b) permitted the judges to determine the issue in private.)

So it is instructive that Lord Widgery prefaced his erroneous observation on this matter with the phrase "it is now revealed that . . ." Had the judges checked this for themselves, they would immediately have appreciated that nothing of the kind was revealed. They must have been working directly from the police report, which would explain both this gaffe, and the next one.

(iii)   In his first (1969) statement, Lawrence said, accurately, that he had been to court with McMahon three times. In his second (1977) one, just once. Further, he said that they had then gone in the Mercedes, when the journey had been by mini-cab.

Widgery said that the statements were "inconsistent . . .

as to means of transport to and from the court". This is inaccurate. Although Lawrence had overlooked the outward journey by mini-cab, they had indeed returned in the Mercedes. The other disparity is easily reconciled. Of the three trips to the court, only one [10 September 1969] was an *afternoon* visit; so that was clearly the one to which the 1977 statement referred.

The problem with relying on the police to investigate post-trial evidence is that they have, as it were, already entered the lists on the side of the prosecution. The case, from their point of view, has received a satisfactory conclusion. The file is closed. They no more relish reopening it than anyone welcomes the prospect of doing, say, last month's work again. They are, however subconsciously, more concerned with discrediting fresh evidence than examining it impartially. Had the overriding concern here been to establish the truth, then the discrepancies in Lawrence's statement could have been put to him at the time, and he could have explained them there and then.

Instead, they were carefully preserved (and, no doubt, picked out with a highlighter pen). Lawrence did rectify the slips in a brief addendum forwarded through McMahon's solicitors to Scotland Yard, but there is no indication that this was brought to the attention of the judges.

The disparity of treatment accorded by police to potentially 'helpful' and potentially 'unhelpful' witnesses is scandalous. Lawrence was given no opportunity to reflect on a second statement; Mrs Crawley was solicitously guided through fourteen separate ones.

(iv)   The judges said that the new evidence did "not justify an inference' that the events took place on that particular day. This is nonsense: the date was not in dispute. By this time, McMahon, after years of study of his own and other cases, had become a lay authority on the law. He wrote to *The Times* summarising the deficiencies in the findings of the fifth court. With regard to this, he noted that "the facts only allow a choice between whether the events occurred, or whether the parties concerned fabricated them". McMahon made three appearances at Thames magistrates court, only one of which was in the afternoon. "This is a matter of public record," wrote McMahon, "not the partisan memory of sympathetic witnesses."[15]

(v) No doubt, though, many accepted the logic of the final point: that evidence materialising so belatedly could hardly be accepted at face-value.

But why not? The circumstances were fully explained by Hurn and Lawrence. No one was able to contradict them. The incident, anyway, was quite plausible. Hurn had confused the ownership of the car; perfectly understandable, since Cooper's car was parked outside McMahon's house. He produced documentation relating to the subsequent sale of his Volvo.

There was a simple explanation as to why Hurn had not previously come to McMahon's aid. He did not interest himself in news events, and knew nothing of the Luton murder case. Even if he had read the reports, he would not have been able to identify McMahon whom he knew only as 'Mackie'.

No single aspect of this fifth-court judgment bore close scrutiny. But even this has not exhausted the unfairness of it. Lord Devlin pointed out that the judgment of the fourth court, Lord Roskill's, contradicted that of the second, Lord Widgery's. For Roskill to be contradicting Widgery was one thing; what the judgment of the fifth court represented was Widgery contradicting Widgery.

The opening point was the "inhibiting distance" one. In 1973, Terence Edwards had alibied Patrick Murphy in Hackney for about 4.30 that afternoon, some thirty minutes earlier than Hurn's alibi for McMahon. In giving judgment on that occasion, Widgery had said, "Although he [Murphy] might conceivably have got to Luton by 6 o'clock, it is quite clear that he was not taking part in the procedure prior to the events . . . for Murphy to be in Hackney at 4.30 or thereabouts was something inconsistent

with the general history of the matter as spoken to by
Mathews."

According to the Lord Chief Justice, the self-same
grounds on which he had upheld an appeal in 1973 were
"valueless" in 1978.

The subsequent intervention of Lord Devlin (see p. 148)
put fresh heart into the Free McMahon/Cooper Campaign
committee. The Home Secretary, however, was unmoved
by the mounting public and parliamentary disquiet. Wendy
Mantle recalled, "I used to get furious with Merlyn Rees'
sheer paralysis over this case." Magee told him bluntly in
the Commons, "The case will not lie down or go away. It
will not stop being a focus of public attention until the two
men are released."

On 26 June 1980 a book entitled *Wicked Beyond Belief*
was published. It contained brief contributions from some
of those closely identified with the long campaign – Lord
Devlin, Tom Sargant, MPs Magee and McDonald, and
solicitors Mantle and Peirce – and the central narrative
was constructed around two lengthy manuscripts independently written by McMahon and Cooper. On these
grounds, the man whose book it actually was – Ludovic
Kennedy – generously ascribed to himself no more than
the role of editor. I intend him no discourtesy in asserting
that the book's most resonant passage flowed from the pen
of Lord Devlin:

> There are occasions, however rare, in all our affairs,
> legal, political or domestic, when things get into such
> a tangle, when the disentangling would take so long
> and cause so much additional misery that the only
> decent and humane thing to do is to cut the knot. We
> have here a prosecution which has been dogged by
> misfortune, a witness upon whom almost all depends
> and whom no court can feel to be generally reliable,
> a police officer who turns out to be a lamentable

exception to his calling, an unprecedented series of
references by the Home Secretary. Doubts do not just
lurk; from the first they have flown about the case like
bats in a belfry.

If the Home Secretary cuts the knot, I do not believe
that there is a voice in England that would be raised
in protest.[16]

The knot, at last, was cut. With dramatic suddenness,
Cooper and McMahon were released from prison on 18
July 1980. The Home Secretary, William Whitelaw, had
asked the Queen to remit the remainder of their sentences.
"This morning I was serving a life sentence with a rec-
ommendation of 20 years," McMahon told the press later
that day. "Now I am free." There was not a voice in
England raised in protest.

In the Commons, Whitelaw explained the reasoning
behind the decision. "I have now considered all the aspects
of the case and I have had the benefit of the views of
the Lord Chief Justice [Lord Lane]. The case is wholly
exceptional and I judge that there is a widely felt sense of
unease about it. I share that unease.

"I have concluded that in view of my responsibility for
the maintenance of public confidence in our system of
criminal justice the matter should now be resolved."

Whitelaw said that the Lord Chief Justice agreed with
him that the history of the case now put it into a category
of its own. It was therefore appropriate that it should be
settled outside the usual system. His action was not to be
taken as a precedent. Crucially, however, he stressed that
his intervention did not imply that he was satisfied that the
men were innocent.

So what on earth did it imply? As Ludovic Kennedy
remarked, "You can't keep men in prison for ten and a
half years and then simply say maybe you have made a
mistake and let them go." McMahon, no stranger to the
correspondence columns of *The Times*, penned another
letter. Was it fair, he asked, that he and Cooper "should

live the rest of our lives with this cloud of doubt hanging over us?"[17]

The Times itself failed to fathom the logic in Whitelaw's action. "If the men are guilty of what was a most brutal murder, then they have not served enough time in prison. If they are innocent they should not have served any time there at all. The Home Secretary can be interpreted as saying that because he is not sure whether or not they are guilty, he is willing to split the difference. That is offensive to the English concept of justice."[18]

Clearly, if the jury had felt the "unease" which now troubled Whitelaw, there would have been no conviction in the first place.

The anomaly was crystallised in the fact that no conditions were attached to the release of the two men. All prisoners released from life sentences, irrespective of the duration of their imprisonment, are automatically on licence for the rest of their lives. Cooper and McMahon, uniquely, were not.

In the weeks following their release, they spoke with some intensity of their commitment to ensuring that the whole matter was satisfactorily resolved – whether by the setting up of a public inquiry, or some other means. However, they found themselves up against an intractable problem: fighting a current injustice is difficult enough; fighting a retrospective one is almost impossible. In order to forestall further developments, the bureaucracy can call upon inexhaustible reserves of lethargy. The further into the past a matter recedes, the less reason there is ever to do anything about it. Cooper and McMahon found that many supporters, thinking a job half-done better than one not done at all, drifted away. It goes without saying that they had no financial resources of their own to conduct a campaign.

They marked the first anniversary of their release with a small demonstration; they climbed scaffolding outside the House of Commons. This attempt to re-engage public sympathies for their cause failed on two counts. The publicity was considerably less than they had hoped; and they were both charged with assaulting a policeman, which they vigorously denied.

They were convicted of the offence at a magistrates court, and given three-month suspended sentences. On appeal, the case went to Knightsbridge crown court, where the convictions were quashed. The two men derived some small satisfaction from the fact that the testimony of five policemen was set aside in favour of their own.

Three men stuck honourably to the pursuit of justice: Ludovic Kennedy, Roy Jenkins and Bryan Magee. In 1983 they approached the Home Secretary, Leon Brittan, who seemed sympathetic and suggested that redress was perhaps possible if something new emerged.

Remote as this prospect must have seemed – fourteen years after the event – there was a fresh development. Out of the blue, Kennedy was contacted by Thomas Weyers, who indicated that he wished to retract the evidence he had given at the trial. He had, he said, perjured himself under police pressure. Kennedy did not view this as especially encouraging; Weyers had never been a satisfactory witness. However, in view of Brittan's interest, he deemed it worth pursuing. Weyers made a statement to Kennedy's solicitors.

Subsequently, the recidivist Weyers was re-arrested. Charges against him were dropped; but Weyers now retracted his retraction, claiming that Kennedy had obtained it from him under duress. Even in the context of the falsehoods that had bedevilled this case, this accusation was outrageous.

Then, on 29 May 1985, Terence Langston made a fresh statement. According to this, Michael Good had said to him, "You know I was on it. Keep your mouth shut."

Wendy Mantle forwarded this to the Home Office. The immediate response at least had the merit of surprise: an official telephoned to say they were not familiar with the case.

*   *   *

As I indicated at the outset, the Luton post-office murder was so straightforward it was dull. The fascination that surrounds it concerns not the crime itself, but the official reaction to it. Why did the police never prosecute those responsible? And why did the Appeal Court refuse to concede, in the face of an Everest of evidence, that two of those convicted could not have been culpable?

To tackle the questions in reverse order:

One factor which apparently troubled the appeal judges was how on earth could Mathews possibly incriminate three totally innocent men; how could he conceivably have known that they did not have cast-iron alibis? The answer is that the alibis had been checked out long before charges were laid. McMahon was surprised, one afternoon in October 1969, to receive a visit from Michael Good, whom he hardly knew. Good informed him that they were both suspects in the Luton case. McMahon told him what he had been doing that day. In retrospect, McMahon believed that the sole purpose of Good's visit had been to ensure that he, McMahon, could be 'fitted up'. Good certainly was a police informer, and would have been able to take back to Drury the welcome news that McMahon had only a 'family' alibi.

Why would Drury have wanted to do this? One theory is that he had set up the Luton post-office job. On one occasion, James Humphreys dropped the very large hint that Mathews was "instructed to organise the raid". In the House of Commons, Dr Oonagh McDonald elaborated on this. "There is evidence that at least one senior officer, and possibly more, in the Flying Squad was actively involved with top criminals. They set up and staged robberies and other crimes. The police arrested the petty criminals involved; and the others were allowed to escape and the proceeds were shared between the criminals and the police."[19]

This interpretation is credible. The would-be robbery was well timed; the post-office was certainly worth robbing.

This suggests inside information of some sort. Yet nothing about this was ever said at the trial.

It is simply not possible to believe, from the way the investigation was carried out, that the police were genuinely looking for those responsible. Alfred Mathews owned the car, and Michael Good the gun, used in the robbery. From the outset, they would have been the prime suspects. Yet, as Stephen Murphy later discovered, residents in the block of flats where Mathews lived were never interviewed about his movements on that day.

The case of Michael Good is even more extraordinary. Not merely were no inquiries carried out with regard to him; but there seems to have been a concerted effort to create the impression that he was in prison at the time of the crime. For years afterwards, this is what most of those involved in the case believed. In February 1971 the first Appeal Court described him, at the time of the crime, as "a man serving seven years for robbery". Apparently, this was said in all good faith; but it was untrue.

According to Langston's 1985 statement, Good admitted his involvement. Langston, somewhat surprised, then said to him, "How come you were in on it? You were inside at the time." Good retorted, "That's what every cunt thought."

Had the investigation been properly conducted, forensic science should have provided the police with the bulk of their evidence: they had the abandoned van, the gun, the hold-all, as well as Mathews' hat and spectacles. They would have had complete sets of fingerprints of Mathews and Good on file. Yet no forensic evidence at all was produced at the trial (except an abandoned pillow-case, which presumably had nothing to do with the crime).

The police knew that Mathews' 'parcels story' was a complete fabrication. Would a gang of hardened, serious criminals – like post-office robbers – take a complete stranger along with them just for the ride? The police had unique experience of the mentality of criminals. They could never have believed this.

According to the 'parcels story', McMahon did three things after the crime had been committed: he put on a particularly vivid boilersuit, saying, as he did so, "I've got blood all over me"; he forced his way into Mathews' car; and he left it a short time later while they were still in Luton.

So: a murder had been committed; a man in conspicuous blue clothing was wandering the streets, a long way from home. The police never attempted to establish where in Luton McMahon left Mathews' car, and carried out no house-to-house interviews with regard to this incident, an indication that they knew it had never happened.

There can be only one reason why the police in charge of the investigation were willing to go along with a palpably bogus story: they themselves had as much to hide as the men who had been involved in the planned robbery. When it went so disastrously, so publicly wrong, it became necessary to find complete outsiders to carry the can. Once it is realised that the 'parcels story' was a joint conspiracy between Drury and Mathews, it becomes easier to understand why the latter was able to sustain it, to the limited extent that he could, for so long.

Cooper and McMahon fared as they did because they had become pawns in a power struggle between the executive and the judiciary. "The appeal court judges regarded it as an impertinence that the case kept being brought before them," said Gareth Peirce, "and so were determined to resist it."

Whether the judges had some inkling of the Pandora's box that would be opened if the appeals were upheld, one can only speculate. Certainly, the entire case stains the popular perception of the scrupulous fairness of British justice more thoroughly than any other. (At least in the Birmingham pub-bombs case the police did not arrange for the real bombers to be financially rewarded.)

Consider, again, the position of Michael Good. On 24 October 1969, shortly after the Luton crime, he received a seven-year sentence for a post-office robbery. When the

Luton case was heard, he gave evidence for the prosecution. His own robbery offence then went to appeal before Lord Justice Fenton Atkinson, Mr Justice Lawton (as he then was) and Mr Justice Geoffrey Lane (as *he* then was). The conviction was quashed.

Consider the experience of Thomas Weyers. At the Cooper–McMahon trial, he gave evidence for the prosecution. On 29 May 1970, his own case went to appeal before Lord Justice Phillimore, Mr Justice O'Connor and, again, Mr Justice Geoffrey Lane. A thirty-three-month term of imprisonment was reduced to eighteen months.

It seems, as they say, a rum business.

What should never be forgotten is that, as a society, we continue to countenance this absurd perversion of the judicial system. Through no fault of their own, Cooper and McMahon have lost over ten years; years when they should have been shaping their lives. When McMahon was first arrested, his girlfriend Sue (who is today his wife) was three months pregnant. She lost that child. She and McMahon finally started their family in 1982 when their son was born. John Disher, as Cooper is once again known, is a less naturally resilient character than McMahon, and has suffered great hardship trying to put his life back together.

Both are determined that, one day, they should establish their innocence once and for all – not just with the ordinary people of this country (they have already more than adequately achieved that), but with its governing authorities. It is the very least they are owed.

Eight

Elizabeth Thompson

People in the case

Peter Stanswood — murder victim
Elizabeth Thompson } __ jointly charged with murder of
Joseph 'Ken' Fromant }   Stanswood
Heather Pridham — wife of Peter Stanswood
Ken Thompson — husband of Elizabeth Thompson
Mr Justice Talbot — judge
Arthur Gavin — brother-in-law and work-mate of Fromant
Barbara McLaren — friend of Heather Pridham
Iris Smith }
Isobel Morgan } — work-mates of Elizabeth Thompson
Beryl Ford — friend of Elizabeth Thompson
John Platts-Mills QC }
Ian Peddie } — counsel for Elizabeth Thompson
Ian Lloyd — MP for Havant

On 5 November 1971 the body of Peter Stanswood was discovered in the front passenger seat of his own Austin 1800 car, parked by the side of Purbrook Heath, north of Portsmouth. He had been stabbed several times, and had died the previous evening, probably some time after 10.00 p.m.

The Hampshire police launched a massive murder hunt. Twenty thousand interviews, 2,500 statements and over three and a half years later, Heather Pridham and Joseph Fromant were jointly charged with the murder.

Pridham, otherwise Mrs Stanswood, was the dead man's widow. The marriage had been in difficulties for some time. Stanswood, who worked in Portsmouth and also operated a beach concession on the Isle of Wight, was a notorious womaniser. Apart from the two children born to Heather and himself, he had also fathered at least two illegitimate children – to different mothers – and a third was born within weeks of his murder. He had had countless affairs, and in November 1971 was regularly seeing at least two other women.

Pridham never concealed her antipathy towards him. Only the weekend before his death, Stanswood had persuaded his wife and children to leave the house on the pretext of his doing some building alterations. When they returned, after having stayed at the home of a friend, Elizabeth Thompson, in Waterlooville, Pridham discovered no sign of any construction work, but obvious tell-tale signs (including stained bed-linen) to indicate that Stanswood had spent the weekend there with one of his mistresses.

Not that Pridham didn't enjoy extra-marital affairs of her own. When, following the murder of her husband, the police asked for the identities of her lovers, she supplied them with a dozen names.

One of those was Joseph Fromant, usually called Ken. He was one of a team who had been working in the area for some time, converting homes to natural gas.

A great deal of blood had been spilt in Stanswood's car – most of it the victim's own. Blood of a different, and particularly rare type, was found over both front seats, and on the hilt and handle of the murder knife, which had been left protruding from the body. Fromant's blood belonged to the same rare group.

The police were in due course acquainted with other seemingly relevant factors. The affair between Pridham and Fromant had been serious in the months prior to the murder. Although Pridham had always ruled out a divorce on the grounds that her standard of living would fall, she expected to benefit substantially from her husband's death through a number of life insurance policies. Stanswood, while sitting in the driver's seat of his car, was stabbed in the back, suggesting that his attackers were known to him.

Pridham and Fromant were charged on 19 May 1975 with Stanswood's murder and remanded in custody.

Out of the blue, on 9 July, Pridham made a statement implicating Elizabeth Thompson, known to her friends as Lizzie. Her husband, also named Ken, worked with Stanswood on the Isle of Wight from 1969 to 1971. The two women had been close friends since 1955.

At committal proceedings on 14 July, Fromant was sent for trial, but Pridham was discharged when the magistrates ruled there was no case for her to answer. During the course of the hearing, the prosecution stated that, despite the statement on 9 July, there was insufficient evidence to bring any charges against Thompson.

Pridham quickly made good this deficiency with a second, more detailed statement on 25 July. On the basis of what she said Thompson was arrested on 5 August and charged with murder. At the time of the second statement the Crown had been deliberating whether to take out a voluntary bill of indictment against Pridham, which would have had the effect of annulling the magistrates' decision. Now, a bill of indictment was instead taken out against Thompson, so that she could be jointly charged with Fromant.

The trial opened at Winchester crown court on 21 October, before Mr Justice Talbot, who rejected applications from counsel for each of the defendants that they should be tried separately.

Much of the background to the case concerned the carnal appetites of a clique of women from the Portsmouth area, and their entanglements with the natural-gas men. In newspaper terms, it was sensational. With the lure of so much sex and violence, could the *News of the World* be far away? Hardly. An acquittal was anticipated, and the Sunday newspaper had laid on champagne, a limousine and a hotel-room in the hope of inducing Lizzie Thompson to tell her story.

There was, however, no acquittal. After a lengthy and complicated trial, the jury retired at 10.27 on the morning of Friday 14 November 1975. They returned at 5.35 to find both defendants guilty of murder. Fromant was convicted on a majority verdict of ten to two; the verdict against Thompson was unanimous. Both were sentenced to life imprisonment.

The case was unusual, not least for the lengthy delay in bringing any charges, when almost from the outset the police appeared to have sufficient forensic and circumstantial evidence to form the bones of a strong prosecution case. Another oddity was that the woman originally charged with the crime should have emerged as the chief prosecution witness.

The bulk of Pridham's evidence against Thompson, virtually all of which Thompson contested, consisted of conversations between the two women in which Thompson allegedly described in detail the sequence of events before and after the murder. Pridham recounted that she and Fromant had been lovers throughout the previous summer, and had regularly made up a foursome with Thompson and Arthur Gavin, who was Fromant's brother-in-law and another member of the natural-gas crew.

At a pub on Priddy's Hard in Gosport, Thompson said that somebody should push Stanswood over a cliff, and that she knew someone who would do it for £1,000. Thompson and Fromant had each asked Pridham if she really wanted her husband dead, and she had replied that she did. After that, Fromant had insisted that he would do it, and then on Tuesday 2 November, Thompson had rung to say, "We are going to do it on Thursday." Pridham said she then deliberately made an alibi for herself by arranging to take her two children to the cinema.

After the murder, Thompson had instructed Pridham to say nothing, but had admonished her for including Fromant's name on the list of lovers she had handed to the police. Subsequently, Thompson advised Pridham to get rid of a pair of earrings which Fromant had sent her as a present from Spain.

Thompson's QC, John Platts-Mills, did not dispute the details, but argued that the roles had been reversed, and that the reason Pridham was able to relate so much about the circumstances of the murder was because it was *she* who had acted in concert with Fromant.

Elizabeth Thompson testified that she had known Fromant since the previous winter. He had originally had an affair with another woman, Beryl Ford, before becoming involved with Pridham. On the evening before the murder, Wednesday 3 November, he had arrived at Thompson's house at about 8.30 p.m., and forced his company upon her and her visitors, the Sansburys, to their embarrassment, so that they departed. Fromant then seduced Thompson and stayed the night with her. He had never previously made advances and, in the light of what followed, she felt that he had probably been trying to establish an alibi for the night of the murder (when he was going to pretend that he had been at Thompson's house all evening).

On Thursday 4 November Thompson stayed at home with her three children (all boys – Martin, Gary and David;

a girl, Rachel, was born to her and Peter Jackson in 1974).
She had gone to bed when Heather Pridham and Fromant
called at about 11.15. Pridham said merely that they had
been to the pictures. They asked to use the bathroom, and
also asked if Fromant could stay the night. Thompson
assumed this must be because Stanswood was at home.
She put Fromant up – although nothing happened between
them – and he left the following morning.

At that time, Thompson was employed potato-picking.
As a large field had been virtually cleared the previous
day, she had been given the Friday off. While she was out
shopping she was told of Stanswood's murder. Thinking
Fromant and Pridham to have been involved, she resolved
to say nothing of their late-night visit the previous evening.
She also concealed the exact nature of their relationship
from the police. Nevertheless, she refused Pridham's request to say that Fromant had been with her throughout.

Heather Pridham's evidence formed the bulwark of the
prosecution case. She admitted that she "disliked her
husband to the point of hatred", and also agreed that her
sole motive in mentioning Thompson had been to extricate
herself from a murder charge. Prior to 9 July 1975 she had
made sixty separate statements to the police; in none of
these had she implicated Thompson.

Her story was considerably knocked about in cross-
examination. In particular, in a passage of some confusion
since she twice collapsed in the witness-box, Pridham
admitted that it was she who first thought of pushing her
husband over a cliff, when she was walking alone down by
the cliffs on the Isle of Wight. She then conceded that what
Thompson actually said was, "It's entered Heather's head
– pushing Pete off a cliff."

She contradicted herself over whether or not she and
her husband had planned a divorce; whether her husband
was involved in drug trafficking; and when she first met
Fromant.

She also suggested that Thompson wanted to make
contact with Fromant after the murder, and to do so invited

Pridham to write a card on her behalf asking him to telephone a friend's home number. Thompson denied this, and Pridham failed adequately to explain why, if what she said were true, the card was signed "Fred", a nickname she herself used, and why it was she who took the call anyway.

In yet another example of Pridham's apparently attributing her own behaviour to Thompson, she said that the latter was unwell during Christmas 1971. This suggestion was particularly forcefully rebutted by Thompson herself and other witnesses, who all recalled that it was Pridham who had been ill.

Having once implicated Thompson, Pridham embellished her story on each occasion she was asked to recount it. Her statement of 25 July was more damaging than that of 9 July. In a subsequent statement, there were at least six fresh references to Thompson, all incriminating. Further embellishments were added in her trial testimony.

Pridham also had problems with her cinema alibi for 4 November. Although the plans had apparently been carefully laid, it crumbled the instant it was examined. In an attempt to discover witnesses, the police twice ran appeals on local television. No one came forward who was able to say that Pridham had been at the cinema with her children on that evening, despite the fact that, according to her story, she was standing in a queue for forty minutes.

Further, Pridham, in her various statements, had consistently given different times of departure from her house to the cinema. The day afterwards, she had told the police she left at 7.00. At the trial, she said it had been 6.35. (The programme began at 7.30, and the only bus which could have got her there in time left at 6.40.) However, there were witnesses who claimed to have heard Pridham calling her children after 7.00. Pridham's neighbours also gave evidence, but were able to say only that the house had been in darkness at 8.00 and that they had heard the children at 11.00.

There was another difficulty with the alibi. A week before the murder, Pridham had arranged to take her children to visit a friend, Barbara McLaren, on 4 November. The day before, however, McLaren had rung to cancel the visit because there was a special film she wanted her children to see. Pridham said she too would take her children to the cinema. This exchange conflicts with her earlier evidence (that Thompson had rung on the Tuesday to tell her of the murder plans, and she had then arranged to go to the cinema). In all this, Pridham's own children were unable to be of assistance. For the duration of the legal proceedings, they stayed with relatives in Canada.

Supporting prosecution evidence came from girls with whom Thompson had worked in a local parachute factory, to the effect that a conversation had taken place about murdering one's husband; but at the trial it was conceded that the conversation was a light-hearted one. Two of the girls, Iris Smith and Isobel Morgan, originally stated that Thompson wanted to withhold this conversation from the police. In cross-examination, however, both agreed that it was Isobel Morgan who recommended doing so.

Further damaging testimony came from Arthur Gavin, although his evidence, consisting of conversations between himself and Fromant, was theoretically inadmissible against Thompson. Although the judge did make this clear to the jury, it is hard to see how they could have blocked it from their minds. Gavin related a pub conversation in which Thompson had referred to "pushing Stanswood off a cliff". Thompson admitted making the remark, but always maintained that she had merely been repeating what Pridham had said to her. Gavin also reported that Fromant had said to him, "You must have thought it was my fault, but you should have seen Liz that night." However, when Fromant finally gave his version of events, there was no point at which he had seen Thompson attacking Stanswood.

In any case, Gavin was hardly a reliable witness. At the trial, he said that Thompson had not mentioned the murder to him when he had seen her on 5 November. However, he conceded in cross-examination that he had made a statement to police on 12 December 1971 in which he stated that he knew of the murder because Thompson had told him about it on 5 November.

Once the judge had ordered that the co-defendants should be tried together, Fromant could not be called as a prosecution witness. Thompson's defence lawyers were not aware of the nature of his testimony until the evening before he delivered it, and were therefore unable to cross-examine prosecution witnesses about it.

In his evidence Fromant revealed that he had been present when the murder occurred. He said that he had been with Thompson on a number of previous evenings. On that Thursday he drove to her house in a grey Ford Anglia at 8.45 p.m. She told him she had arranged to go out, but he drove her over to Purbrook Heath at about 10.00 p.m. *En route*, Thompson made a call from a telephone kiosk. Stanswood subsequently arrived, and Thompson went to his car while he, Fromant, stayed in the Anglia. Suddenly, he noticed flailing arms and, thinking perhaps that Stanswood was attacking Thompson, went over. As he put his arm through an open window, it was slashed. He saw a man slumped in the driver's seat, with Thompson kneeling beside him. He then realised that she had been stabbing Stanswood, so he pulled him across to the passenger seat in order to drive him to hospital. Stanswood, however, was already dead. He and Thompson then returned to her house, where she stitched his arm. The next morning, they disposed of their clothing in a laundry-bag, dropping it into the Solent off Southsea. To try to obliterate the cut on his arm, Fromant burned it with a heated screwdriver.

The prosecution had maintained throughout that Thompson had lured Stanswood to the heath, where Fromant had stabbed him. In the context of the trial, therefore, Fromant's story was a maverick one, unsupported by any evidence. The police discovered no one who had seen

Fromant's grey Ford Anglia, a distinctively shaped model because of its inwardly sloping back window, parked outside Thompson's house that evening between 8.45 and 10.00. By contrast, two witnesses gave evidence of having seen a Ford Anglia parked at Purbrook Heath at 8.45 and again at 10.00, when one of them saw a man standing beside it.

Mrs Thompson's eldest son confirmed that no one had called at the house before 10.00. This evidence was corroborated by a near neighbour who had helped Thompson's sons with their bonfire preparations for the following evening.

Similarly, the telephone call which Fromant alleged that Thompson made never happened, because Stanswood's movements between 9.45 and 10.15 that evening were fully accounted for, and he had not taken a call during that period. Fromant also said that he sustained the wound to his left forearm trying to intervene in the struggle between Thompson and Stanswood. Given the position of the wound, this seemed most unlikely. Nor was there any sign of any struggle in the car having occurred.

While those elements in Fromant's story were contradicted by other evidence, the kernel of it was contradicted by logic. Stanswood received seven wounds. Any one of six would have been potentially fatal. The wounds were appoximately 5″ deep, and the blade of the knife was 5⅝″ long. When the knife was removed from the body, it was found to be bent and broken at the hilt, such had been the force of the attack. There were no defensive marks on the body. Stanswood stood over 6′ and weighed 13 stone; Thompson was 5′4″ and weighed 8 stone.

The notion that she could have inflicted wounds of such severity on such a man is patently absurd. Yet that is presumably exactly what at least two members of the jury, who found Thompson guilty but not Fromant, must have believed. In such circumstances, one is bound to say that the verdict of this jury was not merely unsafe and unsatisfactory, but positively perverse.

Even apart from all this, one outstanding mystery remains: what possible motive could Elizabeth Thompson have had for wanting to kill Peter Stanswood? The prosecution inferred that she hated him for enticing her husband away from the marital home to enjoy the rich pickings of summer seasons on the Isle of Wight. The defence, however, was able to show that, while Ken Thompson's lengthy absences undoubtedly precipitated the breakdown of the marriage, there were no hard feelings. Elizabeth Thompson herself was completely reconciled to it and, after all, had custody of the children.

Thompson's main concern seems to have been that her husband should keep up his maintenance payments for their children. The defence produced evidence to show that Stanswood had actually intervened on her behalf to ensure the continuation of the payments – thereby providing a reason for Thompson to feel gratitude; certainly not enmity.

An alternative prosecution theory was that Stanswood had once tried to rape Thompson. This was really clutching at straws. The incident had occurred years earlier, probably in 1965. Stanswood had apparently been drunk at the time, and in no state to press his advances on Thompson, who simply left him to sleep it off.

On the other hand, Heather Pridham had abundant good reasons for wishing her husband dead – her animosity towards him, and the fact that she stood to gain financially from his death. As it happened, Stanswood had cancelled the largest of his life insurance policies just three days before he died. Even so, his widow received just over £4,000 from insurance claims, and a further £12,000 from the Criminal Injuries Compensation Board. Once Thompson's appeal was dismissed she received a much larger amount, as well as two further lump sums which were put in trust for each of her children.

Also, Stanswood had just resumed living at his home and so Pridham, not wishing to give him grounds for divorce, had had to ask Fromant to stop seeing her. The defence was able to call witnesses who testified that Pridham had said that she wanted her husband dead; and two pointed out that after the murder she had boasted that she had "got rid of one man and it won't be hard to get rid of another".

Similarly, Fromant was in a position to benefit – not only in his liaison with Pridham, but also because he hoped to take over the lucrative beach concession. According to Gavin's evidence (on which, admittedly, weight should not necessarily be placed), Fromant told him that "the reason it was done was because of the concessions on the island"; and had added, in further explanation of why he had done it, "I suppose I love Heather."

Fromant also had a previous conviction for violence, having been sentenced in May 1950 to five years' imprisonment – a stiff penalty for the period – for wounding with intent and possessing firearms.

Since Fromant had been so obviously involved in the crime, Elizabeth Thompson was gravely prejudiced by the refusal of the judge to grant her counsel's application for the trials to be heard separately. For what was the exact evidence against her? None, whether forensic or otherwise, linked her with the scene of the crime, the murder weapon, the car used in the crime, the body of the victim or the disposal of the clothes worn by the murderer. Apart from Fromant's evidence (which should not have weighed against her, since he was not a prosecution witness – though clearly it did), Thompson was convicted on the uncorroborated individual testimonies of Pridham and Gavin. Yet, their evidence was discredited to a greater or lesser extent.

On the other hand, Thompson's evidence had been generally reliable and consistent throughout – though with a number of important exceptions.

In four main areas Thompson had, during the course of the inquiry, lied to the police. She had disclaimed all knowledge of the Priddy's Hard outings. "The reason that I denied that I had been there for so long," she explained, "was that the others were telling the police in effect that at Priddy's Hard I had suggested the murder. I was therefore frightened to admit even that I had been there."

She did equivocate about her own relationship with Fromant and had, strangely, exaggerated the extent of her intimacy with him. "I kept saying I had only had intercourse once, and then I thought that if I said I had had an affair with Fromant, I could cover for Beryl Ford" (whose husband was unaware of his wife's impropriety). However ingenuous Thompson's reactions in this regard, they are self-evidently those of an innocent person. No woman who had carried out a murder with a man would deliberately over-emphasise her relationship with him.

She perpetrated her other lies in covering up for Heather Pridham. "Heather used to ask me to promise not to say anything about her affair with Ken Fromant and I never did, for the reason being that she had asked me not to." It was not until the time of the trial that Thompson disclosed the information about Pridham and Fromant calling at her house on the night of the murder. This too she had withheld out of loyalty to her friend – a loyalty that, tragically, was reciprocated not one whit.

No doubt Elizabeth Thompson was what a character like Philip Marlowe would have described unsympathetically as a sap. Nevertheless it should not be the business of the English judicial process to commit such people to life imprisonment. The murder of Peter Stanswood has many of the elements of the *crime passionnel*; it could have been scripted by Emile Zola. All the more baffling, therefore, that a jury should have deemed culpable a man and a woman between whom no liaison existed. If it had, then the couple would have had no conceivable motive in doing away with the victim.

Elizabeth Thompson was not the only one in court stunned by the foreman's announcement of the verdict against her. The judge, too – I have it on good authority – had anticipated a not-guilty verdict, and was astounded. John Platts-Mills QC and Ian Peddie, who had represented her, were particularly grieved by the outcome. "It was the worst few minutes of my career at the Bar," recalled Peddie. "We were all shell-shocked because we had expected there to be an acquittal.

"This was clearly a travesty of justice. We were determined to try to do all we could to reverse it – but we also knew that the judge had given an impeccable summing-up, so that it would be almost impossible to upset on appeal. Lizzie Thompson was terribly, terribly distressed, and all that we could say to her were, frankly, platitudes because we knew that it was unlikely that we could successfully assist her case. We were, nevertheless, determined to do all that we could."

Unusually, therefore, both defence counsel continued to be involved with the case for years afterwards. Peddie drew up very cogent grounds for an appeal, which was heard on 18 March 1977 before Lord Justice Orr, Lord Justice Waller and Mr Justice Griffiths.

Lord Justice Orr, who delivered the judgment, rejected the argument that the judge erred in ruling that the co-defendants should stand trial together: "the interests of justice required that the two accused should be tried together". He also averred that Heather Pridham's testimony had not been greatly damaged in cross-examination, and further that whether or not they considered it to have been was virtually irrelevant anyway: "in our judgment it was for the jury to decide what evidence they considered to have been discredited". Clearly, the jury must have found it credible, argued the appeal judges, just as they must have decided that Thompson would have been better able than Pridham to entice Stanswood to the scene of his death.

This point cannot be roundly repudiated, but it seems so vague, so unprovable that it was hardly worth mentioning at all. The fact that it was raised says far more about the operations of the Court of Appeal than it does about who murdered Peter Stanswood. The court is virtually bound by a jury decision even when, as in this case, it was manifestly wrong. Accordingly, it is characteristic of judgments that isolated factors which might buttress the original verdict are given additional weight; whereas countless others which, either independently or cumulatively, impugn it are conveniently overlooked.

So it was as Platts-Mills and Peddie had feared. The court rejected Thompson's application.

Counsel tried to build up a case for an appeal to the House of Lords. There was, for example, some discussion over whether Fromant's remarkable evidence should have been the subject of a specific warning to the jury. However, the judge could not have done this without prejudicing Fromant's own case. He, too, was innocent until proved guilty. The fact that two jurors seemed to have been taken in by his story was merely unfortunate.

Accordingly, counsel concluded with regret that there were no grounds for making an appeal to the Lords.

In the absence of redress through legal channels, Platts-Mills and Peddie turned to political ones which were to prove no more efficacious. Thompson's MP, Ian Lloyd, was contacted. Unhappily, because of a misunderstanding between him and the solicitors, he approached the Home Secretary, Merlyn Rees, prematurely, before he, Lloyd, had fully appraised Mrs Thompson's case. The Home Office replied in January 1978 to Lloyd's letter of December 1977, assuring him that there were no grounds for reopening the case.

Platts-Mills and Peddie button-holed Lloyd again, to impress upon him the need for a further initiative, one that would be done properly this time. A detailed, thoroughly professional petition was drawn up, and was lodged with the Home Secretary in June 1979. Platts-Mills, pointing out that as a QC who'd been involved in the criminal law for the past twenty years he was not exactly lacking in experience of murder trials, had appended a personal note. "It is not usually very helpful for Counsel to express a personal opinion about a case in which he is concerned," he wrote, "his job being to give a professional view of matters of fact or law that may arise. In this case, I am going to take that unusual course. I formed the opinion throughout, and continue to hold it, that Mrs Thompson was not present at all and knew nothing of the murder until afterwards; that she had no motive for taking any part, and took no part, and is entirely innocent."

The Home Office did not respond for some time. Then, in March 1980, the two barristers were invited to present themselves at the Home Office to argue the case in person. They were received by the then minister of state, Leon Brittan, subsequently to become Home Secretary himself. It was the last card the defence had to play, but it was not a winner. "We got nowhere at all," said Peddie.

The jury made a mistake. Well, it happens. In recent times, no member of the judiciary has ever tried to argue that it doesn't. Yet the judicial process is unable to deal with it. The Court of Appeal made a cursory examination of Elizabeth Thompson's case. If she had actually been guilty, but the judge had made a small error of law in his summing-up, she would have been freed. This was not the position: she was innocent, but the judge's summing-up was beyond reproach, so she served a life sentence for someone else's crime.

She was a provincial housewife, unable to call on any resources that would have enabled a high-profile campaign to be pursued on her behalf. Needless to say, none of the journalists who flocked to Winchester to cover what promised to be a titillating trial had the insight to realise that they had been witnesses to the unfolding of a genuinely dramatic story. "I had not bargained on seeing justice miscarry before my eyes," Ludovic Kennedy once wrote.[1] When it did, he had the wit to recognise it, and the resourcefulness to do something about it.

Not that Thompson's legal advisers wanted to employ journalistic means. They put their trust in the Home Office, a course that its staff have regularly advised. From one point of view, it made sense. A press campaign often seems to alienate the very authorities who are charged with righting wrongs. However, these political channels were no more efficacious than judicial ones.

Rarely has there been such a clear example of the awful inadequacy of the English legal process, its complete inability to come to terms with frighteningly serious mistakes. As a pawn in the great game of pretending that the UK criminal justice system functions smoothly, Elizabeth Thompson was compelled to sacrifice those years of her life which none of us would ever forgo, those when our children are growing up. The system is as heartless as it is inefficient.

Apart from one conviction for a trivial shoplifting offence when she was nineteen, Elizabeth Thompson had never previously fallen foul of the law. All reports indicated that she had been an excellent mother and that her family was close-knit. From 1975, until her release on 13 December 1985, she shouldered the appalling burden of trying to keep her family together from inside a number of prisons, some of which were at the opposite end of the country. These would have been unbearably stressful conditions for her children under any circumstances. In this instance, the grief was only magnified by the fact that her three sons were fully aware of her innocence. They had been with her thoughout the evening of 4 November 1971.

Nine

The Legal & General Gang

People in the case

Billy Moseley — murder victim
Micky Cornwall — murder victim
Bob Maynard ⎫
Reg Dudley ⎭ — convicted of murder
Charlie Clarke ⎫
Kathy Dudley ⎭ — convicted of conspiracy
Ronnie Fright ⎫
Ernie Maynard ⎬ — acquitted of murder and conspiracy
George Spencer ⎭
Mr Justice Swanwick — trial judge
Michael Corkery QC — prosecution counsel
John Platts-Mills QC — defence counsel
Ann Moseley — wife of Billy Moseley
Phil Luxford — car dealer
George Arnold — half-brother of Billy Moseley
Frankie Fright — wife of Ronnie Fright
Ray Baron — boyfriend of Kathy Dudley
Colin Saggs — friend of Micky Cornwall
Gloria Hogg — girlfriend of Micky Cornwall
John Moriarty — friend of Micky Cornwall
Professor James Cameron — pathologist
Commander Albert Wickstead — Metropolitan Police, lead-
                                                  ing murder inquiry
Detective Chief Superintendent Ronald Harvey — Hertford-
   shire CID, leading murder inquiry
Sylvia Maynard — wife of Ernie Maynard
Anthony Wild — prosecution witness
Oliver Kenny — landlord of Brighton pub
Frank Read — prosecution witness
Frank Happer — defence witness
Sharon Saggs — daughter of Colin Saggs; prosecution witness
Charlie Morrish — newspaper-seller; witness

Duncan Campbell   —   journalist following the case
Jonathan Goldberg   —   solicitor for Reg Dudley
Michael Mansfield   —   Dudley's defence counsel
Michael Hill   —   prosecution counsel
Bobby Maynard   —   son of Bob Maynard

ON 17 JUNE 1977, at the end of the longest murder trial in British legal history, the Old Bailey jury reached varying verdicts on the seven defendants. Ronnie Fright was acquitted of all charges, as were George Spencer and Ernie Maynard. Charlie Clarke and Kathy Dudley were found guilty of conspiracy to cause grievous bodily harm. Each was given a two-year term of imprisonment, though in Kathy Dudley's case the sentence was suspended.

Bob Maynard and Reg Dudley, Kathy's father, were found guilty of the murders of Billy Moseley and Micky Cornwall. Both were sentenced to life imprisonment, with a recommendation that they serve at least fifteen years.

The trial attracted sensational, albeit far-fetched, publicity about gangland activity in north London; but for all that there was, as the prosecution counsel admitted, little material evidence against the defendants, and no forensic evidence at all.

The burden of the prosecution case lay in statements which the accused were alleged to have made – and which all vigorously denied making.

Billy Moseley disappeared eight days after being released from Bedford prison on 18 September 1974. He and Bob Maynard – 'Fat Bob', as he was usually known, an epithet that was less unkind than it sounded – had grown up together, having once lived next door to each other in Holloway, north London. From playing truant together during schooldays, they moved on, predictably perhaps, to crimes like shoplifting and breaking and entering. Neither climbed high on the criminal ladder. Their offences, however frequent, were never grave.

They seemed to serve their intermittent prison sentences

alternately. (Once only, back in 1965, had they been convicted together.) "It was a longstanding arrangement," wrote Duncan Campbell, "that whoever was 'out' looked after the interests of whoever was 'away'."[1] During Moseley's latest spell 'away', Maynard had been paying the weekly rent on his Stoke Newington flat.

While in prison, Moseley learned, to his consternation, that his old friend had become – to coin a phrase – thick as thieves with Reg Dudley, who lived in the Finsbury Park area of north London. Dudley made a comfortable living in Hatton Garden, the centre of the country's jewellery trade and an irresistible target for many London criminals. Maynard, who had become less agile, physically and mentally, after suffering serious head injuries in an incident in a Tottenham Court Road club, assisted him in his dealings which were, at best, of borderline legality. Dudley had served innumerable prison sentences for a variety of offences, including one of six years in Dartmoor for slashing his wife's face.

Moseley heard that Maynard and Dudley had been seen so regularly in each other's company that they had been dubbed 'the Legal & General'. The soubriquet had originally been acquired after they had walked into a Kentish Town pub wearing similar overcoats; their appearance had reminded one customer of a Legal & General Assurance Society television advert. It stuck because it was so apposite: while Dudley had a habit of inquiring of any transaction, "Is it legal?", Maynard guardedly used to describe himself as a "general dealer".

The association perturbed Moseley because there were those who suspected Dudley of being a police informer. Nevertheless, it was of no immediate concern to him when he was released. For one thing, Dudley was away in Spain, extricating his daughter Kathy from problems incurred by a failed night-club venture in Lloret de Mar.

Moseley visited his mother, and also his estranged wife Ann, and their three children, the youngest of whom, Bobby, was named after Maynard. One old friend, Micky

Cornwall, was then finishing an eight-year sentence for armed robbery in Hull prison, but Moseley did see others: Maynard; Phil Luxford, a car-dealer who loaned him a Rover; and George Arnold, his half-brother.

Luxford and Arnold were the only ones who knew that Moseley's primary concern after his release was to get together with Frankie Fright, a woman with whom he had been having an affair prior to his conviction for shoplifting in October 1973. In those social circles there were strong sanctions against becoming involved with a woman while her husband was 'away', and the affair had blossomed while Frankie's husband, Ronnie Fright, was in Chelmsford prison, completing a seven-year sentence for robbery. Moseley had violated one of the basic tenets of the underworld's code of ethics. Moreover, Fright, while in prison, found out about the affair.

With Moseley's release, it was agreed that he and Fright should meet to discuss the position. Frankie herself arranged the rendezvous: outside a bookmaker's, the Victoria Sporting Club, in Dalston at 6.30 p.m. on 26 September 1974.

Moseley disappeared after setting out for the meeting. At about the same time, Dudley arrived back in the UK from Spain. A week later, at the funeral of an elderly relative, Bob Maynard and his brother Ernie were overheard talking to George Spencer, who sometimes acted as Dudley's chauffeur. The gist of the conversation was that they could not expect to see Moseley again.

His body – or, to be gruesomely precise, bits of it – turned up on 5 October in the Thames at Rainham, Essex. Though there was some initial speculation that the torso could be that of Kenneth Littlejohn (*see* page 179), it was soon being assumed in north London that the missing Moseley had surfaced.

The local pathologist did what he could with the incomplete cadaver. He was able to confirm to the police that this was a case of murder. Since the head and hands were missing, however, no positive identification could be made.

Scientific ingenuity ultimately triumphed over criminal cunning. Moseley had suffered from a very rare skin disease. With information about this, and that of an unusual gallstone condition which had been registered on a routine X-ray taken in Bedford prison, and of blood samples which were matched with those of his children, Professor James Cameron was able to give the coroner's court the categorical assurance that the body was William Moseley's.

On his release from prison on 18 October Micky Cornwall was greatly distressed to learn that Moseley had been murdered and his body dismembered. Moseley had visited him several times in Hull.

Cornwall was an armed robber, known, on account of his conviviality and his professional fearlessness, as 'the Laughing Bank-Robber'. Far from emerging from prison a reformed character, he returned immediately to crime, as though desperate to make up for lost time. He did house-breaking, and some hotel robberies. (Bank-snatches, which had been all too easy at the time of his arrest, now presented much greater difficulties.) Cornwall was apparently hopelessly trapped in a life of crime.

Some months earlier, in 1974, Kathy Dudley had become involved with Ray Baron, also a bank-robber, whom Dudley had met in prison. (Back in 1962, Baron had been convicted with Cornwall and Colin Saggs – of whom more shall be heard – of a bank-raid in Barnet.) By this time, though, Baron was back inside, doing another stretch for armed robbery. Apparently less chauvinist towards women than his peers, he consented to Kathy having other relationships while he was away. In December Micky Cornwall started seeing her, but it was just a brief fling, and she went back for another spell in Lloret.

In April 1975 Cornwall met Gloria Hogg, a twenty-one-year-old secretary. Their relationship seems to have been a mutually satisfying one, although he never confided in her how he made his living, and she was too afraid of the

answer to ask. They went together to Blackpool, where
Cornwall apparently had associates. He often spoke of
pulling off the big one, the coup that would enable them
to buy a home in the country. He told one friend, John
Moriarty, of just such a job that he had arranged; Moriarty
was taken aback by his indiscretion. It was perhaps no
surprise that the West Midlands crime squad placed
Cornwall under surveillance; they believed him to be
planning a robbery on their patch.

At 5.00 p.m. on Sunday 3 August Cornwall, then staying
with Gloria, was collected by a friend in a mustard-
coloured Range Rover. She saw him again on the Tuesday,
and gathered that 'the big one' had been scheduled for the
following day.

Cornwall had been renting a room from the Saggs family,
Colin Saggs being once again in prison. Cornwall left later
that week, early one morning. He seemed agitated, and
packed hurriedly. Two men arrived for him fifteen minutes
after his departure. Fourteen-year-old Sharon Saggs, who
answered the door, was unable to say where he had gone.

After that, Cornwall was sighted around north London.
As late as 22 August Moriarty saw him standing by a
bus-stop in Highgate. His body was discovered in a make-
shift grave in woodland, just outside Hatfield, Hertfordshire, on 7 September. He had been shot through the
head.

The Hertfordshire police who investigated the murder
discovered that their inquiries kept leading to London;
and that a number of those questioned brought up the
name 'Moseley'. Without solid information to nurture it,
the police investigation into the latter's fate had been
desultory from the start. By now, it was at a standstill.

Some bizarre incidents deepened what now seemed to
be a double mystery. The *Islington Gazette* received a
letter signed 'Fat Bob', which concluded, "It's been said
that Mick was asking too much about Bill's death. The
police seem to have forgotten Billy. They may forget about
Mick."[2] The *Gazette* passed the letter on to detectives.

Maynard subsequently presented himself at the *Gazette* offices, identified himself as 'Fat Bob' and adamantly disclaimed all knowledge of the letter. The paper published an apology, but was somewhat bewildered; the police had told them the letter was genuine. Maynard said, "I have never been interviewed or questioned about this letter or this case. I don't know who wrote it. I certainly didn't."[3]

Nor was this the only matter to disconcert Maynard. He had also received through the post, wrapped in cotton wool, a .22 bullet. So, similarly, had Phil Luxford.

In this atmosphere of intrigue and tension, Hertfordshire police ceded absolute control of the investigation to a special squad of men drawn from both the Metropolitan and Hertfordshire police forces, and headed by Commander Albert Wickstead and Detective Chief Superintendent Ronald Harvey, head of Herts CID.

At this stage, Moseley's body was formally identified. Part of the evidence which Professor Cameron gave at the long-delayed inquest referred to the torture that Moseley had undergone prior to his death. All his toenails had been pulled out, and he had been burned with a naked flame. Cornwall's murder had already been popularly described as "a gangland execution". These fresh revelations lent even more chilling overtones to the investigation.

On Thursday 22 January 1976 eighteen people were taken for questioning to Loughton in Essex. They included the seven ultimately charged, together with Ernie Maynard's wife, Sylvia, and friends of Cornwall such as John Moriarty. The tabloid newspapers had a field-day. "Four Killings Linked as Yard Grab 50" proclaimed the *Sun*, characteristically heedless of accuracy.[4] Other papers suggested that the police were holding professional killers, and breaking up a vast, ruthless crime syndicate. It was believed that "millions of pounds in stolen bullion, diamonds and jewellery are involved".

They were all interviewed over a period of four days. Of the eighteen, eleven were then released. Charges were preferred against the remaining seven, who were remanded in custody.

At the committal proceedings at Epping magistrates court in May, police objected to bail because they said that two others were still being sought in connection with the crimes: "we have been trying to trace them for some months".[5] It was argued on behalf of the police that, if the defendants were granted bail, it would hinder the police search for the other men. Also, it was stressed that witnesses went in fear of the defendants, and one man had disappeared during the committal.

Nothing further was ever heard about either absent witnesses or additional suspects.

The trial opened on 11 November 1976. The prosecution case was that Moseley had had an affair with Frankie Fright, which the north London criminal fraternity had regarded as 'out of order'; that he had fallen out with Dudley back in the sixties; that he had further provoked Dudley by suggesting that he was a grass; that he was sitting on the proceeds of a large jewellery robbery. Cornwall had set out to avenge Moseley's death; he had discovered that Maynard and Dudley were the culprits; and had then attempted to get close to Dudley by striking up a relationship with his daughter.

Clearly, Maynard and Dudley were the central figures. Fright was thought to have been deliberately late for his appointment, and thus helped to lure Moseley to his death. Kathy Dudley was involved through her relationship with Cornwall (which the police believed had been more intimate than she had admitted). George Spencer and Charlie Clarke, a stallholder in Soho's Berwick Street market, were implicated through their friendship with Dudley. Ernie Maynard was alleged to have been involved in the plot against Moseley. It was implicit in the prosecution case that all had been connected with the Legal & General gang. The press was able to take its cue for some extravagant headlines from the opening remarks of Michael Corkery QC, prosecuting, who said that there was "no shortage of horror, appalling cruelty and sheer evil in this case".

In the course of his summing-up, Mr Justice Swanwick told the jury that "without the evidence of the alleged oral confessions, there would not be evidence on which the Crown could ask you to convict". He was referring in part to 'confessions' which were supposed to have been extracted from the defendants under interrogation at Loughton. The police stated on oath that they were accurate; the defendants maintained just as vehemently that they were fabricated. Whom should the jury believe?

The statements included a number of remarks that, although they fell short of straightforward admissions, were damaging at best and damning at worst. Dudley was quoted as saying, apropos of Cornwall's relationship with his daughter: "I told him if he had sex with her, I would kill him." Similarly, Cornwall was supposed to have written to Ray Baron in prison, boasting about his conquest of Kathy (although evidence of the existence of this letter was never produced). Dudley said, "Yes, but Ray never mentioned it to me. If he had, I would have given Cornwall his last rites earlier . . ."

Maynard's interview was also recorded as being self-incriminating. He seemed to contradict himself over whether or not he knew of the liaison between Moseley and Frankie Fright. Also, he was asked, "Did you tell Ronnie Fright to be late at the meet and did you meet Moseley yourself?" He replied: "I'm not answering that, otherwise I'm finished." With reference to the Cornwall murder, it was put to Maynard that "You went to a certain address – the Saggs' house – looking for him?" Maynard responded, according to the statement, "It was business."

The jury was confronted with a mass of statements such as these, the validity of which was fiercely contested by prosecution and defence, and on the interpretation of which, according to the judge himself, the outcome of the trial hinged.

This kind of argument, with defendants disputing the substance of what the police say they've said, is not unfamiliar in the courts. If the prosecution relies for its evidence, in whole or in part, on statements made in police custody, the defence will almost inevitably riposte with an accusation of 'verbals' (underworld slang for concocted statements). Since the police will have worked hard to construct a case against someone they believe guilty, one can sympathise with their weariness when the 'verbals' charge is levelled once again.

In this case the defendants characterised the statements as 'link-verbals', meaning that although they had actually spoken much of what was attributed to them, their words had been put in a different context.

It emerged during the trial that the office in which the contentious interviews were conducted was equipped with tape-recording facilities. The microphone was concealed inside a dummy telephone on Commander Wickstead's desk.

The tape, however, was not used.

Why not? the defence wanted to know. Why have such equipment at all if not to use in the pursuit of those responsible for particularly malicious crimes?

Wickstead replied, "I am a police officer who believes in police methods and tape recorders are not used in police interviews." He explained that the tape was used when people were supplying information.

In response to further questioning, another police officer gave three reasons for not using the tape: that it was not police practice, as the evidence so obtained would have been inadmissible in court; that because of the "street noise on that Saturday afternoon' the answers would have been inaudible anyway; and that also "the noise of the officers in the room scraping their chairs and coughing would interfere with the tape".

The first point again begs the question of why the equipment was installed at all; and the other points beg the question of why such apparently inadequate equipment was installed. The room, in any case, was carpeted.

The most important prosecution evidence apart from the police statements was given by Anthony Wild, an armed robber. He seems to have hitherto enjoyed an extravagant standard of living. However, he claimed to have undergone a spiritual conversion after his last job, a raid on a Securicor van outside Sainsbury's in Redhill, Sussex.

Wild said that he had met Maynard, Dudley and Clarke when they were all on remand in Brixton prison. While playing cards together, they had openly boasted to him of having committed the crimes. In doing so, they employed rather colourful phrases, which testified to the levity with which they regarded the matter.

Wild also related a bizarre anecdote. Dudley, he said, took Moseley's head in a bag to a Brighton pub, the Horse & Groom, where the landlord, Oliver Kenny, was an old friend. Dudley gave him palpitations by publicly producing it in the bar. (This tale immediately gave the underworld rich scope for black humour. "I hear your beer doesn't have much of a head on it," ran one version, "so I brought along one of my own.")

There are grounds for treating Wild's testimony with considerable caution. It seems to have been an open secret throughout the prison that Wild was an informer. Even if the defendants hadn't known this, they would hardly have taken him into their confidence, partly because Wild was a weird personality (described as "a reformed criminal" by the prosecution, and "unbalanced" by the defence); and partly because, as experienced criminals, they would have been very wary of police tactics of this sort.

Nevertheless, Wild's ebullient repartee under cross-examination did have an electrifying effect in court. Lawyers dubbed his performance 'the Wild West Show'. The prosecution took his story about Moseley's head seriously. There was surmise that it had been thrown into the sea at Brighton. A local fisherman was called to the witness-box to describe having seen something which could have been a head bobbing out to sea. Mr Justice Swanwick, in his summing-up, briefly speculated about what the specific gravity of a head might be.

Ronnie Fright was remanded not to Brixton but Pentonville, ostensibly because Bob Maynard had virtually accused him of Moseley's murder, and had threatened him. A prisoner named Frank Read testified that Fright had confessed to him in prison, blurting out the words, "We done one, we sawed one up." However, this part of the case against Fright was effectively demolished. Two trusted prisoners gave evidence that they had offered to help Fright because they were sure that Read was perjuring himself. More importantly, the assistant governor of the prison testified that the police had tried to interfere with prison administration, and had tried to trap Fright by putting him together with a prison grass.

There was another embarrassing moment for the prosecution at this stage of the trial. Another prisoner, Frank Happer, testified that the police tried to recruit him as a grass, asking him to get a confession out of another defendant, George Spencer. The police vigorously denied attempting to construct the prosecution case in this way. However, when asked who had approached him, Happer replied, "That man there", pointing to a plainclothes policeman who was sitting in court with a group of lawyers. The defence asked the jury to consider how, if the incident had not occurred, Happer could possibly have known that the man was a policeman.

The rest of the evidence was wholly circumstantial. Maynard's remarks at the funeral seemed damaging. How could he have been so sure that Moseley was dead even before his body had been found? Maynard argued that he had feared the worst, and what had been said was just pessimistic speculation.

George Arnold, a witness for the prosecution, said that

when he and Maynard went together to look over Moseley's flat after his disappearance, Maynard picked up a key. The latter responded that it was of no significance. Nevertheless, the incident, tiny as it was, launched a thousand rumours.

Another element in the prosecution case was that Dudley had harboured a grudge against Moseley ever since the two had come to blows back in the sixties. However, the two witnesses produced to give details of this incident contradicted each other. One, a man with a hearing-aid who admitted that he was unwelcome in their circle because he interfered with small boys, dated it firmly in 1968; the other was just as certain that it had occurred in 1964.

Sharon Saggs, who was sixteen at the time of the trial, identified the two men who had called at her home two years earlier asking for Cornwall as Maynard and Dudley. This was a positive identification, but unusual circumstances surrounded it. She had identified the men from photographs, and the photograph of Dudley was significantly larger than all the others. Secondly, she was accompanied by her father at the time, even though Colin Saggs was then serving a sentence in a Lincolnshire prison. Why, the defence asked, wasn't she simply given the chance to pick out Maynard and Dudley from an identity parade?

One identity parade did take place. Kathy Dudley was put in a line during her remand at Holloway prison, with the intention of showing that she was still going out with Cornwall in the summer of 1975. Charlie Morrish, a Clapton newsagent, was supposed to have seen them together in a pub. Remand prisoners are allowed to wear their own clothes. As they lined up, Kathy wondered if Morrish might have been told that she was wearing a red jumper, so she swopped with the girl next to her, whose jumper was green. As she did so, she noticed a policeman looking hard at her. When he retreated to fetch Morrish, the girls hurriedly swopped back again. Morrish picked out the girl in the green jumper.

Towards the end of the trial John Platts-Mills QC, defending Spencer, referred with some vehemence to "these piffling pieces of evidence".

Michael Corkery QC, prosecuting, stressed that he was under no obligation to establish a motive for the crimes, but he would nevertheless put forward some possibilities. Moseley was killed either because of his assertions that Dudley was a grass; or because Dudley was taking revenge for the fight in 1964 or 1968; or because he had a key to a secret hoard of valuables (which would explain the torture aspect of the killing); or because of his affair with Frankie Fright; or out of sheer sadism. Cornwall was killed because he tried to avenge the murder; or because of his relationship with Kathy Dudley.

The profusion of possible motives in itself casts doubts on the validity of the prosecution case. After all, a murderer needs only one motive. Here, the prosecution seemed to be clutching at straws. Moseley may have had an 'out-of-order' affair with Frankie Fright, but surely it was no business of Maynard and Dudley's to avenge it. No evidence has ever been produced to substantiate the theory of a hidden cache of robbery proceeds. (For all their allusions to this, the press just as frequently described Moseley as a "small-time crook".) Dudley may not have liked Moseley, but that was hardly persuasive evidence of a murderous intent.

Cornwall seems to have been genuinely, understandably upset about what had happened to his friend, but he didn't seem bent on revenge. If he was, he displayed a procrastination which might have stood him in good stead had he ever been required to play Hamlet, but which was highly unusual in north London gangsters.

In the witness-box, Maynard was reduced to tears when describing the last time he had seen Moseley alive. His longstanding friendship with Moseley was surely a persuasive argument for his innocence. Moseley's widow, Ann, gave evidence for the defence at the trial (and was demeaned by the judge for her pains). After the convictions, she, with her eldest son, was among the first to lend support to the campaign calling for the release of those who, according to the verdict of the Central Criminal Court, had murdered her husband.

A story is told in legal circles of a trial that had been going on, and on, and on. At length, counsel felt obliged to apologise to the judge.

"I'm sorry, m'lud, for taking up so much of the court's time."

"Time?" responded the judge wearily. "You have exhausted time and encroached upon eternity."

The remark was not made during the torso trial, but it could not have been more apposite. The duration of the trial, as preposterous as it was unprecedented, could hardly have benefited the defendants.

First of all, the trial must have become unacceptably arduous for the members of the jury. When they had been sworn in, they were told that the trial would last eight weeks, not seven months, of which twenty-six entire days were spent outside the court while the judge listened to legal submissions. They should not have been expected to scrutinise the ebb and flow of prosecution and defence argument over such a period. At one stage in his summing-up, the judge referred the jury to a point made previously, "which you have probably forgotten and which I ought to remind you of". He was then referring to something mentioned a few *days* earlier in his twelve-day summing-up. If memories needed refreshing in that instance, what about all those pieces of evidence that had been presented *months* before?

Also the tension associated with such a serious matter as a murder trial evaporated. The business took on the languor of a long-running show. Barristers left proceedings in the hands of their juniors, as they were called away elsewhere. Those who could not escape attempted to relieve the boredom with humour. Duncan Campbell noticed that on one sunny afternoon in court, four barristers were all apparently asleep.

Finally, the longer a trial endures, the harder it becomes for the jury to believe that the whole thing could possibly be a gigantic mistake.

As it happens, the verdicts showed that the jury gave rigorous thought to their unenviable task. They spent two nights in a hotel before coming to decisions on all the charges. Ronnie Fright left the court after being acquitted on 15 June, the first day of their deliberations.

The judge had directed the jury to acquit Ernie Maynard, and they also acquitted George Spencer. The other four were found guilty, the decisions against Bob Maynard being majority ones. As his brother, Ernie, stepped down from the dock, he indicated the remaining defendants, and said to the judge, "They are all innocent."

The sense of unreality which had been occasionally noticed during the trial survived its conclusion, and penetrated the post-trial newspaper reports. Generally, the opportunity to put evil-doing into nefarious perspective is enthusiastically seized, as it was on this occasion. But it was clear that even the most seasoned crime correspondents could not agree on what the trial had been about. Gang-land revenge? A secret hoard of diamonds? There was only disharmony in Fleet Street.

Once a miscarriage of justice has occurred, new evidence to confirm the wrongful conviction has to be painstakingly winkled out by assiduous solicitors, legal organisations or journalists. The process is invariably a lengthy and dispiriting one. In the Maynard–Dudley–Clarke case, however, new evidence emerged in quite sensational fashion.

On 28 July 1977, six weeks after the end of the trial, Moseley's head was discovered on a lavatory seat in public conveniences in Barnsbury, Islington. The skull was covered by a plastic bag. Wrapped around the head was a copy of the *Evening News* dated 16 June 1977, when the jury had spent all day considering their verdicts. Those who had anticipated that this development would lead to the expeditious release of the three men were, however, disappointed. The discovery did not seem to galvanise the police. When Duncan Campbell asked Scotland Yard who was in charge of inquiries, he was informed that there were none in progress. Apparently, the police believed that further action was unnecessary, since the head had, in their view, been placed there by associates of Maynard and Dudley in the hope that it would discredit the correct verdict of the court.

This is not a plausible theory.

The inquest did not take place until October at Walthamstow coroner's court, when Professor James Cameron once again gave evidence. He was closely questioned by Dudley's lawyer, Jonathan Goldberg. Though initially reluctant to answer questions ("I have given my report to the DPP, and I shouldn't divulge it until he tells me"), he was instructed to do so by the coroner. The skull had been in "extremely good condition" (as rotting heads go, presumably). His examination revealed that Moseley was not shot, but had choked to death on his own blood and saliva. Cameron was unable to say for certain where the head had been kept for almost three years, although traces of car paint indicated that it may have been stored in a garage. It had also been buried at one point. For much of the time it must have been in a deep freeze; it was thawing out when it was found.

The head thus yielded more forensic evidence than the totality of what had been put before the trial jury, and it comprehensively shattered two elements of the prosecution case. Right from the outset, at the committal hearing, the prosecution asserted that Moseley had died in the same way as Cornwall – with a single bullet through the head. Corkery stated during the trial that he was "98 per cent certain" that Moseley had been murdered in this way. Now that this link between the murders was disproved, the nexus between the crimes was that much more slender. Further, the head had clearly not been washed out to sea at Brighton. The various references in court to this eventuality now seemed jejune.

If accomplices of Maynard and Dudley were in possession of such dramatic evidence, it would have been sheer perversity not to have produced it while the trial was in progress (there was, after all, plenty of time), rather than waiting until the men were convicted.

A different, more credible explanation is that Maynard and Dudley were both innocent. Whoever was guilty wanted to ensure his own safety by waiting until someone else had been convicted of his crime – and was now trying to salve his conscience by offering a public indication that the convictions were erroneous.

It is one of the vagaries of the English judicial system that even such a significant development as the discovery of the head availed the convicted men nothing when their case went to appeal. Nor was it even expected to: however bizarre, it was, in hard legalistic terms, a matter of no great consequence. A court of law could infer from it nothing about the guilt or innocence of the men.

The appeal was argued on different grounds – that the judge should have used his discretion to rule that the two murders should have been dealt with separately; that what was described as the "inordinate length" of the trial unfairly disadvantaged the defendants; and that the evidence of uncorroborated oral confessions was insufficient on which to convict.

Michael Mansfield, appearing for Dudley, also raised the "hostile nature" of the charges. By this he meant that "the murders were of a class which would horrify anyone who read about them and that a jury would approach their task on the basis that it would be utterly wrong if at the end of the trial they were to reach a conclusion that no one was to be punished for these murders". In this respect, the publicity surrounding the case was "highly prejudicial".

An interesting argument, but the court would have none of it. "There are plenty of examples of horrifying crimes going unpunished because the Crown has been unable to adduce proper proof of the guilt of the particular alleged criminal who, on the evidence, has been rightly acquitted."

Lord Justice Roskill, Lord Justice Ormrod and Mr Justice Watkins delivered judgment on 2 April 1979: "the appeals all fail and must be dismissed".

Almost from the moment that sentences were passed, a campaign for the release of the three men was set in motion. At that time, there was probably greater optimism that those wrongly imprisoned would be able to find rapid redress. A number of cases in the mid-seventies had illustrated the uncertainty of the judicial process, and some were remedied.

The MDC campaign was spearheaded by Bob Maynard's wife, Tina. It was very well organised, which perhaps indicated a metropolitan awareness of the advantages of good publicity, and how to get it. Badges and T-shirts were printed with the slogan, "MDC – Not Guilty, Right √". On 18 September 1977 about a hundred people marched in protest from Camden Town to Hyde Park Corner.

Six of the erstwhile defendants lent what support they could. Bob and Ernie Maynard, Reg Dudley, Charles Clarke and George Spencer all took truth-drug tests, and Kathy Dudley a lie-detector test. All 'passed' in so far as those administering the tests were able to report that all had been telling what they perceived to be the truth, and that all had disclaimed knowledge of any events leading to the Moseley and Cornwall murders.

However, this didn't constitute hard evidence as far as the Home Office was concerned.

In August 1980 Anthony Wild was released from prison, and was subsequently interviewed by Duncan Campbell and Graham McLagan, BBC Radio 4's home news correspondent. They found Wild quite willing to discuss the MDC trial. He said that he could get Maynard and Dudley out of prison "tomorrow", because he had given untrue evidence. He claimed – with some pride, apparently – to have invented the story of the head in the Brighton pub: he seemed to think it was a highly imaginative touch.

Campbell and McLagan reported the conversation to the Home Office. The barrister Michael Hill, who had been Corkery's junior at both the original trial and the appeal, was asked to investigate. Nothing resulted from this fresh investigation.

There was some renewed activity in 1984, when Campbell's examination of the case was presented in the magazine *Unsolved*. Bob Maynard's eldest son, also Bobby, purchased eighty copies with a view to arousing new interest. He had been only fifteen at the time of the trial, but now – by trade a butcher in Knightsbridge – he was in a position to play a leading role in the MDC campaign. He stood as a candidate in the elections for the European parliament in June 1984. Reg Dudley persuasively pleaded his innocence in a programme in the BBC 2 series, *Lifers*.

Some cases which have resulted in erroneous convictions remain mysteries. There is no such uncertainty here. The names of those who murdered Moseley and Cornwall are common knowledge among the clientele of several north London pubs. The detection went wrong from the outset because both the police and the press jumped to conclusions. The murders were not linked, nor were they ever the result of gang warfare: there never was a Legal & General gang. The idea that there could have been was simply a notion that took root and blossomed in the media.

Other avenues could profitably have been explored. In particular, Gloria Hogg's statements should have been followed up. However, once the judge had refused a defence application at the start of the trial for the murder charges to be tried separately, then the chances of disentangling the mundane truth from the extravagant myths that enveloped the defendants became remote. In the circumstances, the jury responded with creditable resolution. It wasn't their fault that they got it wrong.

The MDC case also illustrates one of the advantages

which the prosecution naturally enjoys over the defence: that of being able to call witnesses whose testimony is advantageous, and to exclude those whose testimony could prove disadvantageous. Both Colin Saggs and George Arnold were made available to assist the prosecution, although both were serving prison sentences at the time, having been convicted in November 1974 of taking part in an abortive jewellery raid in Southend.

However, Oliver Kenny, the landlord of the Brighton pub, who would have been able to scotch Wild's story about the severed head in his pub, was not available to the defence. He had been taken into custody for an alleged connection with offences that had taken place in 1965. (In the event, Kenny died of a heart attack in October 1977, prior to standing trial.)

A number of interesting parallels can be drawn between the Torso Murders trial, as the Maynard–Dudley proceedings inevitably became known, and one of Commander Wickstead's previous cases. This concerned Arthur John Saunders, who in 1970 was jailed for fifteen years for his part in the Barclays Bank robbery in Ilford. This was especially notorious since its cash haul – over £237,000 – made it the most successful criminal operation of its kind.

In 1972, police arrested Bertie Smalls, who subsequently agreed to turn QE. In return for his own freedom, he provided exhaustive details about a number of bank-snatches and other robberies including the Ilford one. According to *Cops and Robbers*, "Smalls had been involved in the job from the earliest planning stages down to the final share-out for each member of the team. He was adamant that Saunders, who had by that time been in jail for over two years, was not part of the team."[6]

Saunders' case had already been to appeal, unsuccessfully, in December 1971. In view of what Smalls had said, it was reconsidered. On 12 October 1973 Lord Widgery, Lord Justice James and Mr Justice Geoffrey Lane heard the fresh appeal. Widgery noted that (as in the Maynard –Dudley case) what mattered at the trial was what the defendant was supposed to have said in police custody. According to the judgment, "In the course of this interview as recounted by Police Superintendent Wickstead, one does not find Saunders positively admitting that he had anything to do with the Ilford bank robbery; on the other hand there is a noticeable absence of any positive denial of such association, and indeed many of the answers which I have read, equivocal in themselves, were certainly, one would have thought, answers which did not lie readily in the mouth of an innocent man, who would have asserted his innocence in a positive way."

Widgery went on to comment that the record of this police interview was "in many ways the most substantial contribution which the prosecution was able to make". Soon, he was referring to "the essential weakness of the prosecution case". This is fascinating; the Crown cases in the Saunders and the Maynard–Dudley trials had clearly been cast from the same mould.

Basically, Widgery had to weigh the testimony of Police Superintendent Wickstead against that of the arch-criminal Bertie Smalls. He allowed the appeal, quashed the conviction, and freed Saunders.

In 1985, Wickstead published his memoirs, *Gangbuster*.[7] In view of the way in which the Saunders case had collapsed, it was perhaps not surprising that it did not feature in the book. What was more notable, perhaps, was the complete omission of any reference to the Legal & General gang. After all, the Torso Murders trial had made legal history. Its total cost was in excess of half a million pounds; the court transcript ran to more than three and a half million words. It was the longest murder trial ever to have taken place in the UK. As such, it featured in the *Guinness Book of Records*. How extraordinary that something so significant, so sensational, should apparently have slipped the memory of Gangbuster himself.

Ten

Margaret Livesey

People in the case

Alan Livesey — murdered at his home in Bamber Bridge
Margaret Livesey — his mother, charged with his murder
Bob Livesey — husband of Margaret; father of Alan
Mr Justice Talbot — trial judge
John Hughill QC — defence counsel
Susan Warren ⎱ — next-door neighbours; prosecution
Christine Norris ⎰ witnesses
Ronald Mason — next-door neighbour
Mrs Matthews — resident at No. 63 The Crescent
Leslie Matthews — 18-year-old, who discovered the body
Andrew Matthews — younger brother of Leslie
Mrs Rogers — resident of The Crescent
Tommy Rogers ⎱
Tony Rogers ⎰ — sons of Mrs Rogers
Peter Nightingale — witness for the defence
Raymond Nightingale — brother of Peter
Frank Bamber — alibi witness
John Kershaw — witness
Marion Walker — friend of Margaret Livesey
Tom Sargant — secretary of Justice
Leah Levin — director of Justice
Peter Hill — producer of *Rough Justice*
Martin Young — presenter of *Rough Justice*
Dr Phillips — GP who attended the body
Dr John Benstead — Home Office pathologist
Dr Tapp — pathologist consulted by the defence
James Cameron — professor of forensic science at the University of London
Stan Thorne — MP for Preston
David Mellor — minister of state at the Home Office
William Benion — assistant chief constable of West Yorkshire; head of 1984 inquiry

BETWEEN APPROXIMATELY 10.55 and 11.10 p.m. on Thursday 22 February 1979, Margaret Livesey is alleged to have: arrived home from the local pub; become embroiled in a fierce argument with her 14-year-old-son, Alan; grabbed a knife and stabbed him ten times – six times with great force and four with teasing pin-pricks; placed two socks over the neck wounds; bound his wrists with an elaborate series of knots, culminating with a reef knot; washed the knife with exceptional thoroughness; turned on the gas-taps; walked the long way round the housing estate to give the appearance of not having been home at all; and arrived at the house of a neighbour, Mrs Matthews, in a perfectly composed state.

On the assumption that a scenario of that kind took place, Mrs Livesey was sentenced to life imprisonment for murder at Preston Crown Court, at the conclusion of her second trial on 26 July 1979. The first was aborted at an especially late stage. The jury was stood down after having been out for almost two days, and having by that time been instructed to try to reach a majority verdict, because a relative of one member was taken seriously ill.

The untimely illness of that unknown person hardly assisted Margaret Livesey's cause. She had to endure two virtually consecutive trials. In Britain, a trial is generally reported from the prosecution's point of view. By the time the second jury was sworn in, its members would presumably have been familiar with the lurid gist of the case – the callous murder by a mother of her teenage son – from front-page headlines in the *Lancashire Evening Post* and the rest of the local press. It does seem suggestive that whereas the first jury was still locked in dispute after two days, the second one brought in a unanimous guilty verdict within five hours.

John Hughill QC, Livesey's counsel, could have opted to continue with eleven jurors. In the light of what happened, it is easy to say he should have done so. But James Hanratty, for example, was tried by only eleven (the twelfth became ill at the mention of blood and withdrew almost at the outset); bearing such considerations in mind, Hughill was entitled to believe that he needed a full complement of jurors.

After her conviction, lawyers representing Livesey advised her that there were no grounds on which to lodge an appeal. Belatedly, she did apply for permission, but leave was refused her on 17 September 1980. The case having thus exhausted the formal legal process, it was referred to the Justice organisation whose secretary, Tom Sargant, became convinced that a miscarriage of justice had occurred. He passed it on to the BBC's *Rough Justice* unit, and Peter Hill (producer) and Martin Young (presenter) started to investigate it afresh.

The prosecution case in detail was that Mrs Livesey was given a lift from the Queen's Hotel to the top of her road by Frank Bamber: She went straight home, to 41 The Crescent, Bamber Bridge, to find Alan dressed in his army cadet uniform and boots. He had not been wearing those clothes earlier in the evening, and it was not a cadet night. The fact that he had the uniform on suggested that he'd been out, which she'd expressly forbidden. This latest act of recalcitrance, coming on top of a series of problems – relations between her and Alan were very strained at that time, and they'd been arguing earlier in the evening – enraged her. Her temper snapped, and there was a violent row. She stabbed Alan as he lay on the floor watching television, then as he stood up to try to protect himself, then after he fell down again. When he was dead, she bound his wrists to make it look as though he had been trussed up by an intruder. She then washed the knife and put it back in the kitchen drawer, turned on the gas and went out of the house.

She then turned the 'wrong' way – right, instead of left

– along her horseshoe-shaped road. Walking towards her home for a second time, she noticed two youngsters, Andrew Matthews and Tommy Rogers, playing outside No. 63, where the Matthews family lived. They both ran off, she knocked at the door of the house, and was invited in for a drink. Leslie Matthews arrived home and went off to search for his younger brother, and Tommy; Mrs Livesey asked him to check whether they were with Alan. Leslie arrived back, saying that he was unable to get into No. 41. Mrs Livesey gave him the key. He arrived back, covered in blood and very distressed. He and Livesey returned to No. 41, and then Leslie ran to telephone the police. The call was logged at 11.28 p.m.

The evidence against Livesey consisted in the main of her own confession, made five days after her son's death but retracted soon afterwards. There was also damaging testimony from her next-door neighbours, who alleged that they heard noises of an argument between Alan and his mother shortly before 11 o'clock.

At the outset of their investigation, Hill and Young formed the view that it was unsafe to rely on Margaret Livesey's 'confession'. It was made at a time of great emotional stress, and contained indications that it could not be taken at face-value. One such remark was, "Well, if you say I've done it, then I must have, but I can't remember." Further, it contained errors (Alan's body was lying the wrong way), omissions and, other than in two important respects, displayed only a sketchy knowledge of the crime. Most noticeably, it conflicted with all the available forensic evidence. There was no blood on the walls, the nearby furniture or Alan's boots; there was no sign of any struggle between them – neither bruises, knocks or traces of blood on Mrs Livesey, nor defensive marks on Alan; there was no transference of incriminating hairs or fibres between Livesey and her son or vice-versa. Livesey said that because she could not bear to see her son bleeding she took some thick woollen football socks from the maiden (the clothes dryer) and placed them over Alan's neck wounds. Yet forensic evidence showed beyond doubt that Alan was stabbed through the socks. They were punctured eleven times, and traces of adipose tissue were found on them. Moreover, only if he was stabbed *through* the socks was it possible to explain the absence of blood-splashes on the furniture.

Alan was killed in what seemed a peculiar way. Whereas six of the knife-thrusts were made with great force, four were surface incisions and would hardly have done more than pricked Alan. One of these was particularly purposeful, since it pierced the skin on the eyelid, though without inflicting damage to the eye itself. The 'confession', which implied the kind of frenzied attack which is characteristic of domestic murders ("I was thinking you little bad sod all the time and I had completely lost control of myself") did not begin to account for any of this.

However, Livesey's 'confession' did appear to provide details of the murder weapon and the motive for the crime: two pieces of vital information to which the murderer alone had access. The supposed motive was the increasing friction between mother and son. Mrs Livesey revealed that there had been great strains on her relationship with him – "he was always want, want, want" – and that she was especially worried because he seemed to be taking up petty crime.

She said that to stab Alan she picked up a kitchen knife which she had left in the lounge after peeling potatoes on the sofa. Naturally, the knife was taken away for analysis. As with all the other forensic tests, it failed to provide the 'confession' with any corroboration. The forensic scientist giving evidence for the Crown in court admitted that there was nothing to connect it with the murder.

In fact, the scientific work should have left no one in any doubt that the knife was *not* the murder weapon. No traces of blood were found on it; yet it had a hole in the handle, where the rivet nearest the blade was missing, and bare unvarnished wood was exposed. Had it been the weapon, it is inconceivable that microscopic traces of blood would not have been retained there and thus detected by forensic analysis.

Hill and Young examined the other stanchion of the prosecution case: the evidence of the next-door neighbours, Susan Warren, with whose house the Liveseys shared a party wall, and Christine Norris. In the immediate aftermath of the murder, both made statements to police. Norris said she heard nothing at all prior to the hubbub surrounding the discovery of the body and the arrival of the police. Both Warren and the man with whom she was living, Ronald Mason, remembered hearing noises of "larking about" coming from the Livesey house at around 10.00 p.m. Mason was specific about the time, saying he heard the noises at the end of ITV's nine o'clock programme, *The Streets of San Francisco*, and before the start of *News at Ten*. He heard nothing after that until the noises after 11 o'clock when the body was discovered. He thought he heard Mrs Livesey scream, "He's bloody dead."

Susan Warren's statement more or less confirmed Mason's. She insisted that she heard nothing between the "larking about' and the distressed sounds when and after the body was discovered. The following day (Sunday) the police took a second statement from her, but she was unable to elaborate on her previous one.

Subsequently, Norris and Warren, together with Norris's parents who were at her daughter's house, discussed the murder. The outcome of this conversation was that each decided that she heard Mrs Livesey engaged in a fierce argument with her son at around 10.45 or 10.50. This was damaging enough, but it was not all. Norris also pointed out that relations between mother and son were exacerbated to the point at which someone reported the family to the National Society for the Prevention of Cruelty to Children (NSPCC). Warren corroborated this. They both then made fresh statements to police, incorporating this new testimony. After this, on the Tuesday afternoon, Margaret Livesey was re-interviewed. She broke down and 'confessed'.

Was the Norris/Warren evidence reliable? In its critical aspects, Susan Warren's evidence now conflicted with Ronald Mason's, who maintained throughout that he heard nothing after the "larking about" and who insisted that Warren had said nothing to him about hearing anything else. Mason was one of the few witnesses in this wretched case who gave consistent evidence throughout. He was, though, slightly deaf.

During the first trial, Warren said that she heard the noises just before the end of the programme following *News at Ten* which, she said, finished at 11.00. However, John Hughill was able to show that *The City at Risk*, the programme referred to, finished – unusually – at 11.15. This suggested that whatever noises Warren heard could have been those accompanying the discovery of the body.

Warren's evidence must also be considered in the light of her first two statements. In both, she not only omitted any reference to the argument she subsequently said she heard; but, when specifically asked by police, she unequivocally denied having heard anything at all at that time. ("If anyone had screamed during the evening, I am certain I would have heard them.") At the first trial, the judge, Mr Justice Talbot, asked why she had concealed such obviously important information. She was unable to supply a reason.

By the time of the second trial, Warren had, as it were, got her act together. She was able to eliminate the most telling flaws in her testimony. She reiterated her claims to have heard mother and son arguing, but avoided timing this by the television. She also explained why she had not volunteered the information sooner: she did not want to get involved. In the circumstances, this, which was also the reason advanced by Christine Norris, was the best available excuse. Even so, it lacked credibility. Having freely spoken of the "larking about", she was already involved.

Christine Norris said she heard the row between 10.30

and 11.01 (i.e. she timed it backwards from noticing the time of 11.01 on her digital clock). According to her original statement, she heard nothing during that period. Even in her revised statement, she was vague both about what she heard and when she heard it. Hill and Young did establish that Norris used her digital clock throughout the house during the day, moving it from one plug point to another. Presumably, it lost time whenever she moved it. She hadn't herself checked its accuracy; nor, seemingly, had anyone else. It seemed possible that she, too, had heard nothing more incriminating than Livesey's distress at finding her son dead.

The allegations of the ill-treatment of Alan were without foundation. Someone had indeed contacted the NSPCC, but the inspector reported that there were no marks on Alan to indicate maltreatment; that he himself repudiated the suggestions; and that Margaret and Bob, her husband, seemed to be caring parents.

Altogether, the combined evidence of Susan Warren and Christine Norris, on which so much of the trial hinged, seemed extremely suspect. Peter Hill then went on to consider two other aspects of the case: did Margaret Livesey actually have time to do it, and, could anyone else have done it?

The timing was very tight. Mrs Livesey said that on her way home from the pub she saw Andrew Matthews and Tommy Rogers fooling around under the front window of the Matthews' house. Because she was concerned about the behaviour of local youngsters, her own son included, and because she knew that Andrew and Tommy should not be out at that time of night, she remonstrated with them. They ran off, and she knocked at the door of No. 63 to report their behaviour. She was invited in for a glass of cider. Mrs Rogers, Tommy's mother, was already there. She noticed a bandage on Livesey's leg.

Leslie Matthews, 18, arrived home – and so began the

sequence of events that culminated in the discovery of the body. Between his arrival home and the telephone call to police at 11.28, Leslie did the following:

1. He chatted to Mrs Livesey after he arrived home.
2. He went out into the street, walking up and down to try to find Andrew, his younger brother, and Tommy.
3. He went home and picked up Tony Rogers and both went in search of their younger brothers, though without success.
4. He went back home again. He and Tony then went to the Liveseys' house to see if they were there. They knocked on the door and searched round the back.
5. Returning home, Leslie stopped to talk to a friend.
6. After chatting to Mrs Livesey back at No. 63, he took the keys to No. 41.
7. He found the body and tried to give Alan the kiss of life.
8. He ran back and told the group at No. 63 that Alan was dead.
9. He went back to No. 41 with Mrs Livesey, where he waited while she tried to revive Alan. They opened the windows, turned off the gas, and Leslie was sick.
10. Leslie ran to the telephone box, which would have taken at least a minute.[1]

Peter Hill and Martin Young thought that this would have taken 23 minutes. Even on the most favourable (for the prosecution) estimate, it must have taken 18. This meant that Livesey must have been at the Matthews' house by 11.10 at the very latest. The calculation fitted in with her seeing Andrew Matthews and Tommy Rogers, who left the centre of Bamber Bridge at 10.55, and would not have dawdled home: it was a very cold night, and in any case they were not supposed to be out at that time.

Margaret Livesey had been drinking at the Queen's Hotel with two friends, Marion Walker and Frank Bamber. Marion Walker said that she thought she waved goodbye at 10.50, at which time Bamber was scraping ice off his car's windscreen. He said he dropped her off at the top of her road at about 11.00. They had a conversation about pay rises, and he remembered reaching home (four or five minutes away) at 11.05. John Kershaw said he saw her walking towards her house at about 11.00. If all these statements are accepted, then Livesey could not have murdered her son. Kershaw's evidence, however, could possibly be accommodated by the prosecution as easily as by the defence. The critical testimony was Bamber's. It turned out that Livesey, taking advantage of her husband's night-shift work at British Leyland, was having an affair with him. Consequently, weight was not attached to his evidence. The prosecution held that twelve minutes were missing from Livesey's timetable, and that everything could have been accomplished in that period.

Could anyone else have killed Alan? Perhaps the most important defence witness at Livesey's trials was 17-year-old Peter Nightingale, also a neighbour, who was educationally subnormal. He told police that he saw a youth leaving the Livesey home by the back door at about 10.00 p.m. He described him as 5'10", with long fair hair, and wearing an anorak. His attention was drawn by the sound of the back-door bolt being pulled back, although, strangely, the kitchen light was not on.

Prior to Livesey's confession, the police took great interest in Nightingale's statement. Once Livesey was charged, however, it was obviously an embarrassment. The following Saturday, the police took a statement from Peter's elder brother, Raymond. According to this, Peter told him that he had lied to the police. Later that day, Peter made a fresh statement, saying that his original one was fictitious.

At the trial, Peter reverted to his original evidence, and claimed the police had intimidated him into changing it. Inevitably, his testimony was compromised by his apparent lack of reliability. It was further weakened by the absence of corroborative evidence.

There was, however, a nagging doubt: Raymond's statement. To all intents and purposes, the police had already cleared up the case – so why was it necessary to take a statement from a fresh witness? It was hard to avoid the suspicion that it was to be able to exert pressure on Peter; or, should he prove stubborn, to nullify his evidence.[2]

Years later, as part of his *Rough Justice* inquiry, Peter Hill studied scene-of-crime photographs with a magnifying glass and noticed a packet of Benson & Hedges cigarettes. This was puzzling. The reports used at the trial referred only to two kinds of cigarette: Player's No. 6, which Alan smoked; or Dunhill's, which the rest of the family smoked. After further investigation, *Rough Justice* learned that the Benson & Hedges packet was taken away for analysis, but subsequently omitted from the list of exhibits presented in court. The packet in turn raised questions about cigarette stubs near to the body which were also visible on the photographs. It seemed that these were not examined forensically. This was a murder inquiry, so that was a serious oversight.

The cigarette evidence had potentially been of immense significance, since it seemed to provide corroboration for Nightingale's evidence. If Nightingale was right, however, and if the intruder he saw was the murderer, then death must have occurred at about 10 o'clock. The BBC took the papers on the case to James Cameron, professor of forensic science at the University of London. From the circumstances of the murder, he straightaway described it as a homosexual bondage case. He then examined the various postmortem reports and concluded from the state of digestion of the stomach contents that death almost certainly occurred near to 10 o'clock.

On 26 October 1983, a *Rough Justice* programme on the Livesey case, which assembled much of this information, was transmitted. Justice delivered a detailed petition on the case to the Home Office on 9 November. On 15 November David Mellor told Stan Thorne (Labour MP for Preston), Mrs Livesey's MP, that the Home Secretary had ordered a fresh police investigation, though this did not get underway until 18 December, when William Benion, assistant chief constable of West Yorkshire, was asked to head the inquiry. On the basis of his report, the Home Office decided not to intervene, and communicated their decision to Justice on 20 December 1984.

By this time, Tom Sargant had retired as secretary of Justice, whose director, Leah Levin, then set up a miscarriages-of-justice sub-committee (see page 482). The Livesey case was the first about which its members felt sufficiently concerned to feel it essential to forward a fresh memorandum to the Home Office, challenging the negative response of its 20 December letter. This was despatched on 24 July 1985, and was closely followed by a second *Rough Justice* transmission on the case (12 September 1985), in which fresh queries were raised about the time of death.

Finally, on 15 January 1986, the Home Office referred the case to appeal, specifically requesting the court to examine the precise time of death of Alan Livesey; and the presence in the house of unaccounted-for cigarettes.

The appeal, which opened on 8 December 1986, was heard by Lord Lane, the Lord Chief Justice; Mr Justice Simon Brown; and Mr Justice McCowan.

Margaret Livesey had a complete alibi for all but about ten or fifteen minutes of the entire evening, so the time of death was clearly important. Since the body was discovered (by anyone's reckoning) relatively quickly, it should not have been too difficult to make an educated guess. A Home Office pathologist, Dr John Benstead, took the body temperature at 2.40 a.m. and from that determined that Alan died three-and-a-half hours earlier – i.e. at 11.10 p.m., an unhappy calculation from Mrs Livesey's point of view. (He then allowed an hour each way, and fixed the period within which death occurred as 10.10 p.m.–12.10 a.m.)

However, the rate of cooling of a body is influenced by several factors, including whether and how it is clothed, and the temperature of the surrounding area. In 1979, Dr Tapp, the pathologist consulted by defence lawyers, concurred with Benstead's time-of-death estimate. Six years later, however, he learned that Benstead had measured the room temperature at 54°F. This disconcerted Tapp. Knowing that the windows in the house had been thrown open to the cold night air (in order to get rid of the gas), he had assumed a room temperature of 40°F. Using the fresh information, he re-calculated the time of death as four to five hours before the body temperature was taken – i.e. that a median time of 10 o'clock was much more likely than one of 11. This new estimate seemed especially significant because it dovetailed with the work done by Professor Cameron, who had arrived at the same result by a different route.

The appeal judges, however, rejected Dr Tapp's new line of argument, partly because he could not exclude the possibility of death having occurred at 11.10, even though the earlier time was more likely. "He agreed that he was dealing with calculations that were necessarily imprecise and were based on a number of imponderables," said Lord Lane. This sidestepped the point that the original Crown case used a more or less precise time of death; and ignored altogether the fact that Tapp's estimate was more scientifically tenable than Benstead's. The latter simply used the standard formula for determining time of death (a body cools not at all for the first hour, and thereafter at the approximate rate of 1°C per hour) and entirely failed to take into account the variables that were present in this case: the relative warmth of the room and the heavy clothes on the body.

The second reason for the dismissal of Tapp's evidence was that the emergence of the room temperature was "not a new fact at all". Lord Lane said that the evidence "had been given by Dr Benstead at the first trial in July 1979. The information was consequently available to the defence at all times thereafter, and certainly at the date of the second trial."

This depends on the interpretation of the word "available". Benstead omitted the information from his postmortem report; his statement was never put in evidence. So the defence did not have the opportunity to assimilate the information beforehand. If it was mentioned at the first trial (as Lane asserted), it was not only the defence team which failed to grasp it. *Neither did the trial judge.* In his summing-up, Mr Justice Talbot said, "The time of death depends upon the ambient room temperature. He [Benstead] *could not say what it was in this case.*" The judge was in the dark about the point; so was the jury; so, evidently, was the Home Office, else it would not have wasted Lord Lane's time by bringing the matter to his attention. Most importantly, so was Dr Tapp. He did not attend either trial, so there was no realistic way in which he could have known the room temperature. Moreover, the information was not referred to during the decisive second trial; not even Lord Lane claimed that it was. Bearing all this in mind, it seems extraordinary that such a relatively arcane piece of information should have been described as "available".

To buttress the original estimate of Dr Benstead, Lord Lane referred to the testimony of Dr Phillips. Driving through Bamber Bridge on that Thursday evening, Dr Phillips was flagged down by a police constable on patrol, who had just received radio instructions to go to No. 41 The Crescent. As it happened, Dr Phillips was better qualified than almost any other passing motorist to attend the scene of the crime: he was both the local police surgeon and the Livesey family's own GP.

He examined the body at 11.37, and pronounced life extinct. He subsequently made two statements – one, the day after the murder; the other to the Benion inquiry – in which he said that death had occurred within the previous hour. Lord Lane referred to these statements as "potent evidence supporting the views of Dr Benstead". However, Phillips reached his conclusion on the basis that the body still felt warm, and that the blood was wet and glistening. In these respects, he displayed an ignorance of pathology. He could not gauge time of death by mere impressions of warmth; he needed actual temperatures, which he didn't have. Nor was he aware that Leslie Matthews had attempted to give Alan Livesey the kiss of life, as a result of which blood spurted from Alan's fatal wounds. Matthews was himself covered in blood when he arrived back home. This explained why the blood was glistening when Dr Phillips looked at the body.

The whole episode is reminiscent of the Luvaglio–Stafford case, in which the authorities relied for information about time of death on the observations of a GP, who wasn't trained in such matters. The evidence to determine time of death was simply not available to Dr Phillips. He himself noted shortly after Livesey's conviction that he was concerned only with the state of the body, and made no notes about time of death. Whether he would have been surprised at the importance attached to his comments by the Lord Chief Justice, we will never know. By the time of the 1986 appeal, he had died.

John Rowe QC, counsel for Livesey, then raised the matter of what he termed the "rogue packet of cigarettes". He was startled when his prosecution colleague, Ben Hytner QC, rose to say that the Crown did not contest that someone had been in the house that evening.

This was an electrifying moment for those of us in court. At both trials, the prosecution took pains to portray Peter Nightingale as a liar. Now, at appeal, the substance of his evidence was not challenged – an implicit acknowledgment that it was accurate.

Two considerations inevitably followed. Firstly, serious doubts were raised about the honesty and proficiency of the police murder investigation. If Nightingale was telling the truth about the visitor, was he also telling the truth when he said that he was pressured into changing his initial testimony? And why had this visitor – the last person, presumably, to see Alan alive – not been traced and eliminated from inquiries? Secondly, if the jury had known that there was a visitor in the house that night, to which both witness and forensic evidence could have attested, might not their assessment of the case have been radically different?

Crucial as this area of evidence seemed, the court dealt with it in a remarkably cursory way. Lane did concede that the extra packet of cigarettes "did not appear in the police reports" – that "there was also no report on the fact that there was a quantity of cigarette stubs also on the floor"; and that "no saliva tests had been carried out on the stub ends".

This amounted to gross negligence as far as the police investigation was concerned, and a serious failure to disclose evidence as far as judicial ethics were concerned. Lord Lane, though, uttered no word of criticism of the prosecution. Instead, he suggested that the concealed items were "apparent from examination of the photographs". This was not true. They only became "apparent" under detailed and microscopic examination, and after the photographs had been enlarged at the request of defence solicitors by the Director of Public Prosecutions. In normal conditions, they were not visible.

Lord Lane then turned to the matter of the saliva tests: "If the stubs had been tested and found to bear traces of saliva inconsistent with the grouping of any of the Liveseys, once again, beyond showing that someone else had at some time been in the house, it would have done nothing to help the case for the defence." Yet the whole point was that if someone else had been in the house, then the case ineluctably took on an entirely fresh perspective.

The main reason why their Lordships dissented from this interpretation was that in her 1984 re-investigation statement, Mrs Livesey said that the back door was bolted when she returned home. Never mind that this contradicted all her previous testimony: according to her evidence-in-chief, she said she went in through the back door; under cross-examination, she insisted that she had done so. Never mind that, because the house was an end one, the visitor could have left by the front door and walked round the back. Never mind that it could simply have been an inaccurate recollection. This proved "beyond peradventure", as Mr Justice McCowan put it, that the visitor could not have been the murderer. Livesey was, in the opinion of Leah Levin, "doomed out of her own mouth both at her trial and at her appeal". Theoretically, one of the safeguards of English justice is that people do not bear witness against themselves (which is why defendants are not obliged to give evidence). In Livesey's case, this fundamental safeguard seemed to have been removed.

Because Peter Nightingale specifically referred to the sound of the back-door bolt being drawn back, Livesey's 1984 statement clearly created some confusion. Had the evidence been tested, an explanation might well have been forthcoming. The evidence, however, was not tested: neither Mrs Livesey herself nor the officers who took it gave evidence concerning it. Surely, then, it was inadmissible?

The problem for the defence was that Rowe sought to refer to the re-investigation statement of Frank Bamber, the man who had given Livesey a lift from the pub and with whom she was having an affair. According to this, he drove her to the top of her road, and said he dropped her off just *after* 11.00. He could now be certain of the time because, after racking his brains, he had remembered that the conversation about pay rises (to which he alluded in his original statement) had been stimulated by an item on the BBC radio 11.00 p.m. news bulletin. Mr Justice Simon Brown remarked that, "Bamber's evidence, if established, is clearly fatal to the Crown."

The evidence was independently verified. Livesey's solicitors checked with the BBC and learned that Bamber's evidence was spot-on: the lead item in that bulletin concerned pay awards. There was no conceivable way in which Bamber himself could have discovered this.

Lord Lane hardly bothered to consider the point. "If that was so," he said about the BBC corroboration of the evidence, "it seemed incredible that he [Bamber] made no mention of such a vital fact in 1979 at the trial." At such a moment, Hugo Young's assessment of the performance of Lord Widgery, Lord Lane's predecessor, at the 1974 Luvaglio–Stafford appeal came irresistibly to mind: "there was no subtle forensic examination; just the blunt instrument of judicial assertion".

Lane concluded: "We have carefully considered all these matters, and are not of the view that this conviction was in any way unsafe or unsatisfactory. We add only this. If, as Mr Rowe suggests, it is legitimate for us to look at the 1984 re-investigation evidence for items favourable to the appellant [i.e. Bamber's statement] it is equally legitimate to look at other evidence from the same source favourable to the prosecution." Thus, Bamber's statement became not merely unavailing, but positively disadvantageous, as their Lordships trawled through the 1984 file for material damaging to Mrs Livesey (like a statement from Mrs Matthews saying that Livesey only ever called in the most exceptional circumstances; like her own about the back door being bolted).

There was one simple reason why this judicial manoeuvre was grossly unfair: *Frank Bamber was dead*. Consequently, Rowe had no alternative but to refer to his 1984 statement. The other witnesses were all still alive. If necessary, their evidence could have been tested in court.

Meanwhile, the mere fact of Bamber's death speaks volumes about review procedures in the UK criminal justice system. When *Rough Justice* alerted millions of viewers to the possibility of a miscarriage of justice over three years earlier, he was still alive. Livesey's chances of a successful appeal were seriously handicapped by his death. In that respect, she became another victim of the scandalous dilatoriness of British bureaucracy.

There are compelling grounds for believing Margaret Livesey innocent of the murder of her son. There was simply no time available in which she could have murdered him. She did not leave the pub until closing-time; that was not in dispute. At that time, the licensee of the Queen's Hotel had lately been prosecuted for serving drinks after hours. Both the prosecution at the trial and the appeal judges emphasised that in those circumstances the pub would have closed promptly (as bar-staff said it did). However, an equally valid interpretation is that, in those circumstances, they would certainly not admit that the pub failed to close promptly.

In any case, there is no dispute that Margaret Livesey and Frank Bamber were the last to leave the car-park that night. The parts of Livesey's timetable – leaving the pub, waiting while Bamber scraped the ice off the car, chatting to him in the car, walking round to the Matthews house where she stopped to talk to the two boys before ringing the bell – fit coherently together. There is no missing twelve-minute period.

There was no forensic evidence of any kind against Livesey, even though the circumstances were such that one would have expected to find a great deal. Criminals who have all the time in the world to remove vital clues will find it impossible to destroy all the evidence. Not that Livesey had all the time in the world; even the prosecution admitted that she had barely any time at all.

On arriving at the Matthews house, she appeared perfectly normal – no one suggested otherwise. She had a bandage on her leg. She made no attempt to conceal it – it was the subject of some conversation – and it was not blood-stained.

The knots around Alan's wrists were complicated and would have taken some time to do, even if his mother would have been capable of tying them, which seems unlikely. There is no evidence that she knew how to do reef knots; the 1984 re-investigation surmounted this difficulty by suggesting that they could be tied by accident. Her original deposition, made the morning after Alan's death when the questioning was not hostile, was a detailed one. Its timetable was subsequently confirmed by seven separate prosecution witnesses. Had she been concocting a false story, it is unbelievable that it would have received such precise corroboration. According to the prosecution, she turned right when she left her house after committing the murder and walked the long way round her road. Yet the prosecution could discover not a single witness who saw her do this. Everyone who saw her after she left the pub saw her at a spot which coincided with the defence case.

Had she committed the murder, there was no earthly reason for her to present herself at a neighbour's house straightaway afterwards. Her husband was safely out of the way on his night-shift and her two older children had left home. She could have given herself time to attempt to destroy incriminating evidence and to plan a story.

There are, however, innumerable indications that Alan Livesey was the victim of an attack by a youth at about 10 o'clock that evening. Dr Tapp and Professor Cameron believe that death occurred at around that time, shortly after Susan Warren and Ronald Mason heard the "larking about" noises – and shortly before Peter Nightingale saw a youth leaving the house. The cigarette evidence – and, more importantly, the fact that it was suppressed – pointed to the presence of someone else in the house. Ultimately, indeed, the Crown did not dispute that someone else had been there.

If this was indeed a homosexual bondage case, then everything falls exactly into place. It explains why Alan changed into his cadet uniform. The idea of a kind of torture game, which the surface cuts suggested, could perhaps have come from a copy of the *Daily Mirror* which was lying in the room and which contained a feature about torture methods used by paramilitary groups. Alan then allowed his arms to be pinioned, and his attacker sat astride him. That would explain the absence of blood splashes on the walls and the furniture: he was never standing up. It would explain his inability to defend himself, even with his heavy boots; and it would explain the fact that his clothing was rumpled at the stomach, indicating that he had arched his back as the only defensive option open to him.

Two considerations remain. If Margaret Livesey was innocent, what reason would Christine Norris and Susan Warren have had for concocting what the Lord Chief Justice said would have been "a wicked and false story about the appellant"?

The mistake lies in believing that the story must either have been true, or else have been "wicked and false". It was false, certainly, but not wicked. In conversation, they obviously just convinced themselves that it was true. It is by no means unknown for people to share a common delusion, using someone else's mistaken belief to reinforce their own. Thus, the cycle of self-deception becomes self-perpetuating. That, indeed, is the prime reason why witness evidence should be regarded with special caution.

The Lord Chief Justice acknowledged that Norris and Warren were "very confused as to the times", but he nevertheless relied on their evidence. In doing so, he automatically rejected Ronald Mason's, on the grounds that he was slightly deaf. If, however, Mason was slightly deaf, then surely his evidence is significant not for what he did not hear, but *what he did hear* – i.e. the "larking about" at 10 o'clock.

Then, there is the 'confession'. During the eighties, for the first time, serious research has been undertaken in criminal psychology into the reasons why some people in police custody make false confessions. These fell broadly into three categories. Freely volunteered statements from those who are mentally ill – a syndrome which has long been known about. Compliant statements made under some form of pressure; people set aside long-term considerations for short-term benefits (like getting bail, going to sleep, or merely being asked no more questions). The false confessions in the Maxwell Confait case come into this category. Thirdly, those which result from the person accepting under questioning – however temporarily

– that he or she has committed the crime. Such 'confessions' are generally the result either of a mental handicap, or of a short-term mental state of particular distress. The circumstance most likely to trigger this is bereavement, in the aftermath of which people are frequently both distressed and self-critical. Margaret Livesey's seems a classic case of the third type. Indeed, her 'confession' appears to have been extracted in parallel circumstances to that of Timothy Evans (*see* Chapter 1).

The Lord Chief Justice Lord Lane was persuaded by the fact that within forty-eight hours of her 'confession' she repeated it both to her elder son and her husband, and to her solicitor at the magistrates court.[3] However, all this proves is that she was continuing to suffer from the same short-term mental disability (known to psychologists as an acute adjustment reaction). Three days later, she 'came to', as it were, and has protested her innocence ever since. Evans was convinced of his guilt for a similar period, until he recovered his full mental faculties.

The appeal was dismissed on 16 December (judgment having been reserved for a week). Margaret Livesey was returned to Styal prison, Cheshire, the victim of a family double-tragedy: the son murdered, the mother erroneously convicted of his murder. In all, she had endured two trials and two attempts at appeal. Such is the decrepitude of the British judicial system, her case has yet to receive a fair hearing.

Part Two

The Irish Cases

In the just struggle against terrorism we vitiate our cause unless we do all within our power to keep the sword and scales of justice clean and unsullied.

Sir John Biggs-Davison
(Conservative MP for Epping Forest)
House of Commons
4 August 1980

Eleven

Background

In 1974 the IRA pursued a major terrorist campaign on the British mainland. On 5 October bombs were placed in two Guildford pubs, the Horse & Groom and the Seven Stars. Both were popular with young Guards recruits from Pirbright and Aldershot, and girls from the WRAC training camp at Stoughton, near Guildford. The Horse & Groom bomb exploded at 8.30 p.m., killing five people, including four army recruits, and injuring many more. By the time the Seven Stars bomb went off an hour later the landlord had cleared his pub, and there were no casualties.

One month later, at 10.00 p.m. on 7 November, a bomb was hurled into the King's Arms in Woolwich, opposite the Royal Artillery depot. It contained two pounds of commercial plastic explosive, with nuts and bolts packed round it. Two people were killed. Again, there were many injuries.

Then, on 14 November, a Birmingham IRA man, James McDade, blew himself up while attempting to plant a bomb outside the Coventry telephone exchange. It was apparently in response to this setback that the IRA wreaked its cruellest havoc. On 21 November, the day that McDade's remains were being flown to Belfast, two bombs, placed in popular pubs in the centre of Birmingham, exploded at about 8.20 p.m. The one in the Tavern in the Town killed eleven people; the one in the Mulberry Bush, built on the basement level of the Rotunda, a distinctive local landmark, took ten lives. There were in addition 161 serious injuries. The victims were mainly young people.

Birmingham has traditionally been host to a large Irish community – which numbered around 100,000 at this time – and anti-Irish feeling has long been latent. This outrage brought it welling up spectacularly. Appeals from both the

Prime Minister, Harold Wilson, and the Home Secretary, Roy Jenkins, not to embark on reprisals against Irish people went unheeded. The Irish Community Centre, an inevitable target for petrol-bombing, was hit twice. Less inevitable a target, perhaps, was a Roman Catholic junior school, though it too was attacked; as was the College Arms, a pub in the Kingstanding district known to attract a large Irish clientele.[1] On Friday 22 November there were fisticuffs between English and Irish workers on the production line at British Leyland's car assembly plant at Longbridge. A company spokesman explained that the men "had expressed their disgust at the reprehensible events of the night before".[2]

Anti-Irish hysteria, albeit most prominent in Birmingham, flared up across the nation, and quickly made itself felt in parliament. The Home Secretary introduced the Prevention of Terrorism (Temporary Provisions) Bill within a week of the bombings in what, retrospectively, seems like indecent haste. The Bill made membership of and support for the IRA an offence. It also introduced exclusion orders which gave the British government powers to restrict the movements of designated citizens within its own borders. Additionally, the police were empowered to arrest without warrant anyone they reasonably suspected of being concerned in terrorism, but against whom they had not assembled sufficient evidence in regard to a specific offence. Police could detain someone arrested under this provision for forty-eight hours; but the Home Secretary could permit an extension of the detention for a further five days – so that the bill encroached upon the traditional liberty of *habeas corpus*.

The Prevention of Terrorism Act, as it became, went through all its stages in the Commons in twenty hours, and passed unamended through the Lords in just three minutes. It came into force at 9.25 a.m. on Friday 29 November. Hitherto, the initials PTA had stood, totally uncontroversially, for 'Parent–Teacher Association'; now they took on an almost sinister aspect.

The passing of the PTA, to assuage public opinion, was the overt reaction to the bombings. There was also a covert one. Dialogue with the IRA was resumed. All it took was a call to the Northern Ireland office from a Belfast telephone-box. Within a month, Irish Republican leaders and British government officials were engaged in discussions in Feakle, County Clare and on 22 December, the IRA declared a Christmas cease-fire.

The negotiations got nowhere. The bombings restarted and continued throughout 1975. This phase of the IRA terror campaign was only brought to a halt with the Balcombe Street siege in December, and the arrests of Joseph O'Connell, Eddie Butler, Harry Duggan and Hugh Doherty.

Twelve

The Arrests

THE FIRST person arrested under the PTA, within hours of its receiving the Royal Assent, was Paul Hill. Belfast-born, he lived in a squat in Kilburn, north London, but was picked up at the Southampton home of the parents of his girlfriend, Gina Clarke. On 30 November another friend from Belfast, Gerard Conlon, who had spent some time in England from August to October 1974, was arrested at the family home in Cyprus Street, Belfast, and taken to Springfield Road police barracks. From there he was flown to England and taken to Guildford police station.

At Guildford, Surrey police obtained from Hill and Conlon not only confessions to the Guildford bombings, but also a long list of friends, relatives and acquaintances supposedly involved in IRA activities. Conlon provided the crucial name of his aunt, Annie Maguire. A large number of people were then rounded up, including thirty-eight from Kilburn squats. Among these were Patrick Armstrong, another lad from Belfast, and his English girlfriend, Carole Richardson. They, together with Hill and Conlon, ultimately stood trial for the Guildford and Woolwich bombings.

Hill and Conlon also provided addresses of what were supposed to be two bomb factories. Hill referred to visiting a Brixton flat, where explosives had been stacked in a corner. There the police discovered only an elderly couple, and decided not to pursue inquiries.

The other address – 43 Third Avenue, Harlesden, north London – was where Conlon's aunt Annie Maguire lived, together with her husband, Paddy, three sons – Vincent (born August 1958), John (born July 1959) and Patrick (born March 1961) – her daughter, Anne-Marie (born October 1966), and her brother, Sean Smyth. On 3

December they were joined by Guiseppe Conlon, who was married to Paddy's sister, Sarah.

Conlon snr was born in Belfast in 1923, and christened Patrick Joseph. Because his godfather, Joe Roffe, was an Italian who owned a chip shop in Divis Street, 'Guiseppe' was added to the birth certificate; and, presumably to distinguish him from everyone else christened Patrick Joseph, that is what they all called him.

During the war Conlon served in the Royal Marines. By the seventies, however, he was very frail. For his various illnesses, which included pulmonary tuberculosis, he was prescribed twenty-six tablets a day. He had not worked for fifteen years, and rarely left his home.

When his son Gerard was arrested and, protesting his innocence, flown to England, Guiseppe determined, despite his incapacity, to do all he could to help him. Through the offices of a Belfast solicitor, Ted Jones, a London firm of solicitors was contacted. A telegram was also sent to the Maguire household. Conlon and Jones arranged to meet at the offices of the solicitors – Simons, Muirhead and Allan – on 3 December. Jones was subsequently informed by Surrey police that no one would be allowed to see Gerry Conlon until later in the week. He consequently delayed his own trip – sending a second telegram to the Maguires, to inform Guiseppe.

By then, however, Guiseppe was already on his way, having disregarded the advice of his doctor (Joe Hendron, who also happened to be a local SDLP councillor) that he was too ill to travel; and having informed the RUC of the purpose of his trip. He asked neighbours to drive him to the ferry and reached Heysham, Lancashire, at 5.30 the following morning. He exchanged a few words with an immigration officer, and then boarded the London train. He fell asleep on the journey, and arrived at Euston at about noon.

Despite the telegram to Annie's home, he had hoped to contact first of all another brother-in-law, Hugh Maguire. However, he failed to reach him by telephone, and accord-

ingly took a taxi to Harlesden. When he arrived between
1.10 and 1.30 only Paddy was at home to receive him. As
Guiseppe feared, Paddy immediately enticed him down to
the local pub, the Royal Lancer.

When they returned at closing-time, Annie showed
Guiseppe the telegram informing him that he would be
unable to see Gerry for a day or two. Then while Annie
cooked a meal in the kitchen Paddy telephoned the London
solicitors, and Guiseppe spoke to them. A meeting was
fixed for the following day. For the remainder of the
afternoon, Guiseppe hardly moved from the living-room.
He just dozed in an armchair in front of the television.

There were some comings and goings. Annie and Paddy,
a warm-hearted couple, were generous with their hospi-
tality. Sean Tully, a friend of Hugh's, made two separate
visits, and just after 6.45 another friend, Pat O'Neill,
arrived. His visit was entirely fortuitous; although, in the
circumstances, the word should perhaps be 'inopportune'.
His wife, expecting their fourth child, had been admitted
to hospital because of complications with the pregnancy.
O'Neill had therefore asked her sister to take care of
their three children while he was at work. However, his
father-in-law was then taken seriously ill, and his sister-in-
law had returned to Ireland. So he had collected his children from school and then gone to Annie's because she
had agreed to help him out and look after them for him.

At 8 o'clock he spoke to his wife in hospital, no doubt
reassuring her that all was well. At 8.15 he, Paddy,
Guiseppe and Sean Smyth, who had lately returned from
work, all went to the pub.

The police officers keeping watch outside incorrectly
noted the time of departure to the pub as a quarter to eight
(7.45) instead of a quarter past eight (8.15). It was a simple
error which had unforeseen consequences.

The Maguires' eldest son, Vincent, returned home from
evening classes at a quarter to nine, and noticed a large
number of police cars parked outside with their lights
switched off. Moments after he had entered the house, the

police rang the doorbell and were admitted without demur. Annie and her children were taken to Harrow Road police station. John Maguire showed two police officers the way to the pub. The four men were taken in for questioning from there, just as they were about to start the second round of drinks. They, too, offered no resistance.

The task of rounding up the suspects had been carried out by Surrey CID. The chief constable of Surrey was apparently determined to show that his men could take responsibility for the whole operation. Indeed, when the Kilburn squatters were taken in, Surrey police carried their weapons into an area of Metropolitan Police jurisdiction without first receiving clearance to do so: a remarkable occurrence.

As part of the wide seizure, Hugh Maguire, his wife and a friend had all been held for questioning; hence their absence when Guiseppe Conlon had tried to telephone them. They were all released after a week in custody. Friends of those netted in the raid on Annie Maguire's home assumed theirs would be a similar fate. At a time of escalating antipathy towards those of Irish origin, seven dispiriting days in custody seemed almost par for the course.

Subsequent events, however, were nothing if not unforeseen. Firstly, Pat O'Neill was released on the following day: a Wednesday. He renewed his search for someone to take in his children while his wife was in hospital. Having accomplished this successfully, he returned to work. Three days later, at 7.00 a.m. on Saturday morning, the police pounded on his door and re-arrested him.

The Maguire youngsters were released, but the others were taken to Guildford and held on remand there. (Annie was held at Godalming and Guildford police stations.) Their weekly court appearances, too, were made in Guildford, a city which none of the family had been to before.

The four men were charged with possession of explosives. Annie Maguire was charged with murder in connection with the Guildford and Woolwich bombing offences. At that time, the police were holding eight people on that charge: the four who eventually stood trial; Annie; and John McGuiness, Brian Anderson and Paul Colman, three others from Kilburn.

Annie did have an alibi for the evening when the Guildford bombs had exploded. By chance, 5 October happened to be the birthday of her neighbour's daughter, two days before Anne-Marie's. So, they could remember being together in the early evening. The police checked this alibi, and found that it was watertight.

Because Annie also refused to allow herself to be cajoled or bullied into fallacious admissions, there wasn't a scrap of admissible evidence against her, or, indeed, against McGuiness, Anderson or Colman either. On 3 February 1975, Michael Hill, for the Director of Public Prosecutions, told the Guildford court that it had been decided not to press further with charges against these three, who were all awarded costs out of public funds.

Annie Maguire was held in custody on the murder indictment until 24 February when, on her thirteenth appearance before magistrates, the prosecution finally dropped the charge. Annie, however, was hardly in a position to celebrate. She was still remanded on a charge of possessing explosives; and two of her children, Vincent, sixteen, and Patrick, thirteen, were taken back into custody and similarly charged. They were both admitted to a juvenile remand home, which caused her great distress.

It was a time of rare celebrity for Guildford Guildhall, where committal proceedings were held. On 19 March, Hill, Conlon, Armstrong and Carole Richardson were sent for trial; the following day, so were the seven defendants in the Maguire case.

Annie remained in custody until 15 April when her solicitor finally obtained bail for her, to allow her to look after eight-year-old Anne-Marie.

Thirteen

The Guildford and Woolwich
Pub-bombs Case

People in the case

Paul Hill
Gerard Conlon
Patrick Armstrong — charged with Guildford & Woolwich bombing offences
Carole Richardson

Mr Justice Donaldson — trial judge
Sir Michael Havers QC — prosecution counsel
Lord Wigoder QC — defence counsel
Eric Myers QC — defence counsel

Annie Maguire
John McGuiness
Brian Anderson — implicated by statements given in police custody
Paul Colman

Gina Clarke — girlfriend of Paul Hill
Detective Chief Superintendent Walter Simmons — head of Surrey CID, leading bombing inquiry
Detective Inspector Blake — Surrey police officer
Alastair Logan — solicitor for Armstrong
Brian McLoughlin — prosecution witness
Frank Johnson
Lisa Astin — defence witnesses
Jack the Lad — folk/rock music group
Brian Shaw — former British Army soldier; murder victim

Joseph O'Connell
Harry Duggan
Hugh Doherty — IRA personnel, known as the Balcombe Street Four
Eddie Butler

Brendan Dowd
Sean Kinsella — IRA terrorists

Commander Jim Nevil
Detective Chief Superintendent Peter Imbert — bomb squad officers

Frank Maguire — MP for Fermanagh & South Tyrone

James Still — retired police inspector
Mr Justice Cantley — judge at Balcombe Street trial
John Mathew QC — prosecution counsel
Richard Harvey — defence counsel
PC Cotton
Inspector Carrington } — police witnesses
Douglas Higgs
Donald Lidstone } — forensic scientists

THE TRIAL of Paul Hill, Gerard Conlon, Patrick Armstrong and Carole Richardson opened at the Old Bailey on 16 September 1975 and lasted until 22 October. All four were found guilty of charges of murder and conspiracy to cause explosions relating to the Guildford bombings. Hill and Armstrong alone were indicted on counts of murder and conspiracy to cause explosions at Woolwich. Both were found guilty, although the Crown contended that Hill only was present at the scene; Armstrong was convicted on the grounds of being what would once have been called an 'accessory before the fact'.

The sentences were noteworthy for being the longest ever handed down in an English court of law, and were in due course entered in the *Guinness Book of Records*. The convicted quartet were all sentenced to life imprisonment, but Mr Justice Donaldson used his judicial discretion to make recommendations of minimum terms. He indicated that Carole Richardson should serve at least 20 years; Conlon not less than 30 years; and Armstrong not less than 35. "I must stress the words 'not less than'," he added. "I do not mean by this recommendation to give you any reason for hoping that after 30 or 35 years you will necessarily ever be released."

He was at his most Draconian, however, when addressing Paul Hill: "In my view your crime is such that life imprisonment must mean life. If as an act of mercy you are ever to be released it could only be on account of great age or infirmity."

Hill was then aged twenty-one, so that he had suddenly become the person condemned to the longest period of incarceration in British penal history. Why, though, had he become the prime target of the police in the first place?

In court, police did not need to reveal what prompted their interest in Hill. They simply said they were acting on "information received". Subsequently, Detective Chief Superintendent Walter Simmons, head of Surrey CID, said on television that he paid £350 to an informer in Belfast for the name. What could possibly have happened is this: Paul Hill seems to have played a peripheral role in the abduction of Brian Shaw, who was taken at gunpoint from a Belfast bar and, on 20 July 1974, found shot dead in a house in the Falls Road area of the city. Press reports portrayed him as an innocent victim of the troubles: a former soldier, from Nottinghamshire, who bought himself out of the army so that he could marry a Belfast girl. The Provisional IRA argued that this story was a cover, and that Shaw belonged to the SAS and had attempted to plant a bomb in a Catholic area. He was kidnapped, 'tried' and executed. Hill, at least, was present in the pub at the time of the abduction.

Afterwards, he took an Armalite rifle from an IRA arms cache, but ran into an army patrol and, after exchanging a few shots, dropped the gun. The IRA seems to have been suspicious of this story; they thought that Hill may have given the gun to the army, and that he could even be an informer. Whatever the exact circumstances, Hill seems to have been in some trouble: wanted by the security services for his role in the Shaw affair; and, according to one former intelligence officer, "in bad odour with the Provisionals". He fled to England, where he kept his head down. During the week he worked on building sites; the weekends he spent with Gina Clarke in Southampton.

On a visit to Belfast, Gerry Conlon seems to have been interviewed by a couple of IRA men, and to have told them about Hill and Clarke. It was shortly after this that Simmons got his tip from an informant, passed on by army intelligence. Perhaps the informant himself implicated Hill in the Guildford bombing just to swell the value of his 'information'; perhaps he was acting for the IRA, who were setting up Hill, to teach him a lesson and/or to divert attention from the genuine IRA active-service unit waging a mainland terrorist campaign.

There is an alternative theory of how Hill's name came to Simmons' attention. Identikit pictures of two girls whom police said they wished to interview were published in all national newspapers on 9 October 1974. One army officer, who worked in intelligence in Northern Ireland, remarked that one of the identikits looked like Paul Hill in drag – and the Surrey police were informed.

Whatever the validity of this, it does illustrate the disarray of the police in the immediate aftermath of the bombings. They soon learned the identities of the two girls, who were victims, not perpetrators, of the bombings: one had been killed, the other seriously injured. The police tried to evade responsibility for this error by maintaining that the drawings had been prepared for their own guidance, were leaked to the press by an over-enthusiastic journalist, and published contrary to the wishes of Surrey constabulary. However, the pictures had also appeared, prominently, in *Police*. "I doubt very much," commented Alastair Logan, solicitor for Armstrong, "whether any enterprising journalist could have achieved that."

In the days after the Guildford bombings, the police tried to establish who had been in the pubs that evening, drawing up charts to show the positions of all the customers. Altogether, over 300 statements were collected from those who were in the pubs that evening. From this information, the police discovered that they were two people (a man and a girl) short in the Horse & Groom; and three people (a man and two girls) short in the Seven Stars. No one who knows anything about the case disputes that these were the bombers.

The police attempted to piece together descriptions of the suspects from statements. This proved not at all easy. Three Horse & Groom witnesses were positive about their descriptions, but these did not tally. Despite this handicap, an artist commissioned to sketch likenesses did produce two drawings. Neither looked like Armstrong or Richardson, the two who had, according to the prosecution, placed the bomb. The drawing even showed a clean-shaven man, though Armstrong had a beard throughout this period.

Eight witnesses from the Horse & Groom failed to pick out Carole Richardson in an identity parade. None of the others was ever put in one – a curious omission in view of the prosecution contention that Armstrong and Richardson had been sitting on top of a primed bomb for at least half an hour in full view of everyone; as had the bombers in the Seven Stars. (The prosecution's case was that Conlon and an unknown girl had planted that bomb, with Hill acting as look-out.)

Consequently, there was no material witness evidence against the four accused; nor was there any forensic evidence. The prosecution case rested squarely on admissions which the four were alleged to have made of their own volition while in police custody.

However, all four entirely repudiated these statements and maintained that they were made under duress. According to Hill, threats of violence were made against him from the outset when, together with Gina Clarke, he was taken for interrogation to Shirley police station, Southampton. From there they were both transferred to Guildford, and driven past the Horse & Groom – "that's the pub you blew up," police told him. At the police station, Hill was subjected to brutal treatment. Not only from Surrey constabulary, but also RUC officers, flown over from Belfast to interview him in connection with the Brian Shaw murder. As a result, Hill claimed, both of the violence he suffered – he mentioned a gun being held to his head – and of threats against Gina Clarke, who was pregnant with their child at the time, he signed statements put in front of him which were full confessions to both crimes.

At the trial, Armstrong said that he was extremely frightened, high on drugs, and being punched by Christopher Rowe, the assistant chief constable of Surrey. Richardson said that she was beaten by police during interrogation and was afraid of what might happen if she did not say what the police wanted her to. She said her statements were virtually dictated to her. She apparently told police, "You know I wasn't in Guildford. I was forced to make this statement." For their part, the police denied reducing her to "an abject state of terror".[1] Lord Wigoder, QC for the defence, put it to police witnesses that Conlon had been slapped in the kidneys and the testicles, and that threats had been made against the Conlon family back home in Belfast.

A number of points can be made about the allegations of police brutality. Annie Maguire had met Hill once previously, at a dance on 11 October. She saw him briefly during the intense questioning at Guildford police station and said that he was beaten so thoroughly he was virtually unrecognisable. (It should also be pointed out that on 19 September the trial resumed forty-five minutes late. When it finally did start, Hill appeared in a somewhat battered condition. Most newspapers commented on the visible damage to his right eye – the result, Hill claims, of ill-treatment by prison officers in Wandsworth.[2])

The defence did score one notable bull's-eye during the trial. Conlon said in evidence that a Detective Inspector Blake had taken off his jacket, rolled up his sleeves and "set about me". Conlon remembered that the man had a tattoo on his arm. The officer was asked to roll up his sleeves in court. He did have a tattoo.

The interrogation of Carole Richardson, only seventeen at the time, breached the judge's rules in that no parent, guardian or legal representative was present. (This issue caused great unease in the Maxwell Confait case, and opened the way for the overturning of the convictions.)

The 'confessions' contained no more information about the crimes than that the police would already have possessed. Richardson was alleged to have drawn a picture of a bomb, but it was the sort of thing a child would have produced, and one Crown witness said he would be hard-pressed to describe it as a drawing of a bomb.

As accounts of the crime, the 'confessions' were seriously flawed. According to them, Annie Maguire, McGuiness, Anderson and Colman had been involved in the bomb attacks. By Conlon's account, Annie travelled with them in the car to Guildford. Yet those charges against the four were all dropped.[3] In respect of the involvement of McGuiness, Anderson, Colman and Annie Maguire, therefore, the 'confessions' were evidently untrue. In respect of Hill's assertions about a bomb factory at the Brixton address, they were evidently untrue. Further, Carole Richardson had confessed to bombing *both* pubs. In this respect, too, they were evidently untrue. Even Sir Michael Havers QC, prosecution counsel, conceded that. He attempted to surmount this difficulty by propounding the theory that this was deliberate misinformation: the Provisional IRA was attempting to outwit police interrogators by answering with a cunning and confusing mixture of lies, half-truths and the truth (though Havers was unable to explain how a relatively simple seventeen-year-old girl could have mastered such sophisticated counter-interrogation techniques). Altogether, there were over a hundred discrepancies in the 'confessions'; Havers told the jury that "their separate stories, given in confessions, fitted together like a jigsaw". The Crown thus argued both that the confessions had an erratic relationship with the truth; and that they were truthful and reliable. In the end, Hill, Conlon, Armstrong and Carole Richardson were convicted on the basis of the 'confessions' being both "voluntary and true".

There was barely any corroborative evidence against any of them. However, the prosecution did call Brian McLoughlin, who also lived in the squat, to testify against Armstrong. He said that Armstrong was always talking about bombings, and had once invited him to "do a pub". He said that altogether he had taken in about twenty parcels for Armstrong. He had once opened one himself, and found it to contain two guns; once, he had seen Armstrong opening one containing cartridges.

This evidence seems implausible; front-line IRA men do not fail to take basic security precautions. In view of the fact that McLoughlin was the token prison grass – he was serving a Borstal sentence at the time – it is probably safe to disregard it.

It is not just the absence of genuine independent evidence which raises doubts about the guilt of Hill and the others. Carole Richardson had an alibi. Originally, when asked what she had been doing on the evening of the bombing, she said she couldn't remember. She would be able to say, however, if she could see her diary. This, it was later learned, had been destroyed in an incident at the squat.

However, on 20 December 1974, Frank Johnson, a friend from Newcastle-upon-Tyne, walked into a police station and said, "One of the people you've got for the Guildford bombings is the wrong person, 'cause I was with her that night."

During the summer of 1974, Johnson, then working for a printer's in Colindale, north London, met Carole Richardson in a Kilburn pub, the Memphis Belle. Having been born in Gateshead, she recognised his friendly Tyneside accent and introduced herself. On 5 October, together with Lisa Astin, Carole's friend, they went to a concert at the South Bank Polytechnic, at the Elephant & Castle in London. Frank was a friend of the members of one of the groups playing there, Jack the Lad, an off-shoot of the popular Newcastle band, Lindisfarne.

He arrived at the pre-arranged meeting-place, the Charlie Chaplin pub, at about 6.15 p.m., ordered a Guinness and put "Geronimo's Cadillac" on the juke-box. Ten or fifteen minutes later, Lisa and Carole arrived. They all went to the concert together, and met the group. The brother-in-law of Willie Mitchell, the lead singer, came from Montreal, Canada, and was paying his first visit to Britain. He took a number of photographs in the dressing-room, several of which included Carole.

In December 1974 Johnson went down to London for a party, and was told of Carole's arrest. On the coach back to Newcastle, he retraced the weeks in his mind. "The police seemed to think it was a long time to be able to remember something, but it was only a couple of months back. Events were still fresh in my mind. I remembered Carlisle [United, the football team] winning at Chelsea and leading the First Division, and also incidents from the general election campaign." Back in Newcastle, he rang Mitchell just to check the group's itinerary against his memory; he did have the right date.

Johnson, who had two convictions for possession of LSD, was disinclined to go straight to the police. He rang the clerk of the court at Guildford, who refused to disclose information about defence solicitors; he rang the NCCL, but didn't get very far. "After a couple of days, I thought this is ridiculous. I went to Newcastle central police station, and asked for the station sergeant."

After being seen by local special branch officers, Johnson went home. A couple of hours later, police telephoned and asked him to meet them. He was taken back to the police station, where he was kept waiting for a few hours, until three officers from Surrey Constabulary's bombings inquiry team walked in. "I could tell that things weren't very friendly."

Johnson's information was not exactly welcomed by Surrey police. The prosecution case, already drawn up, was that Richardson and Armstrong planted the Horse & Groom bomb between 6.30 and 7.00. According to Johnson's statement, he was with Richardson from 6.30 for the rest of the evening.

He was made to go through his story again. It was taken down and read back to him. The police asked if he was sure he knew Carole, and showed him photographs; he confirmed that he did. "Then they said to me, 'look, she's told us she did it. You say, she was with you'. I said, 'yes'. They said, 'well, if you were with her, you must have been in Guildford. We'll just have to charge you with murder.'

I said, 'fair enough'. I thought it was all a big joke really."

Johnson was kept in a cell overnight, given some breakfast, but left on his own until late afternoon. He then made a fresh statement which was taken in the presence of both local and Surrey police. By this time, his story had been checked with members of Jack the Lad, who corroborated it. Johnson was photographed, and then sent home. "They apologised for the fact that there wasn't a car to take me home. For the next few days I listened to the news bulletins, expecting to hear that Carole had been released."

After Christmas, Johnson got a job in an abattoir. One Tuesday afternoon in late January, as he was leaving work, unwashed and smelling of animal fats, a plainclothes detective beckoned him into a police car. He was taken back to Newcastle's West End police station.

"I said, 'I want to talk to a solicitor,' and they said, 'You're not talking to anybody, nobody knows where you are.' They refused even to let me wash, saying, 'You've probably got nitroglycerine on your hands.'"

Once again, police had come up from Guildford. They asked him if he wanted to change his story. Johnson replied that everything happened the way he said it did. He was again kept overnight, only this time instructions were left that he was to have a rough time. The blankets were removed from his cell: "See if you can catch pneumonia tonight," police said.

The next morning he was taken by Surrey police to Newcastle airport. He was handcuffed and, as though a dangerous criminal, taken ahead of other passengers on board a Dan-Air flight to Gatwick, where a car with uniformed policemen was waiting on the tarmac. He was put in the back, and handcuffed to a kind of handle on the floor.

He was taken to Guildford and, like Paul Hill, driven past the bombed pubs. At the police station, he was charged with offences under the Prevention of Terrorism Act. (By that stage, he had already been in police custody for about eighteen hours.)

The police used disorientating interview techniques to interrogate him. He was told to talk to an officer at the far end of the room, while another sat in front of him, a little to the side, clicking his knuckles and making fists, just outside his line of vision. A third officer in the room typed down everything that was said. "I wasn't physically abused at all the first day. There were sideways threats, nothing direct. They removed my glasses, saying 'We don't want to pay for a new pair'."

He was kept overnight again, and the next day subjected to the same kind of treatment – though this time violence was used, and he was punched on a number of occasions by the officer sitting close to him. He was shown the self-incriminating statements of those charged with the bombings – "they were so full of inconsistencies they were obviously made under duress" – and further threats were made: to push him out of the window; to shoot him; most unnervingly, to set fire to his mother, who suffered from multiple sclerosis and was confined to a wheelchair. Eventually, the physical and psychological pressure told. "I thought I'm gonna end up here and be charged and not be of use to anyone. I'm just gonna make an idiot of myself. They kept making it clear that they could simply verbal me if they wanted to, that I had no access to solicitors, that no one knew where I was and that if I didn't cooperate I might not be there for anybody to know about anyway." He agreed to sign a fresh statement which served the interests of the police by giving them about two minutes to spare on their version of Carole Richardson's timetable; and which effectively annulled the previous one because Johnson now said he discussed the alibi beforehand with Lisa Astin. He was then advised to take a holiday on the continent, and told that if he turned up in court to give evidence, they'd make sure he got "at least 17 years for attempting to pervert the course of justice".

He was released about 7 o'clock on the Friday evening, still wearing the same clothes as he had when abducted from work, still without having been allowed to wash. He had been in police custody for about seventy-five hours. The third officer in the interview room, the one at the typewriter, slipped him 50p. He was taken to the railway station, and given a train ticket to Newcastle. It was after midnight when he arrived. As he was walking home, a police patrol car stopped to ask why he was walking around at that hour of the morning.[4]

At the trial, Johnson did revert to his original statement. He explained that he signed an alternative one only under duress, and that he knew Carole could never be involved in anything like a bombing. Nor was his the only evidence on this point. Lisa Astin testified that she had been with Carole throughout that entire Saturday, and that before going to the Poly they had been to Primrose Hill together. The photographs taken in the dressing-room were documentary evidence that Carole was with the group that night. Even the doorman at the Poly could remember that Carole and her friends arrived for the dance at about 7.30. (Being guests of the group, they had complimentary tickets, making it more likely that the doorman would remember their arrival.)

Eric Myers QC, counsel for Carole, pointed out to the court that the alibi evidence had not emerged from the defence, but had been discovered by the police. The defence, however, had not been told for some time about the development. The police and prosecution had not 'breathed a word' about Johnson, or about interviewing the group and taking statements from them. (Members of Jack the Lad were specifically told that they need not forward their evidence to defence solicitors.) "This was straight out of the dirty tricks department, wasn't it?" said Myers.

Confronted with all the alibi evidence, the prosecution really should have dropped all charges against Carole Richardson. By then, however, it was too late. The entire case depended on the fact that the four had acted together.

However, the second statement signed by Johnson gave the prosecution just sufficient room for manoeuvre. The Crown QC, Sir Michael Havers, set to work to reconcile the irreconcilable. He disregarded the evidence about Carole's movements before going to the dance, and argued that she could have left the Guildford pub a little before 7 o'clock and arrived at the dance shortly before 8 o'clock. Under cross-examination, the doorman did concede that she could possibly have arrived at the dance as late as 7.45. This, allowed, say, 50 minutes for the journey from Guildford to the Elephant & Castle. Triumphantly, the police announced that they had timed the run at 48 minutes.

Sadly, the jury chose to believe this.

In fact, it was not possible under normal traffic conditions to get from Guildford to the Elephant in that time. The police never revealed when they did their test run, but it is generally suspected that they did it early one morning, with sirens blaring. They certainly did not undertake the run at a busy period on a Saturday evening. The defence asked Daimler Car Hire to cover the route at that time on a Saturday, as fast as they possibly could. They did it twice, and clocked 64 and 65 minutes.

Even if the police timing is accepted, however, that does not allow for the time taken either to return to the car from the pub or, similarly, the time taken at the other end to walk from the car to the Poly. It does not allow for the fact that bombers were hardly likely to operate to a tight schedule: going into a pub, especially one filled with army personnel who were likely to be wary and suspicious, leaving the bomb, and then dashing out again. Nor does it allow for the fact that Carole must have changed her clothes during this flight back to London.

The basic difficulty with the prosecution scenario, though, is that real terrorists are unlikely to plan such a getaway. Their first priority is to evade capture. That, unfortunately, has never been very difficult. Timing devices on explosives allow bombers to make their escape without arousing suspicion, so that the establishment of a bogus alibi is, at best, a minor consideration. If it is likely, by attracting attention, to destroy the primary objective of a clean getaway, then it is pointless. In this case, to have dashed back to the Elephant at speed, presumably jumping red lights on the way, would have been as foolhardy as it was unnecessary.

There is a further weakness with the prosecution theory. *When Carole Richardson was asked where she was on the evening of 5 October, she said she couldn't remember.* In the absence of her diary, she was simply unable to say where she was. It was only the intervention of a friend at the other end of the country that belatedly brought the alibi to light. If the IRA had really risked everything to give Carole an unbreakable alibi, would she have failed to remember it? If she had committed the crime, would she have completely forgotten the alibi? Why, in any case, would the IRA have gone to great trouble to give an alibi to her, but not to those who planted the bombs with her?

Even this is not all that is strange about the Crown thesis. The dash-back-to-London argument actually conflicts with much prosecution evidence taken from witnesses in the Horse & Groom, some of whom put the departure of the couple as late as 7.45 or 8.00.

Finally, there is one lingering question-mark over the treatment of Frank Johnson. He could have had only three possible motives for walking into a Newcastle police station on that December morning: either he was a relatively harmless trouble-maker, perhaps mentally ill; or he was trying to assist the IRA by securing the release from custody of key personnel, an extremely serious offence; or he was telling the truth. Clearly, he was not mentally unstable, because his story was corroborated in essential respects. If he was seeking to give help and succour to the IRA, *why was he simply released, and never officially charged with any offence*? The only plausible explanation would seem to be that Surrey police knew that he was telling the truth; the corollary would be that they knew full well that they were arranging the lifetime incarceration for horrific crimes of an entirely innocent seventeen-year-old girl.

The four defendants lived in a Kilburn squat. To the average tabloid-newspaper reader, perhaps, it might seem entirely natural that IRA bombers should hole up in such places, but it would have been both dangerous and unnecessary. Squatters realise that they are in limbo between legal and illegal residence, and have to tolerate as a fact of life administrative interest in their affairs, and even occasional police raids. In this Kilburn house raids had been not so much occasional as regular; three in the months prior to the Guildford bombing. Armstrong and Richardson were present on each occasion, and each time they had correctly identified themselves.

When the police do catch genuine Irish terrorists, they usually discover incriminating material of some description in the safe-houses they have been using. No evidence of this kind was discovered in relation to any of the four defendants.

Squats would be absurd places to store the equipment necessary to sustain a terror campaign. In any case, why would IRA personnel have needed to countenance such risks? The IRA has been accused – quite properly – of despicable and barbarous acts. No one has ever accused it of being short of funds.

Two weeks after the Guildford bombing, Armstrong and Richardson went hitch-hiking together. From a public telephone kiosk in Folkestone, Kent, Richardson rang her mother. A drunk, infuriated by the length of her call, opened the door and punched her. Armstrong straight-away dialled 999. When the police arrived they both got into the squad car and toured the streets looking for the drunk. When they found him, they all went back to Folkestone police station where Armstrong and Richardson provided their correct names and addresses. The idea of dangerous terrorists on the run behaving in this fashion is ridiculously far-fetched.

In yet another incident, the electricity meters at the Kilburn house were burgled about a week after the Woolwich bombing. Once again, Armstrong was one of those involved in calling the police.

Perhaps the strangest characteristic of a strange trial was that the Guildford and Woolwich bombings had been linked at all. After all, the IRA committed numerous atrocities during 1974 and 1975, and its members were still active in England during the course of the trial. On what basis were Guildford and Woolwich thought to be associated offences, especially since the Woolwich attack employed an entirely different type of bomb from those used in Guildford?

When reaching their verdicts, though, the jurors must have rejected such unexplained aspects of the trial; just as they must also have rejected the alibis (both Hill and Armstrong, as well as Richardson, had offered alibi evidence); just as they must also have been convinced by the veracity of the 'confessions' (or, at least, those parts of them which the prosecution held to be true).

At the end of the trial, it was revealed that Paul Hill was already serving a life sentence for the murder of Brian Shaw in Belfast.[5] The judge made it perfectly clear to the four young people that, had capital punishment been in force, "you would have been executed".

Fourteen

The Trial of the Balcombe Street Four

ON 12 DECEMBER 1975 Joseph O'Connell, Harry Duggan, Hugh Doherty and Eddie Butler were arrested in London at the conclusion of what has become known as the Balcombe Street siege. After a dramatic car-chase through the West End the previous Saturday, the four had taken refuge in 22b Balcombe Street, Marylebone, the home of an elderly couple, Mr and Mrs Matthews, whom they held hostage for six days.

News pictures of the siege and the final surrender of the four were flashed around the world, becoming some of the most familiar in the history of photo-journalism. The IRA maintained that the reason the men remained so long in the flat, with no possibility of escape, was to win maximum publicity for the IRA cause; and to ensure that after their surrender the men would not be assaulted by either the police or prison staff. (In view of what had happened a year earlier to those accused of the Birmingham bombings – *see* page 381 ff – this seemed a sensible precaution.)

Once safely in police custody, the four gave their names, where they came from, and added that they were all IRA volunteers. Police interrogators Commander Jim Nevill and Detective Chief Superintendent Peter Imbert of the bomb squad asked Butler what was the first job he had done in England. Somewhat to their surprise, he told them. It was the bombing of the King's Arms in Woolwich. "You've already got someone for that," he added.

It soon became apparent that the police had got the break they needed and had captured the Active Service Unit (ASU) responsible for the intensive bombing campaign conducted throughout London and south-east England since August 1974. Their delight at such success, however, must have been tempered by the embarrassment of realising that the Surrey constabulary had got it all wrong. The four jailed for the Guildford and Woolwich bombs had nothing to do with them.

Since the convictions of Armstrong *et al.*, Guildford solicitor Alastair Logan, certain of their innocence, had been exploring any avenue he could for their appeal. Through a solicitor he knew in Eire, he put out feelers to the IRA. "There was no reason why they should have trusted me," he said. "What they effectively told me, via the intermediary, was that those who had been responsible for the Guildford and Woolwich bombings were still operative – which was true. It was only after Balcombe Street that they got in touch with me again."

The four Balcombe Street men, who were being held in Wandsworth, requested a visit from Frank Maguire, MP for Fermanagh and South Tyrone, to raise the conditions of their imprisonment. On 27 May 1976 Maguire spoke to them in the presence of the assistant governor and suggested that they should contact Logan. Three of them, O'Connell, Butler and Duggan, agreed to make statements about Guildford and Woolwich on one condition.

They said that their consent was contingent upon consent also being given by the other man who had been with them at the time. This was Brendan Dowd, who had been arrested a year earlier, on 10 July 1975, in Waterloo, north Merseyside, after shots had been exchanged with the police. He was charged with three counts of attempted murder, convicted, and sentenced to life imprisonment on 11 May 1976.

Maguire went to see Dowd, who was then being held in solitary confinement in Bristol. He, too, agreed. Again, this was in the presence of the prison authorities.

Between 26 October and 9 November 1976 statements were taken from O'Connell, Butler, Duggan and Dowd by Logan and James Still, a retired police inspector.

In their statements, O'Connell and Dowd explained how the bombings had been carried out and Duggan and Butler described their roles in the Woolwich bombing. Each individually said that the first he had known of those convicted was when he had read about them in the papers; and that they were entirely innocent. They did say that others still at large had played a part in the bombings, but understandably refused to name them.

"We found on interviewing these people," said Logan, "that they were highly experienced in urban guerilla warfare and in the construction and detonation of explosive devices. We found that there were certain idiosyncrasies in the methods by which they constructed bombs, things which were peculiar to that particular group, and which continued long after those arrested on the Guildford charges were in custody.

"Certain elements, used in the construction of the Guildford bombs, were duplicated later. These were the presence of a Smith's pocket watch as a timer, and of a daisy-pattern drawing-pin as an interrupter device, placed through the face of the watch, so that when the hand touched it that would complete the circuit and cause the device to detonate.

"Also, the delivery of the bombs. For example, the Caterham bombing, which took place in August 1975, nine months after the arrest of Armstrong, my client, was a carbon copy of the Guildford bombings.

"We found that these people knew a lot about how the bombings had taken place, they knew how they had done the reconnaissance, and how they had arrived at Guildford. They could identify where they had parked, and told us the composition of the Guildford team. They described the containers that the bombs were in. They described the people who sat next to them in the pub while they were planting the bombs.

"They described their method of departure from Guildford, how the bombs had been constructed, and how much explosive had been used. Everything was consistent with the evidence. They were able to give a total picture, including elements subsequently proved to be correct that had never been mentioned in the prosecution case."[1]

O'Connell recalled one small incident. A soldier had

turned to him and asked the time of the last bus to Aldershot. This was found to tally exactly with a soldier's deposition which had never been produced in court as evidence or revealed publicly.

Collusion can be completely discounted. O'Connell, Duggan and Butler were in Brixton; Dowd was by then in Albany on the Isle of Wight; the convicted four were in other prisons. They would have had no opportunity to communicate with each other, even through intermediaries, since an especially high degree of security surrounded IRA prisoners and all their visits were closely supervised.

The Balcombe Street four came to trial at the Old Bailey on 24 January 1977. There were exactly one hundred indictments. Each defendant was charged on a total of twenty-five counts of murder and causing explosions, relating to the period from December 1974 to December 1975. There was no reference to incidents during the autumn of 1974.

In normal circumstances IRA defendants would have refused to recognise the court, and thus declined to take any part in its proceedings. They reasoned that, as Irish Republicans at war with British imperialism, they were hardly likely to secure justice in an English court. On this occasion, however, they opted to become more actively involved: they felt they had been handed the perfect opportunity to demonstrate the hollowness of what they would pejoratively have referred to as 'British justice'. Although they refused to plead, therefore, they did make statements. O'Connell said, "I refuse to plead because the indictment does not include two charges concerning the Guildford and Woolwich pub-bombings – I took part in both – for which innocent people have been convicted." Butler and Duggan made similar statements.

Having decided to take an interest, they asked their lawyers to raise the issues of bias and prejudice. It was pointed out to Mr Justice Cantley, for example, that he was on a list of 'targets' discovered in an IRA hide-out. This was presumably because he had been responsible for trying and sentencing Brendan Dowd, Sean Kinsella and three others in Liverpool. The judge declined the invitation to step down.

(Ten years later, this decision still seems fundamentally incompatible with the principles of British justice. Throughout the trial, the Crown was at pains to disavow the suggestion that there was any kind of political dimension to these crimes: they were purely criminal, and were to be treated as such. Now, suppose that in any other trial, the judge, dealing with a series of murders, had discovered himself to be listed as a future victim. Of course he would have stepped down – in the interests of justice.)

As regards jury selection, the defence complained that they had been given no opportunity to examine the jury panel, whereas the police had had unrestricted access to it. There was a wrangle, which was resolved when all the potential jurors were summoned into court and asked to disqualify themselves if they or their families had been affected, directly or indirectly, by the bombing campaign. About ten people stood down.

The defendants then used their right to challenge jurors merely on their immediate impressions of them – peremptory challenges, as they are called. At that time each was allowed, and each used, seven challenges. As finally constituted, the jury included five women and three blacks. Through one of those flukes of fortunes with which journalists are all too rarely rewarded, one of the twelve was a close friend of the author's.

O'Connell and the others argued that the police and the authorities were engaged in the perversion of the course of justice, through the manipulation of the evidence to omit all reference to Guildford and Woolwich. They instructed their lawyers to offer no piecemeal defence to the charges, but instead to use every opportunity to highlight anomalies in the police and prosecution case.

Prosecuting counsel John Mathew QC ran through the

twenty-five indictments, drawing freely upon statements the four were alleged to have made in custody, but which they all maintained were 'verbals'. Despite this, however, he eschewed all mention of the Guildford and Woolwich incidents until near the close of his speech. "Guildford and Woolwich are not a matter for you," he said finally. "It may be that O'Connell and Butler are anxious to claim their part in other bombings."

During the trial, the defendants did not contest the evidence, except when they were able to pinpoint inaccuracies in the prosecution case. For example, on 26 January, PC Cotton said he had seen a car with four men in it being driven away from the home of Edward Heath, in Wilton Street, where a bomb had been placed. Yet in a statement made at the time he referred only to two men. Asked to explain this discrepancy, he blithely replied, "There were four men in the car and I only mentioned two of them."

In this way, defence tactics of cross-examining selectively were frequently successful. Counsel made another intervention on 26 January when Inspector Carrington was giving evidence about the Hilton Hotel bomb on 5 September 1975. Two people had been killed, and as a result the defendants were charged with murder. They asked their counsel to elicit from Carrington in cross-examination how much warning had been given and why the hotel had not been cleared.

Carrington replied that a warning of 20 minutes was given, that the Hilton's own security officers declined police assistance with the evacuation and that they had failed to clear the hotel. It subsequently transpired that the police had received a warning. They had not telephoned the hotel (a foot patrolman was sent round), or insisted on clearing it.

On 31 January Douglas Higgs, principal scientific officer at the Royal Arsenal Research & Development Establishment, Woolwich, gave evidence. He had drawn up a chart which showed how a series of bombings in the London area had followed a similar pattern, indicating that they had been carried out by the same people. However, he had omitted Guildford and Woolwich, even though they clearly conformed to the same pattern. Under cross-examination, he readily agreed that the Woolwich bomb matched others on his chart. So why had he omitted it? Higgs replied that an officer of the bomb squad had told him to.

Donald Lidstone, a scientist with thirty-nine years' experience, had been the chief forensic expert consulted by the police in relation to the Guildford bombings. He too had compiled a list of fifteen related bombings, from which the Guildford ones were conspicuously absent. He agreed, under cross-examination, that these two "could be connected" with the others.

On 4 February, Commander Jim Nevill, recently promoted head of the bomb squad (re-named the anti-terrorist squad) went into the witness-box. He was asked what he did when told that a statement about Woolwich had been made by prisoners in the dock. He replied that he "could not say' whether he had given any instructions. He then offered two alternative explanations of why he had done nothing. First, he said that he considered it a matter for his subordinates. Then, he said that he had reported it to the DPP, and left it to his discretion. He told the court that the DPP, and barristers acting for the DPP, had instructed him to tell Higgs to alter his statements.

Nevill went on to say that it would have been 'wrong' of him to pursue the matter of the statements relating to Guildford since he was not the investigating officer on that case. An extraordinary reply: he was head of the bomb squad for the whole country.

The prosecution case closed on 7 February. Defence counsel told the judge that no witnesses would be called on behalf of the defence, but that instead Joseph O'Connell would make a statement from the dock. Mr Justice Cantley immediately responded that he would not allow a political speech. O'Connell went ahead regardless.

Of course, most of the speech was political ("We say

that no representative of British imperialism is fit to pass judgment on us." etc.) The part relating to the Guildford and Woolwich trials ran as follows:

> We are all four Irish Republicans. We have recognised this court to the extent that we have instructed our lawyers to draw the attention of the court to the fact that four totally innocent people – Carole Richardson, Gerard Conlon, Paul Hill and Patrick Armstrong – are serving massive sentences for three bombings, two in Guildford and one in Woolwich, which three of us and another man now imprisoned have admitted that we did. The Director of Public Prosecutions was made aware of these admissions in December 1975 and has chosen to do nothing. We wonder if he will still do nothing when he is made aware of the new and important evidence which has come to light through the cross-examination by our counsel of certain prosecution witnesses in this trial. The evidence of Higgs and Lidstone played a vital part in the conviction of innocent people. Higgs admitted in this trial that the Woolwich bomb formed part of a correlated series with other bombings with which we were charged. Yet when he gave evidence at the earlier Guildford and Woolwich trial he deliberately concealed that the Woolwich bomb was definitely part of a series carried out between October and December 1974, and that the people on trial were in custody at the time of some of these bombings. Lidstone in his evidence tried to make little of the suggestions that the Guildford bombs could have been part of the 'phase one' bombings with which we are accused with the excuse, and this appeared to be his only reason, that the bombings in Guildford had occurred a long time before the rest. When it was pointed out to him that there were many clear links between Caterham and Guildford and that the time between Guildford and the Brooks Club bomb with which we were originally charged was 17

days and that Woolwich occurred 16 days later, and that equal time gaps occurred between many of the incidents with which we were charged, Lidstone back-tracked and admitted that there was a likely connection.

This shifty manoeuvring typifies what we, as Irish Republicans, have come to understand by the words 'British justice'.

It is the intention of this book to demonstrate that the erroneous convictions of Hill, Conlon, Armstrong and Richardson do indeed fall into a pattern. A pattern not, as O'Connell and others believe, of the oppression of the Irish; but of the conviction of the innocent.

After the speech, the judge asked the court shorthand writer for a transcript. He wanted to refer to the statement, he said, in his summing-up. Richard Harvey, counsel for O'Connell, then said that he, too, would appreciate a copy.

"What do you want it for?" asked Cantley. "As a memento?"

"I regard that remark in rather bad taste," replied Harvey, who explained that he wished to ensure that the case for O'Connell had been fairly put in the summing-up.

O'Connell and the others were then led from the dock. They re-appeared only briefly for sentencing. In their absence, the judge summed up. At 11.20 a.m. on 9 February, the jury was sent out to consider its verdict.

In the Old Bailey canteen, the police let it be known that they expected the jury to return around 2.00 p.m. A press conference was scheduled for 4.00 p.m., in good time for the evening news bulletins and the following day's papers.

The jury did return quickly, though not with the verdict. On the first occasion, a copy of O'Connell's statement from the dock was requested. Mr Justice Cantley denied this, as it was not an exhibit in the case. The second time they asked for a copy of the *Anarchist's Cookbook* which, according to the prosecution, had been the source of the defendants' knowledge of bomb-making.

As the jury remained out, the police press conference was cancelled. When the jury did return, after 7.00 p.m. they acquitted the defendants on twenty-six of the hundred indictments.

Hugh Doherty, for example, was acquitted on each of the first five counts – of having caused explosions between December 1974 and 27 August 1975 – on the grounds that the prosecution had not proved he was in the country at the time.

All four were acquitted of planting bombs in Putney High Street and at the Charco Grill, Hampstead, on 27 January 1975; and at Caterham on 27 August 1975. This was despite the fact that the police claimed to have discovered their fingerprints on the coverings around the bombs; that they claimed to have statements of admission; and that they had 'proved' that these bombings were part of the overall pattern. The four were also acquitted of bombings at the Trattoria Fiori restaurant, Mayfair, London, on 29 October 1975 – again despite police forensic evidence, and despite police claims that O'Connell had admitted to it.

Additionally, all four were acquitted of murder on the Hilton Hotel bomb charge, and instead found guilty of manslaughter. Clearly, the jury held the police to some degree responsible for the loss of life following the revelation during cross-examination that they had failed to clear the hotel despite the 20-minute warning.

On all the other counts, the defendants were found guilty. It was nevertheless difficult not to regard the trial as a hollow triumph for the prosecution. The defendants had managed successfully to demonstrate falsehoods or inconsistencies in its case. The police were flabbergasted; they made no attempt to conceal their incredulity as the not-guilty verdicts were returned.

Yet the reason why there had been acquittals on charges

like the Caterham bombing was obvious: they were so clearly linked to the Guildford and Woolwich bombings. Since the ostensible perpetrators of those crimes had already been convicted of them, it was difficult to understand how a fresh quartet could also be guilty.

After the verdicts had been delivered, Cantley informed the jurors that they need not return to hear sentence passed. Privately, however, they were informed that it would look bad if the jury-box was empty. In the event, all did return for the conclusion of the trial on 10 February.

A strange incident, which went unreported in British newspapers, followed. The proceedings over and done with, the members of the jury left. The trial had been such an emotionally demanding one, it was not surprising that a sense of camaraderie had developed among them. A number of jurors accordingly went for a drink together, before walking the short distance to St Paul's Underground station. There, four of them were suddenly set upon and harassed by armed plainclothes policemen. The matter was sorted out, but it aroused genuine fear in the jurors – one of whom remembers screaming and trying to escape down the platform; another of whom was roughly handled.

One explanation advanced for this in Irish publications (which did report it) was that the police were acting spitefully. The jury had frustrated their case and deprived them of their hour of glory. There was no back-slapping press conference; the judge had not even thanked them for their work. This seems unlikely. No doubt the whole thing was a genuine mistake. Nevertheless, the fact that members of the jury were apprehended strikingly illustrates the tension under which the police were obviously operating. They were so jittery about Northern Ireland that they were ready to jump on a group of people merely for having an animated pub conversation about the Irish situation. (In retrospect, the jurors realised they had been watched in the pub.) If the police were so highly strung about this aspect of their job (and no one is criticising them for that), it does become possible to understand how the various miscarriages of justice that have occurred in Irish cases could have arisen.

Altogether, the Balcombe Street jury was recognised by many legal observers to be one of the best ever empanelled. In a trial of great political sensitivity and highly charged emotions, it displayed meticulous attention to the niceties of the case and a rigorous determination to try it in the strict bounds of fairness of an English court.

The result was that, in a major trial with political overtones, the jury for once refused to rubber-stamp the prosecution case.[2] Subsequently, the Labour government soon buckled under pressure from the police and Home Office permanent officials and changed the law. By making one of the provisions of the 1977 Criminal Law Act the reduction in the number of peremptory jury challenges allotted to a defendant from seven to three, it ensured that a jury as scrupulous as this one could never again be selected in the same way.[3]

This was not only an abject reaction; it was also quite unnecessary. After all, it wasn't as though the Balcombe Street Four had walked free: each received a thirty-year minimum sentence.

Fifteen

The Guildford and Woolwich Case Goes to Appeal

AFTER THE Balcombe Street trial, and particularly in view of O'Connell's statement from the dock, solicitors acting for Hill, Conlon, Armstrong and Richardson knew that they had reasonable grounds for appeal. Their overall strategy was to try to persuade the Appeal Court to order a re-trial (something which the 1968 Criminal Appeal Act specifically empowered it to do) because this was regarded as a more attainable objective than the quashing of the convictions.

Of the four, only Carole Richardson had originally applied for leave to appeal within the stipulated time-period. However, on 20 July 1977, the four were granted applications for leave to appeal, even though they were out of time. The court nevertheless seemed to regard this initial oversight with some suspicion, just as it did the appellants' unusual strategy of seeking a re-trial.

(In fact, Richardson's position was slightly different. Counsel did argue, in her case, for the quashing of the conviction. She had served notice of appeal correctly, and also had an apparently strong card to play in the strength of her alibi.)

The appeal was heard at the Old Bailey, rather than in the Law Courts, because of "the need for special security".[1]

It opened on 10 October 1977 before Lord Justice Roskill, Lord Justice Lawton and Mr Justice Boreham. Hill, Conlon and Armstrong's cases were argued exclusively on the grounds that new evidence had emerged since the original trial: that the men captured in Balcombe Street had now admitted to carrying out the crimes for which Hill *et al*. had then been convicted.

O'Connell, Duggan, Butler and Brendan Dowd all gave evidence in person. They said that they had been responsible for the Woolwich bomb thrown into the King's Arms; O'Connell and Dowd said that, along with three others who were still at liberty, they had planted the Guildford bombs. These men, who freely admitted their ruthless terrorist activities, disclaimed all knowledge of Hill and the others.

At the Appeal Court, O'Connell explained in evidence how he and Dowd reconnoitred Guildford and selected the target pubs; how the bombs were made by him, Dowd and another man in a house in Waldemar Avenue, in Fulham; how they drove to Guildford and where they parked; how Dowd and a girl went to the Horse & Groom; and how he, together with a man and another girl, went to the Seven Stars; how they planted the bombs and then returned to London; how the third man left them at a pub in the Fulham Road; and how he and Dowd then drove the girls home to an address in north London. The cars used for these Guildford expeditions were hired from a leading car rental company, Swan National.

For the Woolwich trips they used vehicles stolen by Dowd. They staked out the area, and again selected a target pub. A would-be raid made on 6 November 1974 in a white Ford Corsair was aborted because the pub was insufficiently crowded. The bombing was done the following evening, this time in a stolen Ford Cortina. The group abandoned the car a few miles away, and returned home by bus and tube.

The Crown contended that O'Connell, Duggan and Butler had indeed been responsible for the Woolwich bomb, but that Hill, not Dowd, had been the fourth man. (At the trial, Hill was the only one convicted of involvement in the actual attack.) As regards the Guildford raids, Sir Michael Havers argued that even if both O'Connell and Dowd had been involved, that did not necessarily preclude the participation of the four already convicted.

At the outset the judges determined the manner in which they would deal with the appeal, by reference to an earlier judgment. "The correct approach which this Court has to adopt in fulfilling its statutory duty," declared Roskill, "has been finally and authoritatively determined by the House of Lords in the case of *Stafford and Luvaglio v. the Director of Public Prosecutions.*" (*see* pages 166–7.)

The court considered at length the arguments advanced by counsel both for the appellants and for the Crown. The thinness of the prosecution case could scarcely be concealed: "there was no evidence whatever against them of identification. Such descriptive evidence as there was was of minimal weight and, as was perhaps inevitable in the circumstances, conflicting. There was no fingerprint evidence . . . no witnesses ever identified Hill as present at Woolwich." The judges were in no doubt that everything hinged on the confessions which were supposed to have been made in custody: "If those confessions were both voluntary and true, the evidence against all the applicants was overwhelming," declared Lord Justice Roskill.

The judgment ran to over fifty pages. On 28 October, the appeals were dismissed. "We are all of the clear opinion that there are no possible grounds for doubting the justice of any of these four convictions or for ordering new trials," stated Roskill.

The crucial factor which enabled the judges to reach their decision was the performance in the witness-box of Brendan Dowd. By pinpointing disparities between his testimony and that of the other three who now claimed responsibility for the crimes, the judges argued that the appeals were without merit. Roskill went so far as to say that Dowd's evidence was "the touchstone by which the credibility of all the new evidence in the relevant respects is to be judged." The appeal judges carefully sifted his evidence to uncover the tiniest error, to the extent even of noting that he had referred to a pavement as a "footpath".

Attention was drawn to three elements of Dowd's testimony which were at variance with the rest of the fresh evidence. Firstly, he said the stolen car used in the abortive mission to Woolwich was an Escort, although he later amended this to a Cortina; in fact, it was a Corsair. Secondly, he said the four men had met in a pub in Knightsbridge, close to the Underground; they had actually rendezvoused at one in Sloane Square. Thirdly, he claimed that the stolen Corsair had been abandoned in Knightsbridge; it was discovered near Vauxhall Bridge. All these points, in the opinion of the judges, were extremely illuminating.

But are they? The make of car? Whether an Escort, Cortina or Corsair, they were all Fords. Sloane Square or Knightsbridge? They are at opposite ends of Sloane Street, and less than a mile apart. It hardly seems a very material mistake for someone from Ireland to have made.

As regards where the car was abandoned, the judges themselves were forced to concede that none of the four were very certain where this had been.

Roskill noted that O'Connell, having already been convicted of six murders, "had nothing to lose by accepting responsibility for a further seven," and went on to formulate the theory that there had been a conspiracy to engineer the release of Hill *et al.*

"We are sure that there has been a cunning and skilful attempt to deceive the Court by putting forward false evidence," he stated. "O'Connell, Duggan and Butler had ample opportunity while awaiting trial to work out how the attempt should be made. Doing so was well within the intellectual capacity of O'Connell.

"The difficulty lay in finding a substitute for Hill. Dowd was brought in for this purpose. Providing him with his lines could not have been easy as he was not, at any material time, in the same prison as the others. He did not, or could not, learn his lines properly. That was the reason why the conspiracy failed."

The appeal judges had entirely failed to consider one single logical proposition. If there had been a conspiracy by O'Connell and co. to get Hill and the others out of prison; and if "the difficulty lay in finding a substitute for Hill" – why didn't they use Hugh Doherty, the fourth man captured in the Balcombe Street siege? They could have pretended that the four had been acting together throughout. No one would have been any the wiser, since the Crown had no proof of the date of Doherty's arrival in England. (Because of this, the Balcombe Street jury had acquitted him on several charges.)

If they had wanted to manufacture a story, they could have said the Balcombe Street four did them all. They wouldn't then have needed to say that Duggan and Butler were involved in Woolwich only, and that Doherty had not been involved in either. If they were simply lying to obtain the release of four colleagues, they could have suggested that they alone were responsible, and then coached each other in their roles. It made no sense to involve Dowd, whom they were unable to contact. They need not have mentioned him at all; or alerted the police to the fact that members of the team (one man and two women) were still at large.

If they were going to coach anybody in a role, Doherty would have been the natural candidate; as the judges admitted, those four had "opportunities of associating together". Roskill understated the facts of the matter when he said that instructing Dowd in a role "could not have been easy". Barring paranormal assistance, it would have been impossible.

It was quite likely that Dowd would have problems remembering precisely what had happened almost exactly three years earlier. The day after his arrest on 10 July 1975 he was admitted to hospital with injuries that included broken bones, a cracked jaw and enlarged bladder. His condition was described as "drowsy and practically unconscious". He was put in solitary confinement in Bristol, both before and after his trial, and subsequently served spells in solitary in Long Lartin and Strangeways. By October 1977 he was clearly not in good shape. *The Leveller* reported that "his disorientation in the witness-box was clear".[2]

Bearing all this in mind, his testimony was probably

more illuminating for its consistencies than its inconsistencies.

One point seemed especially significant. Dowd recalled
that, driving away from the scene of the Woolwich bombing, he forgot to put on his lights and was flashed by an
oncoming car. Among the witness statements taken by
police afterwards, to which their lordships had access, was
one from a driver saying he remembered flashing a car
without lights coming towards him.

The Court of Appeal did concede that members of the
Balcombe Street ASU had played a part in the terrorist
activities at Guildford and Woolwich. They took the view,
however, that all of these people had been in it together.

This was hardly a credible conclusion, because there
wasn't a scrap of evidence to show that Hill *et al.* had ever
been in contact with O'Connell *et al.* The appeal judges
ingeniously surmounted this hurdle by elevating an
apparently inconclusive exhibit to a position of prime
importance.

Prior to the arrest of the Balcombe Street ASU, the
police discovered one of their safe-houses – 39 Fairholme
Road, Earl's Court – from which they had fled. A letter
was found there, bearing the fingerprints of O'Connell,
Butler and Duggan, which read in part: "Dear Joe, Get
those two Belfast fellows home – clean them up, change
them a bit, send them singly (singley) through Glasgow
unless you can think of something better."

O'Connell declined to offer any information about this
letter, beyond admitting that it had been sent to him. The
judges affirmed that the letter was of "great significance".
In their opinion, it established "a clear link" between the
two groups. Hill and Armstrong, they pointed out, "both
came from Belfast".

Here, the assumptions are tremendous. The hypothesis
that the letter referred to Hill and Armstrong was based
on neither facts nor evidence, but the wildest conjecture.
It is also known that in the months prior to Hill's arrest he
had been keeping close company with Gerry Conlon – also

a Belfast boy; so why, if the letter did refer to them, did it not mention *three* 'Belfast fellows'?

It is astonishing that so much could be inferred from so little.

The judges made a further *faux pas* in considering the Guildford bombings separately from the Woolwich one. Had both the O'Connell and the Hill factions been involved, two cars would have been needed to ferry them from London to Guildford and back.

Dowd said he had hired a Hillman Avenger, in the name of Michael Moffitt. This was found to tally with Swan National's meticulous records. On examining the fleet books, police discovered that another car had been hired out for roughly the same period in the name of Moffat. If this was the second car used by the bombers, the apparent difference in the names could be explained by a minor spelling mistake.

A close inspection of Swan National's detailed rental agreements would have confirmed whether both cars had been hired by the same person. Unfortunately, this was not possible. The sheets for those particular days were missing. Swan National had accurate records stretching back for years. The company had never previously mislaid a single sheet. How very curious . . .

The Appeal Court determined, nevertheless, that those two cars had been hired by Dowd, and used to transport this bombing party to Guildford. "We feel *no doubt* that the former car" – the yellow Cortina hired under the name "Moffat" – "was hired by Dowd for the purpose of the Guildford bombings." (Author's italics.)

This cast-iron certainty of the appeal judges raises two points. The first is that Hill, in his 'confession', had said that a yellow Granada had been used for the Guildford trip. The court was now suggesting that it was a yellow Cortina, but that because in both instances the car was a Ford this verified the 'confession'. Earlier, however, when considering Dowd's evidence, the court had taken *precisely the opposite view*: because, amongst other things, Dowd had confused various Ford models, his evidence was held to be invalidated.

Secondly, solicitors for the appellants did eventually succeed in tracking down R. C. Moffat. He was alive and well and then resident in South Africa. He confirmed that he had hired a yellow Cortina from Swan National for the period in question.

Another brick was removed from the prosecution's already crumbling wall.

The abiding memory, however, is of the appeal judges averring that they had *no doubt* that this car had been hired by Dowd when, in this as in so many other details, the evidence was not merely slender; it was non-existent.

After considering, and rejecting, Carole Richardson's alibi evidence, the judges deemed their task completed. But a great deal had not been thought about at all. The number of people involved in O'Connell's scenario tallied exactly with conclusions drawn by the police, whereas the Appeal Court's bewildering theory envisaged the participation of considerably more personnel. Nor, apparently, was it thought in any way strange that Hill *et al.* should have been convicted on confessions alone, and that there was a void where the corroborating evidence should have been.

The manner in which the appeal was conducted was open to criticism on precisely the same grounds as Lord Devlin later criticised the fourth Court of Appeal in the Luton case. (Lord Justice Roskill and Lord Justice Lawton were on the bench on both occasions.) The judges had been presented with important new evidence. Instead of either quashing the convictions outright, or ordering a re-trial, however, they reached their own verdicts on the credibility of this evidence. But it was no part of their remit to determine this. As Lord Devlin argued, the appeal process had now become "one of imperfect re-trial by judges, in which the normal appellate reviews have been swallowed up".[3] The court was simultaneously abrogating to itself powers which parliament had never intended it to exercise; and neglecting to discharge those functions with which it had been endowed. Given such constitutional violations, O'Connell's description of it all as "shifty manoeuvring" seems commendably restrained.

Sixteen

The Maguire Family

People in the case

Annie Maguire — charged with explosives offences
Paddy Maguire — husband of Annie; co-defendant
Vincent Maguire ⎱ — sons of Annie and Paddy; co-
Patrick Maguire ⎰ defendants
Sean Smyth — brother of Annie; co-defendant
Guiseppe Conlon — brother-in-law of Annie; co-defendant
Pat O'Neill — family friend; co-defendant
Mr Justice Donaldson — trial judge
Sir Michael Havers — prosecution counsel
Dr John Yallop — forensic scientist (defence witness)
Douglas Higgs — forensic scientist (Crown witness)
Hugh Maguire — brother of Paddy
Sean Tully — friend of Hugh Maguire
Sarah Conlon — wife of Guiseppe
Gerry [Lord] Fitt — MP for West Belfast; now member of
House of Lords

THE MAGUIRE family came to trial at the Old Bailey on 14 January 1976. In all, there were seven defendants: Annie Maguire; her husband, Paddy; her sons Vincent and Patrick; her brother Sean Smyth and brother-in-law Guiseppe (sic) Conlon; and a family friend, Pat O'Neill. All were charged with possession of explosives (nitroglycerine).

Because of the sensational remark which Gerry Conlon was alleged to have made, and which had been well publicised – that he had learned to make bombs in his Aunt Annie's kitchen – the Maguire trial was umbilically connected to the Guildford and Woolwich one. Moreover, the same figures were involved. Mr Justice Donaldson, who had handled the first trial, made it clear that he wanted to take this one as well, and Sir Michael Havers was again engaged as the prosecuting QC.

At the outset, he outlined the Crown case. After the arrest of Gerard Conlon in connection with the Guildford bombings, a telegram was sent to the Maguire home from Northern Ireland. With its arrival, explained Havers in phrases which reverberated throughout the trial, "alarm bells had started ringing". The game was up; it was "all hands to the pump". The nitroglycerine had to be removed to a place where it was not likely to be discovered. Havers promised that evidence would be given during the trial to show that all the accused had not only handled a quantity of explosive, but had "kneaded and manipulated' it to pack it into small bags.

Donaldson made it clear that all references to "Aunt Annie's bomb factory", or similar, were inadmissible evidence. Conlon would not be appearing as a witness. He had repudiated his confession at his own trial, and would undoubtedly do so again. What he was supposed to have said was therefore hearsay, at best. So all concerned had to perform one of those feats of mental gymnastics of which the English legal system is so ridiculously proud, and pretend not to know what they most surely did know. Havers actually stressed throughout the course of the trial that there was no suggestion that any of these defendants had been concerned with the Guildford bombing.

The prosecution evidence consisted almost entirely of the results of forensic tests on the defendants. After the arrests on 3 December 1974, swabs were taken from the palms of their hands and scrapings from underneath their fingernails. These were analysed at the Royal Arsenal Research & Development Establishment (RARDE) at Woolwich, south London. Thin Layer Chromatography (TLC) tests proved positive for six of the seven, indicating, or so the Crown contended, the presence of nitroglycerine.

The exception was Annie. However, a copious supply of plastic disposable gloves was discovered in a kitchen drawer at the house. (Annie suffered from dermatitis and used the gloves when doing housework.) The supply was taken to New Scotland Yard (strangely, because all other items for analysis were taken direct to Woolwich). On 9 December it, too, was subjected to forensic tests. A positive result was obtained, though it could perhaps have been from only one glove. Mr Elliott, one of the Crown's principal scientific witnesses, further admitted that the contamination might have been on the outside of a used glove; or the inside of a used glove; or the outside of an unused glove.

Nitroglycerine is absorbed into the skin of anyone who handles it. Naturally, therefore, there should be a method of detecting its presence in the skin. In a TLC test, the swabs are immersed in an ether solution, so that the substance being tested is distilled out. A spot of the solution is treated with silica gel, a substance capable of drawing up liquid by capillary action. The plate containing the sample is put in a tank containing a liquid eluant. Next, it is sprayed with a Griess reagent. The solution will have travelled across the plate, and if nitroglycerine is present a pink spot will form at a particular level.

So much for the theory.

The problems began where practice and theory diverged. In the first place, the tests were carried out by an eighteen-year-old who had only been employed at RARDE for nine weeks, and who was described by the judge as "an apprentice". In a case of such importance, this was very odd.

Further, in doing the tests, the youngster used up all the samples. This was contrary to routine scientific procedure under which samples are sub-divided so that confirmatory tests can be made. It was also contrary to specific regulations for conducting tests of this kind. The director of RARDE had ruled that the samples should always be divided so that cross-checks could be done and the TLC test was never the only one carried out. It was moreover contrary to forensic procedure since all the evidence had now been destroyed. Neither were the results photographed. Exhibit A – the first, the foremost, the only one that mattered – no longer existed.

The test, nevertheless, had proved positive. So was it reliable?

Someone who thought not was Dr John Yallop, who appeared at the trial for the defence. His testimony should have been accorded particular attention. After all, he was the former director of RARDE and the man who had devised the TLC test.

Dr Yallop had prepared an explanatory paper for the defence, in which he expatiated on his test. His conclusion had the merit of plain speaking: "no competent scientist could do other than conclude that the hypothesis is incorrect; namely, that the pink spot is *not* due to nitroglycerine. To do otherwise would be unscientific, illogical and pig-headed."

In fact, in the years that have elapsed since the trial, no competent, independent scientist has ever concluded differently; conversely, no competent, independent scientist has ever declared that the results were – to lapse into legal jargon – safe and satisfactory.

Defence witnesses contended that the test was capable of proving positive for other explosive substances, including one called PETN, which was used in commercial blasting and had never at any time been associated with the IRA. It was only with some reluctance that the prosecution agreed that these two substances gave identical readings.

This fact alone should have destroyed the entire case against the Maguire family, because it undermined the Crown theory that the position of nitroglycerine in toluene (the eluant used in this case) was unique. Two chemically dissimilar substances gave identical readings in the TLC test. It was therefore no longer possible to say for certain that the substance isolated in the TLC tests was nitroglycerine. The judge entirely failed to put before the jury the significance of this. (Indeed, it seems from his summing-up that he did not understand it himself.)

The results were also inconsistent among themselves. Some of the defendants, for example, seemed to have nitroglycerine under their fingernails, but not on their palms. The tests on Paddy Maguire's hands were inexplicable. The dry swab – a preliminary test, literally, a dry run – was positive, but the ether swab was negative. Yallop explained to the Court that nitroglycerine is absorbed into the skin very rapidly, and therefore one would expect the ether swab to be positive if the dry one was.

Yallop also said that, in the absence of any others, he would have regarded the findings of a mechanical sniffer (a hand-held explosives detector) as a confirmatory test. In fact, the sniffer had failed to register the presence in the house of any explosives materials. "This is a reasonable condition under which to use a sniffer," Yallop explained, "and to expect to get a positive response. The fact that it gave a negative one is, to my way of thinking, another factor to add to Mr Maguire's hands pointing away from the interpretation of nitroglycerine."

The prosecution pointed to tests of 916 people to demonstrate that this supposedly random sample did not yield equivalent results in the TLC test. However, at no stage was the defence allowed to scrutinise the results of these tests, nor to have them independently examined.

The TLC test is essentially one for nitrates, not for explosives. In evidence, it was maintained that other, entirely innocuous substances such as household cleaning agents and tobacco smoke could give positive readings on the TLC test.

There is an even more interesting point. The police already had information that the TLC test was capable of giving misleading results. At lunchtime on 10 September 1973 a small bomb, believed to have been planted by the IRA, exploded at Euston station in London, though without causing significant damage or injury. That evening two girls, Judith Ward and Eileen Gately, then living in a hostel, were discovered acting suspiciously at the station. They were taken in for questioning, given swab and fingernail tests, and released the following day.

In February 1974, in the wake of the horrific M62 coach-bombing, Ward was arrested. She was later charged and convicted of three bombing offences, including the M62 and the Euston one. After her arrest, detectives re-interviewed Gately at some length. They showed her the results of the TLC tests done the previous year, which had proved positive for nitroglycerine for Ward on her right hand only, but positive for Gately on both hands and under the fingernails. Apparently, Gately had been contaminated to a far greater extent than Ward. In fact, the 'evidence' against Gately was actually greater than against any of the Maguire household. Yet Gately was never arrested or charged with any explosives offence. (Nor is anyone suggesting that she should have been.)

Other factors suggested that the TLC tests on the Maguires had yielded unreliable results. For example, since nitroglycerine is rapidly absorbed into the skin, it very quickly causes severe headaches. None of the

Maguires ever complained of suffering in this way, not even the children.

Leaving the continuing doubts about the efficacy of the TLC tests aside for the moment, there is an even more intriguing question: what had happened to these explosives that had been "kneaded and manipulated into small bags"?

According to Havers, they had been packed up either in the house or in one of the derelict buildings behind it. The charges stipulated possession of nitroglycerine between 1 December and 3 December. Yet the telegram which was presumed to have precipitated the emergency disposal of the explosives had not arrived until 2 December.

If what the prosecution alleged happened had in fact taken place, the police would have been granted a golden opportunity to catch Irish terrorists red-handed. Conlon had told police that he had learned to make bombs in his aunt's kitchen. Her house was indeed under observation for some four hours before the police moved in.

It is important to remember that Guiseppe Conlon reached the Maguire house only at lunchtime on 3 December, but spent barely ten minutes there until the middle of the afternoon. Pat O'Neill arrived only at 6.45 p.m. They, however, were deemed equally culpable.

So: where were the explosives?

The house, like many in London, afforded no escape through the back. It was bounded by the gardens of adjacent houses and by a canal. The empty houses at the back were combed. The canal was dragged. Both searches drew a blank.

Sean Tully, a friend of Paddy's brother Hugh, called at the house in Third Avenue twice in the course of the day. The second time he left just after 7.00 p.m. The policemen keeping watch outside the house noted his car-number and tailed him. His house and car were later searched, but no trace of explosive was ever detected.

The explosives, therefore, had apparently disappeared neither through the front nor the back. The house was also searched. Dogs trained to sniff out explosives, and the mechanical sniffer, were used. Nothing was discovered.

The search, though, was distinctly odd. The police apparently believed that they had chanced upon one of the Provisional IRA's sanctuaries. They might, therefore, have been expected to tear the place apart, yet police activity was uncharacteristically restrained. Carpets were not taken up nor floorboards lifted. No one bothered to check behind boarded-up fireplaces. One policeman was detailed to inspect the loft, but refrained from doing so on the grounds that he might get his uniform dirty. Neither was the garden dug up. When Guiseppe's wife, Sarah, arrived at the empty house a week later, she discovered his coat and unopened bag, the police having apparently paid attention to neither. The judge drew attention to this at the trial. "It was an incomplete search, there is no doubt about that at all," he said. "Large areas of the house were never looked at."

Thus, no explosives were discovered, nor any apparatus that could remotely be thought of as having been employed in the manufacture of bombs. Not even residual traces of explosives. Certainly not on any of the working surfaces in what the popular press had gleefully dubbed "the bomb kitchen"; nor in the drawer where the gloves, including the allegedly contaminated one, had been kept.

Such absolute failure to discover any incriminating material severely holed the Crown case. During the trial the prosecution – with the generous assistance of the judge – made running repairs. In one of his first interviews with the police, sixteen-year-old Vincent, distressed by the hostile and persistent questioning, explained that he'd never seen anything in his house that looked like dangerous explosives – except for a stick of chalk, which his father used to bring home for Anne-Marie from the technical college where he worked. Vincent remembered seeing some pieces under Sean Smyth's bed. He showed the police where, and the chalk was there, exactly as he had said.

Why is this apparently trivial detail deemed worthy of mention? *Because as the trial progressed, this stick of chalk metamorphosed into a stick of dynamite.* In his summing-up, the judge referred to it as precisely that – "a stick of gelignite". In doing so, he was quoting from the testimony of one prosecution witness who averred that that is what Vincent seemed to have been describing (albeit with words the police had put into his mouth). What the judge failed to mention was that this same witness added that of course it could not have been gelignite, otherwise the mechanical sniffer would have detected its presence. Thus did a stick of chalk became a weighty piece of evidence against the Maguires, since it breached the one hitherto impregnable aspect of the defence case, namely that no explosives had ever been discovered. Yet this evidence was literally manufactured as the trial progressed.

Other planks in the prosecution case were as rickety. On arriving at Heysham from Belfast, Guiseppe Conlon had a conversation with an immigration officer. The officer recalled his saying that he was going to Surrey to pick up a vehicle. Conlon protested vehemently that this was wholly incorrect, that he had said he was coming to England to visit his brother-in-law in London, and the officer had confused him with the man standing next to him in the queue.

A bizarre incident was used as additional evidence. When drunk, a couple of years earlier, Paddy had a flaming row with Annie and rushed off to see the council housing officer. He demanded that his name be taken off the rent book, claiming that he could no longer be held responsible because the house might be blown up. This is typical of the kind of evidence on which the prosecution frequently relies in miscarriage-of-justice cases. Anyone but a child would appreciate that such actions, however foolish, are certainly not those of someone with terrorist connections.

The judge referred both to this marital friction and to Paddy's weakness for drink – "I won't say of being an alcoholic, but of taking excessive quantities of drink with the usual obvious results". Judges sometimes cannot resist drawing up adverse character references on defendants for the jury. In this instance, it was grossly unfair. Paddy was a heavy drinker; no one would have quarrelled with that, least of all Paddy himself. What the judge overlooked was that one of the "usual obvious results' was that he was unsuitable for recruitment by the IRA.

As so often in bungled trials, other startling aspects of the case slipped by unnoticed. There was, for example, the arrest, release and re-arrest of Pat O'Neill. Would a real Irish terrorist have behaved in such a sublimely innocent manner? Alarm bells, according to Michael Havers, had been ringing. This particular IRA cell was being flushed out by the authorities. If O'Neill had been engaged in terrorist activities, would he simply have arranged the care of his three children and then returned to work as though nothing had happened? Isn't it more likely that he would have looked for a safe refuge until the storm blew over?

The attitude of the police to Sean Tully was even more baffling. He was never charged with any offence, even though he was present in the house during the period when it was "all hands to the pump" and the other occupants were all "kneading and manipulating". Similarly, the middle son, John, was never charged. This, too, was bewildering. In the circumstances in which the prosecution had alleged that the offences occurred, it was absurd to imagine that John could somehow be innocent while the rest of the family was guilty. Annie's own explanation for this is that when the charge-sheets were prepared, the police simply got mixed up and confused him (John Patrick) with his younger brother (Patrick Joseph).

Were not the circumstances so tragic, the prosecution case against the Maguires, all of whom had consistently and unequivocally maintained their innocence throughout, could have been described as a joke. The only tangible evidence against them had been destroyed in a test to see how far it travelled along a glass plate; and even if it had still existed, it might well have been rejected as "unscientific, illogical and pig-headed".

The case against Annie in particular was so gossamer it beggars the imagination. Traces of nitroglycerine had apparently been found on one glove in the kitchen. She used the gloves, but anyone in the house had access to the kitchen drawer. There was no evidence whatsoever to show that she was responsible for this supposed minute particle of explosive.

The Maguires had to contend with factors other than just the evidence in court. Those headlines of a few months earlier about "Aunt Annie's Bomb Kitchen" could hardly have been entirely forgotten. The trial took place in an atmosphere of extreme public apprehension about and antipathy to the IRA; feelings which could only have been reinforced when on the morning on which the jury was due to deliver its verdict a bomb exploded on the 7.49 a.m. commuter train from Sevenoaks, Kent, to Cannon Street, London (though without causing serious injury). Any jury would have been extremely reluctant to risk freeing anyone tarred with the IRA brush.

Another factor which could have weighed against the family is that much of the trial was taken up with matters of theoretic and applied chemistry. It would not be surprising if members of the jury had not managed to follow all the arguments closely. The judge himself appeared to have some difficulty in doing so, as the following passage from his summing-up indicates. Donaldson is here referring to that part of Dr Yallop's explanatory paper where he is attempting to achieve comparable results for substances other than nitroglycerine in the TLC test:

Then he did the experiment in the same way, using alongside the nitroglycerine nitrobenzene, Dabitoff, Boots' dry cleaner, Targon and dinitrotoluene. Dinitrotoluene produces a spot at 0.61, which suggests

some confusion between dinitrotoluene and nitroglycerine but there does appear to be some distinction
in colour. Of course, dinitrotoluene is an explosive.
Nobody has suggested that in this case dinitrotoluene
was present. His conclusion is . . . I am sorry, I have
misread it. One needs to read 13 as a separate experiment. May I start again on this last one. I think I
misunderstood it and possibly you [the members of
the jury] may have done as well.

The summing-up was open to criticism in further respects.
The judge quoted a comment from one of the Crown's
scientific witnesses, Douglas Higgs, who had said he
thought the TLC test was infallible; Donaldson did not
say that under oath Higgs had expressly withdrawn this
comment.

In another passage, when referring to the discrepancy
between the positive reading from the glove and the negative reading from the drawer in which it had been found,
Donaldson told the jury, "There was the possibility of
using a sniffer, but you have been told that the sniffer does
not really operate on traces but on greater quantities." If
the sniffer was not appropriate for this particular task, why
did the police not subject the drawer to forensic tests of a
suitable nature? The judge, however, did not ask the jury
to ponder this question.

He was absolutely correct, however, when he said to
the jury, "Unless you are satisfied by the scientific evidence
that nitroglycerine was present on those people's hands
(or gloves) it would be quite unsafe to convict any of them.
If you are in any real doubt as to whether the material
which was analysed was nitroglycerine, that must be the
end of the case."

It should indeed have been the end of the case.

On 4 March 1976, the jury returned verdicts of guilty on
all the defendants. They were unanimous in all but one

case. The younger son, Patrick, was found guilty on an 11 –1 majority verdict. Donaldson addressed the prisoners: "You have all been convicted and, in my judgment, rightly convicted, of possessing nitroglycerine for an unlawful object. On the evidence that object can only have been terrorism, and therein lies the extreme gravity of your offence.

"It is not only the man or woman who pulls the trigger or plants the bomb who is the terrorist. Anyone concerned at any stage shares the guilt of using violence for political ends.

"There can be no greater offence than this, for it strikes at the very root of the way of life for which generations have fought and, indeed, died to preserve."

He passed sentences of 14 years' imprisonment, the maximum permitted by law, on Annie and Paddy Maguire. Guiseppe Conlon, Pat O'Neill and Sean Smyth received 12 years. Vincent Maguire was jailed for 5 years, and Patrick was detained under the Children and Young Persons Act for 4 years.

The shock and grief of the defendants must have been terrible. Annie Maguire had to suffer not only her own imprisonment, but the incarceration of virtually her whole family. She was carried from the dock kicking and screaming, yelling over and over again that she was innocent.

Paddy Maguire turned to his sons beside him and apologised. "I always brought you up to respect and honour British justice because I believed it was the best in the world. I'm sorry. I was wrong."

Applications for leave to appeal on behalf of all seven were heard in the Court of Appeal before Lord Justice Roskill, Lord Justice Waller and Mr Justice Ackner from 20 to 29 July 1977.

The judges noted that the jury needed to decide whether the forensic tests had accurately established the presence of nitroglycerine on the hands (or gloves) of the seven applicants. But the latter were not convicted merely of possessing *traces* of nitroglycerine. As a corollary, therefore, the jury needed to decide whether the seven had in their possession a quantity of nitroglycerine of which the traces were but a microscopic part.

The prosecution case "rested almost entirely upon scientific evidence". Roskill noted that, "If the Crown failed to prove the presence of nitroglycerine with the requisite degree of certainty, then the case against all must fail."

The countervailing arguments about the efficacy of the TLC test were put before the jurors. In reaching their verdicts, therefore, the jury must have rejected the evidence of defence witnesses that, for example, a single test for nitroglycerine was insufficient and a confirmatory test was required.

The judges bent over backwards to rationalise the outcome of the trial. Their judgment can be read as a circular argument: because the jury had convicted, the applicants must be guilty; because the applicants were guilty, the jury had convicted them. The judges convinced themselves, if no one else, that justice had not miscarried.

Anyone coming afresh to the Maguire case would probably demand the resolution of three specific problems: were the tests accurate and reliable? If they were, what happened to the quantity of explosive? What was the explanation for the remarkable absence of corroborative evidence?

The Appeal Court addressed itself only to the first question. In doing so, the judges discovered "clear evidence of considerable scientific weight". It is difficult to understand how such hotly disputed forensic data could be construed as "clear evidence".

The judges also found it highly significant that there should have been an unaccounted-for half-hour from 7.45 to 8.15 when the four men could have disposed of the explosives. In doing so they neglected to consider the possibility that the police observers had simply logged the time incorrectly. Let us suppose, though, that the officers were correct. Why were the men not properly followed? How many gift-horses did the police intend to look in the mouth?

All applications for leave to appeal against conviction were refused. In the case of leave to appeal against sentence, the application of Pat O'Neill was granted and, having granted it, the judges then substituted an eight-year sentence. Ironically, even this partial solace turned sour for the luckless O'Neill. When he was released he was made the subject of an exclusion order under the PTA, which meant that he was not allowed to live in the mainland UK. (In 1986, this exclusion order was still in force.) By the time the others were released, the authorities did not exercise the option of making exclusion orders.

Frustrated in their hopes of finding redress in the Appeal Courts, the Maguires could expect only to serve out their lengthy sentences. They had been convicted of possessing a quantity of explosive, even though no one had been able to show that a quantity of explosive had ever been in their possession. That their case had reduced the English legal process to its most fatuous, however, was scant consolation. Few people were aware that a grave injustice had been done. Sadly, it took the death of Guiseppe Conlon to bring the whole matter to some public attention.

On 31 December 1979 Conlon was moved from Wormwood Scrubs to Hammersmith Hospital, in a very poorly condition. A week later, despite being by then so ill that he needed oxygen and a drip feed, he was taken back to prison. His wife Sarah arrived at the hospital to discover the police putting her dying husband into a taxi, with police out-riders. She was told it was believed that the IRA were going to snatch him. She was incredulous. Without medical treatment, Conlon would certainly have died within hours. "If you saw him," said Sister Sarah Clarke, of the Prisoners' Aid Committee, "you knew he was gone. He was just two big eyes and a shock of hair." His condition was described by the prison doctor as "chronic". On 18 January 1980 he was re-admitted to the hospital.

It has been mentioned earlier that Conlon's doctor at home was Joe Hendron, an SDLP local councillor in Belfast. Hendron had always been disturbed by the convictions, and had long ago shared his concern with Gerry Fitt, Independent MP for West Belfast, who for some time waged virtually a lone battle to try to arouse interest in the case. In view of Conlon's dramatically deteriorating condition, he at last began to make some headway. A number of other MPs, most prominently Sir John Biggs-Davison (Conservative) and Christopher Price (Labour), were impressed by Conlon's strenuous protestations of innocence. Cardinal Hume, Archbishop of Westminster, expressed his concern. The case was brought as a matter of urgency to the attention of the Home Secretary, William Whitelaw.

On 23 January 1980, Whitelaw decided that if Conlon recovered sufficiently he would be offered parole on the grounds of ill-health: a piece of Home Office logic that would have slotted seamlessly into the script of BBC TV's *Yes, Minister*.

This, though, was no comedy series. Whitelaw gave humanitarian consideration to the case, but he was pathetically dilatory in doing so. Within hours of his decision, Guiseppe Conlon was dead.

Conlon reaffirmed his absolute innocence, over and over again, as dying declarations. He also asked Gerry Fitt to make every effort to clear his name posthumously. Fitt promised that he would. "I still cling tenaciously to that commitment," he was to tell the House of Lords in May 1985.

In the wake of Conlon's death, Eddie Butler, Joseph O'Connell and Harry Duggan issued a fresh statement from prison. "We repeat," they said, "Paul Hill, Patrick Armstrong, Gerard Conlon and the English girl Carole Richardson are innocent victims. We have decided to reissue this statement after the death of Guiseppe Conlon who only came to England to visit his son Gerard who had been charged with operations which we carried out, and because new scientific tests have emerged which also support this man's innocence and the innocence of other Irish victims of British racism."

Gavin Esler reported on the case for the BBC's Northern Ireland programme, *Spotlight*, and also contributed a piece to the *New Statesman* (21 March 1980).

On 4 August 1980 the matter was debated in parliament. Fitt, Price and Biggs-Davison all took part, urging the Home Secretary "to review all the circumstances of this case". (In this debate Christopher Price first publicly raised the possibility that the Birmingham pub-bombers had been wrongly convicted.)

Unhappily, the Home Secretary was not in the House to hear the arguments for himself. The government's reply was given by the minister of state at the Home Office, Leon Brittan. He refused to consider the representations, arguing that "nothing new has been put forward" on behalf of Conlon and the others which had not already been heard both at the trial and at the Court of Appeal. "There are no grounds," he concluded, "on which my right honourable friend the Home Secretary would be justified in taking any action. If something new emerges, it would most certainly be considered with the care with which we consider any of these matters."

Nevertheless, Fitt, who was ennobled after losing his seat in the 1983 general election, continued to campaign for justice. "I have been a member of deputations to a succession of Home Secretaries," he said, "and we have been met with the usual Civil Service jargon from those civil servants who accompany the Minister." One such deputation, in December 1983, was rebuffed by David Mellor, under-secretary of state.

Television sporadically devoted attention to the case. It was considered on *Panorama* (BBC 1, 18 April 1983) in the context of a programme about the hazards of forensic science evidence; and, more crucially, by *First Tuesday*

(ITV, 6 March 1984), which asked Dr Brian Caddy, of Strathclyde University, a leading independent forensic scientist, to assess the scientific evidence. Caddy reported that the TLC test used in the Maguire case was doubly unreliable: the results should have been confirmed by an additional test; and the test as performed was deficient in not applying enough safety standards. Caddy's conclusion was that "sufficient evidence was not presented that this compound was nitroglycerine".

Annie Maguire was the last of the seven – or six, since Conlon's death – to be released. Her period on bail in 1975–6 meant that she was detained for about ten months longer than Paddy, and she was freed on 22 February 1985, having served her complete sentence, with standard remission. It was put to her on many occasions that she could be considered for earlier parole if she expressed contrition for her crimes. She always replied that it was logically impossible to be contrite for crimes one had not committed.

Upon release, Annie and Paddy soon became minor media celebrities. In England, they were featured with Robert Kee on *Seven Days* (Channel 4, 20 April 1985) and with David Frost on *Good Morning, Britain* (TV-am, 28 April). Annie appeared in radio and TV chat-shows in Ireland. Radio Telefis Eireann made a major documentary about the case, which provoked a strong reaction in Eire and was screened in the UK by Channel 4 on 13 May. Lord Fitt ensured that the case was debated in the House of Lords later the same week. In the matter of public speaking, most members of parliament are artisans; Fitt is one of the artists. His lucid and passionate entreaty on behalf of the Maguire family lasted for forty-five minutes and deserved to be heard by more than the sparse gathering of a dozen members.

He carefully exonerated from blame those who had been protagonists in the early stages of this drama. "I believe that the police honestly believed that they were dealing with people who had been engaged in preparing substances which could be used to cause explosions. I believe that the judge was right in his own belief that these people were guilty. I believe that Sir Michael Havers was totally convinced of the guilt of Annie Maguire and her relatives. What I am saying to them all today is that they were all so terribly wrong."[1]

During his peroration, Lord Fitt asked three specific questions of the Home Office: was it true that a parallel case would not now be brought forward on the strength of forensic tests alone, but that corroborative evidence would be required? Was it true that a parallel case would not now be brought without evidence that someone had had in his possession sufficient quantity of explosive actually to cause an explosion? Was it true that charges were not preferred against a suspected PLO terrorist because there was insufficient evidence to put before a jury, even though (as in the Maguire case) TLC tests had proved positive?

Fitt was supported by four other peers, among them Earl Attlee and Lord Annan, who also contributed a persuasive speech. "If authority has any conscience," he said, "it will now concede that the case which eleven years ago looked so watertight has sprung a leak." He could not have believed that authority was susceptible to attacks of conscience; for he concluded, "I await the noble Lord's reply with intense interest and boundless despondency."

The noble lord to whom it fell to substantiate that boundless despondency was Lord Glenarthur, parliamentary under-secretary of state at the Home Office. He said that the Home Secretary's view that there were no grounds for re-opening the case remained unchanged. Of Fitt's three questions, he was able to answer only the first. He did confirm that "it is standard practice that tests are corroborated." All he could positively offer was an invitation to anyone with fresh scientific evidence to submit it to the Home Office "without delay". Subsequently, David Mellor, minister of state, wrote to Lord Fitt, saying that the Home Office could not "find sufficient reason to recommend the Home Secretary to intervene".

Thereafter, the Maguire case became part of the more general campaign to rectify all the Irish cases (*see* Chapter 18).

On the morning after the Maguire trial ended at the Old Bailey, *The Times* told its readers that "members of Scotland Yard's anti-terrorist squad and Surrey Constabulary are convinced that Mrs Maguire was a vitally important cog in the Provisional IRA network in London". According to this scenario, Annie was giving tuition in bomb-making to people like Paul Hill and Gerard Conlon. "Watch carefully, you may have to do this yourselves one day," is one of the remarks attributed to her.

Rarely can the myth and the reality have been so utterly at odds. If, indeed, she was "a vitally important cog in the Provisional IRA network", then the police drag-net operation must rank as the most incompetent in the history of the fight against terrorism. Fortunately, this is not a cross the police have to bear.

That same *Times* piece also recorded that "to neighbours and friends, Mrs Maguire was a wonderful mother, who kept open house to anyone who needed help". This is, at last, the truth of the matter. Apart from anything else, Annie Maguire didn't have time to be a terrorist. She had three part-time jobs, she kept her house spotlessly clean and she invariably found herself looking after more than just her four own children. She was a member of Paddington Conservative Club, and both she and Paddy held vociferously anti-Republican views. Paddy had served in the British Army. They had sailed for England on their wedding night, 26 September 1957. The Crown had no more loyal subjects.

Seventeen

The Birmingham Pub-bombs

People in the case

Paddy Hill
Gerry Hunter
Richard (Dick) McIlkenny — jointly charged with Birmingham pub-bombings
William Power
John Walker
Hugh Callaghan

Mr Justice Bridge — judge
James McDade — IRA activist, killed on 14 November 1974
Harry Skinner QC — prosecuting counsel

Michael Murray
Michael Sheehan — jointly charged with explosives offences
James Kelly (Woods)

Dr Frank Skuse — Home Office forensic scientist (from Chorley laboratory)
Dr Hugh Black — defence forensic consultant

Douglas Higgs
Donald Lidstone — Home Office forensic scientists (from RARDE, London)

Dr Arthur Harwood — doctor from Winson Green prison, Birmingham

Thomas Watt
Hilda Wickett — prosecution witnesses

Julia Vines — barmaid at New Street station
David Owen — assistant chief constable of Lincolnshire
Dr David Paul — defence witness at prison officers' trial
Mr Justice Swanwick — judge at prison officers' trial

A TELEPHONE call from an alert booking-clerk at Birmingham's New Street station seems to have given police the vital information that a group of five Irishmen had purchased tickets to Heysham a little while before the bombs in the Mulberry Bush and the Tavern in the Town exploded.

On arriving at Heysham, the men left the train and made their way to the ferry. One, Paddy Hill, had his luggage checked and was waved through ahead of the others. He boarded the boat, went to the bar and bought himself a drink. The other four, thinking him behind them, idly chatted to a Special Branch detective while waiting to embark. When asked the purpose of their trip, each said he was visiting relatives; none mentioned that he was going to the funeral of an IRA man.

They were joined by another detective, who'd received the phone call and news of the Birmingham bombings. The men were asked if they would mind giving forensic tests so that they could be eliminated from inquiries. They offered no objection. Hill was brought back off the boat, and they were all taken to Morecambe police station.

The men had all lived in the Birmingham area for some considerable time. Gerry Hunter came to England in 1963, and married a local girl, Sandra, in 1966; Dick McIlkenny arrived in the country in 1956, Paddy Hill in 1960, William Power in 1963, and John Walker, who came from Derry and had attended the same school as John Hume, the much-respected SDLP MP, in 1952. A sixth, Hugh Callaghan, who had not taken the train from Birmingham, had been in England since 1947.

Unlike Annie and Paddy Maguire, who were vehemently anti-Republican, some of these men probably did have Republican sympathies. Nevertheless, none was especially interested in politics, and all deprecated the methods of the IRA. They were all married, with children.

Gerry Hunter was very friendly with James McDade. The two had attended St Gabriel's Secondary School, in Crumlin Road, Belfast, and had met again when both lived in Birmingham. Hunter had on one occasion got McDade a job with the firm he was working for. Their wives, too, knew and liked each other.

Power also went to the same school, but he knew neither Hunter nor McDade well until he came into contact with them in Birmingham in the early seventies. They lived close together in the Aston district, sometimes worked on the same painting jobs, and often went drinking together. Hill had also been at the same school. He, Walker and McIlkenny were all drinking companions at the Crossways public house.

In 1973 Hunter and Walker tried to organise a pub team to play Don in a local Sunday league. (Don, alternatively called Dom Pedro, is a card game.) This scheme fell through, but Hunter and Walker had already begun organising a raffle to raise funds to get the team under way. They decided, therefore, to run the raffle anyway, and send the proceeds to the Prisoners' Dependants' Fund, a charity which helped the relatives of internees in Northern Ireland. Hill and McIlkenny both helped to sell tickets. (Two of McIlkenny's brothers had been interned; he did not know why, and they never faced any charges.)

This straightforward humanitarian gesture inevitably took on a malevolent political character at the men's trial.

The death, on 14 November 1974, of James McDade (*see* page 299) shocked the Hunters. They knew him very well, and they also knew that his brother had been shot in Belfast four years earlier while engaged in IRA activities. Nevertheless, they had not suspected either that he was involved in terrorism, or that he was an IRA member. Other friends were equally astonished. McDade, an Irish folk singer who performed regularly at local dances, had been a popular and well-known figure.

Hunter decided to go to Belfast for the funeral. It seemed the right thing to do. In any case, he had another reason for going. The previous month his father had died, and he wanted to bring his mother back with him so that she could enjoy a break and be with her grandchildren. His only problem was that he had been out of work for a few weeks and had no spare cash.

"Funeral-going is part of the ghetto culture of Northern Ireland," wrote Michael Farrell in the *Sunday Tribune*. "It does not necessarily imply support for the deceased's political views."[1] Power, Walker and McIlkenny all confirmed that they too would try to go to the funeral. In McIlkenny's case, this was out of respect for McDade's parents, whom he had known well in Belfast. Power had put up the McDade family at his home in late 1973, though they had moved to different parts of the city after that, and hadn't seen each other since January 1974. Hill, too, thought that he would probably attend the funeral, though, like Hunter, he had an additional reason for travelling. He wanted to visit a sick aunt in Belfast.

After the shock of McDade's death, the Hunters put up three members of his family for a few days, and Power's wife took in his infant son. Gerry Hunter tried to organise a collection for Mrs McDade (as is traditionally done in such circumstances), but it proved difficult since everyone was so short of money. They did, though, arrange to take Mass Cards with them. They purchased these from the shop in St Chad's Cathedral, and during the week took them to the Crossways so that everyone could sign them.

On Thursday 21 November Walker and McIlkenny collected their week's wages from Forgings & Pressings Ltd (part of the GKN group) in Witton. Walker had agreed to lend Hunter the money for the fare. At 4 o'clock, Hugh Callaghan, another patron of the Crossways, walked round to Dick McIlkenny's house to repay a trifling debt, and stayed playing with the children. He couldn't afford to go to Ireland (he was on social security; a stomach ulcer kept him off work), but decided to see McIlkenny and the others off at the station.

At 6.00 p.m. they both went round to Walker's house and, twenty minutes later, the three called on Hunter. They all then set off. As they were walking towards the bus-stop, two of Hunter's children came running after him with an extra pound that Sandra had managed to find for him.

They caught a bus to Colmore Row, hurried down past New Street, and discovered Power waiting for them at the station. He had been the only one to arrive in good time. At that instant the 6.55 train they had intended to catch was just leaving the station. This wasn't a serious problem. Providing the 7.55 was running on time, they would still be able to make the connection with the Heysham boat.

With an hour to wait, they adjourned to the Taurus, the station bar. Hunter made a couple of phone calls to ensure that someone would be able to meet them off the boat. They did not believe it was safe to be without transport for the journey across Belfast.

At about 7.45, Hill turned up. At the last minute he had managed to borrow enough money for the trip from the nuns at the Convent of the Little Sisters of the Assumption.

The train left on time, with five of them aboard and Callaghan left behind on the platform. They changed at Crewe. Paddy Hill risked a British Rail steak-and-kidney pie, which crumbled in his hands. They all played cards, and reached Heysham without incident.

Once in Morecambe police station, they were all put in separate rooms. At about 3.00 a.m. the Birmingham police arrived, and later on Dr Frank Skuse carried out the forensic tests.

In view of what happened later, the situation in which the police found themselves needs to be fully understood. The bombs which had gone off in the two pubs a few hours earlier had been horrific. The investigating officers had been to the scene and witnessed for themselves the blood-shed. Such wanton murder, such appallingly dreadful violence, must have seemed the quintessence of evil.

While waiting to be swabbed, Hunter and the others were naturally nervous. As Walker subsequently explained, however, this was due not to feelings of guilt, but merely to the apprehension which anyone forced to spend several hours at the dead of night in a police station is bound to experience.

The men's accounts of their movements could have seemed suspicious. They had waited for an hour at New Street Station, just a couple of minutes' walk away from both the pubs. They *could* have slipped out of the station bar for a few moments, planted the bombs, and returned almost before anyone had noticed they had gone. By the time the bombs exploded, they would be twenty miles away. Moreover, the police, so it was later claimed at the trial, already had Walker and McIlkenny earmarked as IRA suspects.

While the five were detained at Morecambe their baggage was searched again, this time more thoroughly. The Mass Cards were found in Walker's bag. To the police, this must have seemed doubly incriminating. Not only had all five lied about the purpose of the journey to Belfast but that purpose was to attend an IRA funeral.

It is all too easy, with hindsight, to see that the suspicious chain of circumstances was more persuasive of the innocence than the guilt of these men. The real IRA bombers would have appreciated only too well that all routes back to Ireland would be sealed that day because McDade's body was being flown back to Ireland. Elmdon airport was heavily policed. Both New Street station and the sea routes would be closely watched. Genuine IRA men, knowing that this surveillance would be intensified once the bombs had exploded, would not have risked returning to Ireland. Why, in any case, would they need to? It would be easy enough to lie low in the city.

However, this analysis of events is perhaps a sophisti-

cated one. In the immediacy of the situation, reeling from
the searing horror of the bomb blasts, the police jumped
to conclusions. They thought they'd got their men. Once
Dr Skuse's forensic tests yielded some positive results,
they were certain of it.

After waving goodbye to the others, Hugh Callaghan
wandered back into Birmingham city centre. Within no
time at all, he'd been in and out of two pubs; each was
cleared because of bomb scares. Back in New Street he
noticed a commotion by the Odeon cinema (i.e. in the
vicinity of the bombed Mulberry Bush) and decided it was
safer to return home. He stopped off at the Lozell's club
for a drink, and was told there about the explosions. By
the time he arrived home shortly after 11.00 p.m. he was
emotionally drained. This could be attributed partly to
shock at realising how narrowly he'd missed the bombs
himself, and partly to self-reproach for having forgotten it
was his wife's birthday.

The homes of Gerry Hunter and the others were all
raided and searched by police between 3.00 and 5.00 a.m.
on Friday morning. This was before the men had been
questioned or the results of the forensic tests become
available. The wives assumed that similar treatment was
being meted out to other Irish families in the area. By and
large, it probably was. This was just thorough police-work
in the aftermath of a national tragedy.

In the morning, Callaghan called on Sandra Hunter. He
felt he needed to assure her that, despite the bombings,
her husband had got safely away to Belfast.

It was a bewildering time for all the wives. They noticed
they were followed as they did their Saturday shopping,
and again on the Sunday when they went to Mass. The
first they knew that their husbands were being held was
when the names were read out on the television news on
the Sunday evening: a traumatic moment, indeed, for any
mother and her young children.

The six accused of the Birmingham bombings were sent for trial by magistrates on 9 May 1975. Hunter, Power, Hill, McIlkenny, Walker and Callaghan were all accused of murder. There were three co-accused of conspiracy: Michael Murray, Michael Sheehan and James Kelly.

Counsel for eight of these nine (Murray refused to acknowledge the court and played no part in the judicial proceedings) immediately requested that, in view of the wave of public outrage which had followed the bombings, Mr Justice Bridge should move the trial away from Birmingham.

In granting the application, Bridge observed that, "I cannot escape from the conclusion that those accused might reasonably apprehend, even if it be contrary to the fact, that a Birmingham jury would be unable to bring to the trial that degree of detachment that is necessary to reach a dispassionate and objective verdict."

Accordingly, the trial was moved to Lancaster's 900-year-old castle, a building which was felt to be suitable because it accommodated a medium security prison.

The biggest mass-murder trial in British criminal history duly commenced on 9 June 1975. From the outset, the prosecution linked the bombings to the death of James McDade the previous week. Harry Skinner QC told the jury that the bombs might have been planted "in some illogical way' to avenge or commemorate his death. Skinner stated that all nine were part of an IRA team which included McDade and which had made and planted eleven bombs in the Birmingham area, including the two that had been so wickedly placed in those crowded pubs. "And what were the accused doing?" asked Skinner rhetorically. "Five of them were on the train to Heysham, playing cards, and were described by people who saw them as being in a jolly mood." This is one of the few points about which there was no dispute whatsoever.

The evidence against the accused men fell into three categories: the forensic tests; evidence of association with the IRA; and the 'confessions'.

In the Maguire trial, the tests were disputed on the grounds both of their unreliability and of the competence of the technician who performed them. In the Birmingham case, Dr Skuse's professional experience was beyond question. Argument therefore centred on what, if anything, his results proved. He had, quite properly, submitted the swabs to three different tests. In the cases of Hill and Power, he had obtained positive results in the Griess test; on the TLC and the more sophisticated Gas Chromatography Multiple Spectrometry (GCMS) he got a negative reaction for Power and a doubtful positive one for Hill.

Those were the tests for nitroglycerine. He then tested for another component of explosives: ammonium nitrate. Now, he got positive reactions for Hill and Power, as well as one for Walker; *but he also got a positive reaction for himself.* Skuse told the court that, in Walker's case, contamination from his (Skuse's) own hands could have contributed to a positive reaction.

The tests for Hunter and McIlkenny had proved negative throughout. (So did those on Callaghan, who had been swabbed in Sutton Coldfield.) The results of the tests on Walker were so uncertain that no judicial weight could have been attached to them. Skuse, however, declared himself "99 per cent certain" that Hill and Power had been handling explosives.

The defence called Dr Black, an independent consultant who had been, until 1970, HM Chief Inspector of Explosives for the Home Office. He maintained that the tests were unreliable because, apart from nitroglycerine and ammonium nitrate, other substances, notably nitrocellulose, could produce the same results. Nitrocellulose has a number of industrial applications. It is contained, for example, in paints and varnishes used for public-house furniture and bars. Black maintained that the nitrates the test was attempting to isolate could be found in varnishes, insecticides, fungicides and in petrol additives, as well as in the soil and in the atmosphere. He said that ammonium ions and nitrate ions, the constituent parts of ammonium nitrate, could come together on a man's hands quite by accident. He also insisted that, when testing for nitroglycerine, if the subsequent GCMS or TLC tests gave a negative reading then that totally invalidated a positive result from the preliminary Griess test. Overall, Black told the court, Skuse's tests had not succeeded in identifying nitroglycerine.

Apart from the scientific value of the tests, there was a separate and crucial factor. On the train journey, the five men had, as the prosecution told the court, been playing cards. Accordingly, if one person had traces of explosive on his hands, they all should have them. The cards, too, should have provided positive reactions in tests. According to police, however, tests proved negative. Subsequent independent tests could not be carried out because the pack was mislaid.

The trial hinged overwhelmingly on the 'confessions' which had been obtained in police custody. When he examined the case some years later, Lord Denning commented that "apart from those confessions, the police had no sufficient evidence on which to charge, let alone convict the men." The 'confessions' were strenuously challenged by defence barristers during a week of legal argument while the jury was stood down. In the end, the judge ruled that they were admissible. He subsequently, however, refused the jury permission to see them.

If the 'confessions' had been properly studied, their inherent weaknesses would have become only too apparent. They provided no information about the crimes other than that which the police already possessed, or could have surmised. They were contradictory, illogical and utterly improbable.

According to these statements, Power said that he alone planted the Mulberry Bush bombs; Callaghan said that it was he and Hunter who put the bombs there; Walker said that he and Hunter put the bombs in the Tavern in the Town; McIlkenny said he and Hill did that job.

Further, some of what was 'revealed' in the 'confessions' was shown by subsequent forensic work to be erroneous. Power, Callaghan and McIlkenny all said that the bombs had been placed in plastic bags. (Previous IRA bombs in the Midlands had been in plastic bags; so had a third bomb discovered in the Hagley Road, fortunately before it exploded, on the evening of the pub-bombings.) Both Douglas Higgs, in charge of the Tavern in the Town forensic work, and Donald Lidstone, who was involved in the parallel investigation in the Mulberry Bush, confirmed that D-type handles had been found in the debris – indicating that these bombs had been in suitcases or hold-alls.

The men who had made 'confessions' all repudiated them at the trial, saying they had been extorted under physical and psychological duress. According to their testimony, early that Friday morning, 22 November 1974, they were plunged into a nightmare from which none has yet emerged.

They were given breakfast, and then told to remove their clothes for forensic analysis. Hunter was taken into a cell. Two police officers came in and, he told the court, "they started to hit me." He said that he was slapped and punched throughout the rest of the day, and endured "a long mental and physical torture". He was deprived of sleep throughout the weekend, until he had made a court appearance on Monday morning, and was given no food or drink between Friday's breakfast and a light meal on Saturday evening. The psychological pressure was, if anything, worse. He was told that his house was surrounded by a screaming mob and that his wife and children were being attacked. On the Sunday evening, in his cell, the police both threatened him with a gun and dangled a noose in front of him.

Walker's testimony was similar. The police had threatened to shoot him, too. One policeman had kicked him on the legs and in the genitals. Another burned his foot with a lighted cigarette. Walker removed his shoe and sock to show the court that, months later, his foot was still badly swollen. He said that on the way back from Morecambe to Birmingham he was punched unconscious. His black eye was the only visible injury suffered by the six. According to them all, the police were careful not to mark their faces.

Like Hunter, Walker was told that his family was being attacked, but that they would be given protection if he signed a statement. That was why, he said, he had signed it.

Hill also showed the court lingering injuries which he said he had sustained while in police custody. Several times a gun was put in his mouth and the trigger pulled. During the journey from Morecambe, he was repeatedly hit on the testicles with a truncheon. Power was told he would be thrown out of the car on the motorway, and that it would afterwards be said that he had been trying to escape. He said he had signed a statement because "I had been beaten up and my wife and children had been threatened." McIlkenny testified that "I was constantly punched and slapped and eventually I broke down completely." He said he signed a statement because "I had just given up – I couldn't take any more."

Callaghan was arrested at his home when he came in at about 11 o'clock on the Friday evening. The police had waited there for him since the afternoon. He was taken to Sutton Coldfield police station where he was made to stand naked, with just a blanket around him, and was given no food until Sunday evening, which weakened his resistance considerably. He said that one detective had been shouting at him "like a raving lunatic" and that he had signed a statement only because he was terrified by the interrogation.

After making court appearances on the Monday morning, all were taken to Winson Green prison. Callaghan had already heard a policeman say that a reception had been arranged for them. Walker suffered physical injury before even entering the prison. As he moved to get out of the police van, he was pushed from behind, and landed face-first on the pavement.

From the moment of their arrival in the prison, all six were assaulted indiscriminately by both warders and other prisoners. Walker lost several teeth after being punched in the mouth by one prisoner. "We ran the gauntlet of a lot of officers all the way through the reception area," recalled McIlkenny. "We were all in a bad state. We were taken into D Wing and at the top of the stairs there was a crowd of convicts who appeared to be waiting for us. One of them shouted, 'Right, lads, let them have it.'" As part of this 'reception' each in turn was pushed into a bath of scalding hot water. The prisoner instructed to clean out the bathroom area afterwards found the water red with blood. Throughout the afternoon the six were forced to stand to attention in their cells, with the blood and water dripping down their naked bodies.

Their wives were allowed to see them for the first time the following day. They found them almost unrecognisable.

Neither the solicitors nor the doctors involved with the men during this period emerge with credit. When the solicitors first saw their clients on the Monday morning, they should have refused the police further access to them until they, the prisoners, had been properly photographed and thoroughly examined by a doctor. The solicitors, though, could hardly be blamed; the pressure inside the police station must have been immense. Only solicitors of vast experience and great strength of character would have been emboldened to take such a course.

As it happens, some photographs were taken. Walker clearly had a bruise under his right eye. Both solicitors reported that the men had sustained injuries; in particular, scratches on their chests. Nevertheless, the first time they were medically examined was in prison on the Monday afternoon by Dr Arthur Harwood, the prison doctor.

As a defence witness, he was in an invidious position.

There was no escaping the fact that the men had been maltreated. Harwood's testimony would therefore fix the blame either on his colleagues in the prison service; or on the police; or both. So, he fell into the trap of telling the truth, but not the whole truth. He said that the defendants' injuries had been at least twelve hours old when he saw them on the Monday. The inference was that they had been sustained in police custody. However, Harwood declined to assert this himself. In doing so, he created a poor impression in two respects: he seemed either to be covering up for his colleagues; or admitting to gross negligence in not ascertaining the origins of the injuries he said he saw on the men. In the event, his testimony at Lancaster did the defence great damage.

After his harrowing experience at the trial (*see* page 405), Harwood then contrived to create an entirely different impression in giving evidence to the Owen inquiry (*see* page 407), when he attributed the injuries entirely to innocent causes.

Walker and McIlkenny were seen by an independent doctor on the Tuesday. Bruises and skin lesions on both were noted; one bruise on Walker's chest "could have been caused three to four days previously". Power was examined on the Thursday, after the men had made their second court appearance of the week. The doctor identified thirteen separate areas of wounding, and reported that some "could have been inflicted as long as a week ago".

The remainder of the prosecution evidence presented at Lancaster was either wholly circumstantial or distinctly odd or both.

A special dock had to be built at Lancaster to accommodate the nine accused, the others being Michael Murray, Michael Sheehan and James Kelly.

Murray is the only one of the team responsible for the Birmingham pub-bombings to have been captured –

captured, but not, since he was never charged with the offence, brought to justice. He was known to be an IRA member. In May 1975, just prior to the Lancaster trial, he was convicted on conspiracy charges connected with several of the earlier explosions in the Birmingham area. Thus, when he appeared in court in Lancaster, he was just beginning a twelve-year sentence. In time-honoured IRA fashion, Murray refused to recognise the court and kept silent throughout.

When giving evidence Walker told of a sensational meeting with Murray in the exercise-yard at Winson Green. Murray, he said, apologised about Walker and the others becoming involved in something which didn't concern them. "Nothing went right that night," he quoted Murray as saying. "The first telephone box we got to was out of order." Walker replied, "What are you on about? Are you telling me that you did those bombs?" He said that he was shocked when Murray answered, "Yes".

Walker said he later learned the identity of the team responsible for the bombings: Murray, and three others who were by then in Eire. He sent the four names to the Home Secretary, Roy Jenkins.

While Murray was, perhaps, an enigmatic defendant, Thomas Watt was an enigmatic prosecution witness. Watt worked at the Witton factory with Walker, McIlkenny and Murray. He suspected some IRA sympathisers among them, and accordingly coaxed Walker into doing a drawing of how he imagined a bomb was constructed. Walker did so. Watt then took it to the police, sometime around June 1974, using it as documentary proof to back up his suspicions. The police, so he said, were grateful and asked him to keep an eye on his work-mates.

Watt's evidence contained a number of other significant, and very prejudicial, observations. He said that his work-mates warned him to stay indoors on the night of the bombings; that Walker had admitted planting other bombs; and that he had asked Watt where he could buy cheap alarm clocks.

None of this is necessarily inconsistent with Walker's innocence; trouble in Birmingham that evening was widely expected among the security services and the Irish community. As for planting other bombs, no one who had done so would refer to it in casual conversation. Probably Walker had just been having him on; Watt seems to have been, on the most favourable interpretation of his behaviour, a rather credulous individual.

What lent the evidence a certain ambiguity, even apart from these reservations, was the revelation during the trial that at the time of the bombings Watt was giving shelter to Kenneth Littlejohn, then notorious in Anglo-Irish affairs.

On 12 October 1972 Littlejohn had been a member of a gang involved in an armed robbery in the Irish Republic. Although the apparent purpose of this was to obtain cash to finance IRA activities, it is widely believed that it was staged by British intelligence in order to discredit the IRA. A week later Littlejohn and his brother were arrested in England on an Irish warrant. The Dublin government successfully pleaded its case for extradition. The Littlejohns appealed, and in February 1973 argued that they had infiltrated the IRA and had been working for British intelligence at the time. The Appeal Court rejected their submissions, and Littlejohn was returned to Ireland where he was convicted and given a twenty-year sentence.

Within a year, he was back in the headlines. On 11 April 1974 he escaped from Mountjoy prison and disappeared. At the time of the Birmingham bombings, therefore, he was being actively sought by both the British and Irish security services. (He was in fact arrested on 12 December.) That one of the major prosecution witnesses at this trial had been giving him shelter, but was never charged with any offence in connection with it, seems to suggest that it would be naïve to take his evidence at face value.

James Kelly, one of the three additional defendants, also had a bizarre story to tell. For a start, it turned out that his real name was not Kelly, but Woods. He had changed it after deserting from the British Army – the Royal Corps of Signals – in Germany in 1964. He was an Orangeman (i.e. Protestant) from Portadown, and said he had been trying to infiltrate the IRA. He said to the policeman who arrested him, "It is imperative that I see your assistant chief constable. I have some valuable information about the IRA."

Kelly said that he had first conceived the idea after meeting Sheehan, who worked for the same Birmingham firm. Apparently, his opportunity occurred when Walker and Sheehan asked him to take charge of bags containing, he said, guns and explosives. However, he did not even contact the police, much less pass on information to them. He said his nerve failed him. He simply returned the bags.

Similar pieces of evidence would have been damaging to Walker in particular and, by extension, to all six. Hilda Wickett, one of his neighbours in Kingstanding, gave evidence that both she and her son had seen Walker and other men carrying large cement bags into the house late at night. She also said that after every Birmingham explosion Walker seemed to disappear for two or three weeks.

Evidence also came from a man who was drinking at the College Arms in Kingstanding when Sheehan came in with a cardboard box, joined Walker, opened the box, and took out an alarm clock. Apparently, Walker wound the clock up, held it to his ear, and then said, laughing, "Isn't that a beautiful tick?"

Walker's explanation was that when he took over from Hunter the job of organising the raffle, Murray gave him an address in Dublin to which the money, for the Prisoners' Dependants' Fund, should be sent. He also told Walker how prizes could be purchased wholesale from a local warehouse. They were the sort of meretricious items that one might see being offered as fairground prizes: lamps, teddy bears, table lighters, and various clocks, including alarm clocks and watches. Murray said he could purchase these for Walker, because his wife had a membership card, and then pass them on either at work, or in the pub nearby called the Yew Tree. On one occasion, though, Murray had taken the prizes round to Walker's home address.

James McDade also helped sell the tickets. Once, in May 1974, he went round to Walker's house, carrying a bag which he asked if he could leave. Walker said he didn't look inside the bag, which was collected the following evening by Sheehan. He and Walker took it by car to a house which, Walker supposed, could have been Kelly's. At the time, he was not really interested; he had only asked for a lift to the pub.

As usual in miscarriage cases, the evidence which the prosecution didn't provide is the more telling. According to its scenario, and according to those wretched 'confessions', the six men who met at New Street station made brief excursions to plant the bombs, and then re-assembled there.

A number of people were in the Taurus bar on that particular evening. In their statements (these are the *bona fide* statements, made of their own volition), the men described some of them: the barmaid; a couple who seemed to have a quarrel and then kiss and make up, and so on. The prosecution, however, called no one who had been in the bar. This omission knocks a sizeable hole in the prosecution argument. Surely someone who had been there at the time must have noticed these men slip out and then return some minutes later.

The sum total of Crown evidence about this part of the case was a statement from a barmaid, Julia Vines, which was read out in court, and according to which her colleague served drinks to a man with an Irish accent at about 7.45.

Similarly, the men were never put on identity parades, although there was a possibility, however slight, that the bombers might have been noticed in either or both of the pubs. (On 23 November, the *Birmingham Post* carried a story in a special panel at the foot of the front page, to the effect that "a man who missed the Mulberry Bush blasts by seconds last night said he felt sure he could identify the man who placed the bomb.")

The absence of forensic evidence is just as glaring. Even the most meticulous criminal is likely to give himself away, because of the skill of forensic scientists in identifying fibres on clothes, dirt on footwear, and so on. It is a corollary that if forensic science fails to yield one single microscopic factor connecting the accused with the crime then he is almost certainly innocent of it.

In this case, conditions for scientific investigation were practically ideal. All the men surrendered for analysis the clothes they had been wearing when they had supposedly planted the bombs, yet the laboratories were unable to discover anything to link them with the crimes. Nor was there evidence to connect the homes of any of the six men with either explosives or bomb-making equipment. The point bears repeating: in this instance, too, detective work should theoretically have been handsomely rewarded. Police raided the homes in strength within a few hours of the bombings. (The argument that the bombs could have been manufactured elsewhere is a non-starter. Where? And why, if the 'confessions' were as reliable as the prosecution insisted, was no hint of this contained in them?)

Hilda Wickett told the court that Walker tended to disappear for a time after bomb attacks in the area. If this had been true, the prosecution would undoubtedly have been able to produce his attendance sheets from work to corroborate it.

Much was made at the trial of the failure of the five men at Heysham to volunteer the information that they were going to the funeral of an IRA man, but can one seriously imagine that this is indicative of their guilt? However law-abiding their intentions, it would have been a fool-hardy admission. The police would have been almost bound to interpret it wrongly – as, indeed, they did.

And so the contradictions and implausibilities of the prosecution case accumulate.

In the twenty minutes prior to the arrival of Hunter and the three others, Power had been at New Street on his own. He is certain that during that time a Special Branch policeman monitored his movements carefully. (It was only in retrospect that he realised the man was on surveillance duty.) Power has always been convinced that this man must know they are all innocent, because he was in the bar throughout. It would have been grossly negligent of the intelligence and security services to have left New Street station unmanned at such an especially tense time, so Power's suspicions are certainly plausible.

To take this a stage further: a Special Branch officer is on duty at New Street station, specifically assigned to keep a look-out for groups of Irishmen. He sees Walker and friends arrive, carrying a number of bags. He sees them depart for a few minutes, and then reappear with rather few bags. He does nothing at all about it, even though – according to the evidence of Watt, testifying for the Crown – the police had been informed five months previously that Walker and McIlkenny were IRA suspects.

Is this credible?

If the six men were the bombers, then the bombings should never have occurred because adequate security would have prevented them. In another parallel with the Maguire trial, if the prosecution case is true, then the ineptitude of the British security services is beyond belief.

Turning to the considerations which are persuasive of the innocence of the men individually, the positions of Hunter, Hill and Callaghan were particularly strange. The prosecution case rested mainly on the strength of the 'confessions' and the forensic tests. So what was the evidence against Hunter? He had not signed a 'confession' and all his tests proved negative. Hill arrived at the station at 7.45 p.m. – after the time when the bombs were supposed to have been planted. He could account for virtually every minute of his time from 6 o'clock onwards that evening. (He had, for example, called in at the convent to borrow the money for his trip.) He had no opportunity to have planted the bombs. Callaghan was at liberty throughout the following day, Friday. He knew that the homes of all the others had been raided in the early hours. Surely, if he had been a bomber, he would have made himself scarce, instead of following his daily routine, and walking into the arms of the police.

Proceedings at Lancaster were interrupted for a week of legal argument which turned on whether or not the 'confessions' were admissible, and for another week in July when the judge was admitted to hospital suffering from acute gastritis. When he resumed after his illness, he told the court that doctors had advised him to lighten his workload, and the daily sittings would be curtailed by forty-five minutes.

On Saturday 2 August, the *Daily Mirror* devoted its entire front page to what it termed a "Mirror Exclusive": photographs of the six facing the murder charges at Lancaster. They were the "first pictures", boasted the reporter, Paul Connew. It was extraordinary that the paper, then still the country's biggest-selling daily, should have sought to prejudice the outcome of the trial by publishing, let alone giving such prominence to, these photographs. Indeed, the appearance of the pictures was only marginally less bewildering than the judge's oversight in not ordering the *Mirror* editor to be brought before him to explain such a blatant contempt of court.

Even when the end of the trial seemed in sight, with the judge's summing-up under way, there was a further delay. The trial was adjourned at lunchtime one day. The judge was again indisposed, this time with a sore throat.

In his summing-up, Mr Justice Bridge stressed that there was a fundamental conflict over the forensic evidence, but that Dr Black had produced no proof of his theory. (Which was true; the overall presentation of the defence case left much to be desired.) Bridge told the jury, "I have made my views pretty plain over this conflict over forensic evidence, but as an issue of fact, it will be your decision and not mine that will count." Indeed, throughout the trial, he never refrained from making his own impressions abundantly clear to everyone.

He also said that the two accounts – from the police and the defendants – of how the 'confessions' had been obtained were utterly irreconcilable. "Gross perjury" was being committed by one party or the other.

"If the defendants' stories were to be believed," he continued, "many police officers had behaved in a manner that recalled the Star Chamber, the rack and the thumbscrews of four or five hundred years ago. At the very least, their [the defendants'] account was that they were subjected to gross violence and brutality."

Mr Justice Bridge's strongest strictures were reserved for the hapless Dr Harwood. His attack was so trenchant that it was the main headline story in *The Times* the next day. He maintained that it was clear that the six men had been the victims of "a series of quite outrageous assaults' soon after arriving in Winson Green. He suggested, therefore, that the doctor must be covering up for his colleagues. "If Harwood came to this Court deliberately to give you [members of the jury] false evidence to protect his cronies in the prison service," Bridge said, "not only is he not fit to be in the prison service but he is also not fit to be a member of the honourable profession upon which – if he did commit perjury – he has brought such terrible shame."[2]

The jury deliberated for six and a half hours, and on 15 August 1975 returned verdicts of guilty on all the 126 murder charges. The judge said to the six, "You have been convicted on the clearest and most overwhelming evidence I have ever heard in a case of murder." He sentenced them all to life imprisonment. What he did not do was to recommend minimum terms.[3]

Of the three additional defendants, Murray was found

guilty on the conspiracy charge, and given a nine-year sentence to run concurrently with the twelve-year one he was already serving. Sheehan was convicted on charges of conspiracy and possessing explosives, and given concurrent terms of imprisonment of nine and five years respectively. Kelly was found not guilty on the conspiracy charge, but guilty of possessing explosives. The judge said that the time he had already been held on remand was equivalent to a twelve-month sentence, and that this could be regarded as adequate punishment. Accordingly, he was set free. No action was taken against him for desertion in 1964.

Two interesting points emerge. The first is that the two men found guilty of possessing explosives in this case received sentences of five years and twelve months. The defendants in the Maguire case, convicted of the same charges, received twelve- and fourteen-year sentences. Secondly, why did Murray have to face these additional charges at all? There was no penal reason for bringing him forward: the sentence he was already serving was longer than the concurrent one imposed for equivalent offences by Bridge. However, the presence of a genuine IRA man in the dock must have cruelly handicapped the abilities of the others to plead their case successfully.

Finally, the judge said, "I am entirely satisfied, and the jury by their verdicts have shown they are satisfied, that all the investigations were carried out with scrupulous propriety." The Birmingham pub-bombs trial concluded, and the six men were taken away to serve their long, and possibly unending, sentences. Meanwhile, senior officers of the West Midlands police force advised the press that they were still looking for at least three more men. The ones they had in mind, presumably, would have been the actual bombers.[4]

Mr Justice Bridge had said that he hoped those responsible for administering the "quite outrageous assaults" on the prisoners would themselves be brought to trial. An editorial in *The Times* echoed this: "one of the most critical tests of any judicial system is that standards are upheld to the full for those least deserving of sympathy . . . The final judgment on this whole affair ought to be that justice was done to and for these men."[5]

Inquiries had already been set in motion. On 14 December 1974 the *Irish Press* published a report in which an Irishman lately released from Winson Green prison said he had witnessed the full severity of the beatings received by the six men. Robin Corbett, the Labour MP for Hemel Hempstead, was sent a copy by an Irish constituent.[6] The *Guardian* published the story, and Corbett took up the issue in the Commons. Roy Jenkins responded by setting up an internal investigation headed by David Owen, then the assistant chief constable of Lincolnshire. He was instructed to look into both the press allegations of maltreatment in prison, and the prisoners' allegations of maltreatment in police custody.

The Owen inquiry concluded that there had been no breach of police discipline. A report on the conduct of the warders was forwarded to the Director of Public Prosecutions on 13 May 1975, but was then left to gather dust. The publication in the *Guardian* on 29 November of a letter from Jacqueline Kaye of the Prisoners' Aid Committee seems to have aroused officials at the DPP belatedly to acknowledge their public duties. By the end of the year it was announced that fourteen prison officers were to be charged with assault. They were all suspended on full pay from 30 December.

The appeals of the six men were heard on 30 March 1976 before the Lord Chief Justice, Lord Widgery, sitting with Lord Justice Lawton and Mr Justice Thompson. They were dismissed.

Only two points of interest emerged from the judgment. Mr Justice Bridge was reprimanded, both over one aspect of his summing-up – "it is difficult to say exactly what he was instructing the jury upon" – and over his ruthless attack on the character of Dr Harwood. "He invited the jury to consider whether Dr Harwood had committed perjury, which was an observation not called for in the circumstances, and went on to imply that he was not fit to be a doctor of medicine, to which the same comment can be applied."

The forensic evidence which had been heard at the trial was virtually set aside. Widgery noted that the scientific tests for explosives had given positive reactions for Hill and Power. "This is not a point, as we see it, of great importance in the case because there was no trace of explosives found on the other hands and even in the case of Hill and Power a subsequent and, one understands, more precise and accurate test failed to confirm the original one."

In the narrow terms of the appeal, this availed the appellants nothing. Their counsel were unable to advance fresh theories about the pack of cards on the train on the basis that this whole issue was effectively a red herring anyway. "The traces of explosive played such a small part," reiterated Widgery.

In the context of the case as a whole, however, Widgery's remarks were extraordinary. At the trial, Dr Frank Skuse had testified that he was "99 per cent certain" that Hill and Power had been handling explosives. For the jury, this must have been persuasive evidence, particularly since Dr Black, the defence witness called to repudiate Dr Skuse's conclusions, was denigrated in the judge's summing-up.

Further, Widgery's comments would have been sufficient, *mutatis mutandis*, to destroy the Crown case in the Maguire trial, which had concluded at the Old Bailey earlier in the month. Those seven defendants were convicted on 4 March, as we have seen, on the basis of tests which, by 30 March, suddenly didn't seem to make much difference one way or the other.

As regards the Birmingham bombs case, the crux of the

matter was now indubitably the 'confessions'. The appeal judges didn't concern themselves with these, though Widgery did make a passing reference to the fact that Walker had a black eye, "the origin of which I have forgotten, but I do not think it matters very much anyway". The whole exercise was par for the Appeal Court course: the unimportant was considered at some length, before being dismissed as irrelevant; and the important was brusquely swept aside and not considered at all.

It could perhaps be argued that the judges were unable to give proper consideration to the 'confessions' lest their deliberations impinged upon the forthcoming trial of the prison warders. This, of course, raises the question of why the appeal, which came to court relatively speedily, was held prior to the warders' trial.

The manoeuvres which preceded the warders' trial were not without significance. The DPP decided not to call the Birmingham men as witnesses. As far as one can tell, the decision was a final one, for the DPP wrote to Anthony Curtis, who was acting as solicitor for three of the men, explaining that it had been reached after "long consideration".

One can only speculate whether the intention was to deprive the six of an additional opportunity to reiterate publicly both their own innocence and the flagrant abuse they had received at the hands of the police. Certainly, their absence would nevertheless have made a farce of the proceedings. Once the decision had been leaked to the *Guardian*, which disclosed it in April 1976, the DPP had to backtrack. On 5 June the newspaper announced that the men would, after all, be called as witnesses.

The trial was held in Birmingham, illustrating a convenient inconsistency in judicial policy. The main trial had been switched from Birmingham to Lancaster, to avoid a possibly biased jury.

The trial of the fourteen Winson Green prison officers that opened before Mr Justice Swanwick on 10 June was technically the second one. The previous day's proceedings were aborted, because of what the *Guardian* described as "remarkable confusion" over the empanelment of the jury.[7] A fresh twelve were sworn in.

Altogether there were ninety separate charges of assault. The Crown's case was that "a catalogue of beatings, screams, blows and blood" had occurred after the admission of the six to prison. None of the prison warders charged went into the witness-box, though a number made unsworn statements. "I saw officers that I knew to be quiet and docile lose control of themselves," said one. "Their actions were the result of the emotions aroused by the murders and mutilations of the previous Thursday night. I do not condone their actions, but I could understand them."

On 15 July all the defendants were found not guilty. Since there was by now absolutely no dispute that Hill, Hunter, McIlkenny, Walker, Power and Callaghan had been brutally attacked inside prison, one explanation of these seemingly perverse verdicts could be that the jury appreciated that those on trial were not solely responsible for the harm done to the six men.

During the trial, the defence called Dr David Paul, a former surgeon with the Metropolitan Police and at that time coroner for the City of London. He studied photographs of the men taken before and after their arrival in prison, and deduced from them that although the men had sustained injuries around 24–27 November, they had also suffered injuries previously – i.e. while in police custody. Also, when the prison governor first carried out an internal inquiry into maltreatment of the prisoners, his officers made statements confirming that the men had been bruised and injured when brought to prison. Three of these officers made their statements available to solicitors of the six men.

On 14 November 1977, armed with such apparently persuasive testimony, the six men took out writs for assault against the Lancashire and/or West Midlands police forces, and also against the Home Office. They were granted legal aid to bring the action. A year later, on 23 November 1978, Mr Justice Cantley firmly dismissed an application by the West Midlands police authority to strike out the statement of claim.

The police authority appealed against this decision. So the matter was determined in the Court of Appeal on 17 January 1980 by the Master of the Rolls, Lord Denning, sitting with Lord Justice Goff and Sir George Baker.

Counsel for the police argued that the issue of threats and violence had been decided in their favour at the trial and should not now be reopened. In legal terminology, their case was that the men were 'estopped' from raising again an issue already determined by Mr Justice Bridge; and, further, that the men's action was "an abuse of the process of the court".

Issue estoppel applies only in civil, and not criminal, cases. It is the technical term for what is actually a kind of legal full stop. In a branch of law which thrives on the interminable, it is almost unique in carrying the weight of finality.

It was basically on the issue of estoppel that Denning did allow the police appeal, thereby thwarting the attempts of the men to find legal redress for their grievances. He affirmed that the jury's conviction had acted as confirmation of the judge's ruling on the admissibility of the 'confessions', since the jurors must have agreed with him in believing the police and disbelieving the men; and that the new evidence which the men had hoped to bring forward – Dr Paul's, for example – could not be considered because it could have been available for the trial had 'reasonable diligence' been used.[8]

Denning's judgment included the following passage:

Just consider the course of events if their [the men's] action were to proceed to trial . . . If [they] failed it would mean that much time and money and worry would have been expended by many people to no good purpose.

If they won, it would mean that the police were guilty of perjury; that they were guilty of violence and threats; that the confessions were involuntary and improperly admitted in evidence; and that the convictions were erroneous. That would mean that the Home Secretary would have either to recommend that they be pardoned or to remit the case to the Court of Appeal.

That was such an appalling vista that every sensible person would say, "It cannot be right that these actions should go any further." They should be struck out either on the ground that the men are estopped from challenging the decision of Mr Justice Bridge, or alternatively that it is an abuse of the process of the court. Whichever it is, the actions should be stopped.

The impression given by those final sentences is that Denning is not certain exactly *why* he is striking out the claim. It might be on some grounds; or it might be on others. Whatever the ostensible reason, however, the actual reason seems to be that the consequences for the English legal system would be so tremendous that the courts must shrink from them *irrespective of whether or not the men's cause is just.* "An appalling vista" it may be; but if it is a landscape that must be surveyed, then the law must survey it. Not to do so brings into focus an even more appalling vista.

Ultimately, the judgment is intellectually dishonest. For all its erudite consideration of past issues of estoppel, it is seemingly based on gut emotion, not fine legal analysis.

Lord Justice Goff parted company with Denning, saying he "could not agree that the judgment of Mr Justice Bridge alone created an issue of estoppel sufficient to bar the plaintiffs' claims", though Goff did uphold the police case on other grounds. His dissenting legal interpretation was read out on his behalf by Sir George Baker, for Lord

Justice Goff had been suddenly taken ill. It fell to Denning, at the end of the appeal, to announce his death.

Denning concluded his judgment by saying that "the cases showed what a civilised country we were": through the facility of legal aid, we had allowed the six Irishmen a generous crack of the judicial whip.

I beg leave to differ, Your Lordship. The cases showed what a wicked, wicked country we can be.

Eighteen

The campaign

FOR A decade, the monstrous injustice of the Birmingham case escaped public notice. The long-drawn-out judicial proceedings inhibited press comment, though the English media were in any case hyper-sensitive to any story concerning Northern Ireland. When news editors did decide to publicise such matters, the Maguire case inevitably received preference. The overriding consideration, though, was the feelings of bitterness and anger which "the most wickedly indiscriminate mainland British bombing of the post-war era" still engendered – especially in Birmingham itself – and which virtually precluded the notion that those imprisoned for the offences were not, after all, the perpetrators of them.[1] Against such a tide of opinion – or, perhaps, prejudice – a "Rough Justice" campaign, launched in Birmingham, could make little headway.

Two Irish priests, Father Denis Faul and Father Raymond Murray, understood what had happened. They had the courage and initiative to produce *The Birmingham Framework*, their own independently-published account of the case. On 19 February 1980 David Leigh reported in the *Guardian* on the gathering doubts surrounding the forensic evidence presented in court; it was an isolated piece of media concern. On 18 November 1984, the tenth anniversary of the bombings, Michael Farrell analysed the convictions in detail in the Dublin *Sunday Tribune*; but even in Eire interest was slight.

The picture was changed by the spirited campaigning journalism of independent television, and in particular of two programmes – *World in Action* (Granada), edited by Ray Fitzwalter, and *First Tuesday* (Yorkshire), edited by John Willis. On 28 October 1985 *World in Action* broadcast an hour-long special on the Birmingham pub-bombings. The researchers, Chris Mullin and Charles Tremayne, had made significant progress in their examination of the case. They obtained copies of statements which the prison warders who stood trial had made to their solicitors, and which had never previously been made public. They have the ring of truth, if only because the warders make damaging, self-incriminating statements in the course of them. They also say, quite categorically, that the prisoners had been seriously assaulted before arriving at Winson Green. One prison officer asserted that "Their bodily markings were at least one or more days old. These were consistent with a systematic beating below the neck while in police custody."[2] These observations paralleled those of Dr David Paul – also interviewed on the programme – who reiterated that he was "completely confident" that the men sustained injuries to their faces prior to their arrival in Winson Green.

Mullin and Tremayne also exposed the inaccuracy of the forensic evidence. At the trial Dr Black, for the defence, suggested that Dr Skuse had failed to confirm the presence of explosives because other substances – and in particular nitrocellulose – would give the same result in tests. This assertion, however, was not scientifically verified, a shortcoming which allowed Mr Justice Bridge to dismiss Black's testimony out of hand.

Granada took the problem to two independent scientists. Dr Brian Caddy of Strathclyde University in Glasgow, who runs the country's only academic forensic science unit, confirmed what Black and many others had long maintained: that nitrocellulose would have yielded indistinguishable results. He tested items such as a pack of cards (most packs are coated with nitrocellulose) and got a positive response. He then asked a lab assistant to shuffle the pack, after which Caddy tested his hands. Once again, a positive result was obtained.

The new research illustrated that Dr Skuse's evidence had been scientifically invalid, and completely vindicated Dr Black, who told the *Observer*, "I felt upset about the trial because I thought the evidence I gave was not being given the weight that it merited and now it seems to have been borne out. Too often at these trials the word of the prosecution scientist is taken as gospel."[3]

There was one conundrum, however. How was it that although all five had been playing cards, positive results were obtained from the hands of only two of them? "This was answered," wrote Tremayne, "by the discovery of a Home Office circular which warned scientists that the Griess test was only 30 per cent accurate."[4]

David Baldock, a former senior scientific officer with the Home Office now working in Nottingham, confirmed Caddy's findings. He explained the limitations of the Griess test – "it proves only that the substance you suspect could be present, not that it is present" – and also revealed some startling information. In the mid-seventies Home Office scientists were frequently asked to test for samples of explosives that were simply too small to register in tests. They devised an ingenious, albeit devious, solution. By saturating the gas chromatograph beforehand with the substance in question (say, nitroglycerine) it was possible to detect an infinitesimal additional quantity. Tests in terrorist cases were sometimes done in just this way. It seems a dangerously uncertain method of testing. Had it been revealed, it would surely have aroused public disquiet. It is doubtful if any jury would have convicted anyone on the basis of 'evidence' thus obtained. Baldock confirmed to Tremayne that "Crown scientists were rather relieved that it was never challenged in court".[5] He also said that, because of unease within the Home Office, the practice was discontinued.

World in Action also exposed one of the dirty tricks of the prosecution. The only witness evidence about the presence of the six men in the Taurus bar at New Street station was contained in a statement from the barmaid, Julia Vines. However, she declined to assist the prosecution case in Lancaster because she said she could not be certain of her evidence. Nevertheless, Crown counsel read out her statement in court and the defence, having no reason to doubt it, allowed it to pass unchallenged.

The programme was less directly concerned with under-mining the 'confession' evidence – no doubt in deference to the Home Office's narrow definition of what constitutes genuinely fresh evidence – but in this regard there was an interesting coincidence. On the day of the *World in Action* transmission, seven British servicemen stationed in Cyprus were acquitted of spying charges at the Old Bailey. All had made detailed 'confessions' which formed the prosecution case. The jury, in acquitting them, must have concluded that these were worthless. The outcome of the trial gener-ated enormous interest, and the similarity of the case to the Birmingham one could not have passed unnoticed.

The evidence assembled by *World in Action* was more than enough to convince Sir John Farr, Conservative MP for Harborough (the constituency which takes in Gartree prison, where Paddy Hill was held) and Roy Jenkins, Home Secretary at the time of the original events, that the case should be reopened. Douglas Hurd, the then recently-appointed Home Secretary, received further rep-resentations from John Hume, leader of the SDLP in Ulster, who had been disturbed about the case since visit-ing John Walker in prison in 1983.

Within a week of the transmission there were two devel-opments, the one predictable, the other less so. Hurd ordered a "painstaking investigation of the new evidence produced"; and Dr Frank Skuse was told to take early retirement from his job with the north-west division of the Home Office's forensic science services in Chorley, Lancashire.

The Maguire case had been seeping into the public con-sciousness over a period of years. After *World in Action*, the Birmingham case attracted widespread attention. On 1 July 1986 First Tuesday's *The Guildford Time Bomb* was shown. Finally, all three cases had been placed, as it were, in the public domain.

As television material, the Guildford case presented two distinct problems. Paul Hill did seem to have had IRA connections at some stage. This, together with the petty-thieving and drug-taking background of the other three involved, would tend to alienate audience sympathy. Also, there was no longer even a remote possibility of uncovering the kind of new evidence which the authorities deem the *sine qua non* of reopening a case. Evidence of the most compelling nature had already emerged: the frank confessions of three of the Balcombe Street gang and Brendan Dowd. If that had not served to raise doubts at the Court of Appeal, then nothing would. In such circumstances, it was immensely creditable of Yorkshire to grasp this particular nettle.

The programme surveyed the lack of forensic and identification evidence, Carole Richardson's near-watertight alibi, and the statements of O'Connell, Dowd and the others. James Still, the retired Metropolitan Police superintendent who helped to take them, said, "I am satisfied from the detail they gave me that they were the people who committed the offences. They provided a coherent, logical story that fitted all the facts. What they said couldn't have been from imagination; it had to be from experience."

That left the 'confessions', which Grant McKee (producer) and Ros Franey (researcher) took to two leading forensic psychologists, Professor Lionel Haward of Surrey University and Barrie Irving, the director of the Police Foundation.

During the eighties, for the first time, research has been undertaken into why some people held in custody do make false confessions. One cause was the overwhelming anxiety felt by people under interrogation, which perhaps leads them to escape the short-term effects of their predicament regardless of the long-term consequences. "Armstrong's case fits this pattern almost exactly," said Haward.

Irving studied confessions like Armstrong's before submitting evidence to the Royal Commission on Criminal Procedure. "My conclusion was that without corroboration one is on very dangerous ground. In this case, the unease is only increased by the additional problems concerning the way the interviews were handled." Irving considered that suspects should not be interrogated while under the influence of drink or drugs (as Armstrong was); and should be denied neither nourishment and adequate rest (as Armstrong was), nor access to a solicitor (as Armstrong was). Overall, Irving concluded, Armstrong's was a classic example of the kind of statement which should not be admitted in evidence without corroboration; and there was none.

(For the sake of legal argument, these observations sidestepped the main point: whether the confessions were extorted by physical intimidation.)

The day after *The Guildford Time Bomb* was shown, Hurd ordered a review of this case also.

By this time, MPs, among others, were beginning to wonder what had happened to the investigations into the Birmingham case, 'urgently' launched some eight months earlier.[6] While official inquiries seemed to be bogged down, journalistic ones were proceeding apace. Chris Mullin, who originally persuaded Granada to take up the case, had written a book about it, and was thus operating a kind of one-man pincer movement on the authorities.[7] On the whole, the book, *Error of Judgement*, reassembled the evidence which *World in Action* had drawn together the previous October, but Mullin made three important strides of his own. He presented in detail police statements relating to the way in which the 'confessions' were obtained, which allowed readers to judge their credibility for themselves. They do not pass muster: would callous bombers have been so spontaneously overcome with remorse? Would police officers, many of whom had witnessed the carnage of the bombings, have behaved towards those whom they believed responsible with a solicitousness that, in the circumstances, was almost saintly? ("Compose yourself, Dick," one officer supposedly said to Richard McIlkenny, "and I'll get some tea.")

Secondly, he disclosed that one of the policemen on duty at Queen's Road police station when the men were brought in, Detective Sergeant Brian Morton, had since been convicted of, and imprisoned for, beating up a suspect while obtaining a 'confession' in another case.

His other piece of extraordinary individual initiative was simply to have made contact in the Irish Republic with the members of the four-man team who admitted having perpetrated the bombings. They were still at liberty. Though this section of the book was not of strict legal usefulness (since Mullin had pledged never to reveal their identities), it did create a powerful impression when the book was published on 14 July.

Mullin's account of his meetings with the real bombers was contained in the two closing chapters of the book. Not wishing to hold back important material while publication was pending, Sir John Farr, who played an increasingly prominent role in the public campaign, had on 12 May forwarded a draft of these to the Home Secretary. He received a reply on 20 May:

> the material and claims in the extract from *Error of Judgement* raise matters which are wholly new and which present a completely different approach to the whole question of whether the six men may have been wrongfully convicted . . . you will understand that I shall need to consider the implication of what Mullin has to say very carefully . . . encourage Mullin to make available as quickly as possible any relevant material he may have.

As a result, a further letter was despatched on 26 May in which Farr and Mullin agreed to go to Queen Anne's Gate to meet the Home Secretary. This was followed by a more characteristic Home Office response – a lengthy silence – until a meeting was eventually scheduled for 9 July; not

with the Home Secretary himself, but with his minister of
state, David Mellor. However, on 7 July, Mellor's office
contacted Farr and asked him to go alone.

It was not only the Home Office that seemed reluctant
to learn at first-hand what Mullin had found out. Douglas
Hurd's initial reaction on receiving the book material from
Farr had been to pass it on to the West Midlands police
and ask them to investigate it. They, too, made no attempt
to contact Mullin; though, according to Harry Cohen,
Labour MP for Leyton, Geoffrey Dear, the Chief Constable, "replied with a longer letter that poured scorn on
the book and I understand that he even questioned Mullin's
motives".[8]

In a written answer on 26 June, the Home Secretary
told parliament for the first time that he had "asked the
police for a report [on Mullin's meetings with the alleged
real bombers]".[9] It was on 24 July that Mellor, his junior,
admitted *which* police force had been asked to carry out
these further investigations. Brian Sedgemore (Labour MP
for Hackney South & Shoreditch) immediately put down
a question, inquiring why such a task was not entrusted to
an outside police force. "We saw no reason to approach a
different police force," Mellor replied. "It seemed sensible
to seek this from the force which was most closely involved
in the investigations and which has most knowledge of the
case."[10]

During this period, in the immediate wake of publication
of *Error of Judgement*, ministers were under constant
pressure in the Commons. In another part of Mellor's reply
of 24 July, he said,

> I assure the House that no one has any interest in
> prolonging these matters. We recognise that there is
> a double public interest – in ensuring that people are
> not wrongly convicted and, equally, in ensuring that, if
> people are rightly convicted, orchestrated campaigns
> should not undermine the integrity of those convic-
> tions.[11]

There was indeed a "double public interest": of ensuring that innocent men were released from prison; and guilty ones called to account for their crimes. The kind of public interest identified by Mellor had not noticeably occurred to anyone outside the Home Office. Harry Cohen was quick to point out that if the campaign to which Mellor had referred with such calculated disdain was indeed "orchestrated", then it was orchestrated by, to name but a few, "the government of the Republic of Ireland, the Archbishop of Canterbury, the Archbishops of Westminster and Armagh, and the Bishops of Down and Connor and Derry".[12]

Cohen opened a lengthy debate on the case in the House on 25 July (his interest being that Patsy Power, the sister of William Power, was one of his constituents). He made it plain that he understood the difficulties facing the administration. Referring back to the comment of Lord Bridge, the trial judge, that if the police were lying it would represent "a conspiracy unprecedented in the annals of British criminal history", Cohen insisted that there had indeed been "a world record quantity of perjury" at the trial. More than twenty officers, ranging in rank from detective constable to assistant chief constable, testified that they "had not laid a finger on the men". Nevertheless, Cohen emphasised, prison staff throughout the country knew that these six men were entirely innocent; unlike other Category A (i.e. most dangerous) prisoners, they all received unsupervised visits. (Something which Mullin had taken advantage of to make a tape-recorded conversation with Paddy Hill, which *World in Action* then used to good effect.) Basically, Cohen wanted to know why the inquiry was proceeding "at a snail's pace".[13]

Bob Clay (Labour MP for Sunderland North) referred to the political difficulties which surrounded the case – namely, the implications for the vexed issue of extradition from the United States and Eire. Tam Dalyell (Labour MP for Linlithgow) asked a number of specific questions about the forensic tests, and wanted an explanation of the disappearance of the two sets of playing cards used by the six men on their train journey to Heysham.

David Mellor explained that the Home Secretary was trying to make "what is often an invidious decision" about whether to refer the case to appeal. "What would be inappropriate would be for him to seek to review cases, and interfere with the decisions of the courts, on the basis of his own or someone else's view of the facts and arguments which have already been considered. He cannot exercise his powers on the basis of concern, doubt, rumour, suspicion or unsupported claim. He should not intervene merely because, if the decision had rested with him, he might have taken a different view of the facts than the jury."[14]

Of the specific questions put to him during the debate, virtually none were answered. He did say that he decided against seeing Chris Mullin, but offered him instead a meeting with Mr B. M. Caffarey, the assistant secretary in charge of the Home Office's criminal justice division. Mellor seemed to forget that it was the Home Secretary who had originally issued the invitation; and to be unaware that Mullin, in being passed down the line of Home Office seniority like an embarrassing problem, was being treated with a shabby lack of courtesy.

A number of influential figures began to make their voices heard. Private doubts quickly gelled into massive public concern. On 7 October Lord Scarman wrote to *The Times*, saying that "there would appear to be grounds for querying the justice of the convictions in the Guildford and Maguire cases".[15] Cardinal Hume then wrote, explaining that he visited Guiseppe Conlon on a number of occasions in Wormwood Scrubs: "I became absolutely convinced of his innocence and because of that developed profound doubts about the justice of the Maguire convictions." These doubts were echoed by an accompanying *Times* leader.[16] Cardinal Hume called for both the Maguire and Guildford cases to be referred to the Court of Appeal, but on 15 October Lord Devlin pointed out that the arrogation of judicial power which he had discerned in the fourth Luton appeal (see page 206) also marked the first Guildford appeal:

> The evidence of the [Balcombe Street] gang was heard by the Court of Appeal, which had power either to reject it out of hand or to order a new trial by jury of the whole case. Instead of this they treated it as an issue which they had power to determine themselves and which they decided against the accused. Thus what was truly an indivisible case was tried in two parts, one by a jury and the other by judges.

Devlin believed that, in the circumstances, a fresh reference-back would be unsatisfactory: "to do justice in every individual case is sometimes beyond the reach of the law: it is the very thing that in the last resort the Royal Prerogative is fashioned to attain."[17]

This correspondence coincided with the publication of Robert Kee's *Trial and Error*, which examined the Guildford and Maguire cases and argued the innocence of those involved. "It is time to recall the ancient precept," wrote Kee, "*fiat justitia et ruant coeli* – let justice be done though the heavens fall."

The next development indicated that there was no immediate danger of the heavens falling. The *Independent* reported that David Mellor, minister of state at the Home Office, had written to Richard Shepherd, Conservative MP for Aldridge–Brownhills, saying that *World in Action*'s assertions about the scientific evidence put forward in the Birmingham case were flawed because the programme used an "almost certainly" incorrect formula for its tests.[18] George Walker, the director of the Chorley laboratory, had, it seemed, provided Granada with incorrect information. David Baldock had written to him in 1985, asking the precise formula of the concentration used in the test.

The director had replied that Skuse swabbed the hands of the six men with a caustic soda solution of 1.0 per cent. Chorley now thought that the concentration was 0.1 per cent. Baldock agreed that, had the test been carried out in that way, it would have yielded different results.

Mellor also confirmed that Dr Skuse's original case notes were not clear enough to determine the "exact procedures" he had used. This was extraordinary. The Home Office appeared to be saying that the director of the Chorley laboratory couldn't get his facts right (although Walker had simply been acting on information supplied to him in writing by Skuse); and that vital scientific work in a major criminal case had been carried out in an unprofessional manner. In the circumstances, Dr Skuse seemed to have acted with unwarranted boldness in declaring himself 99 per cent certain of his results. Most astonishing of all, however, was the inference that, far from having been spurred to immediate action by these revelations, the Home Office was using them to discredit Granada, and thus to justify inaction.

On 16 November, Channel 4 broadcast *Beyond Reasonable Doubt*, a minor milestone in the history of independent television (ITV). It was made as a result of cooperation between two separate programme contractors (Granada and Yorkshire), utilising material from both *World in Action* and *First Tuesday*. How heartening that, in the cause of justice, TV companies could set aside long-established procedures; government departments could hardly be said to display a similar sense of purpose.

Beyond Reasonable Doubt also broke fresh ground by undertaking an analysis of all three cases, the first time a TV documentary had bracketed them together. In a panel discussion that occupied the latter part of the programme, Ludovic Kennedy said there was "not a shadow of doubt that justice had miscarried"; the police "deluded themselves into thinking that they'd got the right people". Sir Edward Gardner QC, Conservative MP for Fylde, and the chairman of the Commons select committee on home affairs, retorted, "I find it surprising that you can be certain that people are innocent." He reminded viewers that the cases had been tried at first instance by Mr Justice Donaldson and Mr Justice Bridge, "both of whom are among the most distinguished members of the British judiciary", and had subsequently received "very long and careful" hearings at the Court of Appeal. "It is important that one should bear in mind", he emphasised, "the quality of justice that has been applied so far."

Clare Short, Labour MP for Birmingham Ladywood (the constituency in which the Mulberry Bush and Tavern in the Town bombings occurred) raised the matter in the Commons on 20 November, asking for an explanation of the "inordinate delay". Did the Home Office not know that "there is growing concern throughout the country that six men who were not guilty of this offence have been locked up for twelve years?" David Mellor could reply only that the case was receiving "thorough investigation and consideration". He said also that he found it surprising that anyone, and especially a Birmingham MP, "should state categorically that these men are not guilty. That seems to show an amazingly one-sided view, which I am astonished she can get away with in her city."[19]

The Home Office was only jolted from its lethargy on 1 December when *World in Action* brought forward fresh evidence regarding the case. Tom Clarke, a policeman for nineteen years who had been on duty at Queen's Road police station when the six alleged bombers were brought there from Morecambe, swore an affidavit saying that while in police custody the men were subject to physical assaults and psychological pressure. "I formed the opinion that they were going to be asked to make statements under extreme duress; that was the object of the whole exercise." He said they were physically maltreated; he noticed bruises on their faces, which were "puffed out", and a red weal on the body of one man. They were intimidated by shot guns, hand guns and police dogs, and were not allowed to sleep during the interrogation period. "The judge's rules were non-existent," confirmed Clarke, adding that, because of the behaviour of the police, "I wouldn't have thought for one moment that I was in this country." Crucially, the kind of maltreatment described by Clarke independently confirmed what the six prisoners themselves had alleged from the outset.

Clarke admitted that had he been asked to give evidence to the 1975 Owen inquiry, he would probably have told lies to cover up for colleagues. He said he had chosen to speak out because his conscience had been pricked by letters in the local papers, especially ones from the prisoners themselves, asking for an honest policeman to come forward. Unfortunately, by the time he came forward, Clarke was no longer a policeman. He left the force in disgrace in 1978 after serving a two-month jail sentence for stealing £5 from a prisoner. Clarke was convicted solely on the testimony of a colleague, and maintained that the conviction was a miscarriage of justice. Sir John Farr said that Clarke's statement "bears out that brutality did occur. It's most impressive; I'm shocked by the content of it."

The *World in Action* report did not solely examine Clarke's evidence. It also re-appraised its forensic science investigations in the light of Home Office objections. Throughout the thirteen months of its "thorough investigation", the Home Office had been unable to find records of the "exact procedures" used by Skuse in his 1975 tests; Granada discovered written records within two weeks. They were in the papers of Dr Hugh Black, who had noted in precise detail his consultations with Skuse at the time. These recorded clearly that the caustic soda solution was 1.0 per cent. "It is also revealed," reported the *Independent*, "that the director of the Chorley laboratory had consulted Dr Skuse, then a member of his staff, before telling Granada that a 1 per cent solution had been used."[20] With this information, Dr Caddy was prepared to stand by his own tests: "If 1.0 per cent was used, then such a test would fail to distinguish between cellulose nitrate and the explosive nitroglycerine."

These developments dramatically increased the pressure on the Home Office. On 2 December an all-party committee headed by Farr, Peter Archer (Labour MP for Warley West) and David Alton (Liberal MP for Mossley Hill) held a press conference at the House of Commons, in which they called on the Home Secretary to explain what action he proposed to take over the case. In response to representations about this and the other two cases, the Home Secretary let it be known that he would be studying all the files at home over Christmas and would announce a decision in January. Even before the month was out, however, there was a further humiliation for the Home Office, which, on 18 December, was finally obliged to admit publicly the reason for Skuse's dismissal: "limited efficiency". However, the Home Office had previously assured Tam Dalyell, back on 22 July, that Skuse's enforced retirement had nothing at all to do with the *World in Action* programme. So Mellor, who now conveyed the information, perforce had to add – somewhat disingenuously, it seemed – "that it was limited efficiency at the time that he was retired, not limited efficiency in 1975".[21]

During the year, the campaign to overturn the convictions reached boiling-point because of several interconnected factors. Prime among these was the resolution of the Granada and Yorkshire TV companies.[22] Individual TV programmes, though frequently enormously helpful, are unlikely to be adequate. Lobbying that is not sustained is not likely to yield results. There must be a commitment to see the case through. Independent television in general, and Granada and Yorkshire in particular, displayed that commitment. How ironic that in recent times television has been so much more adept at providing the oxygen of publicity for important causes than newspapers, which are the natural fount of crusading journalism.[23]

This situation was partially offset by the arrival of the *Independent*, which re-asserted some of the traditional strengths of the newspaper. Accordingly, almost straight from its launch in October 1986, it reported diligently on developments in these cases. In doing so, it became an additional pillar of the campaign.

The books by Chris Mullin and Robert Kee played a crucial part, as did the public comments of those eminent figures – like Cardinal Hume, Sir John Biggs-Davison and Lord Fitt – who gave the campaign their staunch support. By November, over two hundred MPs had signed an early-day motion tabled earlier in the year calling on the Home Secretary to take action. As Lord Devlin wrote, "Protestations of innocence by prisoners are common enough. Support for them by distinguished persons is not unknown. But the total effect must be mountainous before it can command attention. Here it is as high as Everest."[24]

There was, though, another consideration, something from which no other UK miscarriage-of-justice campaign has benefited: an international dimension. This was cleverly exploited by Chris Mullin, who promoted his book in Eire and aroused widespread concern there. Irish foreign minister Peter Barry first raised the Birmingham case with the British government the day after the original *World in Action* transmission. On the basis of what he was told, Dr Garrett FitzGerald, the Taoiseach (prime minister) was able to convey to members of the Dail (parliament) the assurance that it was being urgently considered by the Home Office in London.

That was on 5 November 1985. As the months went by, the *bona fides* of the British government seemed increasingly suspect. Neither further top-level interventions by Peter Barry, nor two all-party delegations of rank-and-file Dail members were able to galvanise the Home Office. "Delay really does defeat justice," said Senator Mary Robinson, a senior counsel at the Irish bar.[25]

The significance of the cases was not merely judicial, but political. Under the terms of the Anglo-Irish Agreement, signed by Margaret Thatcher and Dr FitzGerald at Hillsborough on 15 November 1985, Eire would ratify the European Convention on the Suppression of Terrorism, and facilitate the extradition of terrorist suspects from the Republic. However, no one in Eire was likely to feel comfortable about passing a new extradition law if Irish citizens could not be guaranteed a fair trial in Britain. One of FitzGerald's deputies, Alice Glenn, resigned from the government over the issue. FitzGerald nevertheless managed to get his extradition bill through the Dail in December 1986, but one of its provisions was that it would only become operative in twelve months' time. In the meantime, it was implied, Britain was expected to make progress on these cases.

Irish feeling within the UK was channelled through the Federation of Irish Societies, which represented over 60,000 people. Under its auspices, and with the assistance of shadow Home Office minister Clive Soley (Labour MP for Hammersmith), a public meeting was organised at the House of Commons on 17 November. This attracted over a hundred people, a number which vastly exceeded the expectations of the organisers and which necessitated a move to a larger committee room.

In the weeks leading up to Douglas Hurd's announcement, the pressure remained constant. In an *Observer* article, Ludovic Kennedy quoted Lord Denning's "appalling vista" speech (*see* page 411–12), describing it as "the most shocking thing I have ever heard uttered by any English judge. If it does not mean better for them to rot in jail than admit we might have made a mistake, then I do not know what it does."[26]

One of those rotting in jail, Richard McIlkenny, succeeded in reaching the correspondence columns of the *Independent* from Wormwood Scrubs. He suggested that truth drug or lie detector tests should be given to Dr Skuse and the now-retired Detective Superintendent George Reade, the West Midlands policeman who headed the bombings inquiry and who told *World in Action* that "I've always insisted that they weren't [maltreated], because I know they weren't." McIlkenny wrote,

> I can see no reason why these two men should not or would not be prepared to undergo either test in the interest of British justice. I am sure there are many independent experts in this field who would be willing to give their time and knowledge and to act as witnesses to such tests in order to bring out the truth of our case and put an end to this mockery of justice.[27]

Meanwhile, Geoffrey Dear, the West Midlands chief constable, told a press conference that his police force had "nothing to fear from a judicial review" of the case.[28]

On 6 January 1987, a meeting with another all-party delegation of MPs, headed this time by shadow home secretary Gerald Kaufman (Labour MP for Manchester Gorton) had to be fitted into Douglas Hurd's crowded schedule. Two days later, in a letter to *The Times*, even his own predecessor, Leon Brittan QC, recommended that the cases should be sent to appeal.[29] The Home Secretary finally announced his decision on 20 January, almost fifteen months after he set an inquiry in motion. The Birmingham case would indeed be referred to appeal; but, for want of new evidence, no action could be taken in either of the other two cases.

"On the Maguire and Guildford cases," Hurd explained in a ministerial statement to the Commons, "the Maguires were found guilty on a charge of possessing explosives. I have taken considerable trouble to establish that there is no serious scientific questioning on the validity of [the TLC] test. Carole Richardson's alibi was tested repeatedly at great length during the court proceedings. The Balcombe Street and Dowd confessions were similarly tested with great thoroughness by the Court of Appeal." Hurd emphasised that "the question of guilt was in each case properly determined by due process of law." In the Birmingham case, he would ask the court to consider specifically the scientific evidence as well as the testimony of Tom Clarke. The Devon and Cornwall police force was asked to undertake an inquiry into his allegations of police brutality.

Hurd stated that he had acted in accordance with two fundamental principles: that something new was required before a case could be reopened; and that, "where such material is to hand, no consideration of *amour propre* or possible embarrassment should prevent a referral of the case." He concluded, "I believe that by following these principles a Home Secretary can best serve the interests of justice."[30]

The *Guardian* maintained that the disinterested manner adopted by the Home Secretary was bogus. "The nonsense that Mr Hurd tried to perpetrate was that his was a platonic decision unsullied by political considerations. It was no such thing. Few issues have been pursued with such vigour in the Anglo-Irish talks over the past few months . . . In Irish eyes, a reopening of the Birmingham case is one of the central tests of the Hillsborough agreement."[31] Nevertheless, something had at last been done: as little as possible, as late as possible.

The gap between what is and what ought to be sometimes becomes so large that it goes out of focus altogether. An administration which believed, like Aristotle, that "justice is something essential in a state" would have reacted with alacrity to the *World in Action* assertion that six people had already been imprisoned for eleven years for crimes that were none of their doing. The Home Office responded with prevarication. As this book has attempted to demonstrate, this is standard Home Office practice. No one genuinely expects it to behave differently. But that ought not to obscure the fact that it is unprincipled behaviour on any level, and is certainly conduct unbecoming to a democratic society.

The almost pathological reluctance of the Home Office to divulge information was evident in its unwillingness to give the reasons for Skuse's retirement; to disclose that a police inquiry had been ordered into allegations contained in *Error of Judgement*, or to admit which police force was undertaking it; or even to make known to parliament the doubts it was casting on Granada's research. "Is it not extraordinary," asked Bob Clay in the Commons, "that the Minister should write to one of his hon. friends saying that the formula was wrong, but does not inform other hon. members?"[32] In the context of what occurred, this was not so surprising; the Home Office seemed to regard those campaigning on behalf of the men as its adversaries, the prime motive of its investigations appearing to be to demolish their case, not to probe it objectively.

The argument that a miscarriage of justice had occurred was a perfectly straightforward one. On 20 May, the Home Secretary said that Mullin's book raised matters "which are *wholly new* and which present a *completely different approach*"[33]; on 25 July, David Mellor explained that the inquiry was taking so long because of "*further new points*" and that "it would be wrong to deal with a case of this kind in a piecemeal fashion"[34]; on 20 November he told the Commons that "*further important points* have emerged only this month".[35] (Author's italics.) Each additional revelation that should have accelerated the inquiry was used as an excuse to delay it.

Not that delay was ever conceded. The Home Office used every opportunity to explain that, on the contrary, matters were being speedily dealt with. Eight months had already elapsed from the setting-up of the inquiry when, on 26 June, the Home Secretary told MPs that "I shall reach a decision as quickly as possible"[36]; on 24 July he assured the Commons that "I have no desire or interest in delaying a decision".[37] On 20 November, David Mellor said that "we shall announce the outcome of our considerations as soon as possible".[38] When one MP bluntly told him, on 18 December, that the six men were innocent, Mellor replied, "the hon. gentleman has plainly reached his own conclusions. It is not for me to join him in a rush to judgment."[39] Indeed not; it is the very last thing of which anyone at the Home Office could ever be accused.[40]

In the Commons on 20 January, Hurd referred only briefly to his reasons for declining to take action in the Guildford and Woolwich case. For the benefit of MPs, however, he placed a 27-page memorandum in the Commons library which explained in detail why the Home Office reached its negative decision.

This memorandum is riddled with inaccuracies, omissions, misconceptions and occasional pieces of baffling information. It is impossible to outline them all here; four examples must suffice. On page 4, the Home Office said that "the security forces in Northern Ireland had received information from as early as 29 August 1974 that Hill had gone to England". This was news to everyone involved with the case. It contradicted everything the Surrey police had said about this part of it. In the press conference after the end of the trial, it was said by police that Hill came to their attention from a tip-off *after* the bombings; not *before*, as the Home Office now suddenly suggested. Further, if the 29 August date was accurate, then the security service blunders were staggering. If Hill was a leading IRA suspect, why was he not placed under surveillance, and the bombings thereby prevented? And why, after they had occurred, did it take eight weeks for him to be arrested when he was living and working quite openly in London and Southampton?

Drawing on the Court of Appeal judgment, the Home Office said (page 19) that Carole Richardson's alibi was of no value because she was at the Polytechnic "at or around 8 o'clock" and because "both O'Connell and Dowd gave one hour as the time to and from Guildford". The suggested 8 o'clock time is a wilful misrepresentation of Richardson's case, since witnesses placed her arrival at the Polytechnic as no later than 7.45. Secondly, the appeal was dismissed on the basis that the Balcombe Street witnesses were giving fabricated evidence. Dowd, indeed, was described as "a deplorable witness". When it suited them, however, both the Appeal Court and the Home Office were only too willing to rely on what they said.

The Home Office made the astonishing assertion (page 21) that "there was no scientific evidence to link the Balcombe Street gang with the Guildford and Woolwich bombings". In fact, there was overwhelming scientific evidence to link them. This has been publicly known since the Balcombe Street trial in January 1977. Government scientists placed all the bombings in a connected series because of common characteristics. However, they were told – on instructions from the DPP – to omit all reference to Guildford and Woolwich from the trial. The attempt to doctor the evidence was nevertheless admitted (and telltale gaps in the list of bombings prepared by RARDE scientists bear witness to it today).

On page 22, the Home Office, referring to defence arguments, said, "if Dowd and O'Connell were in the Horse & Groom, this left no room for Armstrong"; and added, "but it is not certain that the police succeeded in tracing everyone who had been in the pub". In fact, the Home Office had got the pubs mixed up – a serious mistake, in the circumstances. It was the Seven Stars which O'Connell bombed. Further, the police always contended that they did account for everyone in the pubs. In any case, the suggestion that there could have been somebody else there who was not noticed by anyone at all is incredible.

The Home Office commissioned reports on Carole Richardson from two experts in criminal psychology, Dr James MacKeith and Dr Gisli Gudjonnson of the Bethlem Royal Hospital and the Maudsley Hospital. These were not published, but they were available to the Home Secretary at the time he reached his decision on the case. Their conclusion was that "the validity of the confession must be seriously questioned . . . the statements that resulted in her conviction were very probably unreliable". There was, of course, no other evidence against Carole Richardson. In the course of the 27-page memorandum, there was no reference to these reports. The Home Office later explained that the Home Secretary thought it "inappropriate".

On 3 March 1987, *First Tuesday* returned to the attack, with a programme entitled *A Case That Won't Go Away*, which produced a fresh witness. At the original trial, Paul Hill provided an alibi for the evening of the Woolwich bombing: he was watching television with his aunt and uncle, Anne and Frank Keenan, at their home in Camden Town (twelve miles from Woolwich). The bombings occurred at 10.17, and *News at Ten* carried a report at 10.26. Hill did leave the house (to phone Gina Clarke), but only for a short period and was in the house when the newsflash was given. The Keenans gave evidence on their nephew's behalf, but it was rejected, as 'family' alibis invariably are. However, there was also an independent witness. Yvonne Fox, a friend of Anne Keenan, was in the house that evening. She corroborated the evidence: "I know Paul was in the house that night, and he was only out for 20 minutes." She said she couldn't understand why she was not called to give evidence at the trial. It does seem to have been a shocking blunder by the defence team.

The programme also included interviews with Cardinal Hume ("I'm convinced that these people are innocent . . . common sense dictates that the cases be looked at again") and Lord Devlin, who identified three points in the case which caused him concern. There was no trial by jury, since half the case was not heard by a jury; the case was split into two parts; and there was no appeal, "because you cannot have the judges deciding an appeal for themselves". Each of these, he stressed, "constitutes a procedural flaw which should by itself lead to the quashing of the convictions. But it is the second one that is a violation of justice on any basis. You can't split a case in half. You can't ask a defence counsel to deploy half his witnesses before one tribunal and half before another."

Nineteen

The Birmingham Pub Bombing:
'Back to appeal'

THE HOME SECRETARY, Douglas Hurd, referred the Birmingham pub-bombing case back to appeal on 20 January 1987. However, such was the amount of material to be assimilated by lawyers of each side that it did not reach the court until Monday 2 November. It was generally anticipated that the hearing would be lengthy; but it turned into a marathon, running at the Old Bailey – where appeals in terrorist cases have recently been heard – until Wednesday 9 December. The three judges – Lord Lane, Lord Chief Justice; Lord Justice O'Connor; and Lord Justice Stephen Brown – heard the equivalent of 12 days of evidence. Speeches from counsel occupied a further 15 days. Judgment was not delivered until the end of January 1988, so that the appeal itself remained a live issue for virtually three months.

Appearing on behalf of the Crown were Igor Judge QC, Stephen Mitchell and John Maxwell. The case for the six convicted men – the appellants – was argued by a hand-picked team of six barristers. They worked in three pairs, each theoretically safeguarding the interests of two appellants: Lord Gifford QC and James Wood (Hunter and McIlkenny); Richard Ferguson QC and Patrick O'Connor (Callaghan and Walker); and Michael Mansfield and Nicholas Blake (Hill and Power). In practice, the divisions of counsel's labour tended to lie between areas of evidence rather than individual appellants.

Grateful as they were for the opportunity of this second appeal, defence lawyers argued at the outset that the case should instead be sent for re-trial before a jury. Mansfield asserted that factors peculiar to this case made it desirable. He pointed out that on both of the major issues, the treatment of the men in custody and the scientific evidence, there had been considerable movement in the years since the trial (1975) and original appeal (1976). He explained that "about a half of the grounds – it is difficult to put a percentage on it – relate to fresh evidence . . . which goes right to the heart of the case". The court would be hearing witnesses giving evidence which might have affected the jury's verdict. It would be impossible, he continued, to assess the value of the new evidence without weighing it against the evidence given at the trial; and moreover, issues of fact and the credibility of witnesses are matters which juries alone must determine. That is the basis of the country's criminal justice system. In 1970, when the case of *R v Merry* went to appeal, the judges ruled that, "If we were to assess the weight of evidence on both sides we would be abrogating to ourselves the functions of a jury, which is not proper." Thus, argued Mansfield, was the rationale behind re-trial succinctly explained.

Nor, were there obvious difficulties in this case to preclude a re-trial. Sometimes – in cases based on eyewitness reports, for example – memories may well have dulled in the interim. This was not such a case. On the contrary, it was one of such moment that all concerned would remember the events vividly for a lifetime. Further, much of the scientific evidence would hinge on the testimony given by two important witnesses, Dr Skuse and Dr Black, in relation to documents which were still in existence. Altogether, stressed Mansfield, the circumstances of the case meant that it was "still ripe" for jury trial.

Nevertheless, re-trial is an option which the appeal court has always been notoriously reluctant to exercise. Apart from anything else, the convictions of the appellants would have to be quashed to enable a re-trial to be held; there is legal provision for suspending sentences, but not for suspending convictions. This is precisely the sort of consideration that judges, given their distaste for terrorist cases of this kind, are unlikely to view with enthusiasm. Indeed, Lord Lane, who referred to it straightaway, did appear to regard it as a major stumbling-block.

In the event, the appeal judges deliberated privately on

Mansfield's arguments and then told the court merely that the case was not "appropriate" for re-trial. The appeal went ahead.

The new evidence presented can be divided into three broad areas: the discovery of a remarkable document which came to be termed "the Reade schedule"; the testimony of witnesses relating to the treatment which the men received in police custody; and queries about the validity of the scientific evidence that had been put forward at the trial.

On 27 January 1987, in the very first week of the investigation ordered by the Home Secretary, the Reade schedule "floated out" from among a pile of papers found by Devon and Cornwall police in a locked steel cabinet at the headquarters of West Midlands police in Birmingham. It consisted of seven pages of A4 paper on which were details of interviews of the suspects carried out between Friday 22 and Sunday 24 November 1974 by police under the supervision of Superintendent George Reade. It was plainly a record of some kind. The key question was: what kind of record?

The schedule was divided vertically into seven columns, with typewritten headings: date, time, officers, prisoners, place, ref and knowledge of. So, it listed who was interviewing whom, and where and when. The details of each separate interview were filled in across the page. It is the "ref" and "knowledge of" columns that are extraordinary. "Knowledge of" refers to the information (for which "ref" provides code letters) that the officers conducting the interviews ought to have been carrying in their heads at that point *if the investigation were being honestly carried out*.

However, one simple consideration suggests that it wasn't: if the investigation was being honestly carried out, then there would have been no conceivable need for a record of this kind. Interviews would have succeeded one another naturally with, presumably, additional information being elicited at each stage. When giving evidence at the trial, police conducting them need only have referred to their notebooks. The Reade schedule would never have been drafted; it would have been superfluous.

Yet it existed. Someone forming an instant impression of it might suppose that it was a guide to assist the author of some fictional work, to ensure that he had his characters in the right place at the appropriate time, and that they knew no more of the proceedings than would logically have been the case. The various crossings-out and annotated additions only reinforce this impression.

That is, in effect, what defence lawyers alleged the Reade schedule to be: a fictional work, a document prepared to assist the fabrication of the record of the interviews conducted by Reade and his team. At the original trial, the judge, Mr Justice (now Lord) Bridge, had emphasised that, for the allegations of ill-treatment to be true, "they [the police] must have spent many hours trying to ensure that their various lies would accord with each other". In his view, it was not feasible that this could have happened; in the opinion of defence lawyers, the schedule now provided clinching proof that it had.

Only if the police were being completely dishonest would they have needed a schedule like this, to ensure – as Bridge indicated – that all the perjured evidence dovetailed. The defence team considered it a rare piece of damning evidence. "Conspirators rarely leave this kind of document behind", observed Lord Gifford.

Anxious as he must have been to dispel this interpretation of the schedule, George Reade made significantly heavy weather of doing so. On 9 June 1987, he was interviewed about it by two Devon and Cornwall officers. He confirmed that he had drawn it up and that all the writing was his. He explained that its purpose had been "to keep a sequence of events as they happened".

The interviewing officers replied that, logically, this couldn't have been the case, because then he wouldn't have been able to include on it times for Dr Skuse's tests, which he would not have known until later. The interview continued:

> Q: So this isn't a log of events, or is it?
> Reade: Probably
> Q: Could it have been a check to ensure the accuracy of the officers' statements when they came in with the file?
> Reade: Probably, that's more like it. Probably done on reflection, to make sure everything they had said and done was correct and tied together.

That was the second explanation. The officers then pointed out to Reade that an interview with Paddy Hill had been first inserted into the schedule, and then crossed out altogether. There was no record of such an interview in police evidence. How was it possible for a non-existent interview to have been written in?

This point alone was sufficient to dispose of the second explanation. Reade, down but not out, then produced Explanation No. 3:

> Reade: On reflection, I think that I made this out as a guide when going through the evidence to give myself a true picture of the evidence and the overall situation as it occurred because it does clarify what happened. I can't think why it [the Hill Interview] was taken out, probably because I had wrong information in front of me and upon checking finding it wasn't so.
> Q: That entry is pretty explicit.
> Reade: Yes
> Q: It gives definite times, says that Detective Inspector Moore, Detective Sergeant Bennett and Detective Constable Brand were present and that DS Bennett left the room between 4.30 and 4.40 when he got information re Callaghan's statement . . . The inference could be drawn that for some reason an interview with Hill had taken place and was deliberately

omitted, or an interview with Hill was concocted and then omitted.

Reade: I follow your point

Q: Similarly, an inference could be drawn that the document was a blueprint as to how officers must prepare their evidence.

Reade: That's certainly not so . . . I can't explain now. I can't. It is as simple as that due to the lapse of time. It was a practice of mine to do this sort of thing to check the evidence in complicated cases. There is nothing sinister in it. I have a vague recollection that I gave a copy of it to Harry Skinner QC, leading counsel for the Crown [at the original trial] to help him understand the evidence.

However intrinsically unlikely, this suggestion – that the schedule was drawn up to assist counsel – had by the time of the appeal, when Reade had had some months to think it over, emerged as his fourth explanation of its existence. Cross-examining Reade during the appeal, Mansfield straightaway raised what was merely the most conspicuous flaw in this argument: Skinner already had a schedule for use in court. In fact Maxwell – the only barrister present who had acted in the same capacity in the original trial – had drawn it up. Moreover, he said that he had no recollection of Reade's document.

The schedule contained some intriguing mis-spellings. Morecambe is spelt wrongly throughout. Detective Sergeant Millichamp is written down as "Millerchamp". Most instructively, Power's surname is sometimes written down as "Powers", and on one occasion as "Powers" with the 's' crossed out. This suggests that Reade was uncertain about what the surname actually was; or, perhaps, that he was struggling to correct an initial impression that it was "Powers". Altogether, the mis-spellings suggest that he could not have compiled the schedule from other documentation, but must have made it at a very early stage, before official papers had been drawn up.

Also, there is one interview which did take place that is not mentioned at all. Callaghan was arrested at about 11.00 pm on the Friday night, and questioned about 12.30am.

> Mansfield: If your document is a trial document, how do you explain that you did not manage to get it in?
> Reade: I can't explain that.

The striking out of the Hill interview, to which the Devon and Cornwall police referred ("OUT" in capitals, underlined three times had been written across the centre, and everything scribbled over) adds further weight. Reade insisted that this was because the interview was "a mistake". Yet how could he have made such a detailed mistake, especially if he was working just prior to the trial, with documentation available?

The inference was that this was an interview which *had* happened, but which had to be deleted because the police were going to suggest that Hill had confessed prior to this. Accordingly, there would have been no need for this interview to have taken place at all, and it was removed from the record. This was crucial because exactly what had occurred during interviews at Morecambe and Queen's Road (Birmingham) police stations was a hotly-contested issue at the trial. Both Hill and Hunter alleged not only that they had been assaulted, but that the police falsely claimed that they made verbal confessions.

The deleted section concerning the Hill interview was especially significant, because what was originally written down provided reasonably precise corroboration of Hill's own evidence at trial. Yet West Midland police officers said on oath that no such interview took place.

The entry immediately following refers to a Callaghan interview at Sutton Coldfield. In the "Officers" column, Reade wrote DS Hornby, and then "DC". This was crossed out, and "& crew" substituted. Once again, the logic is inescapable: if Reade was compiling this, as he said, for the trial, then the names of the interviewing officers would have been available to him. However, he seems not to have known them. This could indicate that the record was a contemporary one, and that the missing names were to be filled in later. In fact this is borne out on the last page of the schedule, at the bottom of which the names "Davies and Bryant" – the "crew" in question – are written down, in this context: "Mick Hornby OK. 1pm. Davies & Bryant. Will be OK."

"What do the words 'be OK' mean?," asked Lord Gifford. "We submit that officers were being checked out as to whether they would agree to whatever aspect of the fabrication they needed to agree to."

In the details of one interview session, Reade had written, "Remember Power with DS Watson at 9.30". "The more you look at this document", continued Gifford, "the more curious it becomes. What honest purpose is there is Reade reminding either officers or himself – *Remember* – of this particular fact. Of course, if the purpose is dishonest, it would be extremely important for a number of officers to be told to remember that the scenario was for Power to be with DS Watson at 9.30."

Lord Justice Stephen Brown remarked that, if the document had the status which the defence attached to it, "a heinous crime" had taken place. It is hard to conclude otherwise. There seems no conceivable honest explanation of the Reade schedule – but a readily apparent dishonest one. The Lord Chief Justice put it to the appellants' lawyers that they were making the grave accusation that it constituted what he described as "a master perjury plan"; and Mansfield conceded that this was indeed the case.

Just as the police evidence was discredited by the appearance of the Reade schedule, so the prisoners' allegations of maltreatment were supported, to a greater or lesser extent, by the fresh evidence of seven independent witnesses. At the trial, these allegations were largely, though not entirely, unsupported: the testimony of Ian Gold and Anthony Curtis, the two duty solicitors who saw the men directly after their weekend in police custody, contained indications that the prisoners may have endured some rough treatment (Curtis noticed scratch marks on Walker's chest, and Gold saw signs of discoloration on the chests of Hill and Power); evidence from Dr Alan Cohen (the doctor whom the solicitors brought in to examine their clients on the Tuesday afternoon) referred in particular to the chest injury suffered by Walker (his evidence was not heard by the jury it formed part of the trial-within-a-trial, in which the admissibility of the "confessions" was thrashed out). This meant that three witnesses in all considered that the men had sustained injury in police custody. A fourth emerged afterwards, at the trial of the prison warders, when Dr David Paul offered his professional opinion that the men had suffered bodily harm prior to their arrival at prison.

The first of the new witnesses was William Bailey, who was employed from 1971 to 1976 as a cleaner/supervisor at Morecambe police station. He stated that on the Friday he had noticed that two of the men were unsteady on their feet as they were led from the station to West Midlands police vehicles; and that when on the Monday afterwards he went in to clean the cells where the men had been held, he saw blood in them. Then, Paul Berry, a former West Midlands police constable who left the force in 1978, saw a man with facial injuries – swollen lips, and a puffed-up left eye – at Queen's Road. Kenneth Garrington, who retired from the West Midlands force in May 1986, saw the six men standing in line "as if to attention", with an "expressionless glare" on their faces.

Two of the prison officers placed on trial had also agreed to give evidence on behalf of the men: Brian Sharp referred to having seen injuries on Walker's body; and Peter Bourne described how the police had insisted on waiving the standard procedure for the handing-over of prisoners, thereby avoiding the need to place their physical condition on record.

Then, there was the crucial testimony of Tom Clarke,

the former policeman whose appearance on *World in Action* had forced the Home Secretary's hand in sending the case back to appeal. Clarke said that both officers with guns and a dog-handler with his dog had been called in at that time – bearing out the remarks of the appellants that both guns and dogs had been used to frighten them. Clarke claimed that the prisoners were clearly "petrified" and "scared out of their wits". He indicated that they had been subject to considerable psychological duress – instructions were given, he said, that they were not to be allowed any sleep – and had also received a physical pounding. "They had been hammered, hit hard. There was puffiness over and under the eyes, red faces". One injury, which looked like a weal or a rope burn (presumably a reference to Walker), looked so bad that Clarke was worried in case the liver was ruptured.

Clarke explained that he was moved to come forward after reading a letter in the *Birmingham Post* from one of the prisoners, Hill. Unfortunately, he first tried to sell his story to the *Daily Mirror*, but was offered only £2,000. He then did tell his story, for no monetary reward, to Chris Mullin. However, the newspaper episode, together with his earlier conviction for theft, was bound to undermine his credibility as a witness.

Joyce Lynas, a former policewoman who left the force in 1980 to start a family, gave evidence in the first week of the appeal. Beyond saying that she had seen the appellants at Queen's Road being treated "very roughly" – not, in the circumstances, a very damaging accusation – she seemed to have little of value to impart. The Lord Chief Justice became impatient. "Are we concerned with this?", he asked, referring to her inconsequential testimony.

But at the start of the following week, in very exceptional circumstances, Joyce Lynas was recalled to the witness box. She now explained that, after being asked to make a statement to the Devon and Cornwall inquiry, she had telephoned Queen's Road to ascertain former colleagues' reaction to it. They said to her, "You know what you saw", and "Remember we all have families". She nevertheless made her statement, as a result of which defence solicitor Gareth Peirce asked to see her. After the meeting, which took place at Worcester police station, she received an anonymous telephone call at home. The caller said simply, "Don't forget you have got children". It was as a result of that call, in a state of some fear, that she was somewhat selective with her memory in originally giving evidence.

She now explained that over the weekend, she had watched a television programme about bullying in the army, and young soldiers being too frightened to speak out. She and her husband then decided that she should have said more. Consequently, she contacted Mr Peirce with a view to giving additional evidence.

On her return to the Old Bailey, she was more forthright.

Q: What did you omit to tell the court on the last occasion?
Lynas: That there were armed officers in the cell block area. On one occasion, when I went to one of the interview rooms upstairs, I saw one of the defendants being assaulted . . . There were at least three officers in the room. One of the officers said something and then kneed the man in the groin while the other two held his arms.
Q: What was said?
Lynas: He said, This is what we do to fucking murdering bastards.

In the end Joyce Lynas seemed an impressive witness. Her revised evidence confirmed the kind of allegations made by the six men. In the course of his concluding speech, Lord Gifford said: "The return of Mrs Lynas to the witness-box was one of the most dramatic episodes in this case . . . To write off her evidence must encourage all who put pressure on witnesses not to speak the truth. It is only because of her moral courage that such pressures may not have succeeded."

Arguments about the validity of the scientific evidence occupied several days of the appeal, with Drs Skuse and Black once again the central combatants. The points at issue included whether or not nitrocellulose could give a positive reaction on the Griess test at room temperature, as Baldock and Caddy had claimed in the *World in Action* programme; if so, then the tests that Skuse had carried out were not, in fact, specific to nitroglycerine. The Home Office had asked the Aldermaston Forensic Science Laboratory to carry out a re-appraisal of the Griess test to determine whether this was indeed the case, and whether, accordingly, Skuse's results carried something less than the 99% certainty he had claimed for them.

Aldermaston confirmed that this could be so, though only under very particular circumstances, one concerning the strength of the caustic soda solution used, and the other whether the swabs were re-dissolved in ethanol. Unfortunately, Skuse's original notes could shed light on neither of these points. Regarding the caustic soda solution, Dr Black's own contemporary notes indicated that Skuse told him that the figure was 1.0%. This was also the figure which the director of the Chorley laboratory had passed on to Baldock. Yet Skuse himself now insisted, as he had since October 1986, that the solution was 0.1%.

Moreover, he then proceeded to move the goalposts altogether by claiming that the tests were not carried out at room temperature at all, but at a sub-ambient (below room) temperature. This directly conflicted with his evidence at the trial. On five separate occasions he said that the tests were carried out at room temperature. He even referred to the actual temperature: 15° Celsius.

The scientific case was now so weak, argued Mansfield, that it could not withstand serious examination. It had been shown that nitroglycerine was not the only substance capable of giving a positive reaction on the Griess test; and that in any case the Griess was only a screening test which required confirmation. This was not forthcoming, other than through one reaction on the GMCS test which was so doubtful that Dr Black said he thought it was probably caused by urine.

Mansfield also pointed out that Skuse had been accorded great respect throughout the trial, and treated as an authority of unblemished reputation, whereas Black was regarded with "extraordinary hostility" by the judge. A role reversal had now taken place; Black had given clear and consistent evidence throughout, but Skuse's was characterised mostly by imprecision. Several times his answers during the appeal contradicted those given at the original trial. He had further admitted not only having altered his notes about the times he carried out the tests, but of not really having a clue about the times because he was not watching the clock. On top of all this there was the question of his enforced early retirement, ten years ahead of schedule, and the fact that he was extremely evasive about the reasons for this under cross-examination.

An additional ground of appeal was that serious prejudice to the chances of the men receiving a fair trial had ensued from the fact that they were indicted with three others, one of whom, Michael Murray, was a confessed IRA man who in typical IRA fashion refused to recognise the court; and none of whom had any direct connection with the planting of the bombs.

Other, lesser points were adduced on the appellants' behalf. Bishop Daly, the Bishop of Derry, took the stand to confirm that no sinister motive could be attached to the fact that, when arrested, the men had been on their way to an IRA funeral. "There has always been a very strong tradition of attending funerals," he said. "The service is a plea for God's mercy on the person who has died. It is not a matter of tribute or any kind of honour to the individual."

At just after 12.30 on Wednesday 9 December, the Court rose at the conclusion of the appeal. Lord Lane explained that judgment would be reserved until after Christmas – "there is obviously a great deal which we have to consider" – and went on to thank all counsel for their hard work. "We realise it [the appeal] has involved a tremendous amount of labour on everybody's part, but it is labour which has been very usefully spent."

When judgment was delivered on 28 January, the Court upheld the convictions of the six men. The three judges began a very lengthy (169-page) judgment by elaborating on their reasons for refusing a re-trial: "It would, as a matter of practical politics, be highly unsatisfactory, if not unjust, 13 years or more after the event, to hold a re-trial. Suffice it to say that this is the sort of case in which there is no halfway house."

There was a certain wry amusement to be derived from the judges' apparent admission that their deliberations were subject to considerations of "practical politics", but the important point is that their reasoning in regard to this matter was hopelessly flawed. In the first place there is nothing intrinsically unjust about holding a re-trial 13 years after the event. At the time of the appeal, the Home Secretary, Douglas Hurd, was talking about bringing Nazi war criminals to trial in Britain. Also, straight after the conclusion of this appeal, an IRA terrorist, Thomas Quinn, was tried on charges relating back to 1975. Relevant evidence was missing, and prosecution witnesses were exempted from answering certain questions on the grounds that they couldn't remember, but there seemed no difficulty about going ahead with that trial.

Moreover by deciding to hear the appeal, with the extensive new evidence and new witnesses, the Court itself had created a 'half-way house'. One tribunal had heard one part of the evidence; another had examined the rest. It was not merely an unsatisfactory situation; it was an absurdity.

In other respects, the appeal judges were no more enlightened. They decided that the six appellants had been lying in their allegations of police brutality. Of the fresh evidence brought forward, Bailey's "did not support the [other] evidence", and Sharp's was dismissed out of hand: "we did not believe him". Clarke was given equally short shrift. He had "invented" his stories, and was "a most unconvincing witness . . . an embittered man . . . we have no doubt that his evidence was false."

Considering the evidence of Joyce Lynas, the judges said, "There was nothing in the remark, 'Don't forget we all have families' which constituted a threat"; and asked why she had not been more forthcoming when making her statement to the Devon and Cornwall enquiry. This latter point was hardly adequate to dismiss her testimony. In any case, her inquiry statement had been enough to alert the defence solicitor. Since the judges were hearing the appeal proper, the critical matter was to consider her evidence in court, and her reasons for amplifying it. In that context, the threat was not the first remark (which the judges in any case misquoted): remember *we* (i.e. the police still serving at Queen's Road) have got families. The threat was "don't forget *you* have got children"; it would – and should – have created anxiety in any parents of young children. Having thus ignored the vital part of her evidence, the judges delivered the coup de grace, and dismissed her as "a witness not worthy of belief", a verdict which doubtless encouraged all those who put pressure on witnesses not to speak the truth.

The Reade schedule was "an informal document" having the characteristics of an aide memoire, and did not serve the purpose which the defence attributed to it. "We are quite certain that Mr Reade did not seek to deceive the Court."

With regard to the scientific evidence, the judges said that "it may well be that the tests at Morecambe were carried out without ethanol and using 0.1% caustic soda, but there is so much doubt, particularly as to the strength of caustic soda, that in our judgment the Griess tests at Morecambe should not be regarded as specific for nitroglycerine."

This, however, was as much headway as the appellants were allowed to make. The judges declared themselves sure that on the basis of fresh evidence regarding the

GCMS test from Dr Janet Drayton, who in 1974 was a senior scientific officer at the Aldermaston forensic laboratories that "Hill's left hand is proven to have had nitroglycerine upon it for which there is and can be no innocent explanation"; and further determined on the basis of tests conducted at Aldermaston that the substance giving the positive Griess tests at Morecambe could not have been nitrocellulose which indicated to them, notwithstanding their earlier comment, that it was nitroglycerine after all.

However, the Aldermaston re-appraisal of the Griess test also affirmed that, in carrying out the Griess test in the way he did, Skuse was using a relatively insensitive method; in other words, considerable quantities of nitroglycerine must have been present for it to be detected at all. This raises two points of common sense. Where had the nitroglycerine come from? There was no evidence whatsoever that any of the six had been engaged in bomb-making. The prosecution alleged only that they had planted bombs. So had the handles of the bags been heavily contaminated? It seems highly unlikely. Secondly, why, if a large quantity was present, were subsequent more sophisticated tests not able to confirm its presence beyond a shadow of a doubt? Out of all the tests done, only three were positive: the Griess test on the right hands of Power and Hill; and the GCMS test on the left hand of Hill. This point had particularly exercised Mansfield: why had the confirmatory tests on the right hands of Power and Hill registered negative for nitroglycerine?

The only way the judges could deal with this indubitably logical point was by dispensing altogether with logical argument. "It all depends on what quantity was reabsorbed into the swab", they explained, "*remembering that nitroglycerine is a highly volatile substance*".

Surely, even these judges might have realised how absurd this was. If nitroglycerine was "highly volatile", wouldn't Dr Skuse have lost his samples long before the tests got under way? How did they imagine that, in such circumstances, the nitroglycerine had remained on the hands of the appellants throughout the train journey? To take it a stage further, how on earth did the judges imagine that such a substance could be safely manufactured and incorporated into blasting explosives?

The truth, of course, is that nitroglycerine is an *involatile* liquid. This is precisely the characteristic which enables forensic scientists to test for it in the first place.

The Court concluded by saying that "as has happened before in references by the Home Secretary to this Court, the longer the hearing has gone on, the more convinced this Court has become that the verdict of the jury was correct." This hardly invited fresh references from the Home Office. Yet Lord Lane himself had been party in 1983 to a Home Office promise to the House of Commons to be 'more ready' to send cases back to appeal; just as he had then promised on his own behalf to examine "more readily" the arguments for re-trial. Nothing in his approach to this case indicated that he was vigorously seeking to implement those promises.

The appeals were dismissed. On 14 April 1988, a committee of law lords then dismissed a further application by the six to be allowed to take their case before a full hearing of the House of Lords. Legally, that seemed to be the end of the road.

Meanwhile, there remained two outstanding matters concerning the seemingly accident-prone Dr Skuse. He claimed that some of his important papers had gone missing during the appeal, and the matter was investigated by the City of London police. Secondly, documents from the hotel where he stayed during the appeal were passed to Chris Mullin. These showed that Skuse had twice telephoned Reade in the middle of the night during the appeal. This was also investigated by the City of London police, who reached the conclusion that no improper motive could be attached to these telephone conversations.

Admittedly, because of the way the hotel night clerk

had logged the calls it was impossible to tell whether they were made before or after Skuse completed his evidence. However, the Lord Chief Justice was explicit in his warning to Skuse: "Dr Skuse, you will not discuss this case with anyone at all." Skuse replied, "I understand, my Lord." It would surely be reasonable to argue that, irrespective of whether Skuse had actually finished his evidence, he should not have been in contact with another of the crucial figures in the case; he might, after all, have been re-called. In any case: could there really have been an innocent explanation of middle-of-the-night calls such as these?

Amnesty International, which had delegated a Greek lawyer to be present throughout the appeal hearing, produced a short report in March, followed by a lengthier one in August, stressing its continuing concern over the case.

> In Amnesty International's opinion, the Court consistently refused to give the prisoners the benefit of the doubt on any important point. It is striking overall that the Court did not specifically deal with the cumulative effect of the testimony supporting the prisoners' allegations. It is also striking that even though according to the Court the prisoners' convictions rested on their confessions, the testimony of every fresh witness in support of the submission that the confessions was involuntary, was dismissed as being either dishonest or mistaken or irrelevant.
>
> Amnesty International believes that the most grave doubt remains regarding official denials that these prisoners were ill-treated while in police custody, and hence regarding the safeness of allowing the confession evidence against them to stand.
>
> Amnesty International believes that the case should not be closed, and that the allegations of ill-treatment must be subject to further review.

Despite Amnesty's concern, however, the fact is that the case *is* officially closed. The English authorities have successfully sealed all routes by which the six men could hope to secure justice. Even though the Crown case has been shown to be threadbare, there are simply no designated legal or political avenues left open to the men.

What the appeal represented was the total eclipse of matters of justice by matters of political expediency. The Court of Appeal was revealed, more nakedly than ever, as a tribunal of the establishment. The judgment in the Birmingham case must have extinguished the last vestiges of faith that even abnormally optimistic citizens might have placed in it.

One way or another, the powers-that-be must be shamed into conceding that they cannot continue to incarcerate innocent men just because the administrative embarrassment of admitting error, as well as the political fall-out, would be so considerable.

The case *will* be resolved.

Conclusion

"Truth is a luxury. We can only afford it now and then."
Olivia Manning, *The Great Fortune*

No ONE working within the judicial system would dispute the
contention that miscarriages of justice can, and do, occur.
Lawyers, judges and juries may make mistakes; so, of course,
may expert witnesses (sometimes with appalling consequences).
The potential for human error in the legal process cannot possibly
be eliminated.

In response to this observation, defenders of the judicial faith
would doubtless chorus: this is precisely why we have the Court
of Appeal; its existence demonstrates that the legal process is
functioning efficiently, and that any public anxiety is misplaced;
justice will prevail – ultimately, if not initially.

Lay observers could be excused for regarding such assurances
with the deepest scepticism.

The Court of Criminal Appeal was only established after a
long struggle, in 1907. Throughout the nineteenth century, judges
had strenuously resisted its introduction, despite the emergence
of an accumulating number of evident miscarriages of justice. As
far back as 1845, a Royal Commission deprecated the lack of any
machinery for correcting mistakes in criminal trials. Subsequently, 31 bills proposing some form of court of appeal were
unavailingly introduced in parliament. In the end, it took the
scandal of the Adolf Beck case (1896–1901) to force the capitu-
lation of the judiciary.[1]

The Court specifically, logically, was created to remedy miscarriages of justice; understandably, the British public believed that
to be its *raison d'être*. In practice, it has never fulfilled that
function. "The Court of Criminal Appeal was a compromise and

a misnomer," explained Lord Paget QC in parliament. "It has never been a court of appeal. Under a series of Lord Chief Justices, its original function was forgotten. The Court confined itself to points of law. Unfortunately, guilt or innocence is not a point of law."[2]

The concern which had been evident prior to the celebrated Beck case began, in due course, to re-surface. In the Evans case the Court merely rubber-stamped the trial verdict and was of no use whatsoever; in the Rowland case it did have the opportunity to be of service, but the judges abdicated their responsibilities.

The organisation Justice, the British section of the International Commission of Jurists, was founded in 1957 by a number of concerned lawyers. In general, its purpose was to tackle the whole field of law reform, but under the determined helmsmanship of the redoubtable Tom Sargant, its secretary from the very start, Justice took a keen interest in judicial miscarriages.

In October 1961 it began a full-scale investigation into the operations of the Court of Appeal. The chairman of the committee of inquiry was Edward Sutcliffe QC, and members included Gerald Gardiner QC, Niall MacDermot QC, Sebag Shaw QC and Sargant.

Doubtless realising that the committee's conclusions would be both authoritative and cogent, the government of Sir Alec Douglas-Home pre-empted it in January 1964 by setting up the Donovan committee to conduct a parallel inquiry into the Court of Appeal.

The Justice report appeared later in the year,[3] but attention had by then switched to the Donovan commission. By the time this reported, Gerald Gardiner had become Lord Gardiner, Lord Chancellor.[4] Armed with its recommendations, he was able to guide an important new Criminal Appeal Act on to the statute book in 1968.

There are four fundamental reasons why, historically, the process referred to in legal circles as judicial review, and outside them, as 'going to appeal' has been so narrowly circumscribed. Firstly, legal and political administrators, for fear of an open-ended system, have always been anxious to impose a point of termination on the criminal trial process. If a series of tribunals was sifting evidence and calling witnesses, cases would be heard over and over again. Each verdict would become merely one station *en route* to the next, the terminus never in sight. Justice would never be administered at all, just perpetually deferred. This would be self-defeating, impractical, and also absurdly expensive. Although it is almost offensive to talk about criminal justice in terms of economy, this is hardly an insignificant consideration for the Treasury when it already funds the system to the tune of £137.4 million a year in legal aid.[5]

Secondly, there is the fear of flooding. "The legal authorities don't want the system to work well," explained Peter Ashman, legal officer of Justice, "because they think they'd be inundated with time-consuming appeals – both from those prisoners with legitimate grievances, and from those who, even without just cause, would attempt to take advantage of it." Whether or not this fear is well founded, it parallels the bureaucratic disposition to fight shy of any proposed remedy for anything on the grounds that it would 'open the floodgates'; civil servants have attested to hearing the phrase used regularly and indiscriminately by superiors.

If a case of particular political or commercial importance, say, is fought out in the civil courts, then the original verdict is virtually an irrelevance. Each side understands that the loser will merely appeal to a higher court. The legal establishment has always deplored the possibility that criminal-court verdicts would ever be treated in like fashion – particularly as they had been determined not by a judge, but by a jury. This brings us to the critical reason for judicial aversion to judicial review: it undermines the role of the jury. If jury verdicts were regularly overturned, they would be devalued. Perhaps if juries came to believe that the outcome of their essentially amateur deliberations would, as like as not, be countermanded in due course by the professionals at the appeal court, then the scrupulousness with which they (theoretically) applied themselves to their tasks would be diminished. This would jeopardise the entire criminal justice system; the jury, after all, is the rock to which it is anchored.

A flourishing appeals system might have the disadvantage of allowing barristers to tackle their own briefs less assiduously. Most of us, lawyers included, approach our daily tasks with some reluctance; matters which can be put off to another day frequently are. But in the criminal justice system, it is a pillar of faith that a barrister is presenting his client's case to the very best of his ability; no allowance is made for a less than perfect performance. We shall return to this important point.

So, for these reasons – cost, practicality, the inviolability of the jury, and the firm belief that no one should be tempted to view the trial as merely a dress rehearsal – the appeal court determined neither to 'usurp the functions of the jury', as it has frequently put it, nor to allow the appeal to become simply a replay of the trial.

It had painted itself into a corner. How could a court which had heard merely an abridged version of the proceedings, usually in the form of the trial judge's summing-up, possibly come to the conclusion that a jury, which was not only the real fount of arbitration but which had heard the evidence and seen the witnesses, got it wrong?

Of course, it couldn't. The appeal court, as Lord Paget pointed out, eschewed considerations of fact and confined itself to ones of law. In effect, it was reduced merely to ascertaining that trial etiquette had been properly observed. It disqualified itself from doing the very thing for which it had been created: remedying miscarriages of justice. Throughout this century, appeal court judges have ducked the responsibilities which parliament prescribed for them and which the country expected of them.

The 1968 Act was a laudable, if doomed, attempt to come to terms with the transparent shortcomings of the system. Section 17 was the crucial one. If a case had exhausted the normal appeals procedure, but nevertheless continued to cause concern, the Home Secretary was empowered to do one of two things. He could, for instance, act entirely on his own initiative, though it was thought seemly to camouflage such a direct governmental intrusion into the judicial process. So what he did was to recommend the Royal Prerogative of Mercy. The Queen could then grant a full pardon; a conditional pardon[6]; or order the remission of the remainder of a prisoner's sentence. Alternatively, the Home Secretary could refer the case back to appeal – put the ball in the Court's court, as it were. The act permitted an appeal to be upheld if the judge had made an error of law in his summing-up; or if there was some material irregularity in the course of the trial; or if, in the light of all the circumstances, the guilty verdict was held to be 'unsafe and unsatisfactory'.

The overwhelming odds against an appellant's success were

marginally less formidable if the appeal could be contested on either of the first two grounds. For an appeal to succeed via the third channel, the appellant generally needed to bring forward 'fresh evidence'. Section 23 of the 1968 Act stipulated conditions for admissibility: that such testimony was likely to be credible; and that there was a 'reasonable explanation' of the failure to adduce it at the time of the original trial. You didn't need to be a legislator to spot that the pregnant issues were the definitions both of 'reasonable explanation', and of 'fresh evidence' itself.

The Criminal Appeal Act received the Royal Assent on 8 May 1968. Within three months, the judgment in the Luvaglio-Stafford case demonstrated that no heady wave of enlightenment was crashing through the appeal courts; quite the reverse. Judicial heads were still buried deep in the sand. Lord Justice Edmund Davies, who delivered the judgment, Lord Justice Fenton Atkinson and Mr Justice Waller, turned down the applications to call additional evidence on the ground that "public mischief would ensue". (The judiciary has sometimes seemed to conceive of the public as a band of medieval churls, ready to march into London like Wat Tyler's men, sworn to "kill all lawyers and judges".)

Edmund Davies continued, "The legal process would become indefinitely prolonged were it the case that evidence produced at any time will generally be admitted by this Court when verdicts are being reviewed."

This was merely the standard judicial interpretation of the parameters within which the Court of Appeal operated. What made this reiteration of it so remarkable, and so profoundly disgraceful, was that the 1968 Act had clearly been designed to put an end to such hidebound attitudes. "The law had been changed precisely to allow the Court to call new evidence in those circumstances," wrote Sir David Napley. "It seemed odd that the Court should have behaved as if the law had not been altered at all."[7]

The vexing issue at the centre of this was clearly the professional rigour of lawyers. It seems axiomatic that a defendant ought not to be held responsible for the performance in court of his legal advisers: yet of course he is. If the barrister makes a mess of it, if defence solicitors don't use all the available evidence, if tactics are employed which, with hindsight, prove to have been disastrous – then the defendant could well land in prison. The lawyers go home (the good ones resolving to learn from their mistakes).

After 1968, though, it was meant to be different. Geoffrey Rhodes MP wrote that "the Donovan committee had envisaged that the Court of Appeal would henceforward treat the decisions of legal advisers or the inadequacies of their conduct of the case as a *reasonable explanation* of their failure to place evidence before a jury." (Author's italics.)[8]

This was the spirit, if not quite the letter, of the 1968 Act. At the time of the third reading of the bill, the Home Secretary told the Commons that "the governing principle of the admission of new evidence is to ensure as far as possible that there has been no miscarriage of justice". Nor had that been said idly. He indicated that the speech had been sanctioned by the Lord Chief Justice.[9]

Thus, the judgment in the Luvaglio–Stafford case flatly contradicted assurances given to parliament about the way in which the new act would be interpreted, and also illustrated that the Court was quite heedless of the tide of informed opinion that had carried the act to the statute book.

The following year hopes were raised that the appeal system could, after all, function properly. In the case of *R. v. Cooper*, Lord Justice Widgery formulated his famous "lurking doubt" premise. "The court must in the end ask itself a subjective question," he opined, "whether we are content to let the matter stand as it is, or whether there is not some lurking doubt in our mind which makes us wonder whether an injustice has been done."

Hopes briefly raised were as swiftly dashed – not least by Widgery himself. Sir David Napley described "lurking doubt" as "a phrase invented by Widgery but never, as far as I could see, a principle implemented by him".[10] Widgery finally shattered his own doctrine in the second Luvaglio–Stafford appeal judgment (*see* pages 114–16).

Writing in the wake of this in the *Sunday Times*, Hugo Young put the matter characteristically plainly:

"It is a common assumption among ordinary citizens that mistakes made by one court can be rectified in a higher court. We think this is a fundamental protection. This is not merely the layman's opinion. It is also the law. Yet this law seems to have been re-defined . . ."[11]

It was as if the country's senior judges had determined to implement all the laws of the land, with the exception of those that applied to themselves.

The Luvaglio–Stafford case then went to the House of Lords on a point of law, prompting thoughts that the constitutional machinery at the disposal of legitimately aggrieved prisoners was certainly impressive. In this case, it was put to exhaustive use. There was (i) an appeal; (ii) a judicial review of new evidence; (iii) a second appeal; (iv) an application for leave to appeal to the House of Lords; (v) an appeal against the rejection of that application; and (vi) a hearing in the House of Lords.

Unhappily, Luvaglio and Stafford, though plainly innocent, remained in prison. The machinery just *looked* impressive; when put to the test, it failed at each critical point.

The Lords' interpretation of the particular point of law was of immense significance. Viscount Dilhorne argued that "the 1968 act gave wide power to the Court of Appeal, and it would be wrong to place any fetter or restriction on its exercise . . . the act left it to the court to decide what approach to make . . . it would be wrong to lay down that, in a particular type of case, a particular approach had to be followed." This decision, interpreted as giving the Court of Appeal *carte blanche* to behave as it wanted, was cited several times thereafter in an attempt to justify some shocking judgments.

Dilhorne also referred to the "lurking doubt": "this is a reaction which may not be based strictly on the evidence as such; it is a reaction which can be produced by the general feel of the case as the court experiences it." So, after centuries of criminal law, and erudite interpretations of it, the aspect of a case which suddenly merited attention was its "general feel", whatever that was. The use of such an expression betrayed appalling intellectual sloppiness, as well as a fundamental misconception of the nature of the criminal law. The whole point is that cases, at any level, are determined not by hunches, but by rigorous evaluation of the available evidence; not by intuition, but by ratiocination. The phrase "lurking doubt" has legal pertinence, as it dovetails with the standard beyond-all-reasonable-doubt requirement of the law; the phrase "general feel" is meaningless. I mention this only to illustrate how impoverished legal analysis at the highest levels can sometimes be.[12]

The Maxwell Confait case superseded Luvaglio–Stafford as a *cause célèbre*. Lack of space has precluded discussion of it in this book but very briefly, in November 1972 three young boys, Colin Lattimore, Ronald Leighton and Ahmet Salih, of Catford, South London, were convicted of crimes leading to the death of Confait, a homosexual and transvestite known locally as "Michelle".

After leave to appeal was refused in July 1973, a vigorous campaign on behalf of the boys was spearheaded by Christopher Price, the local MP, and Jonathan Caplan, a barrister who investigated the case on behalf of the National Council for Civil Liberties (NCCL) and the *Sunday Times*.

In June 1975, Roy Jenkins referred the case back to appeal. Some months later, in the Commons, he outlined the reasoning behind the decision in reply to a question from Price.

> It would not be right for me to refer a case to the Court of Appeal under section 17 of the Criminal Appeal Act 1968 unless, after full investigation, I was satisfied that there was some new evidence, or other consideration of substance, that had not previously been taken into account by a court and that the Court of Appeal could properly consider. I may need to seek the advice of the Lord Chief Justice on a point of procedure; but, after discussion with him, I have decided that there need not be consultations, as there sometimes have been hitherto, where such a consideration does not arise. The final decision whether or not to refer a particular case rests of course with me.[13]

The appeal was heard on 17 October 1975 by Lord Justice Scarman, Lord Justice Ormrod and Mr Justice Swanwick. Richard Du Cann, Crown counsel, sought to argue that the evidence on which the Home Secretary had sent the case for appeal was inadmissible under section 23 of the 1968 Act. "Mr Du Cann reminded us," said Scarman, "that scientific and medical evidence had been adduced at the trial, and that what now was being sought to be done was to adduce further evidence either modifying the evidence then given or demonstrating that the evidence that had been given had been misunderstood by the trial judge. He submitted that the reception of further evidence by the Court of Appeal in such circumstances and for such purposes was not authorised by statute and was contrary to principle."

Scarman weighed this argument and also considered afresh Lord Justice Edmund Davies' 1968 judgment in Luvaglio–Stafford. He concluded that section 23 (2) laid down a *duty* on the court to admit evidence which passed the stringent tests imposed. Nevertheless, the court itself had *discretion* under section 23 (1), he insisted, to hear any evidence – even that which, technically, was not new – if it was in the interests of justice that it should. "The discretionary power is very much older," said Scarman, "it was originally conferred by subsection (1) of section 9 of the 1907 Criminal Appeal Act."

Taken together, these developments should have represented a giant leap forward for the judicial system. The Home Office and the Court of Appeal had simultaneously adopted an enlightened approach. The Home Office no longer demanded the emergence of new evidence as the pre-condition for referring cases back. Jenkins had added a notable factor: "*or other consideration of substance*". This was necessary to justify his action in this case, where the evidence was not really new at all, and it did introduce a precedent which should have benefited future petitioners. Scarman had not only made it clear that the court should accept such evidence, but had also reminded his colleagues about "the interests of justice", the thought which should always have been uppermost in their minds, but which hardly ever was.

The other matter to emerge from Jenkins' Commons statement (it could be described as a concealed revelation) was that it had hitherto been the practice – "a matter of routine" as Home Office officials subsequently confirmed[14] – for a potential Home Office referral to be sent to the Lord Chief Justice for his private opinion. Alex Lyon, minister of state at the Home Office at this time, later explained that if the Lord Chief Justice gave it the thumbs-down, that was "in effect, a veto".[15]

That Jenkins proposed to terminate this practice was welcome news. What was outrageous, though, was that this clandestine policy should ever have been in operation at all. It was constitutionally improper. The appeals procedure was designed so that particular cases could be considered independently by Home Office personnel (the executive) and by judges (the judiciary). After all, the separation of powers is theoretically at the root of the English constitution; it is the particular provision which underpins the liberties of the individual. If the executive and the judiciary are secretly in cahoots, then precious constitutional freedoms are being eroded.

In any case a pragmatic point can be set beside the constitutional one. Once the Lord Chief Justice has considered these cases in advance, a casually-proffered piece of advice has become decisive; and the process of appeal becomes bogus. Most section 17 references would be heard by the Lord Chief Justice; if he has previously advised against a particular case, the appeal is hardly likely to be productive.

In spite of the Jenkins/Scarman initiatives, though, trials continued to go awry – the most notorious in the late seventies being the Carl Bridgewater murder case – and the Appeal Court resumed its intractable ways. In the civil division, Lord Denning, the Master of the Rolls, declined to allow the Birmingham pub-bombers to bring forward evidence on the grounds that it could have been produced at the trial had 'reasonable diligence' been used (*see* page 411). This was further proof that the courts were ignoring the 1968 Act, and raised again the distinct possibility that defendants in British courts could be sentenced to prison *sine die* because of the incompetence of their lawyers.

An entirely separate example of the way the Court of Appeal shamelessly snubbed parliament was provided by the 're-trial' fiasco. Under the 1968 Act the court was empowered either to quash a conviction, full-stop; or to quash it and order a re-trial. It is astonishing to recall now the vigour and acrimony with which the idea of a second trial was debated in parliament, the legal profession, and the correspondence columns of *The Times*; "perhaps no other topic has given rise to so much controversy", reported Justice.[16] Even the members of the 1961–4 Justice inquiry found themselves at odds over the issue. Those opposed to re-trial argued that its absence was actually "a humane feature" of the English criminal procedure. "It ensures that once the jury has given its verdict the accused person cannot be subjected a second time to the ordeal of a criminal trial." Conversely, the reformers, in favour, believed that a re-trial gave a wrongly convicted person the opportunity to be properly and publicly acquitted.[17]

An earlier attempt to give this discretion to the court was defeated in the Commons in 1948. In the fifties the Tucker committee advised that appeal courts should be empowered to order fresh trials, but there was no real likelihood of this being implemented until the Aloysius Gordon case focused public attention on the issue.

On 7 June 1963, Aloysius "Lucky" Gordon, a jazz musician, was sentenced at the Old Bailey to three years' imprisonment for assaulting Christine Keeler, a former lover. This was no ordinary case, but a high-profile event in the long-drawn-out scandal of the Profumo affair. The Gordon case, like the Stephen Ward trial and the Denning report, was just one of its constituent parts.

Gordon's conviction was quashed at an extraordinary nine-minute hearing of the Court of Appeal on 30 July. The Court acted on the statements of witnesses not called at the trial, and on the transcript of a tape-recording. But the three judges – who included both the Lord Chief Justice, Lord Parker, and his eventual successor, then Mr Justice Widgery – did not disclose what these contained. Justice was accordingly dispensed, but in a secretive fashion.

The reason for this behaviour was that the tape-recording – of a conversation with Keeler – revealed that she gave perjured evidence at the Gordon trial. The judges could not reveal this without prejudicing – indeed, destroying – the Crown's chances of a conviction in the Stephen Ward trial, then in progress. Ethically, of course, the Ward trial should have been halted at the same time as the Gordon appeal was allowed, but ethical considerations do not inevitably trouble the appeal court.

"What the Court did," explained Sydney Silverman in *The Times*, "was to act upon the unsworn evidence of un-cross-examined witnesses to the prejudice of other proceedings without even reading it in open court and without it having reached the stage of being evidence at all."[18] The judicial manoeuvre not only allowed the Ward trial to continue, but gave its prosecution counsel Mervyn Griffith-Jones the opportunity to say that the success of Gordon's appeal "does not mean to say that the Court of Appeal have found that Miss Keeler is lying. As I understand it, the Lord Chief Justice said that it might be that Miss Keeler's evidence was completely truthful."[19]

Patrick Gordon Walker, a shadow minister, said that "the public has as much right to know this new information as they had to know the original evidence that led to the jury's verdict. It was, I believe, the Court of Criminal Appeal that first made the famous dictum that justice must not only be done but must manifestly be seen to be done."[20]

The overwhelming public feeling was that the principle of justice had been put in jeopardy. Sydney Silverman put down a motion in the Commons deploring the conduct of the Appeal Court and questioning the legal validity of the procedure adopted. The Liberal leader Jo Grimond commented that the argument in favour of re-trial had strengthened, and *The Times* took up the theme: "What this case does so pointedly illustrate is the need for reform of the powers of the appeal court. Justice would have been done to all had the court had power to order a new trial."[21] So, from this unlikely context of sex scandals in high places, arose an irresistible call for the English law to make provision for re-trial – a facility which appeal courts in most Commonwealth countries had had throughout the century. (The further from home they travelled, the purer the principles of British justice often seemed.) Re-trial was thus incorporated into the 1964 Criminal Appeal Act, though only after further stubborn parliamentary resistance, this time in the Lords.

What the protagonists in the argument failed to take into account, however, was the ability of the courts to ignore legislation they did not like. The Justice reformers anticipated that "under the rules at present governing the admission of fresh evidence, the number of new trials ordered is likely to be negligible – and the beneficial effect of a much-needed reform thereby minimised."[22]

This was a shrewd forecast, but it did not go far enough. Despite the long and bumpy road to the 1964 Act, despite the landmark 1968 Act, despite the 1975 Scarman ruling about fresh evidence, the Court of Appeal declined to order re-trials. Clearly, the power was one to be used sparingly; but the court used it so exceptionally that this important legislative change was nullified.

Were there particular occasions on which it should have done so? Yes. The most notable was at the appeal of the Guildford and Woolwich pub-bombers after the confessions of O'Connell and the others. The failure of the Court in this regard remains one of the darkest shadows cast over the English judicial process.

Ever since becoming secretary of Justice in 1957, Tom Sargant had worked assiduously to rectify miscarriages. Though he carved out a niche for himself as the *eminence grise* of this field, his task was, literally, thankless. His efforts, officially at least, were unappreciated. They also went largely, though not entirely, unrewarded. Nevertheless, while many others trimmed their sails to the prevailing legal and political winds, he stubbornly pursued the goals of truth and justice. Finally, he received an opportunity to put his case-work before the public. Having been approached by the BBC, he enthusiastically agreed to co-operate with producer Peter Hill on a series of programmes about judicial miscarriages. The result was *Rough Justice*, the first three editions of which were transmitted in April 1982. Two of the cases concerned people erroneously convicted of murder, in each of which Hill and his collaborator, Martin Young, had successfully discovered the identity of the real murderer.

Naturally, this provoked extraordinary interest. The transmission of these initial programmes led directly to an examination of miscarriages of justice by the House of Commons select committee on home affairs. The chairman was Sir John Eden (Conservative MP for Bournemouth West; now Lord Eden of Winton); its members included Labour MPs Alex Lyon (York) and Alf Dubs (Battersea South), and Conservatives John Wheeler (Paddington) and Jill Knight (Birmingham Edgbaston). The committee took evidence from three senior civil servants at the Home Office; from David Jeffreys QC and Jonathan Caplan, representatives of the Criminal Bar Association; and from Sargant, Lord Gardiner, the former Lord Chancellor, and solicitor Bernard Sheridan, representing Justice. There was also a written submission from Sir David Napley.

In its report, published in October 1982,[23] the committee recommended that section 17 of the Criminal Appeal Act should be scrapped – or, at least, mothballed. Cases which gave cause for particular concern should instead be referred to an extra-judicial body: an independent review panel, consisting of up to a dozen members, a number of whom would be criminal lawyers.

This was by no means an original idea (the committee never suggested that it was). Curiously enough, its virtues had been apparent to a former Lord Chief Justice, Lord Parker. In 1966, when dealing with the reference-back to the Court of Appeal of the notorious case of Alfred Hinds, he observed, "When you get a reference of this sort, it does not seem to me that this Court is the proper body to deal with it; we have not got the inquisitorial powers that a commissioner or tribunal set up to hear it would have." The concept was then firmly espoused by Justice in 1968,[24] and endorsed in 1976 by the Lord Devlin committee which examined erroneous convictions resulting from mistaken identity.[25] The theory behind this was that although the Court of Appeal might be a good vehicle for determining issues of law (although many would dispute even that), it was a poor one for determining issues of fact. An independent body, unencumbered by legal niceties such as the complexities of admissible and inadmissible evidence, could perhaps arrive at the truth.

The House of Commons committee asked the Home Office officials who appeared before it whether the idea of an independent review tribunal had ever been seriously considered. "It certainly was," replied the most senior of them. "The outcome of that consideration by the government of the day was that they could not adopt it."[26]

Having received this fresh cue, the Home Office considered it afresh, as well as giving thought to the select committee's recommendations for improving its own performance in this field.

A prisoner petitioning the Home Office must satisfy two fundamental criteria. His case must have exhausted the formal appeals procedure; and the petitioner must be able to show that there has been a development of some sort in his case – whether it be as concrete as 'new evidence' or as nebulous as 'a consideration of substance'. Because one or other of these conditions is not met, an overwhelming proportion of inquiries are rejected at the outset.

The remainder are sifted in C5, the Home Office department responsible for these matters. C5 is staffed by a dozen people, one of whom explained that "In looking at these cases, we are trying to achieve justice; we are not in any way circumscribed by rules of evidence or anything like that."[27]

This would appear to indicate a proper sense of priorities. Indeed, there can be no argument about the theory behind the system, only about how it works, or does not work in practice. Sir David Napley explained to the Commons committee that "over a long period of time I have made representations to the Home Office on behalf of various persons who allege that they were the victims of injustice. I cannot recall a single case where the Home Office has, as a result of its own investigations, felt able to recommend a pardon or any other recognition that a conviction was necessarily wrongful."[28] Innumerable other lawyers are similarly unable to 'recall a single case' where Home Office channels have proved efficacious.

These procedures fail, partly because of the mere insufficiency of the system. As the solicitor Brian Raymond has written, "Many thousands of petitions are received each year, only to be dealt with by a small, overworked staff with limited resources for expert legal advice and no facilities at all for investigation."[29] Partly, it is due to the inherent secrecy and conservatism that pervades the Home Office. Partly, it is the dogmatic implementation of civil service codes of behaviour, and the discouragement of individual initiatives. Unless there is such pressure of publicity that holding the line becomes impractical and it is simply easier to make a calculated retreat (and that hardly ever happens), there is no incentive for officials or ministers to stick their heads above the parapet.

In the Timothy Evans case, R. A. Butler was quoted as saying, "*I am advised* I cannot say Evans was innocent" (author's italics), implying that he wanted to, but that the permanent Home Office staff discreetly dissuaded him. This does not absolve Butler of blame. To overcome such built-in resistance, those holding high government office need to be made of sterner stuff. In post-war years only one Home Secretary, Roy Jenkins, has had sufficient strength of character to overcome the drag of the bureaucratic machine.

Moreover, Home Office procedures betrayed a fundamental principle of English law. Justice was never seen to be done. The Home Office explained neither its eventual decisions nor the Byzantine delays in reaching them.

Deliberate delaying tactics are a unique impediment to justice. In general it helps to hold up petitions because the wind is taken out of the sails of those trying to mount a campaign; but, over and above this, particular campaigns might be irreparably harmed. In the Jock Russell ("handful of hair") case, the BBC *Rough Justice* team disclosed that the hair clutched in the hand of the murdered girl did not belong to Russell, who had been convicted of her murder; but could easily have come from the head of a suspicious character called Michael Molnar, who had by then died of natural causes. To check this, Tom Sargant applied to the Home Office for an exhumation order, and even offered to bear all the costs himself. Hair decays, so obviously the matter was urgent. For months and months, though, the Home Office simply would not come to a decision.[30]

In April 1986, in the House of Lords, Lord Glenarthur, under-secretary of state, urged that all those with genuine grievances should seek the immediate assistance of the Home Office. "I must emphasise that representations about wrongful convictions are considered on exactly the same basis whether the representations come direct from the aggrieved person, via his Member of Parliament, from one of your Lordships, from a solicitor, from the media or from any other source. Once there is reason to believe that a miscarriage of justice might have occurred, the Home Secretary will, if necessary, instigate full and urgent inquiries into the case."[31]

"Full and urgent inquiries"? When has the Home Office ever conducted "full and urgent inquiries"?

As the arm of government responsible for the reputation of both the police and the criminal law, it is – understandably – unlikely to look favourably on any development which undermines the authority of either. Yet incorrect convictions necessarily evince both bungling in police work and deficiencies in the administration of justice. It is hard to avoid the conclusion that the Home Office is saddled with incompatible duties, invigilating a system whose integrity it must protect. In any case, the Home Office and the police are too closely connected. When examining petitions, for example, Home Office staff do no field-work of their own: "generally speaking, we are working on impressions and reports and statements collected by the police."[32] This vitiates the entire system.

Police antipathy to post-trial investigations is well understood. At its least culpable, it represents merely a natural reluctance to reopen closed files. This reluctance, however, can be taken too far. In the Cooper–McMahon case, the second appeal court quashed the conviction of Patrick Murphy (*see* page 193). This meant, logically, that one of the gang of four must have escaped capture. Yet the police undertook no inquiries to discover the identity of this fourth man. According to the *Guardian*, the police decided to disregard the court verdict. It reported that, "In a letter, Scotland Yard's Assistant Commissioner (Crime), John Wilson, writing on behalf of the commissioner, Sir Robert Mark, said, 'on the facts known to the police there is no doubt that Murphy was present and consequently there have been no further inquiries to establish the identity of any other person'."[33] If the country's senior police officers can simply ignore High Court verdicts which don't suit them, it is no wonder that the criminal justice system is falling into such disrepute.

There was also the discovery of the severed head after the verdict in the Maynard–Dudley–Clarke case. Once again, the Metropolitan Police did nothing – a quite extraordinary dereliction of their professional duties. If a severed head is not a matter for police investigation, then what is?

A more prominent factor in the unwillingness of police to think again about technically closed cases is the refusal to uncover anything which might reflect adversely on colleagues, whether in the same force or a different one. In the A6 murder there were two police inquiries into Hanratty's alibi; in the Maxwell Confait case, there were two police inquiries into improper conduct by officers investigating the crime; in the Carl Bridgewater murder case, there have been two police inquiries into post-appeal developments.[34] None discovered even the smallest lapse of professionalism in police behaviour – or anything which led to the genuine resolution of the crime.

The relationship between the Home Office and the courts is likewise not conducive to a solution of the miscarriages of justice problem. For a start, the staff at Queen Anne's Gate behave as though in awe of the legal machinery. Despite specific legislative provision for the Home Office to act on its own, it nearly always defers to the courts in what are, after all, matters of judicial concern. Sir David Napley told the Commons committee that "on a number of occasions officials have quite freely expressed to me their sense of disquiet about particular cases but have pointed out that since appellate courts either on appeal or on reference under section 17 have refused to interfere with the verdicts they felt themselves unable to intervene."[35]

Over and over again, Home Office ministers have explained in parliament that they are unable to do anything about a particular case because it is a matter for the courts – and for the Home Office to tread on their toes would be unthinkable. "The independence of the judiciary is a fundamental constitutional principle," explained Lord Glenarthur. "It is one to which successive Home Secretaries have always had due regard."[36]

So to say that Home Office powers – to grant a pardon, for example – are sparingly used misses the point. As far as serious criminal cases are concerned, they are vestigial.

Thus, the executive will not intervene in what it takes to be judicial matters; nor will judges intrude into what are seen to be executive affairs – as was demonstrated by the appeal judgment in the civil case brought by Hanratty's parents against the Home Secretary (*see* page 128). Wrongful convictions slip into this constitutional crevice between the judiciary and the executive, like tennis balls despatched straight down the middle of a doubles court for which neither partner assumes responsibility.[37]

An underlying tension between the two further inhibits the possibilities of justice. The Home Office is disinclined to refer back a case if it fears the appeal will be dismissed; it will be made to look foolish. (This perhaps explains – though not condones – the erstwhile practice of playing safe by seeking the Lord Chief Justice's private opinion in advance.) Naturally, if that does happen, the advocates of caution inside the Home Office will be in a stronger position. The Court of Appeal, on the other hand, will resent repeated references-back by the Home Office, with the implied criticism of its judgments. This happened in the Luton murder case.

Very occasionally, a convenient escape-route has been to set up inquiries. These have been almost unanimous in reaching the wrong conclusions. Presumably, the legal and political establishments have nevertheless been able to draw comfort from the facts that the conclusions, however wide of the mark, have been the ones which best suited them, and from which they were absolved of all responsibility.

The type of inquiry carried out is immaterial. The Hawser inquiry into the A6 murder was a solo undertaking. Hawser, a leading QC, was simply required to sit in his chambers and study the available documentation, without benefit of counsel. In the end, he got it completely wrong, but this should not have been surprising. Ten years earlier, Lord Denning conducted an inquiry of the same kind into the Profumo affair. In his final report, he wrote:

"This inquiry has two great disadvantages: first, being in secret, it has not had the appearance of justice; second, in carrying out the inquiry I have had to be detective, inquisitor, advocate and judge, and it has been difficult to combine them . . . My inquiry is *not a suitable body to determine guilt or innocence*. I have not the means at my disposal." (Author's italics.)[38]

In the light of Denning's prior evaluation, the major share of blame for the failure of Hawser's inquiry should be borne not by the man asked to sail such an unseaworthy ship, but by the one who launched it.[39]

The Fisher investigation of the Maxwell Confait case was a full inquiry, with counsel, solicitors and witnesses. Nevertheless this too went spectacularly awry. The final report re-incriminated two of the three boys who had already been absolved at the Court of Appeal. The result was that they had to be cleared all over again, this time by Attorney-General Sir Michael Havers in the House of Commons.

Ultimately, perhaps, the real explanation for the failure of such proceedings was disclosed in the BBC's *Yes, Prime Minister*, a kind of documentary series masquerading as Light Entertainment. Sir Humphrey Appleby was upbraided by Jim Hacker for having conducted a curiously myopic inquiry some years earlier. "But, prime minister," protested Sir Humphrey, "the whole point of an inquiry is not to find anything out."[40]

For all these reasons, the setting-up of an independent review tribunal to act as a fail-safe device seemed an attractive proposition. The Home Office, though, would have none of it. "It is better that miscarriages of justice which occur within the judicial system should, so far as possible, be corrected by that system, which itself embodies high and long-established standards of openness and independence. [The government has concluded] that it should not establish an independent review body. As a matter of principle, priority should be given to improving and enhancing the part played by the courts in these matters, rather than curtailing the present arrangements."

This response was contained in a White Paper, published in April 1983.[41] As a direct response to the considered deliberations of a group of prominent MPs, it was disgracefully patronising. The issues did not seem to have been seriously examined. The crux of the Home Office argument was this: "it cannot be assumed that where the judicial process might have failed to arrive at a just solution, an alternative arrangement can be devised which will be certain to get it right."

It is characteristic of bureaucratic dialectics that some points of argument are firmly rebutted, even though they have never been proposed. No one was ever foolish enough to suggest that a review tribunal would be "certain to get it right". The other objection to this piece of prime Home Office humbug was equally obvious; had civilisation advanced on the premise that only developments "certain to get it right' were to be implemented, then it would not have got very far.

Writing in *The Listener*, Geoffrey Robertson, the barrister and author, was scathing in his criticism. "This White Paper response is breathtaking in its ignorance of the causes of injustice and the proven inability of the judicial system to rectify cases . . . It is a tepid and devious document, which pretends that a few tinkerings with existing rules will produce justice."[42]

One or two quite unexceptionable points were conceded – the Home Office undertook henceforth to provide prisoners with both an explanation of the delay in attending to their petition, and a summary of the reasons for its failure – but the only significant comment occurred in paragraph 10:

"As to greater use of the procedure for reference to the Court of Appeal, the Home Secretary will in future be prepared to exer-

cise his power of reference *more readily*; and the Lord Chief Justice, who has been consulted about this reply, sees room for the Court to be *more ready* to exercise its own powers to receive evidence, or, where appropriate and practicable, to order a re-trial."
(Author's italics.)

Promises, promises.

In the wake of this, there was some movement in the House of Lords. In the case of *R v. Chard*, Lord Diplock ruled that on appeal "the whole of the case" must be considered by the Court, and this must embrace all questions of fact and law involved in the case.[43]

Now, the relevant 1968 Act, and the 1956 Act from which the phrase had been extracted, clearly referred to "the whole of the case", a term which, or so the average person would assume, left no room for ambiguity. The Appeal Court, however, moves in mysterious ways (its blunders to perform). It had been considering not "the whole of the case", but only those parts of it explicitly referred to in the Home Secretary's letter of reference. Lord Diplock said that the Court's interpretation hitherto of its duties in this regard was "in my respectful view, wrong". Nothing ambiguous about that. In effect, the Lords determined that the Appeal Court had been artificially circumscribing its own powers for the past 27 years.

As a result of these 1983 developments – the White Paper pledges and the Diplock ruling – what benefits have accrued to wrongly convicted prisoners? The answer is plain: none.

Because the situation remained worrying, the director of Justice, Leah Levin, set up a sub-committee to consider miscarriages of justice. Its members included Sir Denis Dobson, former permanent secretary to the Lord Chancellor; Sir George Terry, former Chief Constable of Sussex; James Cameron, professor of forensic medicine at the University of London; and Ludovic Kennedy. The first case about which the committee felt sufficiently strongly to make representations to the Home Office was Margaret Livesey's (*see* Chapter 10), which was subsequently referred to appeal – in January 1986. Since the case had first received national attention as a possible miscarriage of justice in October 1983, this hardly confirmed that the Home Office was doing what it said it would, and referring cases "more readily".

The programme immediately following the Livesey one in the *Rough Justice* series concerned Ernie Clarke, who was convicted in 1979 of the murder in 1970 of a girl he hardly knew.[44] The Crown case, at best, was gossamer. It depended on the allegation that

Clarke was seen disposing of some of the dead girl's clothing. *Rough Justice* proved that the 'clothing' was an industrial rag (precisely what Clarke had said at his trial) and that it had been discarded prior to the girl's disappearance. The critical evidence was not only destroyed by the ingenuity of the BBC investigation; it was expressly withdrawn by the Crown at the appeal in February 1986.

What did the court, in its state of being "more ready" to admit new evidence and to consider "the whole of the case" do then? It dismissed the appeal. Since this was transparently a travesty of justice, the judges should not be allowed the shelter of anonymity. They were Lord Justice Lawton, Mr Justice Michael Davies and Mr Justice Mars-Jones.[45]

One might have thought that such oppressive odds against wrongly convicted prisoners were adequate for even the most implacable administration. Throughout 1985 and 1986, however, it became clear that the government was manoeuvring to make things yet more difficult for them. On 15 January 1976, Roy Jenkins said that cases would be referred to appeal if there was "new evidence, or other consideration of substance". Though the latter condition was clearly introduced by Jenkins to validate his referral of the Maxwell Confait case, it made sense in broader terms because many miscarriage-of-justice campaigns had foundered on the "new evidence" rock. So, the phrase "or other consideration of substance" was distinguished from "new evidence"; and was not itself qualified by the word "new". It was introduced at a time of growing public disquiet about the steady stream of miscarriages and in the knowledge that the particularly narrow interpretation generally placed upon "new evidence" by the courts and the Home Office had prevented the 1968 Act from being as effective as parliament had intended.

After Jenkins – and his minister of state, Alex Lyon – had moved on from the Home Office, however, this ancillary condition was ignored. (In a letter to the *Guardian*, Lyon said that over half the 46 referrals made during the 1972–81 period had been made by him in just two years, from 1974–76.)[46] A decade later, Home Office officials insidiously began to nullify Jenkins' initiative.

On 17 May 1985, Lord Glenarthur, under-secretary of state at the Home Office, spoke of cases being referred on the basis of "*significant* new evidence or *material* consideration of substance".[47] Then, on 24 July 1986, the grounds were further qualified. David Mellor told MPs that "the Home Secretary can consider intervening only if some new evidence, or some *new and material* consideration of substance comes to light".[48] This change in the rules, which passed virtually unnoticed at the time, was absolutely critical. Mellor reiterated on 18 December that there must be "new evidence or *new* considerations of substance".[49]

This was a kind of semantic subversion of justice. It is obvious that the phrase "considerations of substance" requires no qualification whatsoever. Material? It is bound to be that. Similarly it will by definition be "new" too; if a "consideration" is "old" it is unlikely to have "substance". The only explanation of the deliberate introduction of the word "new" was to sabotage the principle. Put in those terms, a new consideration is likely to be as elusive as new evidence; likely, indeed, to be the same thing.

The simple truth at the root of the original phrase was that a trial could take on an entirely different complexion in hindsight. By negating it, the Home Office had to realise that it was bound to create difficulty in cases like that of the Maguire family, where the particular circumstances virtually precluded the emergence of anything "new". In making the application of justice more difficult, the government brazenly disregarded Scarman's 1975 judgment and also broke the pledge – minimal as it was – contained in the 1983 White Paper to "refer cases more readily".

The judicial process cannot be forever relitigating cases. Nor would it be prudent to deprive jury verdicts in any way of their special significance, thus undermining public confidence in the system and endangering trial by jury. These points are incontestable. It is nevertheless unpardonable that appeal judges have allowed such considerations an overriding importance, with the result that the channels of judicial review have effectively been sealed. As Lord Chuter-Ede observed, the law exists to serve justice. As things stand at present in Britain, it baulks it.

Further, the crude belief that this is the way to preserve public faith in the system is ill-founded. The populace is not as dim as senior judges seem to imagine. "Whereas some years ago the public would have been very surprised to learn that the police get up to dirty tricks or that juries make mistakes," said Peter Ashman, legal officer of Justice, "today there is a much greater awareness of the things that can and do go wrong." In their mistaken efforts to pretend that everything is shipshape, the judges are increasing, not diminishing, public misgivings. Moreover, to quote Ashman again, "the kind of appeal actually conducted by the Court of Appeal [i.e. on errors of law] undermines trial by jury far more than appeals judged on merit. What it generally means is that someone who is guilty can get off on a technicality, while someone who is clearly innocent, and in whose case the jury simply arrived at the wrong verdict, has his appeal dismissed."

Ultimately, the public has been sold a lie. The system which perpetrates miscarriages of justice does not, despite appearances, have a self-correcting mechanism. (Prisoners have long been aware of this. Jimmy Boyle wrote that the ones he knew always regarded the appeal process as "an exercise in futility".)[50]

How many miscarriages occur? It is impossible to tell, especially since the field can hardly be adequately researched. Arthur Koestler made a persuasive point in 1956 when he commented, apropos of the Evans case, that "it is not unreasonable to assume that the number of undetected errors may be greater than we believe".[51] Whenever a judicial error came to light, the temptation in those days was to regard it as exceptional. Wrong, argued Koestler. The correct inference to draw was not that the occurrence itself was exceptional; but that it required exceptional luck to be able to detect one.

Research by Dr John Baldwin and Dr Michael McConville into cases before Birmingham Crown Court in 1975–6 led them to estimate that at least five per cent of defendants were convicted in doubtful circumstances. They added that, "the offences in question were far from trivial". This research may not seem up-to-date, but it remains valid because it is the last allowed by the Lord Chancellor's department. Perhaps the less than comforting results, published in *Jury Trials*, explain why no further work has been sanctioned. Baldwin and McConville established that:

> Juries were thought by respondents [i.e. other key participants in the trial] to have reached wrong or questionable conclusions on the evidence with a surprising frequency. The jury appeared to be insufficiently prepared to protect the possibly innocent . . . The infrequency of appeals reflects a realistic appraisal of an appeals procedure which inhibits, except on technical grounds, an effective review of the question of guilt . . . That the Court of Appeal is reluctant to interfere with a jury's verdict cannot be doubted. If the reason for the Court's reluctance is a general confidence

in the precision of jury trial or a belief that jury waywardness operates only to the advantage of the defendant, then it is perhaps time to reassess this assumption.[52]

Miscarriages of justice, in the first instance, frequently seem to be the result of a shared delusion on the part of the police. They simply convince themselves that they have caught the criminal(s). This syndrome is not particularly unusual. In his book, *Selling Hitler*, about the forged Hitler diaries, Robert Harris showed how a large number of highly intelligent people could foster a common delusion. We live in a world in which a widespread credence has been given to rumours that Paul McCartney was dead, to the Bermuda Triangle, and to MIAs (American GIs missing in action and supposedly surviving in South-East Asia). The unwitting creation of elaborate fantasies goes on around us all the time.

The major problem when it happens in miscarriages of justice is that to acknowledge the case as such would inevitably involve admitting to a catalogue of serious errors in the detection of crime and the administration of justice. The authorities are loath to countenance this. What the Americans call a mind-set then seems to develop, with the result that, as in the Margaret Livesey case, even allowing murderers to go free and commit further crimes becomes a small price to pay for the maintenance of the façade of judicial infallibility.

It is not simply that the average miscarriage of justice is not rectified. Not even the *causes célèbres* are overturned. Of the cases discussed in this book – a fraction of those available – only in the Timothy Evans case has judicial error been officially admitted. To reach that stage took thirteen years of dedicated and selfless work by a group of unusually committed people.

Sometimes, it is thought, especially intractable cases would be rectified if only the real criminal came forward and confessed. The 1977 appeal in the Guildford and Woolwich case makes it clear that *not even in those circumstances* will the courts allow justice to be done.

Further, the treatment of fresh witnesses who try, merely as a matter of civic conscience, to alert the authorities to judicial error is in itself a scandal. The experience of Frank Johnson (*see* pages 321–5) is a grievous indictment of the state of British justice. Witnesses who do have information about a case which conflicts with police or prosecution assumptions should on no account confide it to the police or the Home Office but should instead contact a reputable solicitor.[53]

As things stand at present, the best chance a wrongly convicted prisoner has of compelling the authorities to take positive action about his case is to persuade Ludovic Kennedy to write a book about it.[54] Failing that, one can attempt to make headway by going directly through Home Office channels (as Lord Glenarthur recommended) without creating any fuss, in deference to the widespread assumption that a public clamour only alienates the authorities. ("British justice," wrote the American novelist Marilynne Robinson, "grows squeamish at the thought that the legal process should be adulterated by publicity."[55]) This approach, which was tried in the Elizabeth Thompson case, is almost invariably unsuccessful.

The alternative method is to go public, bang a big drum and arouse as much media interest as possible. This approach, too, is almost invariably unsuccessful, yet it is essential that it be adopted. It is the only one with even a faint hope of being availing, and it is clearly in the public interest that information of this nature is disseminated. The sickness of the country's judicial system is the concern of us all.

It would be better if miscarriages of justice simply did not happen. That must be an unobtainable utopia, but a couple of specific observations can be made. The first concerns evidence from inside prison, from prison grasses. This can never be untainted, and it has been instrumental in securing a disturbing number of wrongful convictions (Hanratty, Maynard–Dudley–Clarke, McMahon–Cooper, Michael Hickey and the others convicted of the murder of Carl Bridgewater – the list is a long one).[56] Moreover, the practice has frequently led directly to the absolute perversion of the judicial system, with the innocent being imprisoned and the guilty doing deals to secure their release. The mere presentation of such evidence is a pointer to a jury that the "not-guilty' verdict is the correct one. Realising that this kind of testimony will inevitably be regarded with the deepest suspicion, the Crown will attempt to introduce it only when it has been unable to assemble a sufficiently strong case from the genuine evidence.

Secondly, so-called confessions which are repudiated by the defendant must automatically be scrutinised with great caution. Not until the police oblige by agreeing to videotape the taking of crucial statements in important cases will juries be able to assess properly the evidential weight of contested 'confessions'. (Fortunately, the jury in the Cyprus secrets trial at the Old Bailey in October 1985 was alert to the possibility that 'confessions' could be extracted under physical or psychological duress, and thus be completely fraudulent.)

Gerald Kaufman, the shadow Home Secretary, wrote in the *Guardian* that "it is essential to change the practice by which confession statements are made and which can later be used as evidence against those who make them. We must move as speedily as possible to the audio-recording of all interviews with alleged offenders, certainly in the case of serious crimes punishable by long prison sentences. However, the only way to dispose of the possibility of physical brutality will be by video-recording such interviews."[57] The police remain hostile to any such development and, even if it was introduced, would doubtless try to circumvent it. "When a Scottish police force experimentally introduced recording at its police stations," wrote the barrister Stephen Sedley, "suspects suddenly began confessing in the police vehicle on the way to the station."[58]

In the Commons on 20 January 1987, Nicholas Fairbairn (Conservative MP for Perth and Kinross) drew the attention of the Home Secretary to the Evidence Act of 1895 which the law of England imposed not in Britain, but in its dependent colonies. "Under section 25 and 26 of that Act, no confession made by a person to a police officer while in custody is admissible in evidence, and no confession to any other person except a magistrate while a person is in police custody is admissible as evidence. That is still the law of most of our now independent colonies. Might it not be a good idea, if the law of England thought it fit to impose those provisions on dependent colonies in 1895, to introduce them in England in 1987?"[59]

The Home Secretary did not agree. He referred to the provisions of the 1984 Police and Criminal Evidence Act, which imposed some restrictions on the police but in the final analysis left it to the courts to determine whether such confessions were admissible as evidence.

However, even if juries were fully attuned to all these considerations, wrongful convictions would continue to occur. It is impossible to eliminate human error, and they are probably, as Baldwin and McConville said, "an unavoidable by-product of the system".[60]

How ironic, for example, to consider that in future years the

1974–77 period may well be regarded as the short-lived golden age of the British jury. Between April 1974, when all property qualifications were abolished and anybody of voting age (subject to certain restrictions) could become a juror; and June 1977, when the Criminal Law Act reduced the number of peremptory challenges from seven to three, a defendant had a historically unique opportunity of being judged by his peers, by a group of twelve over whose selection he, like the prosecution, could hope to exercise a measure of influence.[61] Yet this 1974–77 period saw some of the most astonishing miscarriages of justice: all the Irish cases, Maynard–Dudley–Clarke, and poor Elizabeth Thompson, whose conviction could be attributed to nothing other than jury error.

"The abolition of capital punishment has perhaps taken the edge off our fear of erroneous convictions," wrote Stephen Sedley. "We need to remember that hanging is not the only way in which the law can take life."[62] The situation continues to deteriorate. Miscarriages doubtless pile up, and yet the channels through which victims of justice are encouraged to plead their case – the executive and the judiciary – lead nowhere. "No one inside or outside government except those with mischievous intent, has an interest in creating a judicial system which is unfair or inhumane, or in which miscarriages of justice are swept under the carpet," said Lord Glenarthur.[63] But such reassurances ring hollow, because that is precisely what is happening today, and what has been happening in this country since the Second World War and, for all we know, what has been happening for centuries.

If the UK is indeed a nation which does not sweep miscarriages under the carpet, it is time that the government and the judiciary provided effective proof of that. A start could be made by acknowledging that the cases outlined in this book are all miscarriages of justice. The integrity of the country's judicial system is seriously in doubt. It is going to take determined measures to restore its reputation.

Truth does periodically surface in the judicial review process (as in the Confait case), but it is very much the occasional luxury, certainly not a built-in feature. The paramount concern of those operating the system is to conceal its valetudinarian condition. "I sit in this cell now," wrote Michael McMahon in Long Lartin prison in 1977, "not because of any evidence against me, but because of the legal establishment's pretensions to infallibility."[64] The interests of justice and the interests of the judiciary have for too long been confused.

Cyril Connolly suggested in the *Sunday Times* in 1961 that the real test of a country's justice "is not the blunders which are sometimes made but the zeal with which they are put right".[65] By that criterion, the UK's judicial system is in a wretched state.

It is wrong to keep innocent people in prison. That is a truth so basic that no amount of politics, of bureaucratic expediency and judicial casuistry, can alter it. Yet the shaming fact is that the continued incarceration of the innocent is nothing less than national policy. There can be no sadder reflection on the state of Britain today than that there seems to be no one in the legal or political hierarchies with the moral fibre, with the simple human decency, to want to do anything about it.

Notes

1. This is an important quotation. As I have condensed it slightly for narrative clarity, I must also give it in full:

    With regard to the other matter [i.e. the Evans trial], I would prefer not to say any more about it. My learned friend is perfectly right to say it is not a relevant consideration in this case, directly relevant, as to what happened in another trial. But I think you will understand how, especially in my position – my learned friend talked about politicians; I do not think he meant that. I think that what he means was in a governmental position – it is most important that nothing avoidable should be said in Court which might cast an unjustified reflection on the administration of justice; and therefore it is most important that one should scrutinise most carefully what is and what is not proved with regard to a case of this kind.

    Rather a clever piece of rhetoric, this. At the same time as he is actually introducing extraneous political considerations into a trial, Heald is carefully denying that he is doing any such thing. He got away with it at the time. Today, though, there is probably no one in the country who could accept that MPs in positions of government are somehow divorced from the political process.

2. This has absolutely no relevance to the theme of miscarriages of justice, but readers might like to compare the backgrounds and characters of John Reginald Halliday Christie and Peter Sutcliffe, the Yorkshire Ripper, as they are presented in, respectively, Ludovic Kennedy's *Ten Rillington Place* and Gordon Burn's . . . *Somebody's Husband, Somebody's Son: The Story of Peter Sutcliffe* (Heinemann,

1984). The parallels are striking. Moreover, Sutcliffe also pleaded insanity, but the Attorney-General of the time (Sir Michael Havers) successfully contested this line of defence. Nevertheless, Sutcliffe, who is now in Broadmoor, was, of course, insane; as was Christie. ("He was an unpleasant bore, but not a monster," wrote Dr Jack Hobson. "A man sick in mind. In the Christie–Evans case, we should have not one, but two men on our conscience.")

3. The case of George Beattie was examined by Peter Hill and Martin Young for their television series, *Rough Justice* (BBC1). It is documented in *More Rough Justice* (Penguin, 1985). To be strictly exact, Beattie's statement was not a confession, but, forensically, it served the same purpose. At the trial, the judge told the jury that "it is as if the accused had made a confession".

4. Letter to *The Times*, 17 April 1971.

5. I'm here trying to recall the values of the time. Personally, I don't believe that executions are compatible with humanitarian considerations of whatever kind.

6. Hansard, 29 July 1953, vol. 518, col. 1464.

7. *The Times*, 15 September 1953.

8. Lyrics © Harmony Music Ltd.

9. *The Times*, 16 September 1955.

10. *The Times*, 17 September 1955.

11. Sir Harold Scott, *Scotland Yard* (André Deutsch, 1954). The actual quote is crystal-clear:

The records showed that when the police were investigating the murder of a Mrs Evans at the same address in 1949, they had learned that Christie's dog had dug up a skull in the garden and that Christie had thrown it into the basement of a bombed house, where it had been found by the police in 1949.

12. Letter in the *Sunday Times*, 5 March 1961.

13. Letter in the *Sunday Times*, 12 March 1961.

14. Hansard, 16 March 1961, vol. 636, col. 142.

15. Hansard, 15 June 1961, vol. 642, cols. 664, 672, 702.

16. Hansard, 4 February 1965, vol. 705, col. 256.

17. Hansard (H.L.), 18 May 1965, vol. 266, col. 361.

18. Harold Evans, *Good Times, Bad Times* (Weidenfeld, 1983).

19. Ludovic Kennedy, *Ten Rillington Place*: preface to the 1971 edition (Panther).

CHAPTER 2 pp 51–84

1. R.T. Paget and S.S. Silverman, *Hanged – And Innocent?* (Gollancz, 1953).
2. Patrick Devlin, *Easing the Passing* (Bodley Head, 1985).
3. Percy Hoskins, *Two Men Were Acquitted* (Secker & Warburg, 1984).
4. Jolly died in January 1950.
5. Hansard, 6 December 1951, vol. 494, col. 2553.
6. For details of the Derek Bentley case, see David Yallop, *To Encourage The Others* (W.H. Allen, 1971).

CHAPTER 3 pp 85–110

1. This proved an extraordinary example of the power of media myth. For years afterwards (and, perhaps, still today) it was commonly believed that Gregsten and Valerie Storie had been a hitch-hiker's victims. I remember it cropping up regularly in conversation during my own hitch-hiking days in the mid-sixties. It made drivers especially wary about whom they picked up; and I, of course, was not sufficiently well informed to disabuse them.
2. *Daily Sketch*, 19 February 1962.
3. In 1971 Ewer told Paul Foot that none of this was accurate. He blamed it all on the fertile imagination of the press. However, Fleet Street was no street of shame in those days. The *Daily Sketch* piece was given considerable space on the back page of the Monday edition following the end of the trial on the Saturday. So, it is a piece the *Sketch* must have researched and prepared some time earlier; and it included no fewer than 17 paragraphs of direct quotes from Ewer. If the crime reporter concerned, Peter Duffy, had invented all this, it is surprising – to say the least – that no complaint was ever made.
4. Hansard, 2 August 1963, vol. 682, col. 819.
5. Paul Foot, *Who Killed Hanratty?* (Cape, 1971), p. 126.

CHAPTER 4 pp 111–138

1. Hansard, 2 August 1963, vol. 682, col. 829.

2. *The Times*, 19 July 1967.
3. *The Times*, 13 May 1967.
4. *The Times*, 4 September 1967.
5. Hansard, 1 November 1967, vol. 753, cols. 2–3.
6. *Who Killed Hanratty?* (p. 398) *op. cit.*
7. *The Times*, 30 March 1971.
8. *The Times*, 13 May 1971.
9. Hansard, 6 May 1971, vol. 816, col. 424.
10. Hansard, 20 May 1971, vol. 817, col. 1509.
11. *Sunday Times*, 4 July 1971.
12. Hansard, 28 October 1971, vol. 823, col. 2052.
13. *The Times*, 17 March 1974.
14. Peter Hain, *Mistaken Identity* (Quartet, 1976).
15. *Private Eye*, 18 April 1975. The unsigned piece had, of course, been written by Paul Foot.

CHAPTER 5 pp 139–168
1. Sir David Napley, *Not Without Prejudice* (Harrap, 1982).
2. All quotations from the trial transcripts.
3. David Lewis & Peter Hughman, *Most Unnatural: An Inquiry into the Stafford Case* (Penguin, 1971), p. 109.
4. "A Strange Kind of Justice", *New Statesman*, 26 November 1971.
5. *The Times*, 24 October 1969.
6. *The Times*, 9 July 1971.
7. Letter in *The Times*, 27 January 1972.
8. *Most Unnatural*, Chapter 8, *op. cit.*
9. "Widgery and the Doctrine of the Lurking Doubt", *Sunday Times*, 28 January 1973.
10. *Not Without Prejudice, op. cit.*
11. *Sunday People*, 28 September 1980. I do not believe that Stafford's 'confession' raises any doubts at all about the case. The factors consistent with his innocence (e.g. the absence of any forensic evidence) remain as convincing; so do those suggesting that he and Luvaglio were framed (e.g. the apparent disappearance of the E-type while they were inside the Bird Cage Club, and the telephone call to police later in the day). Some newspapers do offer very tempting sums for criminal confessions; Stafford, who went abroad anyway after his release, would have had little to lose by taking the money.

CHAPTER 6 pp 169–86

1. *News of the World*, 28 May 1972.

CHAPTER 7 pp 187–222

1. Ludovic Kennedy and others, *Wicked Beyond Belief* (Granada, 1980).
2. *Wicked Beyond Belief*, ibid.
3. *News of the World*, 20 April 1975.
4. It was, of course, the third time the case had been referred back to the Court of Appeal, so Lawton's statement was judicial hair-splitting. The first time the court had been concerned with Murphy's conviction, and had refused to consider McMahon and Cooper.
5. *The Times*, 2 August 1976.
6. *The Times*, 21 August 1980.
7. *The Times*, 2 August 1976.
8. Records showed that Mathews had £300 in cash when he was first arrested. It is believed that this was a normal amount for him to carry. By withdrawing £700, he would therefore have been able to pay Drury £1,000 in cash.
9. Quoted in *The Times*, 3 May 1978.
10. *The Times*, 8 November 1977.
11. The sentence was reduced, on appeal, to five years.
12. The background to this sordid business is fully covered in *The Fall of Scotland Yard* by Barry Cox, John Shirley and Martin Short (Penguin, 1977).
13. Hansard, 14 December 1977, vol. 941, col. 877.
14. According to Mathews' 'parcels story', Cooper had called on him at 2.30 to initiate the Luton expedition. At that time, Lawrence had been with Cooper, and that is why he was cited on his behalf. (In the event, of course, Lawrence was behind bars by the time of the trial, which probably explains the decision not to call him.)
15. From an addendum to McMahon's manuscript, written in Long Lartin prison and supplied by Wendy Mantle.
16. *Wicked Beyond Belief, op. cit.*
17. Letter to *The Times*, 8 August 1980.
18. *The Times*, 21 August 1980.
19. Hansard, 14 December 1977, vol. 941, cols. 868–9.

CHAPTER 8 pp 223–42

1. Ludovic Kennedy, *The Trial of Stephen Ward* (Gollancz, 1964).

CHAPTER 9 pp 243–68

1. Quote from the Duncan Campbell–Peter Chippindale manuscript.
2. *Islington Gazette*, 19 September 1975.
3. *Islington Gazette*, 3 October 1975.
4. The *Sun*, 23 January 1976.
5. *The Times*, 19 May 1976.
6. John Ball, Lewis Chester and Roy Perrott, *Cops and Robbers* (Penguin, 1979).
7. Commander Bert Wickstead, *Gangbuster* (Futura, 1985).

CHAPTER 10 pp 269–93

1. Timetable taken from *More Rough Justice*, p. 48.
2. Subsequently Peter Nightingale and Margaret Livesey herself lodged complaints under section 49 of the Police Act. These were studied by the DPP, but no action was taken.
3. According to Lord Lane's judgment (p. 8a), this conversation at the magistrates court, which he deemed so damaging to her case, took place on 29 February 1979, a non-existent date.

CHAPTER 11 pp 297–302

1. In August 1984 Paul Jessimer, Adrian Roberts and William Everill received suspended prison sentences for hurling petrol bombs into the College Arms and causing more than £6,000-worth of damage.
2. *Birmingham Post*, 23 November 1974.

CHAPTER 13 pp 311–30

1. *The Times*, 2 October 1975.
2. See, for example, *The Times*, 20 September 1975.
3. Nor were any of the others mentioned in Hill's statement deported under the PTA.
4. From author's interview with Frank Johnson, December 1986.

5. This conviction falls outside the purview of this book. However, Hill has maintained his innocence of this as much as of the Guildford bombings. It is perhaps relevant that there was no hard evidence to link him with the Shaw murder other than the statement he signed at Guildford – as he claimed, under duress. He consistently pleaded not guilty to the Shaw charges. Of the three co-defendants at the trial, two were found not guilty and the third was convicted only of membership of the IRA. In subsequent analyses of the Guildford and Woolwich case, it has frequently been assumed that Hill had an 'IRA history'. In letters from prison, Hill has repeatedly stressed that this 'IRA history' only started at Guildford police station.

CHAPTER 14 pp 331–44

1. *The Irish Prisoner*, April 1980.
2. In the years since, juries have tended to become increasingly sceptical of the Crown case, even in high-profile 'political' trials. This was borne out by the acquittals in the prosecutions under the Official Secrets Act of Clive Ponting (February 1985) and the seven Cyprus airmen (October 1985).
3. A previous Labour administration – the post-war Attlee government – had enacted the previous reduction in the number of peremptory challenges, from twenty to seven, in 1949. In November 1986, the Conservative administration of Margaret Thatcher proposed to abolish them altogether.

CHAPTER 15 pp 345–56

1. *The Times*, 10 October 1977.
2. *The Leveller*, December 1977.
3. Quoted in *The Times*, 3 May 1978.

CHAPTER 16 pp 357–80

1 Hansard (H.L.), 17 May 1985, vol. 463, col. 1385.

CHAPTER 17 pp 381–414

1. *Sunday Tribune*, 18 November 1984.

2. *The Times*, 15 August 1975.
3. There was enormous speculation, apparently orchestrated by Airey Neave, opposition spokesman for Northern Ireland, about the omission of a minimum sentence recommendation. It was inferred, for example, that the 'bombers' might in the future benefit from some kind of political deal. All of this was completely misinformed. (After all, there had been no recommended minimum sentence in the Moors Murders case either.) Yet such was the agitation that Mr Justice Bridge took what he described as the "wholly exceptional course" of writing to *The Times* to clarify the position. He explained that he could see no reason "to anticipate that either the Parole Board or any Home Secretary in future years will need reminding, by the presence of a recommendation on the file, of the enormity of the crime." (*The Times*, 21 August 1975).
4. *The Times*, 16 August 1975.
5. *The Times*, 16 August 1975.
6. Robin Corbett is now MP for Birmingham, Erdington.
7. *Guardian*, 10 June 1976.
8. According to Chris Mullin's *Error of Judgement*, there was indeed no reason why Dr Paul could not have been called at the original trial. Solicitors for the men could have contacted the Royal Academy of Forensic Science or the Forensic Science Society, he said. "So far as I know, we had no inquiry." (p. 234).

CHAPTER 18 pp 415–440
1. Quote from the *Guardian*, 30 October 1985.
2. *Listener*, 31 October 1985.
3. *Observer*, 27 October 1985.
4. *Listener*, 31 October 1985.
5. ibid.
6. The Home Office assured the Irish government that the inquiry was urgent: *see* p. 432.
7. Chris Mullin was the Labour party's Member of Parliament candidate for Sunderland South.
8. Hansard, 25 July 1986, vol. 102, col. 798.
9. Hansard, 26 June 1986, vol. 100, col. 272(w).
10. Hansard, 25 July 1986, vol. 102, col. 383(w).
11. Hansard, 24 July 1986, vol. 102, col. 582.

12. Hansard, 25 July 1986, vol. 102, col. 799.
13. Hansard, 25 July 1986, vol. 102, col. 798.
14. Hansard, 25 July 1986. vol. 102, col. 810.
15. *The Times*, 7 October 1986.
16. *The Times*, 13 October 1986.
17. *The Times*, 15 October 1986.
18. *Independent*, 1 November 1986.
19. Hansard, 20 November 1986, vol. 105, cols. 678–9.
20. *Independent*, 1 December 1986.
21. Hansard, 18 December 1986, vol. 107, col. 1334.
22. According to the *Independent* (20 January 1987), one government minister complained that the issues were "whipped up by contentious mass TV programmes".
23. See the *Listener*, 14 November 1985: Bob Woffinden, "What The Papers Don't Say".
24. *The Times*, 15 October 1986.
25. *Beyond Reasonable Doubt* (Yorkshire/Granada), Channel 4, 16 November 1986.
26. *Observer*, 21 December 1986.
27. *Independent*, 24 December 1986.
28. *Guardian*, 23 December 1986.
29. *The Times*, 8 January 1987.
30. Hansard, 20 January 1987, vol. 108, cols. 735–9.
31. *Guardian*, 21 January 1987.
32. Hansard, 20 November 1986, vol. 105, col. 679.
33. See Hansard, 25 July 1986, vol. 102, col. 798.
34. Hansard, 25 July 1986, vol. 102, col. 810.
35. Hansard, 20 November 1986, vol. 105, col. 679.
36. Hansard, 26 June 1986, vol. 100, col. 272(w).
37. Hansard, 24 July 1986, vol. 102, col. 586.
38. Hansard, 20 November 1986, vol. 105, col. 679.
39. Hansard, 18 December 1986, vol. 107, col. 1335.
40. In other contexts, however, the Home Office can sometimes act with extraordinary despatch – for example, when deporting those whom it deems illegal immigrants.

CONCLUSION pp 463–90
1. Adolf Beck was twice the luckless victim of mistaken identity.
2. Hansard, 9 April 1986 (H.L.), vol, 473, col. 279.
3. *Criminal Appeals*: a report by Justice (1964).

4. Cmnd 2755, August 1965. Report of the inter-departmental committee on the Court of Criminal Appeal. Chairman: Lord Donovan. (Official Reports, vol. xiii, p.1).

5. 1984/85 figures for legal aid in criminal cases from the Lord Chancellor's department for Crown and magistrates courts combined. The 1985/86 figure for Crown courts only was £75.29 million (compared with an 84/85 figure of £68.02 million).

6. A left-over from the days of capital punishment, a conditional pardon referred to the power to commute a death sentence to one of life imprisonment.

7. *Not Without Prejudice* (Harrap, 1982).

8. *New Statesman*, 26 November 1971.

9. *New Statesman*, ibid.

10. In conversation with the author, December 1984.

11. *Sunday Times*, 28 January 1973.

12. Viscount Dilhorne was the former Lord Chancellor and Attorney-General, Sir Reginald Manningham-Buller. "Most of his convictions were wrong-headed," wrote Lord Devlin in *Easing the Passing* (pp. 39–40).

13. Hansard, 15 January 1976, vol. 903, col. 194 (w).

14. House of Commons official paper, HC 421 (see below), para 69.

15. ibid., para 61.

16. *Criminal Appeals*, para. 77.

17. This contrasts with the device of the Queen's Pardon, which is not really acceptable. The use of the word 'pardon' implies a prior state of guilt, yet in the UK people receive official pardons precisely because they are *not* guilty. (President Ford's pardon of ex-President Nixon may have been hasty and ethically dubious, but it did have the merit of semantic accuracy.) Interestingly, the Home Office White Paper of April 1983, so unyielding in its totality, did leave the door to reform ajar in this one respect.

18. *The Times*, 17 August 1963.

19. Ludovic Kennedy, *The Trial of Stephen Ward* (p. 200) (Penguin, 1965).

20. *The Times*, 12 August 1963.

21. *The Times*, 15 August 1963.

22. *Criminal Appeals*, para. 85.

23. House of Commons select committee on home affairs: sixth report 1981/2. HC 421 (published 20 October 1982).

24. *Home Office Reviews of Criminal Convictions* Justice (1968).

25. This has an unwieldly title: Report of the departmental committee on evidence of identification in criminal cases, HC 338. (vol. xix of the Official Reports, pp. 177–382.) Published 26 April 1976.

26. HC 421, para 23. The "government of the day" referred to the Callaghan administration; Merlyn Rees was Home Secretary.

27. ibid., para. 29.

28. ibid., appendix.

29. *The Times*, 29 July 1980.

30. see HC 421, para. 128.

31. Hansard (H.L.), 9 April 1986, vol. 473, col. 296.

32. HC 421, para. 75.

33. *Guardian*, 26 February 1976.

34. A third police inquiry into the Bridgewater case was ordered in October 1986.

35. HC 421, appendix.

36. Hansard (H.L.), 9 April 1986, vol. 473, col. 296.

37. Nor does this consideration affect solely the rectification of miscarriages of justice. According to *Rebel Advocate*, the biography by Muriel Box of her husband, Lord Gardiner, "somewhere between the Lord Chancellor's office and the Home Office is a large hole where projects for the reform of our criminal law lie deeply interred".

38. Cmnd 2152, September 1963. Official Reports, vol. xxiv, p. 349.

39. This was Roy Jenkins. Elsewhere I have been unstinting in his praise, so I feel no compunction in averring that his handling of the A6 murder goes to the debit side.

40. *Yes, Prime Minister*, "One of Us", BBC 2, 27 February 1986.

41. Cmnd 8856.

42. *Listener*, 8 December 1983.

43. Weekly Law Reports, November 1983.

44. The Clarke case is described in *More Rough Justice* by Hill, Young and Sargant.

45. See the *Listener*, 13 February 1986. When Lord Justice Lawton – "Fred' to his friends – retired on 19 December 1986, the tributes were fulsome. Lord Lane, the Lord Chief Justice, said, "If Fred has ever made a mistake, I have yet

to come across it. He has in the words of the Collect for Whit Sunday, 'a right judgment in all things'. His judgments have brought enlightenment to us all. I should add that as well as those which appear under his name there are a number of crypto-Fred judgments, where the apparent author has nipped down the corridor to have a word with Fred before, so to speak, going on the air." (*Guardian*, 20 December 1986.) So, no mistakes, but rather uncharitably the *Guardian* immediately pointed to what some might regard as 'a teeny-weeny lapse' in 1936, when Lawton was selected as prospective parliamentary candidate for Hammersmith North for Sir Oswald Mosley's British Union of Fascists. It is also not clear whether Lane included amongst the "judgments that have brought enlightenment to us all" those in the Ernie Clarke case, the Guildford and Woolwich case, and the fourth Luton appeal.

46. *Guardian*, 30 January 1987.
47. Hansard (H.L.), 17 May 1985, vol. 463, col. 1404.
48. Hansard, 24 July 1986, vol. 102, col. 810.
49. Hansard, 18 December 1986, vol. 107, col. 1335.
50. Jimmy Boyle, *A Sense of Freedom* (Pan, 1977).
51. Arthur Koestler, *Reflections on Hanging* (Gollancz, 1956).
52. John Baldwin and Michael McConville, *Jury Trials* (Clarendon, 1979).
53. In the Carl Bridgewater case, a letter from a witness to the Home Office resulted in the setting-up of a second police inquiry. Its contents have never been revealed. Working in secrecy, the police and the Home Office were thus able to claim that there was no need to do anything about the case. Yet the letter must clearly have been of importance and authority, else an inquiry would not have been initiated in the first place.
54. Kennedy is the doyen of this business. He has written *Ten Rillington Place* (1961), *A Presumption of Innocence* (1976), about the Patrick Meehan case, and *Wicked Beyond Belief* (1980), all of which have led to administrative about-turns (pardons for Evans and Meehan, and the release of Cooper and McMahon). "It is a strange system," the solicitor Brian Raymond wrote to *The Times*, "that requires the publication of a paperback book to secure the release of an innocent man." (29 July 1980).

55. Marilynne Robinson "The Waste Land", *Granta 15* (Penguin, 1985).
56. For information about the Carl Bridgewater case, see Paul Foot's *Murder at the Farm* (Sidgwick & Jackson, 1986).
57. *Guardian*, 13 October 1986.
58. *London Review of Books*, 5 March 1987.
59. Hansard, 20 January 1987, vol. 108, col. 744.
60. *Jury Trials*, ibid.
61. In fact, the prosecution's rights always outstripped those of the defence. Prosecution counsel could ask would-be jurors to "stand by for the Crown", which is a kind of unlimited peremptory challenge. From the end of the seventies, the prosecution has additionally been allowed access to confidential government records in order to vet juries in a wide range of cases.
62. *London Review of Books*, ibid.
63. Hansard (H.L.), 9 April 1986, vol. 473, col. 298.
64. The McMahon manuscript.
65. *Sunday Times*, 15 January 1961.

Chronology and Sources

	introduces bill to transfer the remains of Evans
16 March	R. A. Butler, Home Secretary, turns down appeals for a fresh inquiry
4 February 1965	Sir Frank Soskice, Home Secretary, refuses renewed pleas for another inquiry
18 May	Debate on Evans case in the House of Lords
21 July	All-party delegation received at Home Office
28 July	Timothy Evans Committee formed. Press conference held in a pub near Rillington Place
19 August	Home Secretary asks Mr Justice Brabin to conduct a new inquiry
December	Evans exhumed and reburied
21 January 1966	Brabin inquiry concluded
12 October	Brabin report published
18 October	On the recommendation of the Home Secretary, the Queen grants Evans a posthumous free pardon

Sources

The Timothy Evans case has been the most thoroughly documented of all miscarriages of justice. The authoritative work of reference is Ludovic Kennedy's *Ten Rillington Place* (Gollancz, 1961). I used the 1971 Panther edition – the one with a picture of Richard Attenborough on the cover. He played Christie – and John Hurt, Evans – in Richard Fleischer's creditable film of the case, also entitled *Ten Rillington Place*.

Also:

Michael Eddowes, *The Man on Your Conscience* (Cassell, 1955).
Ian Gilmour & John Grigg, "The Case of Timothy Evans: An Appeal to Reason' (*Spectator*, 1956).
F. Tennyson Jesse, *The Trials of Evans and Christie* (William Hodge, 1957).
R. T. Paget & S. S. Silverman, *Hanged – And Innocent?* (Gollancz, 1953).
Leslie Hale, *Hanged in Error* (Penguin, 1961).
The Scott Henderson Report (Cmnd. 8896, 1953).

The Scott Henderson Supplementary Report (Cmnd. 8946, 1953).
The Report of an Inquiry by the Hon. Mr Justice Brabin (Cmnd. 3101, 1966).

TWO   WALTER ROWLAND

19 October 1946	Olive Balchin murdered
21 October	Ware surrenders to police in Sheffield
26/27 October	Rowland arrested and charged with murder of Balchin
12 December	Rowland's trial opens at Manchester assizes
16 December	Rowland found guilty and sentenced to death
22 January 1947	In Walton prison, Ware confesses to murder of Balchin
10 February	Rowland's appeal dismissed
21 February	Home Secretary appoints J. C. Jolly to conduct an inquiry
22 February	Ware withdraws his confession
26 February	Jolly's report published. As a result, the Home Secretary decides there are no grounds to justify any interference with the due process of law
27 February	Rowland hanged at Strangeways prison
2 August 1951	Ware surrenders to police for the attempted murder of Adelaine Fuidge
16 November	Ware found guilty but insane of attempted murder
6 December	Home Secretary questioned in the House of Commons about the Rowland case
1 April 1954	Ware commits suicide by hanging in Broadmoor

Sources
The case is fully documented in the "Celebrated Trials' series of the Newton Abbot publishers, David & Charles. *The Trial of Walter Rowland* (1975) was written by Henry Cecil, author of *Brothers in Law* and many other novels. He was the *alter ego* of the respected County Court judge Henry Cecil Leon, who died in May 1976.

It is also included in both *Hanged – and Innocent? op. cit.* and *Hanged in Error, op. cit.*

The Jolly report was published on 26 February 1947, Cmnd. 7049. It can be located in Vol. XIV of the Official Reports, 1946–7, pp. 515–33.

THREE AND FOUR   THE A6 MURDER

22/23 August 1961	Michael Gregsten murdered on Deadman's Hill near Bedford; Valerie Storie sexually assaulted and shot
22 September	Police hold major press conference launching public appeal for information about Peter Alphon, wanted for questioning in connection with the A6 murder inquiry
24 September	Identity parade at Guy's Hospital. Valerie Storie fails to identify Alphon
3 October	Alphon released from custody
11 October	Hanratty arrested in Blackpool
14 October	Valerie Storie picks out Hanratty in identification parade at Stoke Mandeville hospital. Hanratty charged with murder
5 December	Hanratty committed for trial at the Old Bailey
2 January 1962	Trial switched to Bedford
22 January	Trial opens at Bedford
17 February	Hanratty found guilty and sentenced to death
13 March	Hanratty's appeal dismissed
2 April	Home Secretary refuses to grant a reprieve
4 April	Hanratty executed at Bedford
2 August 1963	Commons debate on motion calling for an inquiry
16 October 1964	*Murder versus Murder* published
21 October 1965	*Deadman's Hill: Was Hanratty Guilty?* published
4 August 1966	Lords debate on Lord Russell's motion calling for an inquiry
7 November	Case examined on *Panorama* (BBC)
30 January 1967	Home Secretary appoints Detective Chief Superintendent Nimmo to conduct inquiry into the Rhyl alibi

12 May	Alphon makes public confession to A6 crime in Paris
17 May	Confession repeated on *Dateline* (ITN)
13 July	Home Secretary appoints Nimmo to conduct second inquiry into Rhyl alibi
1 November	Home Secretary refuses calls for public inquiry
16 November	Case examined on *The Frost Programme* (LWT)
28 November 1968	Home Secretary refuses further calls for an inquiry
May 1971	*Who Killed Hanratty?* published
13 May	Mr James Hanratty's writ for damages against Lord Butler struck out in the Appeal Court
28 October	Home Secretary refuses MPs' demands to set up an inquiry
16 December 1972	Fresh revelations published in the *Sunday Times*
7 June 1974	Valerie Storie's original statement published
19 July	Home Secretary appoints Lewis Hawser QC to conduct inquiry
10 April 1975	Hawser report published

Sources

The most important reference is Paul Foot's *Who Killed Hanratty?* (Jonathan Cape, 1971; with postscript, Granada, 1973). He has also written about the case in the magazine *Unsolved* (Orbis, 1984).

Other books:

Louis Blom-Cooper, *The A6 Murder: Regina v. James Hanratty; The Semblance of Truth* (Penguin, 1963).
Jean Justice, *Murder versus Murder* (Olympia Press, Paris 1964).
Lord Russell, *Deadman's Hill: Was Hanratty Guilty?* (Secker & Warburg, 1965).

FIVE   THE ANGUS SIBBET MURDER

| 5 January 1967 | Body of Angus Sibbet discovered in Jaguar car parked in South Hetton, Durham |

	Michael Luvaglio and Dennis Stafford taken in for questioning, and charged with murder
7 March	Trial opens at Newcastle assizes
15 March	Luvaglio and Stafford found guilty of murder and sentenced to life imprisonment
26 July 1968	Application for leave to appeal refused
23 October 1969	Petition delivered to 10 Downing Street
29 June 1971	Home Secretary agrees to study new evidence after meeting all-party delegation of MPs and peers
27 January 1972	Letter advocating an inquiry, signed by a cluster of distinguished people, published in *The Times*
11 February	Home Secretary refers the case back to the Court of Appeal
12 May	High Court rules that new evidence should be heard before a single judge sitting as an examiner
14 November	Appeal Court rules that new evidence should be heard in open court — Examination of witnesses begins
30 November	Examination of witnesses concluded
16 January 1973	Appeal begins
23 January	Appeal dismissed
26 February	Leave to appeal to House of Lords refused
12 April	Leave to appeal to House of Lords granted by Lords appeal committee
11 July	Lords appeal begins
17 July	Appeal concluded. Judgment reserved
18 October	Lords unanimously reject appeal
June 1979	Luvaglio and Stafford released from prison

Sources

David Lewis & Peter Hughman, *Most Unnatural: An Inquiry into the Stafford Case* (Penguin, 1971).
Sir David Napley, *Not Without Prejudice* (Harrap, 1982).
Hugo Young, "Widgery and the Doctrine of the Lurking Doubt", (*Sunday Times*, 28 January 1973).

SIX AND SEVEN   THE LUTON POST-OFFICE MURDER

10 September 1969	Reginald Stevens, postmaster, shot dead in car-park in Luton
22 October	Alfred Mathews taken into custody
25 October	Mathews makes 'parcels story' statement
31 October	McMahon, Cooper and Murphy arrested and charged with murder
3 December	Mathews makes second statement
15 December	McMahon, Cooper and Murphy sent for trial at the Old Bailey; Mathews discharged
26 February 1970	Trial opens at the Old Bailey
19 March	McMahon, Cooper and Murphy found guilty, and sentenced to life imprisonment, with a recommended twenty-year sentence
26 February 1971	Appeal (1) dismissed
27 February 1972	Drury named in corruption scandal in *Sunday People*
25 October	*Midweek* programme on the case
7 December	Murphy's conviction referred to appeal
13 November 1973	Appeal (2): Murphy's conviction quashed
29 May 1974	Convictions of McMahon and Cooper referred to appeal
16 December	At a private hearing, High Court determines that prosecution must provide defence with specific information
10 February 1975	Appeal (3) opens
12 February	Appeal dismissed
5 May	*Panorama* programme on the case
9 May	Leave to appeal to House of Lords refused
June 1976	Drury committed for trial
12 July	Appeal (4) opens
22 July	Appeal dismissed
23 May 1977	Committee to free McMahon and Cooper formed in London
7 July	Drury jailed for eight years for corruption
15 December	New evidence referred to Appeal Court
11 April 1978	Appeal (5): new evidence rejected
2 May	Lord Devlin lecture at All Souls College, Oxford

26 June 1980	*Wicked Beyond Belief* published
18 July	Cooper and McMahon released
15 August	Home Secretary refuses demands for public inquiry
17 July 1981	Cooper and McMahon make small demonstration at House of Commons
29 May 1985	Terence Langston makes fresh statement

Sources

Ludovic Kennedy and others, *Wicked Beyond Belief* (Granada, 1980).

Michael McMahon has also been generous enough to provide me with a copy of his fascinating manuscript which, sadly, remains unpublished.

EIGHT   ELIZABETH THOMPSON

5 November 1971	Peter Stanswood murdered in his car
19 May 1975	Heather Pridham and Joseph Fromant charged with murder
9 July	Pridham makes statement in prison implicating Elizabeth Thompson
14 July	Committal proceedings: Fromant sent for trial; Pridham discharged
25 July	Pridham makes a second damaging statement against Thompson
5 August	Thompson arrested and charged with murder
21 October	Trial opens at Winchester Crown Court
14 November	Thompson (and Fromant) found guilty of murder and sentenced to life imprisonment
18 March 1977	Appeal dismissed
March 1980	Thompson's counsel argue the case for her innocence, unavailingly, at the Home Office
13 December 1985	Thompson released from prison

NINE   THE LEGAL AND GENERAL GANG

| 18 September 1974 | Billy Moseley released from Bedford prison |
| 26 September | Moseley last seen alive |

5 October	Moseley's torso discovered in Thames at Rainham, Essex
18 October	Micky Cornwall released from Hull prison
22 August 1975	Cornwall last seen alive
7 September	Cornwall's body discovered in woods near Hatfield, Herts.
22 January 1976	Eighteen people taken for questioning to Loughton police station, Essex
26 January	Seven people charged and remanded in custody
26 April	Committal proceedings at Epping magistrates court
11 November	Trial of seven accused opens at Old Bailey
15 June 1977	Jury sent out to consider their verdicts
17 June	Maynard and Dudley found guilty and sentenced to life imprisonment
28 July	Moseley's head discovered in public toilets in Islington
18 September	Protest march by MDC – Not Guilty campaign from Camden Town to Hyde Park Corner
2 April 1979	Appeals dismissed
September 1980	As a result of inquiries by Duncan Campbell, Home Office study the case again

Sources

Duncan Campbell, late home affairs correspondent of the *London Daily News*, has done more work on this case than anyone else. He very kindly allowed me access to the manuscript commissioned by Granada Books which he co-authored with Peter Chippindale. Sadly, it remains unpublished.

Campbell has also contributed regular news stories on the whole affair to *City Limits*; and written about it at greater length in *Unsolved* (Orbis, 1984).

TEN   MARGARET LIVESEY

22 February 1979	Alan Livesey found murdered at the family home at Bamber Bridge, Lancashire

27 February	His mother, Margaret Livesey, confesses to murder
1 March	Margaret Livesey charged with murder at magistrates court
2 March	Margaret Livesey retracts her confession
2 July	Trial opens at Preston Crown Court
11 July	A juror is discharged, and the trial halted
19 July	Second trial opens at Preston Crown Court
26 July	Margaret Livesey found guilty of murder
17 September 1980	Livesey refused extension of time necessary to apply for leave to appeal
26 October 1983	*Rough Justice* transmission on the case
9 November	Justice petition delivered to Home Office
15 November	David Mellor assures Livesey's MP in House of Commons that Home Secretary has ordered a fresh police investigation
18 December	Willlam Benion appointed to head fresh inquiry
20 December 1984	Home Office declines to take action in the case
24 July 1985	Fresh petition to Home Office from Justice
12 September 1985	Second *Rough Justice* transmission
15 January 1986	Home Office refers case to appeal
8/9 December	Appeal heard
16 December	Judgment delivered; appeal dismissed

Sources
The Livesey case is one of the three examined in *More Rough Justice* (Penguin, 1985) by Peter Hill, Martin Young and Tom Sargant.

TWELVE, THIRTEEN, FOURTEEN AND FIFTEEN   THE GUILDFORD AND WOOLWICH PUB-BOMBS CASE

5 October 1974	Bombs explode in two Guildford pubs; five people killed
7 November	Bomb thrown into Woolwich pub; two killed
29 November	Prevention of Terrorism Act passed; Paul Hill arrested
30 November	Gerard Conlon arrested
2 December	Patrick Armstrong and Carole Richardson arrested

17 March 1975	Committal proceedings against the four open in Guildford
16 September	Trial at Old Bailey begins
22 October	All four found guilty and sentenced to life imprisonment
12 December	The Balcombe Street Four arrested
10 February 1977	Balcombe Street Four found guilty of terrorist crimes and receive thirty-year sentences
10 October	Appeals of Armstrong *et al.* begin at the Old Bailey
28 October	Appeals dismissed
1 July 1986	*The Guildford Time Bomb (First Tuesday)* transmitted
2 July	Home Secretary orders review of the case
23 July	Cardinal Hume leads delegation to Home Secretary Douglas Hurd
14 August	Home Secretary announces new investigation by Avon & Somerset police
13 October	*Trial and Error* published; Cardinal Hume calls for case to be referred to appeal
16 November	*Beyond Reasonable Doubt* transmitted
17 November	Public meeting in House of Commons
20 January 1987	Home Secretary declines to reopen case
3 March	*A Case That Won't Go Away (First Tuesday)* broadcast

SIXTEEN THE MAGUIRE FAMILY

3 December 1974	Seven members of the Maguire household arrested
20 March 1975	Committal proceedings against the seven in Guildford
14 January 1976	Trial begins at the Old Bailey
4 March	All found guilty of possession of explosives
29 July 1980	Guiseppe Conlon dies
4 August	Case debated in House of Commons
18 April 1983	*Panorama* programme
6 March 1984	*First Tuesday* programme
22 February 1985	Annie Maguire released from prison
13 May	RTE documentary transmitted in Britain
17 May	Case debated in House of Lords

13 October 1986	*Trial and Error* published
20 January 1987	Home Secretary declines to reopen case

SEVENTEEN   THE BIRMINGHAM PUB-BOMBS

14 November 1974	IRA activist James McDade killed by his own bomb in Coventry
21 November	Bombs planted by IRA in crowded city-centre pubs in Birmingham; 21 people killed, 161 injured
22/25 November	Hill *et al.* questioned in police custody
24 November	Hill *et al.* appear before local magistrates, and remanded in Winson Green prison
9 May 1975	Committal proceedings
9 June	Trial opens in Lancaster
15 August	Guilty verdicts returned. All six sentenced to life imprisonment
30 December	Fourteen prison warders charged with assaulting the six men and suspended from duty
30 March 1976	Applications for leave to appeal dismissed
10 June	Trial of prison warders opens in Birmingham
15 July	All prison warders acquitted
14 November 1977	Hill *et al.* take out writs for assault against the West Midlands police, Lancashire police and the Home Office
23 November 1978	Application by West Midlands police to strike out the claim dismissed
17 January 1980	Appeal of West Midlands police against previous High Court ruling upheld by Lord Denning
November 1981	Denning ruling upheld in House of Lords
18 November 1984	Article on the case in the *Sunday Tribune*
28 October 1985	*World in Action* documentary transmitted
July 1986	*Error of Judgement* published
25 July	Debate in House of Commons
1 December	*World in Action* broadcast highlights fresh evidence
20 January 1987	Case referred to appeal
2 November	Fresh appeal opens at the Old Bailey
9 December	Appeal concluded
28 January 1988	Judgment delivered – appeals dismissed

14 April   Leave to appeal to House of Lords refused

Sources

Father Denis Faul & Father Raymond Murray, *The Birmingham Framework* (published privately, 1976); *Synopsis of the Forensic Evidence* (published privately, 1980)

Michael Farrell, "The Other Victims" (*Sunday Tribune*, Dublin, November 1984)

Brian Gibson, *The Birmingham Bombs* (Barry Rose, 1976). "After ten weeks of sitting patiently through a complex trial trying to be an objective journalist," Gibson wrote, "I have not doubted since the very early days that the police got the right men." Gibson should have tried a little harder to be an objective journalist. His book, unfortunately, seems to have had some influence in the Midlands.

Nick Davies and Ros Franey, "The Case of the Guildford Four" (*Observer*, 29 June 1986).

Chris Mullin, *Error of Judgement* (Chatto & Windus, 1986).

Robert Kee, *Trial and Error* (Hamish Hamilton, 1986).

Bibliography

Ruth Brandon and Christie Davies, *Wrongful Imprisonment* (George Allen & Unwin, 1973)

Charles du Cann, *Miscarriages of Justice* (Frederick Muller, 1960)

Peter Cole and Peter Pringle, *Can You Positively Identify This Man?* (Andre Deutsch, 1974)

Patrick Devlin, *The Judge* (OUP, 1979)

Peter Hain, *Mistaken Identity: The Wrong Face of the Law* (Quartet, 1976)

Peter Hain, *Political Trials in Britain* (Penguin, 1985)

Leslie Hale, *Hanged in Error* (Penguin, 1961)

Peter Hill and Martin Young, *Rough Justice* (Ariel, 1983)

Arthur Koestler, *Reflections on Hanging* (Gollancz, 1956)

Arthur Koestler and C. H. Rolph, *Hanged by the Neck* (Penguin, 1961)

David Lewis and Peter Hughman, *Just How Just?* (Secker & Warburg, 1975)

R. T. Paget and S. S. Silverman, *Hanged – and Innocent?* (Gollancz, 1953)

Christopher Price and Jonathan Caplan, *The Confait Confessions* (Marion Boyars, 1977)

Tom Sargant, "The Court of Expediency" (*New Society*, 2 May 1985)

David Yallop, *To Encourage The Others* (W. H. Allen, 1971)

Appendix 1

Post-war Home Secretaries

August 1945:	James Chuter Ede
October 1951:	Sir David Maxwell-Fyfe
October 1954:	Major Gwilym Lloyd-George
January 1957:	R. A. Butler
July 1962:	Henry Brooke
October 1964:	Sir Frank Soskice
December 1965:	Roy Jenkins
November 1967:	James Callaghan
June 1970:	Reginald Maudling
July 1972:	Robert Carr
March 1974:	Roy Jenkins
September 1976:	Merlyn Rees
May 1979:	William Whitelaw
June 1983:	Leon Brittan
September 1985:	Douglas Hurd

Appendix 2

The Lord Chief Justices of England

1940	Viscount [Thomas] Caldecote
1946	Lord [Reyner] Goddard
1958	Lord [Hubert] Parker of Waddington
1971	Lord [John Passmore] Widgery
1980	Lord [Geoffrey] Lane

Index

JULIAN CRITCHLEY

HESELTINE: THE UNAUTHORISED BIOGRAPHY

Adam Raphael's 1987 Book of the Year in *Elle*

Michael Heseltine: mace-waving, hair-tossing emotional darling of the Tory constituency parties. Tarzan, descending on riot-torn Liverpool 8 in a blaze of publicity and storming out of Cabinet, post-Westland, in a blaze of anger.

But also Michael Heseltine, the undergraduate who coolly charted his political ambitions on the back of an envelope. Who made a fortune in property and publishing to further those ambitions and who is still on that original schedule that ended with Downing Street in the 1990s.

Michael Heseltine: now just another ex-Ministerial backbencher? Or a future leader of his party and Prime Minister?

'Amusing and charitable in his judgements'
John Biffen in the *Daily Telegraph*

'A splendid escape from present political tribulations'
Michael Foot in *The Observer*

'Critchley knows his stuff from his own observation'
Jeremy Isaacs in *The Independent*

HODDER AND STOUGHTON PAPERBACKS

THOMAS KARAS

STAR WARS: THE NEW HIGH GROUND

Star Wars: President Reagan's obsession.

Space hardware, lasers, particle beams ... The US military and their political allies clamour for it. The huge aero space industry promises to make all the dreams come true – as long as it is fuelled with endless sums of money. Britain scrambles for a few contractual crumbs.

Yet most scientists simply don't think Star Wars can be a real working proposition, while more and more people now see it chiefly as an obstacle to the disarmament process.

So how did the whole idea come about in the first place, and why?

Dr Karas has ventured into the closed world of US Air Force politics and ambitions. With a sharp eye for paradox and the telling detail, he describes the well-secured civil and military research institutions, the ultra-high technology behind locked doors, the publicly-funded private foundations, the computer-enhanced speculations and the behind-the-scenes pressure groups.

Star Wars: the system that may never work but still have a disastrous effect on all our lives.

HODDER AND STOUGHTON PAPERBACKS

MORE TITLES AVAILABLE FROM
HODDER AND STOUGHTON PAPERBACKS